D1808232

ZAGAT®

Miami/So. Florida Restaurants

2011

LOCAL EDITORS
Bill Citara, Rochelle Koff and Jan Norris
STAFF EDITOR
John Deiner

Published and distributed by
Zagat Survey, LLC
4 Columbus Circle
New York, NY 10019
T: 212.977.6000
E: miami@zagat.com
www.zagat.com

ACKNOWLEDGMENTS

We thank contributing editor Victoria Pesce Elliott, Emily Adams, Jimmy Barron, Linda Bladholm, Simone Diament, Linda Gassenheimer, Carole Kotkin, Kathy Martin, Claire Mitchel, Diane Mooney, Taylor Morgan, Hilda Ruiz, Steven Shukow, Scott Simmons, Davis Ward, Katie Ward, Philip Ward and Heidi Wilson, as well as the following members of our staff: Danielle Borovoy (editorial assistant), Brian Albert, Sean Beachell, Maryanne Bertollo, Jane Chang, Sandy Cheng, Reni Chin, Larry Cohn, Alison Flick, Jeff Freier, Michelle Golden, Matthew Hamm, Justin Hartung, Marc Henson, Anna Hyclak, Natalie Lebert, Mike Liao, James Mulcahy, Jacqueline Wasilczyk, Art Yaghci, Sharon Yates, Anna Zappia and Kyle Zolner.

The reviews in this guide are based on public opinion surveys. The ratings reflect the average scores given by the survey participants who voted on each establishment. The text is based on quotes from, or paraphrasings of, the surveyors' comments. Phone numbers, addresses and other factual data were correct to the best of our knowledge when published in this guide.

Our guides are printed using environmentally preferable inks containing 20%, by weight, renewable resources on papers sourced from well-managed forests. Deluxe editions are covered with Skivertex Recover® Double containing a minimum of 30% post-consumer waste fiber.

SUSTAINABLE FORESTRY INITIATIVE	Certified Chain of Custody
	Promoting Sustainable Forest Management
	www.sfiprogram.org

PWC-SFICOC-260

ENVIROINK™

The inks used to print the body of this publication contain a minimum of 20%, by weight, renewable resources.

Contents

Ratings & Symbols

	Zagat Top Spot	Name	Symbols		Cuisine	Zagat Ratings			
						FOOD	DECOR	SERVICE	COST

Area, Address & Contact

Z Tim & Nina's ◗ *Seafood*

▽ 23 | 9 | 13 | $15

Miami Beach | 21120 Collins Ave. (10th St.) | 305-555-4550 | www.zagat.com

Review, surveyor comments in quotes

Reeling in fish fiends with its "all-around originality", this low-budget Miami Beach–front seafooder in a "wacky setting" (sand on the floor and a "talking stuffed marlin" by the door) features "fabulous" fare like conch-and-crab bruschetta; you may need to "shout your order" above the bar's roar, but the "cheerful mates" will likely be "too busy" to do much about it anyway.

Ratings

Food, Decor and **Service** are rated on the Zagat 0 to 30 scale.

0 – 9 poor to fair
10 – 15 fair to good
16 – 19 good to very good
20 – 25 very good to excellent
26 – 30 extraordinary to perfection
▽ low response | less reliable

Cost

Our surveyors' estimated price of a dinner with one drink and tip. Lunch is usually 25 to 30% less. For unrated **newcomers** or **write-ins,** the price range is shown as follows:

I $25 and below   E $41 to $65
M $26 to $40   VE $66 or above

Symbols

Z highest ratings, popularity and importance
◗ serves after 11 PM
Ⓢ closed on Sunday
Ⓜ closed on Monday
⌿ no credit cards accepted

About This Survey

This **2011 Miami/So. Florida Restaurants Survey** is an update reflecting significant developments since our last Survey was published. It covers 1,075 restaurants in the South Florida area, including 71 important additions. To bring this guide up to the minute, we've also indicated new addresses, phone numbers, chef changes and other major alterations. Like all our guides, this one is based on input from avid local consumers – 6,102 all told. Our editors have synopsized this feedback, highlighting representative comments (in quotation marks within each review). To read full surveyor comments – and share your own opinions – visit **ZAGAT.com,** where you'll also find the latest restaurant news plus menus, photos and lots more, all for free.

THREE SIMPLE PREMISES underlie our ratings and reviews. First, we believe that the collective opinions of large numbers of consumers are more accurate than those of any single person. (Consider that our surveyors bring some one million annual meals' worth of experience to this Survey. They also visit restaurants year-round, anonymously – and on their own dime.) Second, food quality is only part of the equation when choosing a restaurant, thus we ask surveyors to separately rate food, decor and service and report on cost. Third, since people need reliable information in a fast, easy-to-digest format, we strive to be concise and we offer our content on every platform. Our Top Ratings lists (Miami/Dade County, pages 9–17; Key West, page 90; Ft. Lauderdale/Broward County, pages 105–111; Palm Beach County, pages 153–158) and indexes (starting on page 202) are also designed to help you quickly choose the best place for any occasion.

ABOUT ZAGAT: In 1979, we started asking friends to rate and review restaurants purely for fun. The term "user-generated content" had not yet been coined. That hobby grew into Zagat Survey; 32 years later, we have over 375,000 surveyors and cover everything from airlines to shopping in over 100 countries. Along the way, we evolved from being a print publisher to a digital content provider, e.g. **ZAGAT.com, ZAGAT.mobi** (for web-enabled mobile devices), **ZAGAT TO GO** (for smartphones) and **nru** (for Android phones). We also produce customized gifts and marketing tools for a wide range of corporate clients. And you can find us on Twitter (twitter.com/zagatbuzz), Facebook and other social media networks.

THANKS: We're grateful to our local editors, Bill Citara, a food and wine writer; Rochelle Koff, a restaurant critic and editor at *The Miami Herald*; and Jan Norris, publisher of the Florida food website jannorris.com. Thank you, guys. We also sincerely thank the thousands of surveyors who participated – this guide is really "theirs."

JOIN IN: To improve our guides, we solicit your comments; it's vital that we hear your opinions. Just contact us at **nina-tim@zagat.com.** We also invite you to join our surveys at **ZAGAT.com.** Do so and you'll receive a choice of rewards in exchange.

New York, NY
November 17, 2010

Nina and Tim

Nina and Tim Zagat

What's New

With one of the country's highest average meal costs ($39.86, compared with $35.37 nationally), the Miami restaurant scene saw its share of tumult in the past year. But while a number of high-profile eateries closed, a healthy crop of openings (see page 7) kept diners happy.

$ RECESSION REDUX: Hamburgers became hot with the South Beach debut of Danny Meyer's **Shake Shack** chain and a second branch for **Burger & Beer Joint.** Fellow New Yorkers Michael Psilakis and Donatella Arpaia built on the success of their **Eos** in the Viceroy by turning the space into **Bistro e** during the day, serving inexpensive daytime fare. And **Mandolin** (Greek), **Otentic** (French) and **Talavera** (Mexican) brought value meals to wallet-watching diners.

STAR APPEAL: Despite tight economic times, celebrateurs pushed forward with new projects. Leading the pack was **Norman's 180** from Norman Van Aken, who did a 180 from his original posh namesake with this more casual farm-to-table eatery. Nuevo Latino king Douglas Rodriguez opened the upscale **De Rodriguez Cuba,** and is readying the seafood-oriented **De Rodriguez Ocean.** Theatrical restaurateur Barton G. debuted **The Villa By Barton G.,** a glitzy Continental set in the former Gianni Versace mansion.

GONE BUT NOT FORGOTTEN: **Talula** on South Beach shut its doors, though chef-owners Andrea Curto-Randazzo and husband Frank Randazzo landed on their feet at the new **Water Club** in North Miami Beach. Other casualties included **Grass,** Jonathan Eismann's **Pacific Time** and the much-touted **Au Pied de Cochon.**

BROWARD WATCH: Las Olas Boulevard, Ft. Lauderdale's foodie mecca, was hard hit by the downturn, which claimed high-profile (and high-end) spots like **Bova Prime** and **Samba Room.** Hence, a number of entrepreneurs took a more casual approach to their new endeavors: Paula Pace, whose **Las Olas Café** folded, unveiled the homey **Mason Jar** on U.S. 1, while **Casa D'Angelo** chef-owner Angelo Elia opened the hip-but-laid-back **D'Angelo Pizza** in Oakland Park. Meanwhile, gambling gastronomes found a bevy of tasty offerings – including **Brio Tuscan Grille** and **Cantina Laredo** adjacent to the Hallandale horse track and casino.

PALM BEACHED: Even in this ritzy resort land, low-cost crowd-pleasers stepped to the fore at arrivals such as **Relish** in Northwood and Jupiter's **CG Burgers,** the latter attached to **Carmine's Coal Fired Pizza.** Meanwhile, Gary Rack expanded his mini-empire with two affordable Boca arrivals: **Rack's Downtown Eatery + Tavern,** a haven for comfort fare, and **Table 42,** an Italian boîte. And Miami's Allen Susser brought a touch of South Beach to Delray Beach with **Taste Gastropub,** albeit without the SoBe price tags.

Miami, FL   Bill Citara
Ft. Lauderdale, FL   Rochelle Koff
Palm Beach, FL   Jan Norris
November 17, 2010

Key Newcomers

Our editors' take on the year's top arrivals. See page 225 for a full list.

MIAMI/DADE COUNTY

Fin | *Seafood* | Jonathan Eismann's Design District fish house

Forge Restaurant | *American* | A Miami Beach icon's rebirth

Mandolin | *Greek* | Hellenic haven in the Design District

Norman's 180 | *Eclectic* | Return of the original Mango Gangster

Shake Shack | *Burgers* | NYC's patty mecca meets SoBe

STK Miami | *American/Steak* | Sizzling Miami Beacher

Sugarcane Raw Bar Grill | *Eclectic* | Small plates hit Downtown

Villa By Barton G. | *Continental* | SoBe's luxe Continental

Water Club | *American* | Splashy comfort fare in N. Miami Beach

Zuma | *Japanese* | Downtown izakaya with a view

FT. LAUDERDALE/BROWARD COUNTY

Café Europa | *Italian* | Lauderdale classic returns in style

D'Angelo Pizza | *Pizza* | Posh pies in Oakland Park

Elle's | *Asian/Caribbean* | A modern Miramar strip-maller

Il Mercato Café & Wine Shop | *Eclectic* | A wine-centric Hallandale entry

SoLita | *Italian* | Chic eats on Las Olas

PALM BEACH COUNTY

Apicius | *Continental/Italian* | Lantana alfresco charmer

Fiorentina | *Italian* | Small space, big tastes in Lake Worth

Gratify American Gastropub | *American* | West Palm crowd-pleaser

The Office | *American* | Comfort food in Delray Beach

Rack's Downtown Eatery | *American* | Boca scene-setter

BIG-NAME PROJECTS ON TAP:

American Noodle Bar – Michael Bloise's Upper East Side noodle shop

Bazaar – Spanish star José Andrés expands his empire to South Beach

Cecconi's – London Italian import at SoBe's new Soho Beach House

DB Bistro Moderne – Daniel Boulud ventures into Miami's JW Marriott

Deck 84 – Delray hooks a Burt Rapoport fish house

De Rodriguez Ocean – A sustainable seafooder from Douglas Rodriguez in the Hilton Bentley

Eden – Farm meets table in Miami Beach courtesy of NYC's Chris Lee

Katsuya – South Beach sushi palace from LA's Katsuya Uechi

Rocco's Tacos – Ft. Lauderdale outpost of Rocco Mangel's Mexican

Vino e Olio – Alessandro Cecconi brings Tuscan to the Design District

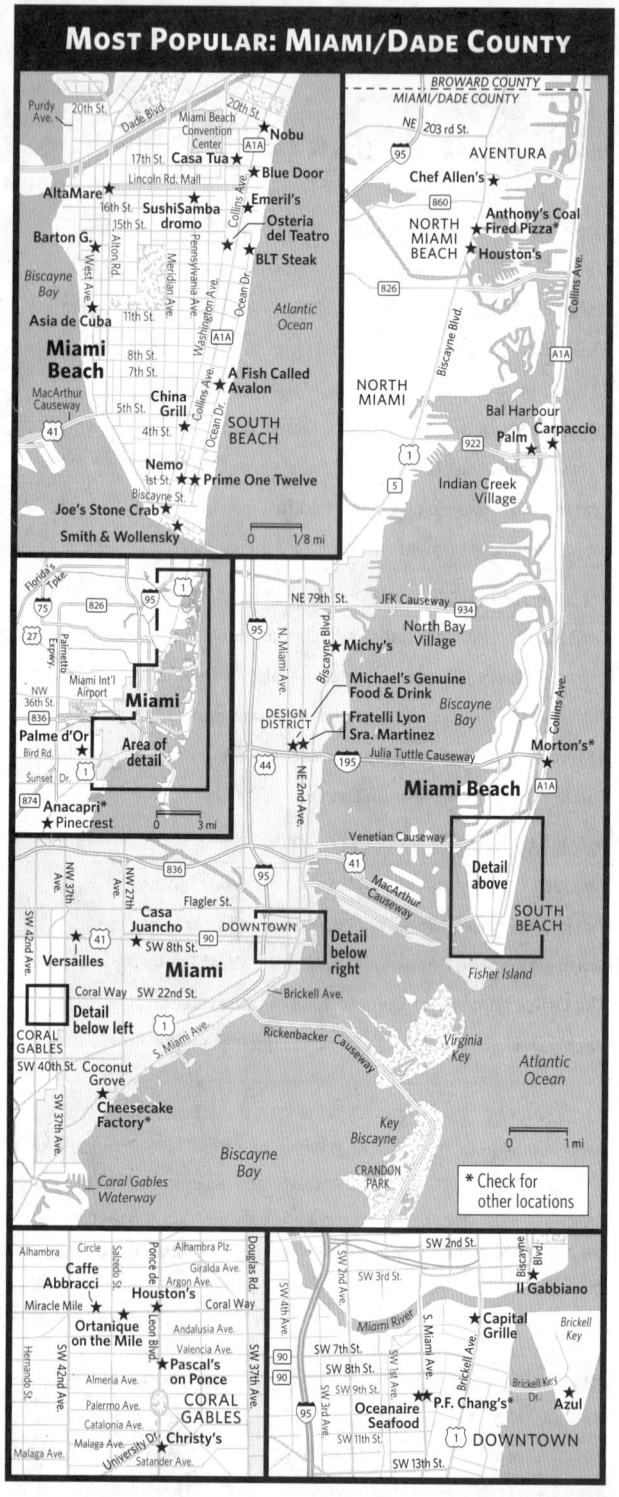

Most Popular:
Miami/Dade County

1 Joe's Stone Crab | *Seafood*
2 Prime One Twelve | *Sea./Steak*
3 Michael's Genuine | *American*
4 Michy's | *American/French*
5 Barton G | *American*
6 Nobu Miami | *Japanese*
7 Chef Allen's | *Seafood*
8 Capital Grille | *Steak*
9 Il Gabbiano | *Italian*
10 Azul | *Mediterranean*
11 Casa Tua | *Italian*
12 Blue Door | *Brazilian/French*
13 Smith & Wollensky | *Steak*
14 Houston's* | *American*
15 Ortanique | *Carib./New World*
16 Cheesecake Factory | *American*
17 Emeril's | *Contemp. Louisiana*
18 China Grill | *Asian*
19 Palm | *Steak*
20 Nemo | *American*

21 Oceanaire | *Seafood*
22 Versailles | *Cuban*
23 Asia de Cuba | *Asian/Cuban*
24 Osteria del Teatro | *Italian*
25 Pascal's on Ponce | *French*
26 SushiSamba | *Japanese/S Amer.*
27 AltaMare | *Seafood*
28 Morton's | *Steak*
29 Christy's | *Steak*
30 A Fish Called Avalon | *Seafood*
31 Anacapri | *Italian*
32 Carpaccio | *Italian*
33 Caffe Abbracci | *Italian*
34 P.F. Chang's | *Chinese*
35 Sra. Martinez* | *Spanish*
36 Casa Juancho | *Spanish*
37 BLT Steak | *Steak*
38 Fratelli Lyon | *Italian*
39 Palme d'Or | *French*
40 Anthony's Pizza | *Pizza*

Many of the above restaurants are among the Miami/Dade area's most expensive, but if popularity were calibrated to price, a number of other restaurants would surely join their ranks. To illustrate this, we have added two pages of Best Buys starting on page 16.

Top Food

<u>28</u> Palme d'Or | *French*	Palm | *Steak*
<u>27</u> Romeo's Cafe | *Italian*	Adriana | *Eclectic/Seafood*
Pascal's on Ponce | *French*	Shibui | *Japanese*
Michy's | *American/French*	Hiro's Yakko San | *Japanese*
Nobu Miami | *Japanese*	Hakkasan | *Chinese*
Hy-Vong | *Vietnamese*	Chef Allen's | *Seafood*
OLA* | *Pan-Latin*	Bond St. Lounge | *Japanese*
Matsuri | *Japanese*	Capital Grille | *Steak*
Joe's Stone Crab | *Seafood*	Andiamo! Pizza | *Pizza*
Azul | *Mediterranean*	Basilico | *Italian*

<u>26</u> Il Gabbiano | *Italian*   <u>25</u> Christy's | *Steak*
Francesco | *Peruvian*   Oishi Thai | *Japanese/Thai*
Osteria del Teatro | *Italian*   Timo | *Italian/Mediterranean*
Prime One Twelve | *Sea./Steak*   Wish | *American*
Michael's Genuine | *American*   Bourbon Steak | *Steak*
Spiga | *Italian*   Scarpetta | *Italian*
Red Light | *American*   Escopazzo | *Italian*
Ortanique | *Carib./New World*   Quinn's | *Seafood*
Cheese Course | *Eclectic*   Captain Jim Hanson's | *Seafood*
Graziano's | *Argent./Steak*   Tropical Chinese* | *Chinese*

BY CUISINE

AMERICAN (NEW)
- <u>27</u> Michy's
- <u>26</u> Michael's Genuine
- Red Light
- <u>25</u> Wish
- <u>24</u> Nemo

AMERICAN (TRAD.)
- <u>22</u> Houston's
- Grill on the Alley
- Joe Allen
- <u>21</u> S&S
- Front Porch Cafe

CARIBBEAN/CUBAN
- <u>26</u> Ortanique
- <u>23</u> Asia de Cuba
- <u>22</u> Las Culebrinas
- Tap Tap Haitian
- Enriqueta's Sandwich Shop

CHINESE
- <u>26</u> Hakkasan
- <u>25</u> Tropical Chinese
- <u>24</u> Kon Chau
- <u>22</u> Tony Chan's Water Club
- <u>21</u> Philippe

DELIS/SANDWICHES
- <u>26</u> Cheese Course
- <u>23</u> La Sandwicherie
- <u>22</u> Enriqueta's Sandwich Shop
- <u>21</u> S&S
- <u>20</u> Perricone's

ECLECTIC
- <u>26</u> Adriana
- Acqua
- <u>23</u> Icebox Café
- <u>20</u> Tantra
- <u>19</u> Balans

FRENCH
- <u>28</u> Palme d'Or
- <u>27</u> Pascal's on Ponce
- Michy's
- <u>24</u> Café Pastis
- A La Folie

FRENCH (BISTRO)
- <u>24</u> A La Folie
- <u>23</u> Le Bouchon du Grove
- <u>22</u> George's in the Grove
- Le Provençal
- La Goulue

Excludes places with low votes, unless otherwise indicated

Menus, photos, voting and more – free at ZAGAT.com

ITALIAN

27	Romeo's Cafe
26	Il Gabbiano
	Osteria del Teatro
	Spiga
	Basilico

JAPANESE

27	Nobu Miami
	Matsuri
26	Shibui
	Hiro's Yakko San
	Bond St. Lounge

LATIN AMERICAN

27	OLA
26	Francesco
	Adriana
23	La Cofradia
	SushiSamba

MEDITERRANEAN

27	Azul
25	Timo
24	Maroosh
23	La Cofradia
22	Bin No. 18

PAN-ASIAN

24	Yuga
23	Lan

	China Grill
	Café Sambal
22	Restaurant at the Setai

PIZZA

26	Andiamo! Pizza
23	Bugatti Pasta
	Anthony's Pizza
	Blú la Pizzeria
	Tutto Pizza

SEAFOOD

27	Joe's Stone Crab
26	Francesco
	Prime One Twelve
	Adriana
	Chef Allen's

SPANISH

25	Casa Juancho
24	La Dorada
	Sra. Martinez
	Xixón
22	Las Culebrinas

STEAKHOUSES

26	Prime One Twelve
	Graziano's
	Palm
	Capital Grille
25	Christy's

BY SPECIAL FEATURE

BREAKFAST

25	Wish
24	A La Folie
23	Blue Door
21	S&S
	La Casita

BRUNCH

24	Nemo
23	Icebox Café
	SushiSamba
22	Joe Allen
21	La Palma

BUSINESS DINING

28	Palme d'Or
27	Pascal's on Ponce
	Joe's Stone Crab
26	Il Gabbiano
	Palm

CHILD-FRIENDLY

27	Joe's Stone Crab
26	Spiga

	Shibu
	Andiamo! Pizza
25	Tropical Chinese

DOCK & DINE

22	Garcia's
	Tony Chan's Water Club
21	Lido at The Standard
20	Red Fish Grill
–	Water Club

EARLY-BIRD

26	Osteria del Teatro
23	Café Prima Pasta
22	Here Comes the Sun
	A Fish Called Avalon
21	Tiramesu

EXPENSE ACCOUNT

28	Palme d'Or
27	Pascal's on Ponce
	Nobu Miami
	Joe's Stone Crab
	Azul

HOTEL DINING

28 Palme d'Or (Biltmore)
27 Nobu Miami (Shore Club)
   OLA (Sanctuary)
   Azul (Mandarin Oriental)
26 Hakkasan (Fontainebleau)

LATE DINING

27 Nobu Miami
26 Prime One Twelve
   Red Light
   Hiro's Yakko
25 Escopazzo

MEET FOR A DRINK

28 Palme d'Or
26 Il Gabbiano
   Michael's Genuine
   Red Light
   Bond St. Lounge

PEOPLE-WATCHING

28 Palme d'Or
27 Nobu Miami
   Joe's Stone Crab
26 Prime One Twelve
   Palm

PRIVATE ROOMS

28 Palme d'Or
26 Prime One Twelve
   Ortanique
   Graziano's
   Chef Allen's

QUICK BITES

26 Michael's Genuine
23 Icebox Café

Bugatti Pasta
Tutto Pasta
La Sandwicherie

QUIET CONVERSATION

28 Palme d'Or
27 Romeo's Cafe
   Pascal's on Ponce
   Hy-Vong
26 Francesco

SINGLES SCENES

26 Prime One Twelve
24 Nemo
   Fleming's Prime Steak
23 Blue Door
   Smith & Wollensky

TRENDY

27 Azul
26 Ortanique
   Bond St. Lounge
25 Scarpetta
   Toni's Sushi

WATERSIDE DINING

27 Azul
26 Red Light
25 Morton's
   Il Mulino New York
23 Smith & Wollensky

WINNING WINE LISTS

28 Palme d'Or
27 Pascal's on Ponce
   Michy's
   Joe's Stone Crab
   Azul

BY LOCATION

BAL/BAY HARBORS/ SUNNY ISLES/ SURFSIDE

26 Palm
   Adriana
25 Timo
   Il Mulino New York
24 Café Ragazzi

BRICKELL AREA/ DOWNTOWN

27 Azul
26 Il Gabbiano
   Capital Grille
25 Morton's
   Acqua

COCONUT GROVE

23 Le Bouchon du Grove
   Jaguar
22 Las Culebrinas
   George's in the Grove
20 Berries

CORAL GABLES

28 Palme d'Or
27 Pascal's on Ponce
26 Francesco
   Ortanique
   Graziano's

Menus, photos, voting and more – free at ZAGAT.com

DESIGN DISTRICT/ UPPER EAST SIDE

- 27 Michy's
- 26 Michael's Genuine
  Red Light
  Andiamo! Pizza
- 24 Sra. Martinez

KENDALL

- 26 Shibui
- 23 Bangkok (Kendall)
- 22 Bonefish Grill
- 21 Los Ranchos
  Fuji Hana

LITTLE HAVANA

- 27 Hy-Vong
- 25 Casa Juancho
- 21 Versailles
  Las Vegas
- 20 Islas Canarias

MIAMI BEACH

- 26 Hakkasan
- 25 Scarpetta
  Morton's
- 23 Café Prima Pasta
  Canyon Ranch Grill

NORTH DADE

- 26 Hiro's Yakko San
  Chef Allen's
- 25 Oishi Thai
  Bourbon Steak
  Captain Jim Hanson's

SOUTH BEACH

- 27 Nobu Miami
  OLA
  Joe's Stone Crab
- 26 Osteria del Teatro
  Prime One Twelve

SOUTH MIAMI

- 27 Matsuri
- 24 Café Pastis
  Old Lisbon
  Two Chefs
- 23 Lan

WEST DADE

- 26 Graziano's
  Basilico
- 25 Tropical Chinese
- 24 Kon Chau
- 23 Anthony's Pizza

Top Decor

28 Palme d'Or	Acqua
27 Restaurant at the Setai	Sra. Martinez
Blue Door	BED
Scarpetta	Ocean Prime
Bourbon Steak	**24** La Cofradia
Casa Tua	Area 31
26 Azul	Philippe
Wish	Gotham Steak
Hakkasan	Nikki Beach
Barton G.	Emeril's
25 Asia de Cuba	Grimpa Steakhouse
Il Gabbiano	Spiga
Red Fish Grill	Smith & Wollensky
Lido at The Standard	**23** Fleming's Prime Steak
Meat Market	Canyon Ranch
Il Mulino New York	Dolores/Lolita
Red the Steakhouse	Tanta
Café Sambal	Prime One Twelve
Grill on the Alley	Oceanaire
Capital Grille	Adriana

OUTDOORS

Ago	News Cafe
Barton G.	Perricone's
De Rodriguez Cuba	Uva 69
Fontana	Water Club
Maitardi	Wish

ROMANCE

Atrio Restaurant	Cioppino
Azul	Escopazzo
BED	Palme d'Or
Casa Tua	Romeo's Cafe

ROOMS

Area 31	Mr. Chow
Canyon Ranch Grill	Nemo
Gotham Steak	Philippe
Hakkasan	Restaurant at the Setai
Mia	Tantra

VIEWS

Azul	Lido at The Standard
Café Sambal	Red Fish Grill
Garcia's	Red Light
Gibraltar	Rusty Pelican
Il Gabbiano	Smith & Wollensky

Top Service

28 Palme d'Or
Romeo's Cafe

26 Christy's
Capital Grille

25 Osteria del Teatro
Il Gabbiano
Michy's
Wish
Azul
Il Mulino New York
Acqua
Pascal's on Ponce
Cioppino
Spiga
Trattoria Luna
Sra. Martinez
Scarpetta
Chef Allen's
Red the Steakhouse

24 Palm

Morton's
Caffe Abbracci
OLA
Ruth's Chris
Fleming's Prime Steak
Grazie Italian
Francesco
Oishi Thai
Michael's Genuine
Bourbon Steak
Caffe Vialetto
Joe's Stone Crab
Fogo de Chão

23 Oceanaire
Ortanique
Barton G.
Quinn's
Casa Tua
Ocean Prime
Cafe Avanti

Best Buys

Everyone loves a bargain, and the Miami/Dade area offers plenty of them. All-you-can-eat options are mostly for lunch and/or brunch.

ALL YOU CAN EAT ($30 AND UNDER)

- 23 Imlee
- Café Sambal
- 21 Atrio Restaurant∇
- 20 Ago
- Bizcaya∇
- 19 Old San Juan∇
- – Neomi's Grill

BURGERS/DOGS

- 20 8 Oz. Burger Bar
- Dogma Grill
- 18 OneBurger
- 14 Scotty's Landing
- – Burger & Beer Joint

CUBAN

- 22 Enriqueta's Sandwich Shop
- 21 Havana Harry's
- La Casita
- 20 Islas Canarias
- Puerto Sagua

DINER

- 22 Jumbo's∇
- 21 S&S
- 20 Original Pancake House
- 19 Big Pink
- 18 11th St. Diner

EARLY-BIRD

- 23 Café Prima Pasta
- 22 Here Comes the Sun
- A Fish Called Avalon
- 21 Spris
- Tiramesu
- 16 Rusty Pelican
- – Morgans

ETHNIC

- 25 Chéen Huaye
- 24 Kon Chau
- 23 Bangkok (Kendall)
- Guayacan∇
- 21 El Toro Taco
- 20 El Atlakat∇

PIZZA

- 26 Andiamo! Pizza
- 23 Anthony's Pizza
- Blú la Pizzeria del Sole
- Tutto Pizza
- 22 Piola
- 21 Big Cheese
- Fratelli La Bufala
- Pizza Rustica
- Mike's Italian Pizza
- 19 Mario the Baker

PRIX FIXE LUNCH

- 26 Ortanique ($22)
- 25 Su Shin Izakaya∇ ($9)
- Il Mulino New York ($20)
- 24 Oceanaire ($22)
- La Dorada ($20)
- Sra. Martinez ($22)
- Two Chefs ($22)
- Fogo de Chão ($27)
- 23 Emeril's ($36)
- Grimpa Steakhouse ($33)

PRIX FIXE DINNER

- 26 Ortanique ($35)
- 24 Oceanaire ($35)
- Maroosh ($25)
- Two Chefs ($35)
- Fogo de Chão ($47)
- 23 Grimpa Steakhouse ($40)
- – Prelude by Barton G. ($39)

PUB GRUB

- 21 Clarke's
- 20 Yard House
- 17 JohnMartin's
- 16 Titanic Brewery
- 14 Gordon Biersch
- – Waxy O'Connor's

SEAFOOD SHACKS

- 25 Captain Jim Hanson's
- 22 Garcia's
- 20 Bahamas Fish
- 15 Monty's
- 14 Scotty's Landing

BEST BUYS: BANG FOR THE BUCK

In order of Bang for the Buck rating.

1. S&S
2. Dogma Grill
3. La Sandwicherie
4. Baja Fresh
5. Lime Fresh Mexican
6. Andiamo! Pizza
7. Daily Bread
8. Pizza Rustica
9. Pei Wei Asian Diner
10. Taco Rico
11. A La Folie
12. Big Cheese
13. Original Pancake House
14. Enriqueta's Sandwich Shop
15. El Toro Taco
16. Anthony's Pizza
17. Here Comes the Sun
18. Sergio's
19. OneBurger
20. Kon Chau
21. Tutto Pizza
22. Chéen Huaye
23. Pasha's
24. Shorty's Bar-B-Q
25. La Casita
26. Piola
27. Bali Café
28. 11th St. Diner
29. Pit Bar-B-Q
30. Las Vegas
31. Blú la Pizzeria
32. Mario the Baker
33. La Casona
34. Bahamas Fish
35. Flanigan's Seafood
36. Tap Tap Haitian
37. Café at Books
38. Islas Canarias
39. Zuperpollo
40. Puerto Sagua

BEST BUYS: OTHER GOOD VALUES

Archie's Pizza
Bangkok (Coral Gables)
Bar-B-Que Beach
Basilico
Berries
Big Pink
Bin No. 18
Botequim Carioca
Bulldog BBQ
Captain Jim Hanson's
Cheese Course
Clarke's
David's Café
Deli Lane Café
Dynamo Café
El Atlakat
El Chalán
El Gran Inka
El Novillo
El Rancho Grande
Garcia's
Guayacan Restaurant
Havana Harry's
Hy-Vong

Indochine
Jumbo's
Khoury's
Lan
Little Havana
Mike's Italian Pizza
Miss Saigon
Mykonos
Off the Grille Bistro
Panya Thai
Paquito's
Paul Bakery
Pilar
Pita Hut
Red Light
Rice House of Kabob
Shake Shack
Soya & Pomodoro
Spris
Talavera
T-Mex Cantina
Versailles
Xixón
Yuga

MIAMI/DADE COUNTY
RESTAURANT
DIRECTORY

Abokado *Japanese/Pan-Latin*
| 19 | 20 | 18 | $42 |

Brickell Area | Mary Brickell Vill. | 900 S. Miami Ave. (bet. 9th & 10th Sts.) | Miami | 305-347-3700 | www.abokadosushi.com

"Mojitos made with sake" and other "ingenious", "beautifully presented" Japanese–Pan-Latin creations – including "always fresh" "sushi that's not what you're used to" – are the hallmarks of this "attractive" wood-and-terrazzo–infused Mary Brickell Villager; an outdoor patio adds to the "pleasant" vibe, but it's not enough for a few foes who fume over "high prices" for "small portions" and service that's merely "ok."

Acqua *Eclectic*
| 25 | 25 | 25 | $65 |

Brickell Area | Four Seasons | 1435 Brickell Ave. (bet. SE 14th Ln. & SE 14th Terr.) | Miami | 305-358-3535 | www.fourseasons.com

"You're likely to meet any number of celebs" or "high-powered movers and shakers" at this "grand restaurant for splurging", where the "impeccable" Eclectic cuisine and "top-notch service" are imbued by the "Four Seasons magic"; it's a "beautiful setting to watch beautiful people", for sure, and if some aesthetes say it "lacks intimacy" (or is even a "little boring"), most agree that overall it's got the "wow!" factor.

☒ Adriana *Eclectic/Seafood*
| 26 | 23 | 22 | $45 |

Surfside | 9477 Harding Ave. (bet. 94th & 95th Sts.) | 305-867-1220 | www.adrianarestaurant.com

The "unique" Eclectic cuisine at this "chic" Surfside "surprise" has diners wondering "is it Peruvian, Chinese, Continental?", but its Lima leanings become apparent with "fantastic" offerings like *lomo saltado* (salted tenderloin), "fresh" seafood and "excellent ceviche" paired with equally "excellent service"; it's "always a nice evening", and thanks to "perfect pisco sours", you may "feel the glow" long after the meal is over.

A Fish Called Avalon *Seafood*
| 22 | 21 | 20 | $52 |

South Beach | Avalon | 700 Ocean Dr. (7th St.) | Miami Beach | 305-532-1727 | www.afishcalledavalon.com

All the "people-watching is almost as good as the food" at this "lovely" seafooder "right in the thick" of South Beach, where the "live music", "ocean-as-decor" ambiance and "handsome waiters" "trying hard to please" add up to "pure Ocean Drive bliss"; not taking the bait are those who sniff it's too "touristy" and "hardly worth the price", but most maintain it's "still a winner."

Ago ● *Italian*
| 20 | 22 | 19 | $63 |

South Beach | Shore Club | 1901 Collins Ave. (19th St.) | Miami Beach | 305-695-3226 | www.agorestaurant.com

The "glitz of South Beach and a little Hollywood" unite at Robert De Niro's "stylish" Shore Club Northern Italian, whose "romantic location" – with a "view of the pool and Sky Bar" – "gives it a bump up" over "good but not wonderful" chow and "uneven service"; you'll be dining with the "cool crowd" (some say "mingling with the pretentious"), and paying "premium prices" for the privilege.

	FOOD	DECOR	SERVICE	COST

A La Folie ● *French*　24 19 18 $20

South Beach | 1701 Purdy Ave. (Abe Resnick Blvd.) | Miami Beach |
305-672-9336
South Beach | 516 Española Way (Drexel Ave.) | Miami Beach |
305-538-4484
www.alafoliecafe.com

As long as you "don't look outside", you'll think "you've been trans-
ported to a Parisian cafe" at this "adorable" (and "affordable") "little
piece of France on South Beach" and its Purdy Avenue sib; the "authentic" French bistro offerings include "outstanding crêpes",
"delicious croque madames" and even service of the "'I weel get to
yoo when I can' variety."

☑ AltaMare *Seafood*　25 15 22 $46

South Beach | 1233 Lincoln Rd. (bet. Alton Ct. & Alton Rd.) | Miami Beach |
305-532-3061 | www.altamarerestaurant.com

"Knowledgeable" servers who "even remember the snowbirds" sup-
plement the "warm" vibe at this "out-of-the-way" SoBe fish house, a
"secret" that locals want kept – if only to keep the "consistently fine
seafood with an Italian accent" for themselves; happily, its new,
larger location should alleviate concerns about tight conditions, all
the better to enjoy the "high-end cuisine at low-market prices."

Anacapri *Italian*　22 18 21 $36

Coral Gables | 2530 Ponce De Leon Blvd. (bet. Andalusia & Valencia Aves.) |
305-443-8388
Pinecrest | 12669 S. Dixie Hwy. (SW 128th St.) | 305-232-8001
Westernmost Dade | 5749 NW Seventh St. (NW 57th Ct.) | Miami |
305-266-1355 ⊠
www.anacaprifood.com

"Hearty" fare that's "thoughtfully prepared" and "served in a
friendly environment" makes this "homey" Italian trio "perfect" for
"family dining or pre-theater"; the "chic" Coral Gables branch
trumps the others' "bland strip-mall" settings, but you'll find "great
value" no matter which you choose; P.S. Pinecrest closed on Tuesdays.

☑ Andiamo! Brick Oven Pizza *Pizza*　26 16 18 $19

Upper East Side | 5600 Biscayne Blvd. (56th St.) | Miami | 305-762-5751 |
www.andiamopizzamiami.com

"The atmosphere isn't great, but who cares?" proclaim pie-lovers
pining for the "best and most creative pizza in Miami", found at this
"funky" former gas station on the Upper East Side with "only a few
cramped tables" inside and an "oasis of an outside patio"; "service
can be frustrating", so "get your car washed" next door "while you
wait" ("only in America!").

NEW Angelique Euro Café *European*　- - - M

Coral Gables | 117 Miracle Mile (Galiano St.) | 305-529-9922 |
www.angeliqueeurocafe.com

A multiculti menu marks this Coral Gables European with chic, contemporary trappings, an exhibition kitchen and live music most
nights during high season; wine lovers from serious oenophiles to

cork dorks will appreciate the fruits of owner Carlos Rossi's labors: more than 40 wines by the glass and wine flights composed of petite (three-ounce) pours.

☒ Anthony's Coal Fired Pizza ◑ *Pizza* | 23 | 16 | 20 | $21 |

NEW **Pinecrest** | 10205 S. Dixie Hwy. (bet. SW 102nd & SW 104th Sts.) | 305-740-5800

Aventura | Aventura Plaza | 17901 Biscayne Blvd. (bet. NE 179th St. & Point East Dr.) | 305-830-2625

NEW **Miami Lakes** | 15492 NW 77th Ct. (NW 154th St.) | 305-558-3950

www.anthonyscoalfiredpizza.com

See review in Ft. Lauderdale/Broward County Directory.

Archie's Gourmet Pizza *Pizza* | 18 | 15 | 16 | $21 |

Brickell Area | 50 SW 10th St. (bet. S. Miami & SW 1st Aves.) | Miami | 305-371-9980

Coral Gables | 166 Giralda Ave. (bet. Galiano St. & Ponce de Leon Blvd.) | 305-444-1557

Key Biscayne | Winn-Dixie Shopping Plaza | 600 Crandon Blvd. (Sunrise Dr.) | 305-365-5911

Westernmost Dade | 9769 NW 41st St. (97th Ave.) | Miami | 305-499-9757

www.archiespizza.com

If you like "no-nonsense" pies with "fresh, creative" toppings and "flavorful salads", these "casual", "kid-friendly" pizzerias deliver the goods; "service is hard to come by" and the decor needs an "update", but at least you'll have "money left over" after paying the tab.

Area 31 *Seafood* | 22 | 24 | 20 | $55 |

Downtown | Epic Hotel | 270 Biscayne Boulevard Way (Brickell Ave.) | Miami | 305-424-5234 | www.area31restaurant.com

Boasting "power views" that make you "feel like you're in a tropical Times Square", this "upscale" Downtown seafooder atop the Epic Hotel is "swank, sexy and scrumptious"; true, a few find the service a bit "lacking", but chef John Critchley's "interesting" cuisine and the "sophisticated atmosphere" hook most; P.S. the fin fare comes from 'Area 31', waters designated ecologically sustainable by the U.N.

☒ Asia de Cuba *Asian* | 23 | 25 | 20 | $65 |

South Beach | Mondrian South Beach | 1100 West Ave. (11th St.) | Miami Beach | 305-514-1940 | www.chinagrillmgt.com

This "stylish" Asian–Latin with "all-white decor" is "what Alice in Wonderland's poolside would look like", a "sumptuous" stage in the "hip" Mondrian Hotel for "pretty people" to consume cocktails and "innovative", "well-prepared" dishes "meant for sharing"; no thanks say skeptics, who slam prices "expensive even by SoBe standards" and "too much attitude"; P.S. it's part of the China Grill empire.

Atrio Restaurant *American* | ▽ 21 | 26 | 23 | $56 |

Downtown | Conrad Miami Hotel | 1395 Brickell Ave. (SE 14th St.) | Miami | 305-503-6529 | www.conradmiami.com

"People looking for spectacular views" of Downtown Miami "must" have a meal at this "romantic" 25th-floor enclave in the Conrad

FOOD | DECOR | SERVICE | COST

Hotel, where "very good" New American chow (much of it locally sourced) and "gracious service" try hard to measure up to that "unsurpassed" vista; it's pricey, though, so the cost-conscious may want to just "splurge on a couple of cocktails and enjoy."

Aura ● *Eclectic*   ∇ 26 | 24 | 21 | $39

South Beach | 613 Lincoln Rd. (Pennsylvania Ave.) | Miami Beach | 305-695-1100

It's "always worth a visit" to this South Beach bistro, if only to enjoy the Morris Lapidus–designed decor and the "people-watching on Lincoln Road"; happily, foodies will find there's also an "interesting menu" of "excellent" Eclectic eats (including the signature pistachio-crusted sea bass) that, coupled with "personal service", make it a "special place for a good meal."

∅ Azul ⊠ *Mediterranean*   27 | 26 | 25 | $74

Brickell Area | Mandarin Oriental Hotel | 500 Brickell Key Dr. (SE 8th St.) | Miami | 305-913-8358 | www.mandarinoriental.com

It "all comes together" at this "stunningly decorated" "gem" in the Mandarin Oriental – a "perfect combination" of "impeccable service", "excellent wines" and "stupendous" Mediterranean cuisine that "blends Asian flavors with European"; "one of the best views in Miami" adds to an atmosphere that's "sooo romantic", "even for those of us who've been married 50 years", and while it may be "made for those on an endless expense account", few deny that it's "worth every penny."

Bahamas Fish Market *Seafood*   20 | 9 | 17 | $19

West Miami | 13399 SW 40th St. (134th Ave.) | 305-225-4932
West Miami | 7200 SW Eighth St. (bet. SW 72nd & 73rd Aves.) | 305-264-1448

"The decor isn't great, but the value is" at these "always packed" West Miami seafooders serving up "delicious" Cuban-style fin fare ("get it grilled or try the specials"); they're part "fish market", so you know everything's "fresh", but be aware staffers "don't speak much English."

Baja Fresh Mexican Grill *Mexican*   18 | 12 | 15 | $13

Brickell Area | 1010 S. Miami Ave. (10th St.) | Miami | 305-523-2393
Coral Gables | 230 Miracle Mile (bet. Ponce De Leon Blvd. & Salzedo St.) | 305-442-9596
www.bajafresh.com

Part of the "new wave of Mexican fast-food joints", this "reliable" chain "lives up to its name" with "fresh" ingredients that provide "cooked-to-order", "relatively healthy" meals for "on-the-go" types; "inexpensive" tabs, "fantastic salsa bars" and a "kid-friendly" vibe trump the "slow service" and "cafeteria-like" looks.

Balans *Eclectic*   19 | 18 | 17 | $33

Brickell Area | Mary Brickell Vill. | 901 S. Miami Ave. (SW 9th St.) | Miami | 305-534-9191
Upper East Side | 6789 Biscayne Blvd. (68th St.) | Miami | 305-534-9191

(continued)

(continued)

Balans

South Beach | 1022 Lincoln Rd. (bet. Lenox & Michigan Aves.) | Miami Beach | 305-534-9191 ●
www.balans.co.uk

"Watch the world go by" – or at least the "unending Lincoln Road parade of people and dogs" – at this "down-to-earth" London import offering "reliable" Eclectic fare and "one of the best Sunday brunches" on South Beach; even if waiters have a little "attitude", admirers aver the "fair prices" make it a "good option"; P.S. fans are "delighted" about the newer Brickell and Upper East Side branches, even though they're "not as picturesque."

Bali Café ⊅ *Indonesian*

| 23 | 14 | 20 | $23 |

Downtown | 109 NE Second Ave. (NE 1st St.) | Miami | 305-358-5751

"If you didn't know how good the food is" at this "cramped yet cozy" Downtown Indonesian, "you'd probably walk by" and miss "authentic", "expertly prepared" dishes at "amazingly low" prices; "quick, friendly service" is another reason to venture to its "out-of-the-way" (some say "dodgy") location; P.S. "cash only."

Bangkok Bangkok *Thai*

| 20 | 16 | 19 | $28 |

Coral Gables | 157 Giralda Ave. (bet. Galiano St. & Ponce de Leon Blvd.) | 305-444-2397

Reliably "tasty food", "reasonable prices" and "efficient service" make this longtime Coral Gables Thai (unrelated to the Kendall venue with the same name) an "oldie but goody"; detractors dis "tired decor" and a "menu that's a bit cliche", but many still deem it a "value find" worth seeking out.

Bangkok Bangkok *Thai*

| 23 | 19 | 21 | $31 |

Kendall | Shops of Kendall | 12584 N. Kendall Dr. (127th Ave.) | 305-595-5839 | www.bangkokbangkok.net

Expect a "great taste of the East" at this "Thailand-in-a-mini-mall" in Kendall, where "dishes you can't find" elsewhere are "consistently delicious", "creatively presented" and "fairly priced"; whether you "sit at tables or on the floor", it's "definitely a place to blow your diet."

Bar-B-Que Beach ● *BBQ*

| 14 | 13 | 15 | $23 |

South Beach | 1555 Washington Ave. (bet. 15th & 16th Sts.) | Miami Beach | 305-538-7201

"Catch a game" while digging into "huge portions" of "decent" "pulled pork and smoked brisket" at this SoBe BBQ "joint" in an "unlikely Polynesian-style setting"; but critics 'cue up to slam "über-cheesy" decor, "hit-or-miss" service and fare they deem "mediocre at best."

⊠ Barton G. The Restaurant *American*

| 23 | 26 | 23 | $71 |

South Beach | 1427 West Ave. (14th Ct.) | Miami Beach | 305-672-8881 | www.bartong.com

"Gaudí meets the Ringling Brothers" at this "unique" SoBe New American in a "festive tropical setting" where "charming" waiters lug "oversized portions" of "elaborately presented" food "so far over the top you need a ladder to eat" ("where else is duck served in a hollowed-out decoy?"); cynics shrug it's "all flash, no substance" and "more show than restaurant", but vets insist that "seeing is believing" – just "close your eyes when paying the bill."

NEW Baru Urbano ● *Pan-Latin* | - | - | - | M |

Brickell Area | 1001 S. Miami Ave. (SE 10th St.) | Miami | 305-381-5901 | www.baruurbano.com

The graffiti-esque decor incorporating Pop Art murals and Latin concert posters is as eclectic as the menu at this hip yet casual Brickell Area Pan-Latin, where arepas (South American corn cakes), ceviches and churrasco steak share space on the menu with Caesar salad, smoked salmon pasta and risotto primavera; P.S. night owls hoot over the 3 AM closing time Wednesday–Saturday.

Basilico ⊠ *Italian* | 26 | 16 | 23 | $31 |

Airport Area | 5879 NW 36th St. (NW 57th Ave.) | Miami | 305-871-3585
NEW Doral | 10405 NW 41st St. (bet. NW 102nd & NW 107th Aves.) | 305-406-3737 Ⓜ
www.basilicomiami.com

Its "strip-mall" perch near the airport "isn't the nicest", but this "little treasure" "more than makes up for it" with "amazing" Northern Italian food (including its signature linguine frutti de mare); the "pleasurable experience" is made even better by "good prices" and "attentive owners" who "treat you like family" "even if it's your first time"; P.S. the Doral branch opened post-Survey.

Bayside Fish Market *Seafood* | ▽ 13 | 10 | 13 | $24 |

Key Biscayne | 3501 Rickenbacker Cswy. (½ mi. south of the bridge) | 305-361-0177

"After the grueling bike ride over the causeway", locals chill with a "cold beer and simple seafood" at this "waterfront" Key Biscayne "hideaway" that's "not on the tourist radar"; then again, cynics snipe its "location is the only positive aspect", citing "long waits" for "mediocre everything."

BED ● *Eclectic* | 17 | 25 | 18 | $60 |

South Beach | 929 Washington Ave. (bet. 9th & 10th Sts.) | Miami Beach | 305-532-9070 | www.bedmiami.com

"Who knew eating in bed could be so much fun?" ponder patrons turned on by this "chic", "upscale" Eclectic that's a "perfect date spot", at least if you want a "South Beach-y experience" with lots of "eye candy" (particularly when it becomes a "full-blown nightspot"); it turns off just as many, though, who target "twin-bed-quality food at king-size prices" and yawn the whole concept "is *so* last decade."

Bella Luna *Italian* | 22 | 18 | 21 | $38 |

Aventura | Aventura Mall | 19575 Biscayne Blvd. (William Lehman Cswy.) | 305-792-9330

"Shop till you drop, then relax" at this "always jammin'" mall-locked Aventura Italian that dishes "affordable, honest" fare ("fish, pasta or just a salad") and gets props for "efficient service", even though it's usually "busy" and sometimes "hectic"; a few "don't get the fuss", but many agree "it sure beats eating in the food court."

	FOOD	DECOR	SERVICE	COST

Berries *Health Food*

	20	17	19	$25

Coconut Grove | 2884 SW 27th Ave. (Coconut Ave.) | 305-448-2111 | www.berriesinthegrove.com

For "unpretentious" dining in a "rustic open-air setting", "tasty" health food "you can actually enjoy" and prices that are "berry, berry good", you "can't go wrong" at this "tucked away" yet "buzzing" Coconut Grover attracting a "friendly crowd"; "attentive" service and "splendid" brunches are other pluses.

Big Cheese *Pizza*

	21	12	20	$18

South Miami | 8080 SW 67th Ave. (U.S. 1) | 305-662-6855 | www.bigcheesemiami.com

"You really get your money's worth" at this "low-key" South Miami Italian where the "pleasant service" and "huge" portions of super-"cheesy pizza", "red-sauce pasta" and "addictive garlic rolls" "never disappoint"; but be prepared for a "mobbed" scene with "over-whelming University of Miami decor."

Big Pink ❶ *Diner*

	19	15	16	$23

South Beach | 157 Collins Ave. (2nd St.) | Miami Beach | 305-532-4700 | www.bigpinkrestaurant.com

"You never know who you're going to see" at this "1950s diner on steroids" on South Beach, where the "super-sized portions" of "reasonably priced" "down-home grub" make it "perfect" for a "bite after the beach" or a "late-night", "I've-partied-my-butt-off break-fast"; detractors beg to differ, citing "lots of noise" and a staff that "always seems to be bothered about something."

Bin No. 18 ⊠ *Mediterranean*

	22	19	21	$29

Downtown | 1800 Biscayne Plaza | 275 NE 18th St. (entrance on Biscayne Blvd.) | Miami | 786-235-7575 | www.bin18miami.com

"Loiter after work with a book or a friend" at chef-owner Alfredo Patino's "welcome" wine bar/Med cafe, a "sophisticated" Downtown "hangout" with a "top-quality" "menu that leans toward tapas" but includes "perfect meat and cheese boards"; round out meals with "hard-to-find wines", all served "with a smile" amid "slightly funky decor" (read: crystal chandeliers and wine barrel tables).

Bistro Bisou *French*

	18	15	19	$35

South Miami | Dadeland Plaza Mall | 9519 S. Dixie Hwy. (Datran Blvd.) | 786-268-0178 | www.bistrobisou.net

It may be "tucked away in the corner of a strip mall", but this "friendly" South Miami French serves up "authentic bistro fare with a Parisian accent" that's "simple, delicious" and "reasonably" priced; even if a handful find it "nothing special", it's "good for the 'hood."

Bizcaya *Continental/Mediterranean*

	▽ 20	25	21	$60

Coconut Grove | Ritz-Carlton Coconut Grove | 3300 SW 27th Ave. (bet. Bayshore Dr. & Tigertail Ave.) | 305-644-4675 | www.ritzcarlton.com

A "delightful" ambiance that's "among the finest in Miami" – "you have to love the little stools for your purse" – garners praise for this Continental-Med in the Ritz-Carlton Coconut Grove; but mixed

FOOD · DECOR · SERVICE · COST

grades for service ("excellent" vs. "a bit slow") and food have some dubbing it a "place that can't seem to get its act together", though kitchen tweaks may fix that.

BLT Steak *Steak* 　　24 | 23 | 23 | $70

South Beach | The Betsy Hotel | 1440 Ocean Dr. (bet 14th & 15th Sts.) | Miami Beach | 305-673-0044 | www.bltsteak.com

Chef-restaurateur Laurent Tourondel's "chic" chophouse in SoBe's Betsy Hotel wins praise for its "perfectly cooked" steaks, "amazing sauces and phenomenal sides", not to mention "fabulous" signature popovers; the "no-attitude" service enhances a "civilized" ambiance that's "at once casual and refined", though a few find the lobby setting a little "weird", and wallet-watchers balk at the "big bill."

⧫ Blue Door at Delano ◑ *Brazilian/French* 　　23 | 27 | 23 | $73

South Beach | Delano Hotel | 1685 Collins Ave. (17th St.) | Miami Beach | 305-674-6400 | www.chinagrillmgt.com

"Cool and sleek like the tan young things at the pool", this Delano Hotel "treasure" remains the "scene of all scenes", where an "attentive" staff makes "everyone feel like one of the beautiful people" as they down consulting chef Claude Troisgros' "delish" New French–Brazilian fare and "rub shoulders with SoBe celebs"; if some say it's "pretentious and pricey", more insist it's still the "place to be" "after all these years."

Blue Sea ◑ *Japanese* 　　▽ 25 | 25 | 24 | $62

South Beach | Delano Hotel | 1685 Collins Ave. (17th St.) | Miami Beach | 305-674-6400 | www.delano-hotel.com

Despite its "simple setting" (a pair of communal tables) in the Delano Hotel lobby, this "creative", "sexy" Japanese is deemed "a must-stop on your visit to South Beach" by devotees; prices can add up, but figure in "excellent sushi and service" and you've got "quite an experience."

Blú la Pizzeria del Sole *Pizza* 　　23 | 18 | 19 | $25

South Miami | 7201 SW 59th Ave. (Sunset Dr.) | 305-666-9285 | www.blurestaurantsgroup.com

"If it has dough and it's Italian", you "can always count" on this "unpretentious", midpriced South Miami "classic" to "make it well"; *amici* aver that its "world-class, thin-crust pizza" is "one of the best" in town, especially enjoyable when you "sit outdoors" and "people-watch" while the "attentive" servers do their thing; P.S. it's a sib of Trattoria Sole.

NEW Bombay Darbar *Indian* 　　- | - | - | M

Coconut Grove | 3195 Commodore Plaza (Main Hwy.) | 305-444-7272 | www.bombaydarbarrestaurant.com

All the classics of the Indian kitchen, from butter chicken to tandoori lamb chops, are plated at this modest Coco Grover owned by a husband-and-wife team from Mumbai; palates from sensitive to asbestos-lined are accommodated by heat levels that begin at mild and build toward three-alarm fire.

☑ Bond St. Lounge *Japanese*

26 | 21 | 20 | $55

South Beach | Townhouse Hotel | 150 20th St. (Collins Ave.) | Miami Beach | 305-398-1806 | www.townhousehotel.com

"For a respite from the madness" of South Beach, raw-fin fans converge on this "*très* hip, *très* sexy" Japanese "hidden" in the basement of the Townhouse Hotel; the "innovative" sushi, including "terrific spicy tuna rolls", is "so good it's worth having to eat at the tiny tables" (read: "uncomfortable"), and even if some sniff you "have to cash in bonds" to pay the tab, most patrons agree it "doesn't disappoint."

☑ Bonefish Grill *Seafood*

22 | 20 | 21 | $35

Kendall | 12520 SW 120th St. (125th Pl.) | 786-293-5713
Westernmost Dade | 14218 SW Eighth St. (bet. SW 142nd & 143rd Aves.) | Miami | 305-487-6430
www.bonefishgrill.com
See review in Ft. Lauderdale/Broward County Directory.

Bongos Cuban Café ☒ *Cuban*

17 | 22 | 16 | $38

Downtown | 601 Biscayne Blvd. (bet. 6th & 7th Sts.) | Miami | 786-777-2100 | www.bongoscubancafe.com

Amigos of Gloria Estefan's Downtowner near American Airlines Arena "love" the "festive" atmosphere, "refreshing mojitos" and "abundant" quantities of "relatively authentic" fare at this "terrific" "place to salsa the night away"; dance but eat elsewhere opine others, because "as a Cuban restaurant, it's a great disco" (and "strictly for tourists" at that).

NEW Botequim Carioca ☒ *Brazilian*

– | – | – | M

Biscayne | 900 Biscayne Blvd. (NE 9th St.) | Miami | 877-902-2224 | www.botequimcarioca.com

Straight from Rio de Janeiro (where it has a quartet of older sibs) comes this casual, pubby Biscayne Brazilian serving midpriced South American tapas like its signature fried salt cod dumplings and such traditional dishes as feijoada (pork and black bean stew); a roster of Brazilian beers and relatively late closing times – midnight on weekdays and 1 AM on weekends – round out the picture.

☑ Bourbon Steak ☒ *Steak*

25 | 27 | 24 | $84

Aventura | Fairmont Turnberry Isle Resort & Club | 19999 W. Country Club Dr. (Aventura Blvd./NE 199th St.) | 786-279-6600 | www.michaelmina.net

Celebrity chef-restaurateur Michael Mina "has done it again" crow carnivores about this "swank" Aventura chophouse, where the "killer" cuts, "superb" wine list and "exceptional" "city-chic" decor by Tony Chi combine to "give new meaning to the American steakhouse"; service is "marvelous" too, but brace yourself for a "breathtaking" experience, "especially when you get the bill."

Bubba Gump Shrimp Co. *Seafood*

15 | 16 | 17 | $27

Biscayne | Bayside Mktpl. | 401 Biscayne Blvd. (bet. NE 4th & 5th Sts.) | Miami | 305-379-8866 | www.bubbagump.com

Boatloads of Bubba-razzi "love" the "cheesy but fun" "family atmosphere" at this "*Forrest Gump*–inspired" chain serving up an ocean of "mostly fried seafood"; but cynics call it an "overpriced" "tourist trap" with a "tired theme" and suggest "Mrs. Gump would be very upset."

Bugatti, The Art of Pasta *Italian*   23 | 18 | 22 | $32

Coral Gables | 2504 Ponce de Leon Blvd. (Andalusia Ave.) | 305-441-2545
"A long-standing Coral Gables staple", this "reliable" Italian "never changes – but that's good", especially if you dig "fresh homemade pasta" delivered by "friendly" staffers; while many insist the "legendary" lasagna (served the "first Wednesday of every month") is the "main thing to go for", thrifty types tout the tabs.

Bulldog Barbecue *BBQ*   20 | 14 | 19 | $24

Aventura | 15400 Biscayne Blvd. (156th St.) | 305-940-9655 |
www.bulldog-bbq.com
The "barbecue with a twist" – plus salads, sliders and a slew of sides – at *Top Chef* contestant Howie Kleinberg's diminutive, "sparsely" decorated Aventura strip-maller proves that "good things can come in small packages", even if "they're still working out the kinks"; work harder plead purists, who find the "untraditional 'cue" only "adequate" and bark "there's not enough bite in this bulldog."

Burger & Beer Joint *Burgers*   - | - | - | I

NEW **Downtown** | 900 S. Miami Ave. (SE 9th St.) | Miami |
305-523-2244
South Beach | 1766 Bay Rd. (bet. Abe Resnick Blvd. & 18th St.) |
Miami Beach | 305-672-3287 ●
www.burgernbeerjoint.com
These aptly named, no-frills SoBe and Downtown multitaskers – part sports bar, part family mecca – serve up burgers featuring some of the best buns on the beach (ciabatta, whole wheat, etc.) and patties (beef, turkey, mushroom) that can be assembled in countless configurations, plus signature creations named after rock oldies; with some hundred bottles of beer on the wall and a decent selection of wines and more potent concoctions, they can get a bit raucous.

Café at Books & Books, The *American*   21 | 18 | 17 | $23

Coral Gables | 265 Aragon Ave. (bet. Ponce de Leon Blvd. & Salzedo St.) |
305-448-9599
South Beach | 927 Lincoln Rd. (bet. Jefferson & N. Michigan Aves.) |
Miami Beach | 305-695-8898
www.booksandbooks.com
Page-turners "always feel more literate" after noshing on the "simple", "well-prepared" New American vittles at these "won't-break-the-bank" cafes affiliated with "high-class bookstores"; faultfinders report "inconsistent service" at both, however, and while noshers are still "surrounded" by tomes at the "cozy" Coral Gables branch, SoBe's titles have moved to a "larger space" a few doors down.

Cafe Avanti *Italian*   22 | 20 | 23 | $39

Miami Beach | 732 41st St. (bet. Chase & Prairie Aves.) | 305-538-4400 |
www.cafeavanti.com
"Feel like a local" (and "part of the family") at this "elegant" Italian in Miami Beach, where "delicious" fare comes with "personal service" by

the "charming" owner and his staff; bonus: there's "easy parking", so "your money will go toward food, not valet."

Café Pastis ⧈ French   24 | 14 | 20 | $36

South Miami | 7310 S. Red Rd. (bet. 73rd & 74th Sts.) | 305-665-3322 | www.cafepastis.com

"Wonderful", "well-priced" French cuisine that "comes out of a kitchen the size of a closet" "transports you to Marseilles" at this "petite" South Miami bistro; service can be "authentically brusque" too, but it's still so "crowded" surveyors advise "don't go without a reservation."

Café Prima Pasta ◑ Italian   23 | 19 | 22 | $40

Miami Beach | 414 71st St. (Abbott Ave.) | 305-867-0106 | www.primapasta.com

"*Molto buono!*" proclaim *paesani* about the "hearty", "dependable" Northern Italiana at this "non-touristy" Miami Beach "favorite" with "decent" tabs and service that's "attentive without being overbearing"; it's filled with "old-world charm", which for some translates into a "clubby" vibe that "feels like you're in a scene from *The Sopranos*."

Café Ragazzi ◑ Italian   24 | 18 | 23 | $46

Surfside | 9500 Harding Ave. (95th St.) | 305-866-4495 | www.caferagazzi.com

"Always crowded, always noisy, always good": that's the word on this "upscale" Surfside Italian where "superb" food and a staff that "makes you feel welcome" spell "la dolce vita"; though some warn of "cramped quarters" and "long waits" ("complimentary wine" helps pass the time), most shrug it off, deeming the "area fixture" a "true pleasure."

Café Sambal Asian   23 | 25 | 21 | $53

Brickell Area | Mandarin Oriental Hotel | 500 Brickell Key Dr. (SE 8th St.) | Miami | 305-913-8288 | www.mandarinoriental.com

It may not be the "newest, hottest, sexiest" scene around, but no matter: "sophisticated" Pan-Asian fare ("from fresh sushi to Kobe burgers"), "stunning" views of Brickell Key and beyond "from the terrace" and "attentive" service make for an "enchanting" experience; plus, compared with its "upstairs" Mandarin Oriental sister, Azul, it's got "lighter fare and prices – and still plenty of panache."

Caffe Abbracci ◑ Italian   24 | 21 | 24 | $52

Coral Gables | 318 Aragon Ave. (bet. 42nd Ave. & Salzedo St.) | 305-441-0700 | www.caffeabbracci.com

A "regular who's who" of Coral Gables descends upon owner Nino Pernetti's "old-school" "stalwart", whose "tried-and-true" Italian dishes and "warm" staffers (you may get a "kiss-kiss reception" if "they know you") "never disappoint"; "old-fashioned" decor and noise levels that "can be high" rankle a few, but the majority says "so what?"

Caffe Da Vinci Italian   21 | - | 20 | $47

Bay Harbor Islands | 1009 Kane Concourse (E. Bay Harbor Dr.) | 305-861-8166 | www.caffedavinci.com

"Large portions" of "solid" Italian fare and a staff "always ready to go out of its way to fulfill special requests" ensure that this "classy", "upscale" Bay Harbor Islands spot (and sib to Oggi Caffe) is "constantly packed"; it's "small", though, so there may be a "wait for a table even with reservations"; P.S. a recent refurb may outdate the Decor score.

Caffé Milano ⏺ *Italian*   19 | 19 | 17 | $49

South Beach | 850 Ocean Dr. (bet. 8th & 9th Sts.) | Miami Beach | 305-532-0707

This South Beach Italian "old-time" destination is "still attracting model wannabes, scenesters and tourists" looking to get in on "all the action on Ocean Drive"; though service can be "distracted" and food ranges from "very good" to "not very good", just about everyone concurs that "with water in your front yard, you can't lose."

Caffe Vialetto *Italian*   24 | 18 | 24 | $48

Coral Gables | 4019 Le Jeune Rd. (Bird Rd.) | 305-446-5659 | www.caffevialetto.com

Take an "amazing trip down taste bud lane" at this "unassuming" nook in Coral Gables where the "creative" Italian fare with a Latin-Caribbean punch packs "explosive flavors"; "spot-on service" and a "solid wine selection" add to the appeal, though "expect your neighbors to overhear conversations" (if it's not too "noisy", that is).

Calamari *Italian*   - | - | - | M

Coconut Grove | 3540 Main Hwy. (Franklin Ave.) | 305-441-0219 | www.calamarirestaurant.com

Another hit by Miami restaurateur Tommy Billante (Carpaccio, Gaia, Il Villagio, Luna, etc.), this bright and bustling Italian seafooder delights Coconut Grovers with its idyllic courtyard adorned with a fountain and comfortably spaced tables and umbrellas; inside, diners can peer into the open kitchen as they dig into a broad selection of midpriced pastas, bruschetta and pizzas; P.S. there's a small market on-site.

Canyon Ranch Grill *Health Food*   23 | 23 | 22 | $53

Miami Beach | Canyon Ranch Living | 6801 Collins Ave. (bet. 67th & 69th Sts.) | 305-514-7474 | www.canyonranch.com

Partisans proclaim that the "yummy" "organic" fare at this "upscale but unstuffy" health-fooder in the oceanfront Canyon Ranch Miami Beach "tastes of real ingredients" and will "almost make you forget it's good for you" (and it's relatively "affordable" at that); still, a few critics sniff that the grub and service "don't live up to the beautiful space", though the "nutritional information on the menu" is a "big plus."

ⓩ Capital Grille *Steak*   26 | 25 | 26 | $65

Brickell Area | 444 Brickell Ave. (SE 5th St.) | Miami | 305-374-4500 | www.thecapitalgrille.com

Sure, "it's part of a chain", but this "swank" "meat lover's paradise" attracts a "well-heeled" horde of South Florida's "movers and shakers" jonesing for "generous portions" of "superb beef" (including a Kona-crusted sirloin) and "to-die-for sides"; it's all accented by an "extensive wine list", "clubby" atmosphere and service that "makes you feel like royalty", which you may have to be to afford the "prime prices", but partisans proclaim you "get what you pay for."

	FOOD	DECOR	SERVICE	COST

Captain Jim Hanson's
Seafood 🅱 *Seafood*

| 25 | 6 | 19 | $22 |

North Miami | 12950 W. Dixie Hwy. (bet. NE 129th & NE 130th Sts.) | 305-892-2812

"Talk about fresh!" – that's how chowderheads describe the "excellent" fin fare at this "funky" North Miami "fish market" whose "no-frills" feasts come with "incredibly reasonable" tabs; "service can be spotty" and "parking is a problem", but at this "price point", loyalists "return time and again."

Captain's Tavern *Seafood*

| 23 | 13 | 20 | $36 |

Pinecrest | 9625 S. Dixie Hwy./U.S. 1 (SW 98th St.) | 305-666-5979 | www.captainstavern.com

The "captain has remained on top of the heap" by serving "fish so fresh it seems to be squirming" at this "throwback" Pinecrest seafooder with "experienced" staffers and a "rationally priced" wine list "that'll bring tears to the eyes of any oenophile"; the "musty" nautical decor "hasn't changed in eons", but "if you can get past that", "it's a treat."

Carpaccio *Italian*

| 22 | 18 | 20 | $45 |

Bal Harbour | Bal Harbour Shops | 9700 Collins Ave. (96th St.) | 305-867-7777 | www.carpaccioatbelharbour.com

"Mall food never tasted so good" proclaim fans of this Italian at the "chichi" Bal Harbour Shops where "fast" service and "fair prices" make it a primo spot for "people- and fancy-car-watching"; it can get "crazy when busy", so "sit outside or you'll be deafened by the noise."

Casa Juancho *Spanish*

| 25 | 23 | 23 | $46 |

Little Havana | 2436 SW Eighth St. (bet. SW 24th & 25th Aves.) | Miami | 305-642-2452 | www.casajuancho.com

With the "look of a true Spanish restaurant" and "superb" cuisine "as genuine as you can get" ("I slobber just thinking about its paella"), it's no surprise this "reliable" Little Havana casa has "been there forever"; but it's the staff that "makes you feel like you're home" and the "roaming musicians" who keep it all "lively and fun."

Casa Larios *Cuban*

| 19 | 17 | 18 | $27 |

South Miami | 5859 SW 73rd St. (SW 58th Ct.) | 305-662-5656
West Miami | 7705 W. Flagler St. (SW 79th Ave.) | 305-266-5494
www.casalariosonline.com

"Hefty" portions of "basic, honest Cuban fare" that's "just like mom would make" explain why these "friendly", "well-priced" South and West Miamians are usually "packed"; cynics snipe about "mediocre" chow and "sloppy service", but they're outvoted; P.S. "live music" on Saturdays at the 73rd Street venue.

Casa Paco *Cuban/Spanish*

| 20 | 16 | 20 | $27 |

South Miami | 8868 SW 40th St./Bird Rd. (SW 88th Pl.) | 305-554-7633 | www.casapacomiami.com

"Family-friendly" and family-owned, this "old-school" Spanish-Cuban "find" in South Miami continues to churn out an "extensive" selection of "authentic" dishes (e.g. tostones, picadillo) in a dark-wooded space; prices that are easy on the wallet and "good service" round out the package.

☑ Casa Tua *Italian* 25 | 27 | 23 | $83

South Beach | Casa Tua | 1700 James Ave. (17th St.) | Miami Beach | 305-673-1010 | www.casatualifestyle.com

A "jet-set" clientele lands at this "intimate" SoBe Northern Italian where "nothing compares" to "amazing" cuisine that "makes you drool just thinking about it" – except, of course, the "classic service" and "gorgeous setting" akin to a "wealthy friend's villa"; even with "outrageously expensive" tabs and attitude "so thick you can cut it with a knife", for most it's a "complete dining experience."

Caviar Kaspia *French* - | - | - | VE

South Beach | The Webster | 1220 Collins Ave. (12th & 13th Sts.) | Miami Beach | 305-674-7899 | www.kaspiamiami.com

Fish eggs with a French pedigree come to South Beach in the form of this cozy sibling of the 1927 Parisian original; located in The Webster boutique, the luxe eatery attracts a fashion-forward clientele that feasts on farmed and wild caviar ($360-an-ounce Iranian golden osetra, anyone?), smoked fish and even grass-fed filet mignon, all enjoyed in a splashy, terrazzo-floored space that was once a hotel lobby.

Charlotte Bistro ☒ *French* - | - | - | M

Coral Gables | 264 Miracle Mile (Galiano St.) | 305-443-3003 | www.charlotte-bistro.com

The quirky decor of this midtier Coral Gables charmer – mismatched tables and chairs, vintage wallpaper, an intricate black-and-white-tiled floor – is reflected in the equally interesting bistro-esque menu of chef-owner Elida Villarroel, who apprenticed with several Michelin-starred French chefs; forward-thinking fowl fanciers flock to dishes like pheasant terrine with cardamom-infused pears and caper-raisin coulis.

Chéen Huaye *Mexican* 25 | 15 | 23 | $25

North Miami | 15400 Biscayne Blvd. (NE 151st St.) | 305-956-2808 | www.cheenhuaye.com

For a "nice change" from the "typical" "burritos and refried beans", amigos detour to this "casual, consistent and cool" North Miami strip-maller dishing out "authentic" "Yucatán-style" Mexican that's "worth the search"; other pluses include "great prices" and "friendly servers" who really care "that you're pleased."

☑ Cheesecake Factory ◐ *American* 20 | 19 | 19 | $29

Aventura | Aventura Mall | 19501 Biscayne Blvd. (NE 195th St.) | 305-792-9696

Coconut Grove | CocoWalk | 3015 Grand Ave. (Virginia St.) | 305-447-9898

Kendall | Dadeland Mall | 7497 N. Kendall Dr. (SW 88th St.) | 305-665-5400 www.thecheesecakefactory.com

"You'll be surrounded by a mountain of food" (and it's "usually pretty good") ordered off a "monstrous menu" at these American chain links, so "be prepared to share or take half home"; it's "always a zoo" and "long waits" are the norm, but "everyone knows what to expect here", and that includes prices that "can't be beat."

☑ Cheese Course *Eclectic*
26 | 15 | 18 | $18

NEW Downtown | 3451 NE First Ave. (Midtown Blvd.) | Miami | 786-220-6681 | www.thecheesecourse.com

See review in Ft. Lauderdale/Broward County Directory.

☑ Chef Allen's *Seafood*
26 | 22 | 25 | $63

Aventura | 19088 NE 29th Ave. (bet. NE 191st St. & 28th Ave.) | 305-935-2900 | www.chefallens.com

"The master is still at work" exalt enthusiasts wowed by the "reinvention" of original Mango Gangster Allen Susser's "expense-account destination" into a "seafood bistro" featuring "fresh, imaginative" fin fare, "striking modern decor" ("a treat for the eyes"), "superb service" and "downscaled pricing"; if a few nostalgists "miss" the "good old times", they're overruled by those who say this Aventura "classic" has "been reborn – and the baby is terrific."

☑ China Grill ● *Asian*
23 | 23 | 20 | $60

South Beach | 404 Washington Ave. (4th St.) | Miami Beach | 305-534-2211 | www.chinagrillmgt.com

For more than a decade, this "still hot" Pan-Asian has been dishing out "glitz" to go with "fun fusion food" served "family-style" in a "stylish" space; it's got "outlandish prices (even by SoBe standards)" and a "deafening" clatter, but the "scenesters don't seem to mind"; P.S. its newer Ft. Lauderdale sib features "gorgeous water views."

☑ Christy's ⊠ *Steak*
25 | 21 | 26 | $55

Coral Gables | 3101 Ponce de Leon Blvd. (Malaga Ave.) | 305-446-1400 | www.christysrestaurant.com

If you're craving "fantastic" filets and a "last-meal-good" Caesar salad, committed carnivores say "forget the chains" and head to this "worth-every-dime" Coral Gables "classic" that's "exactly what a steakhouse should be"; sticklers suggest it's "past its prime (rib)" – particularly the "somewhat stodgy" decor – but a "fabulous" staff that's "been there forever" ensures it's "always a pleasure" for most.

Cioppino *Italian*
23 | 21 | 25 | $63

Key Biscayne | Ritz-Carlton Key Biscayne | 455 Grand Bay Dr. (Crandon Blvd.) | 305-365-4500 | www.ritzcarlton.com

"If you're lucky enough to go on a full moon" and perch on the "beautiful veranda", you'll experience this "romantic" waterfront Italian in the "deluxe" Ritz-Carlton Key Biscayne at its best; "excellent" fare (particularly an "awesome brunch") and staffers who make "you feel like royalty" round out the experience, though "high prices" hinder wallet-watchers.

Clarke's ● *Irish*
21 | 19 | 22 | $29

South Beach | 840 First St. (bet. Alton Rd. & Washington Ave.) | Miami Beach | 305-538-9885 | www.clarkesmiamibeach.com

It may "look more like the grill at a posh country club", but this SoBe "sleeper" is every bit a "damn fine" Irish pub, with the "delicious" grub (including the "juiciest" burgers) and "pints of Guinness" to prove it; "friendly" service and an owner who "rocks" create a "homey atmosphere", while "low prices" make it a "local hang."

Daily Bread Pinecrest *Mideastern*   23 | 9 | 16 | $15

Pinecrest | 12131 S. Dixie Hwy. (SW 121st St.) | 305-253-6115 | www.dailybread2.com

For "fabulous" Middle Eastern "goodies", consider this "reasonably priced" Pinecrester where "people who couldn't be nicer" proffer "fast, healthy" fare; even "industrial-like" decor (it's "more of a market than a restaurant") "doesn't get in the way of an enjoyable meal."

da Leo Trattoria ● *Italian*   17 | 16 | 18 | $37

South Beach | 819 Lincoln Rd. (bet. Jefferson & Meridian Aves.) | Miami Beach | 305-674-0350 | www.daleotrattoria.com

"Unlike many places on Lincoln Road", you'll find "unpretentious service" and "big portions for moderate prices" at this "basic" South Beach Italian with "lovely outdoor seating"; the unimpressed deem it "nothing special", but at least there's "unsurpassed people-watching."

David's Cafe ● *Cuban*   17 | 10 | 16 | $21

South Beach | 1058 Collins Ave. (bet. 10th & 11th Sts.) | Miami Beach | 305-534-8736
South Beach | 1654 Meridian Ave. (Lincoln Ln.) | Miami Beach | 305-672-8707
www.davidscafe.com

To relieve the "club munchies", night owls swoop into these "busy" Cuban cafes offering a "welcome departure from SoBe's high prices"; if some maintain the "uninspired" chow is matched only by a "blah atmosphere", caffeine-hounds herald "cafe con leches done right."

DB Bistro Moderne *French*   - | - | - | E

Downtown | JW Marriott Marquis Miami | 345 Avenue of the Americas (Brickell Ave.) | Miami | 305-350-0750

Set to debut in late October is this sleek, oh-so-moderne French by NYC's celebrated chef Daniel Boulud in the new Marriott Marquis Downtown; the Yabu Pushelberg–designed space boasts 16-ft. ceilings, a wine tower, a trio of dining areas and a street-level terrace overlooking the river, while the menu will feature Boulud's contemporary bistro fare with, of course, his famed truffle-stuffed burger.

Deli Lane Café & Tavern *Deli*   17 | 13 | 17 | $22

Brickell Area | 1401 Brickell Ave. (14th St.) | Miami | 305-377-8811
South Miami | 7230 SW 59th Ave. (SW 72nd St.) | 305-665-0606
www.delilane.com

The "coffee-shop menu on steroids" at these Brickell and South Miami sandwich joints is packed with "reliable" deli fare, plus "excellent breakfast specials"; they're "nothing to write home about", but at least staffers "get you in and out fast."

De Rodriguez Cuba *Cuban* | - | - | - | E |

South Beach | Astor Hotel | 956 Washington Ave. (10th St.) |
Miami Beach | 305-673-3763 | www.drodriguezcuba.com

Douglas Rodriguez, celebrity toque and father of Nuevo Latino cuisine, puts his own spin on the food of his native Cuba at this elegant indoor-outdoor spot in SoBe's tony Astor Hotel; the chef's signature ceviches figure prominently on the pricey menu, as do 'Cuban pizzas' made with flatbreads; P.S. a lounge remodel is due, and a seafood-oriented sibling is set for the Hilton Bentley Miami.

DeVito South Beach ❷ *Italian/Steak* | 21 | 23 | 20 | $80 |

South Beach | 150 Ocean Dr. (bet. 1st & 2nd Sts.) | Miami Beach |
305-531-0911 | www.devitosouthbeach.com

The "celebs eating next to you" are almost as eye-catching as the "over-the-top" decor at actor Danny DeVito's "sexy" Italian chophouse, among the newest "SoBe scenes"; still, voters split on the chow ("wow!" vs. "so-so") and service ("attentive" vs. "snobby"), though all agree portions are "as large as DeVito himself, with prices to match."

Disco Fish *Seafood/Spanish* | 19 | 10 | 17 | $24 |

West Miami | 1540 SW 67th Ave. (SW 16th St.) | 305-266-7323

This "informal" Spanish seafooder in West Miami features a "strange name" (sorry, no dancing) and plates "fresh, well-prepared" fin fare at "good prices"; not so good: decor that "should have stayed in the '70s."

Dogma Grill *Hot Dogs* | 20 | 9 | 15 | $11 |

Upper East Side | 7030 Biscayne Blvd. (bet. NE 70th & 71st Sts.) |
Miami | 305-759-3433 | www.dogmagrill.com

"You can't beat" the franks ("beef, turkey and even veggie") at this "no rush, no fuss" Upper East Side "purveyor of one of America's backyard barbecue favorites"; there's "no real atmosphere", but with "all the toppings in the world" and downright "cheap" prices, no wonder so many are "addicted" to these "top" "dawgs."

Dolores But You Can Call Me Lolita ❷ *Eclectic* | 18 | 23 | 19 | $35 |

Brickell Area | 1000 S. Miami Ave. (SE 10th St.) | Miami | 305-403-3103 |
www.doloreslolita.com

"If the name doesn't get you", the "sizzling" atmosphere will at this "elegant yet casual" Eclectic nestled in a "converted" Brickell firehouse; "satisfying" fare (some say "boring") is "served with a smile" and costs "less than you'd expect", but "ask for a table" on the "romantic" "rooftop terrace", because dining there is "sooo divine."

Doraku *Japanese* | 21 | 20 | 18 | $35 |

South Beach | 1104 Lincoln Rd. (Lenox Ave.) | Miami Beach |
305-695-8383 | www.sushidoraku.com

"Hip without the price tag to match", this "swanky" SoBe Japanese next to a multiplex proffers "innovative sushi" alongside a "solid sake list"; just beware of "loud music" – courtesy of a "good bar scene" – that's sometimes "just plain annoying."

Dynamo Café *Eclectic*

- | - | - | M

South Beach | Wolfsonian Museum | 1001 Washington Ave. (10th St.) | Miami Beach | 305-535-1457 | www.wolfsonian.org

With its "avant-garde feel" and "wonderful salads" and tapas, this "charming", "classy" Eclectic in the Wolfsonian is "not your normal museum cafe"; after all, how many museum cafes show silent movies and feature a 19th-century library shelving system? P.S. closed Wednesdays.

8 Oz. Burger Bar ● *American*

20 | 15 | 16 | $22

South Beach | 1080 Alton Rd. (11th St.) | Miami Beach | 305-397-8246

"Bodacious" burgers with "yummy, creative toppings" (like "Gruyère cheese and fried green tomatoes") and "divine adult milk-shakes" have South Beachers "coming back" to celeb chef Govind Armstrong's "barlike" American; however, naysayers snarl it "doesn't live up to the hype", citing "extras that add up fast" and "slow service" steeped in "dude-itude – shaggy waiters who tell you their outlook on 'life, man.'"

El Atlakat ● *Salvadoran*

▽ 20 | 11 | 17 | $16

Westchester | 9425 40th St. SW (bet. SW 94th & 95th Aves.) | 305-552-9090 | www.elatlakat.com

It's "not fancy", but this casual, airy Westchester Salvadoran serves up "plentiful" amounts of "inexpensive" fare, including some Mexican selections; the "excellent" pupusas are standouts – and easier to order if you speak some Spanish.

El Carajo International Tapas & Wines *Spanish*

▽ 20 | 16 | 20 | $39

Coconut Grove | 2465 SW 17th Ave. (bet. SW 24th Terr. & U.S. 1) | 305-856-2424 | www.elcarajointernationaltapasandwines.com

"Fill up in more ways than one" at this "cozy" tapas bar in the "least suspecting of locations": a Coconut Grove CITGO station where waiters who "couldn't be friendlier" deliver "super" Spanish fare and selections off an "amazing wine list"; throw in "romantic decor", vino tastings and a retail shop, and it's a real gas.

El Chalán *Peruvian*

22 | 8 | 17 | $24

South Beach | 1580 Washington Ave. (bet. 15th & 16th Sts.) | Miami Beach | 305-532-8880
Westchester | 7971 SW 40th St./Bird Rd. (SW 79th Ave.) | 305-266-0212

"You won't go hungry" at this "family-friendly" SoBe and Westchester duo dishing up "heaping portions" of "excellent Peruvian food" for "reasonable" tabs; despite "cafeteria decor" that "needs a lot of help" and "language issues", "you walk away knowing you'll come back."

11th St. Diner ● *Diner*

18 | 15 | 18 | $21

South Beach | 1065 Washington Ave. (11th St.) | Miami Beach | 305-534-6373 | www.eleventhstreetdiner.com

"Affordable" "homestyle" grub that's "classed up a bit" and dished out in an "art deco-esque diner" (moved from Pennsylvania) makes

FOOD
DECOR
SERVICE
COST

this "lively" South Beach "institution" an "ideal" place for a "late-night bite" or "greasy hangover breakfast" before "heading to the beach"; the unenchanted say "nooo thanks" – it's just "so ordinary."

El Gran Inka *Peruvian*   21 | 16 | 19 | $38

NEW **Brickell Area** | The Plaza | 947 Brickell Ave. (SE 10th St.) | Miami | 786-220-7930
Key Biscayne | Winn-Dixie Shopping Plaza | 606 Crandon Blvd. (Sunrise Dr.) | 305-365-7883
Aventura | 3155 NE 163rd St. (Interama Blvd.) | 305-940-4910
www.graninka.com

"It's like being in Lima" without ever leaving Key Biscayne or Aventura insist deep thinkas about these "agreeable" Peruvians; the "courteous" staff and a "big menu with many choices" please most, though surveyors prefer the "above-and-beyond" decor at the 163rd Street branch; P.S. the Brickell venue opened post-Survey.

El Novillo *Nicaraguan/Steak*   22 | 20 | 21 | $31

Coral Terrace | Ludlum Shopping Ctr. | 6830 SW 40th St./Bird Rd. (68th Ave.) | Miami | 305-284-8417
Miami Lakes | 15450 New Barn Rd. (67th Ave.) | 305-819-2755
www.elnovillo.com

"Huge portions" of "mouthwatering food" that'll leave you with "money to spend the next time you visit" is just the ticket at these Coral Terrace and Miami Lakes Nicaraguans; they can get "loud", but the "attentive" service and "traditional" hacienda-like settings have loyalists lamenting "wish they were near my home."

El Rancho Grande *Mexican*   20 | 16 | 19 | $26

Miami Beach | 314 72nd St. (bet. Abbott & Collins Aves.) | 305-864-7404
South Beach | 1626 Pennsylvania Ave. (Lincoln Rd.) | Miami Beach | 305-673-0480 ●
NEW **Kendall** | 1288 N. Kendall Dr. (SW 127th Ave.) | 305-382-9598
www.elranchograndemexicanrestaurant.com

"Magnificent" margaritas "add punch" to repasts at this trio of "always packed" Mexicans where a "festive crowd" digs into "tasty" fare; while a few insist they're "nothing spectacular", even grumps allow they're "fun" places to "grab some cheap eats."

El Toro Taco Ⓜ *Mexican*   21 | 12 | 18 | $18

Homestead | 1 S. Krome Ave. (W. Mowry Dr.) | 305-245-8182
"Hard-core Mexican food lovers" swear it's "worth the drive to Homestead" for the "cheap, delicious" fare at this "foofoo"-free "joint" that's "been around for years"; just take note: "it's BYO."

ⓩ Emeril's Miami Beach *Contemp. Louisiana*   23 | 24 | 23 | $68

South Beach | Loews Miami Beach Hotel | 1601 Collins Ave. (16th St.) | Miami Beach | 305-695-4550 | www.emerils.com
"NOLA meets SoBe" at chef Emeril Lagasse's "irresistible" oceanside outpost offering "first-class" Contemporary Louisiana fare (the "sauces would make an inner tube taste good") and "service that falls all over you"; if a few decree you can get "more 'bam!' for your money

elsewhere" and fault a "tired" "formula" that's "designed for tourists", they're overruled by those who ask "how can you not love it?"

Enriqueta's Sandwich Shop ⊠ *Sandwiches* | 22 | 9 | 18 | $17 |

Wynwood | 186 NE 29th St. (2nd Ave.) | Miami | 305-573-4681
"Affordable, delicious" "comfort food" is why this "trusty Cuban sandwich joint" in Wynwood is always "busy"; be warned it's got a "minuscule parking lot" and a "truck stop" feel, but for a "satisfying" lunch or breakfast, "this is the place."

Eos *Mediterranean* | - | - | - | E |

Brickell Area | The Viceroy Hotel | 485 Brickell Ave., 15th fl. (SE 5th St.) | Miami | 305-503-4400 | www.viceroymiami.com
Famed New York duo chef Michael Psilakis and telegenic restaurateur Donatella Arpaia come south to create this sophisticated Med stunner in Brickell's Viceroy Hotel; dressed in Aegean opulence (lots of gray marble) and tropical elegance (splashes of flowery color), it boasts impressive 15th-floor views that help soften the not-exactly-cheap prices on its tapas-style menu; P.S. at lunch and breakfast it becomes Bistro e, serving quick meals to wallet-watching noshers.

Escopazzo ● *Italian* | 25 | 19 | 23 | $64 |

South Beach | 1311 Washington Ave. (bet. 13th & 14th Sts.) | Miami Beach | 305-674-9450 | www.escopazzo.com
"Behind an unassuming storefront" on a "busy" SoBe street lies this "simple" Italian "oasis" where "charming" chef-owner Giancarla Bodoni ("you can tell she cooks with love") dishes up "blissful" fare made from "organic, locally grown" ingredients; it's all complemented by "personalized" service and a "fantastic wine list", and though a few fume about "small portions" at "hideous prices", more maintain it's a "one-of-a-kind culinary experience"; P.S. dinner only.

Essensia *American* | - | - | - | E |

South Beach | The Palms Hotel & Spa | 3025 Collins Ave. (Indian Creek Dr.) | Miami Beach | 305-534-0505 | www.thepalmshotel.com
South Beach style meets stylish spa cuisine at this elegant (and expensive) American in the Palms Hotel & Spa, where organic produce and hormone-free meats find their way into dishes like sweet squash ravioli with fresh sage and grilled rib-eye with cherry-port wine sauce; diners can choose between a meal in a sleek, earthtoned dining room or on an expansive covered terrace with pool and garden views.

5300 Chop House *Steak* | - | - | - | E |

Doral | The Blue | 5300 NW 87th Ave. (NW 53rd St.) | Miami | 305-597-8600 | www.5300chophouse.com
Located in Doral's Blue resort and overlooking a PGA golf course, this pricey carnivorium attracts eagle-eyed duffers and other hungry sorts craving steaks, chops and all manner of seafood, plus sides like truffled mac 'n' cheese; the dark-brown-and-cream palette and clean lines provide a modern look, which extends into the lounge.

FOOD | DECOR | SERVICE | COST

NEW Fin *Seafood*
- | - | - | M

Design District | 4029 N. Miami Ave. (NE 41st St.) | Miami | 305-227-2378 | www.finrestaurantmiami.com

Fin-fare fanciers find themselves up to their gills in piscine possibilities at chef-owner Jonathan Eismann's low-key, New England-esque seafooder in the Design District where the motto is simple, local and organic; also notable is a wine list that features 29 wines for under $29, a bonus for wallet-watchers already drawn by the menu's affordable prices.

Flanigan's Seafood Bar & Grill ● *American*
20 | 15 | 18 | $23

Coconut Grove | 2721 Bird Rd. (SW 27th Ave.) | 305-446-1114 | www.flanigans.net

"You always know what you're going to get" at this "longtime" Coconut Grove chain link, so if you're hankering for "fall-off-the-bone ribs" and other "consistently good" American grub at "unbeatable prices", acolytes exclaim "this is the place"; even with "up-and-down" service, sports fans give it extra points: there's "plenty of beer, plenty of TVs."

Fleming's Prime Steakhouse & Wine Bar *Steak*
24 | 23 | 24 | $59

Coral Gables | 2525 Ponce de Leon Blvd. (Andalusia Ave.) | 305-569-7995 | www.flemingssteakhouse.com

"*Carpe carne!* (seize the meat!)" cry filet-ophiles when they arrive at this "dark wood"–bedecked Coral Gables steakhouse whose "fine food, polished service" and "imaginative" vinos – particularly the "100-plus wines by the glass" – make it "hard to believe this is a chain"; some may beef it's "just a fancy Outback", but the majority opines it "has a formula, and it works."

Fogo de Chão *Brazilian/Steak*
24 | 21 | 24 | $58

South Beach | 836 First St. (bet. Alton Rd. & Meridian Aves.) | Miami Beach | 305-672-0011 | www.fogodechao.com

Carnivores may want to "fast for a week" before alighting at this "excellent" Brazilian steakhouse on SoBe where the "elite meet to eat meat" that's carted around a "sleek" dining room by "attentive" waiters "practically on a conveyor belt"; while vegetarians will be "pleased" by the "dandy salad bar", budgeteers may begrudge "pricey" tabs.

Fontana *Italian*
▽ 21 | 27 | 24 | $56

Coral Gables | Biltmore Hotel | 1200 Anastasia Ave. (Columbus Blvd.) | 305-445-1926 | www.biltmorehotel.com

"More casual" than some of its similarly expensive Coral Gables brethren, this "beautiful" Italian dining room spills onto a "romantic" "patio with fountains" at the historic Biltmore Hotel and serves up "excellent" cuisine like signature *zuppa di pesce*; "Sunday brunch like no other" and "impeccable" service win high marks too, but even the less gushy can't stop asking "how can you beat the setting?"

	FOOD	DECOR	SERVICE	COST

NEW Forge Restaurant | Wine Bar American

| - | - | - | E |

Miami Beach | 432 41st St. (Sheridan Ave.) | 305-538-8533 | www.theforge.com

Once an actual blacksmith's workshop turned celebrity magnet steakhouse, this Miami Beach icon has replaced tuxedoed waiters, heavy silver gueridons and the caged finches in the ladies room with gleaming enomatic wine dispensers, Helmut Newton nudes and a dazzling blond dining room lighted by Murano glass chandeliers; also somewhat lighter: the tabs and the American cooking (think quinoa pancakes instead of creamed spinach), thanks to veteran Miami chef Dewey LoSasso (ex North One 10).

☑ Francesco ☒ Peruvian

| 26 | 17 | 24 | $53 |

Coral Gables | 325 Alcazar Ave. (bet. SW 42nd Ave. & Salzedo St.) | 305-446-1600 | www.francescorestaurant.com

If you "crave" "quality seafood" and "ceviche that'll blow your socks (and everything else) off", surveyors swear "this place is for you" – a "small, crowded" Coral Gables "knockout" awash in "awesome" "Peruvian flavors"; the ambiance is "lacking", but "you'll forget about [that] once you start eating", and the "welcoming" staff and "solid" wine list don't hurt; all that, and a "bang for your buck" too.

Fratelli La Bufala ◗ Italian

| 21 | 15 | 16 | $29 |

South Beach | 437 Washington Ave. (bet. 4th & 5th Sts.) | Miami Beach | 305-532-0700 | www.fratellilabufala.com

This "unassuming little piece of Italy" on South Beach is "where the buffalo roams" (i.e. "savory" water-buffalo-milk mozzarella), though its home atop "solid", "reasonably priced" pizzas is what has fans crying "*mangia!*"; true, some are cheesed off by "laid-back" service that "really suffers when it's busy", but most just "keep going back."

Fratelli Lyon Italian

| 23 | 21 | 19 | $48 |

Design District | Driade | 4141 NE Second Ave. (bet. 41st & 42nd Sts.) | Miami | 305-572-2901 | www.fratellilyon.com

"You can taste Italy in every bite" of the "delicious" trattoria fare drawn from grass-fed meats and sustainable seafood at this "sophisticated" – and "high-priced" – Design District "breath of fresh air"; despite "inconsistent service" and a "love it or hate it" "über-modern" space in the Driade furniture showroom, the majority maintains it "never disappoints."

Fritz & Franz Bierhaus German

| 16 | 15 | 17 | $26 |

Coral Gables | 60 Merrick Way (bet. Aragon & Giralda Aves.) | 305-774-1883 | www.bierhaus.cc

"Get your schnitzel on" at this "energetic" "beer hall"-cum-"sports bar" in Coral Gables proffering a "classic lineup of gut-busting" German fare and "wide variety" of suds; *futbol* fans take note: with plenty of "wide-screen" TVs, "there's no better place" to watch soccer.

FOOD | DECOR | SERVICE | COST

Front Porch Cafe American
21 | 15 | 16 | $24

South Beach | Penguin Hotel | 1418 Ocean Dr. (bet. 14th & 15th Sts.) | Miami Beach | 305-531-8300

"Linger on the porch" and "people-watch" at this "legend on South Beach" where "huge portions" of "delicious" American chow (including "fantastic" all-day breakfasts) please palates and pocketbooks; service can be "very *manana*" and there's "always a line for brunch" on weekends, but with "all the standards done well" and "ocean views", "what more could you want?"

Fuji Hana Japanese/Thai
21 | 15 | 19 | $31

Aventura | 2775 NE 187th St. (Biscayne Blvd.) | 305-932-8080
Kendall | 11768 SW 88th St. (SW 117th Ave.) | 305-275-9003 | www.fujihanakendall.com

"Cheap, tasty" Thai and Japanese fare – including "fresh-from-the-sea" sushi – makes this Aventura and Kendall duo "well worth" a visit; if the decor "leaves much to be desired", at least improved service from "friendly staffers [who] remember regulars" helps compensate; P.S. 187th Street has a "lovely little outside area."

Gables Diner Diner
16 | 13 | 16 | $24

Coral Gables | 2320 Galiano St. (Aragon Ave.) | 305-567-0330 | www.gablesdiner.com

Coral Gables "does everything a little better" (or at least tries), which explains this "upscale diner" dishing "homestyle" vittles; gourmands grouse it's "expensive for what it is" and knock "inconsistent service", but all in all, it's a "decent" option for a "hearty meal."

Garcia's Seafood
22 | 14 | 19 | $29

Miami River | 398 NW North River Dr. (NW 4th St.) | Miami | 305-375-0765 | www.garciasseafoodgrill.com

There are "no gimmicks" at this "funky", "affordable" seafooder "on the Miami River", just some of the "freshest fish anywhere" (plus an "adjacent market") and "friendly" staffers; it can be "tricky to find", but once you do, "sit outside", "order a beer" and "watch the boats."

George's in the Grove French
22 | 21 | 20 | $44

Coconut Grove | 3145 Commodore Plaza (Main Hwy.) | 305-444-7878 | www.georgesrestaurants.com

"Over-the-top" owner George Farge (ex Le Bouchon du Grove) "sets the bar pretty darned high" at this "fun, delicious" Coconut Grove French where the "complimentary champagne" flows freely and the "high energy" never ebbs; prepare for "reasonable prices", "attentive" service, "impossibly close tables" and lots of "noise" – especially if you "tell them it's your birthday" (hint: it involves a "disco ball" and "singing waiters").

NEW George's on Sunset French
- | - | - | E

South Miami | 1549 Sunset Dr. (56th Ave.) | 305-284-9989 | www.georgesrestaurants.com

Gregarious owner George Farge reprises his never-a-dull-moment Coconut Grove bistro with this wacky South Miamian boasting multiple statues of Buddha along with disco balls and neon lights; just beware that birthday celebrations complete with fog machine and strobe lights compete for attention with the French fare, though a patio provides refuge for those overwhelmed by the frivolity and large central bar.

Gibraltar *American*

`- | - | - | E`

Coconut Grove | Grove Isle Hotel & Spa | 4 Grove Isle Dr. (off S. Bayshore Dr.) | 305-857-5007 | www.groveisle.com

Miami's Grove Isle Hotel & Spa plays host to this pricey New American where the chef turns local bounty into such delicacies as breadcrusted diver scallops and spice-roasted yellowtail snapper; the waterfront setting offers sweeping vistas of Biscayne Bay, and there's a fire pit to warm up windy nights.

Gil Capa's Bistro Ⓜ *Italian*

`▽ 25 | 18 | 21 | $36`

Kendall | Sabal Chase Shoppes | 10712 SW 113th Pl. (107th St.) | 305-273-1102

Proprietor Gilberto Nalli is a "character" who cooks up the "best of everything" in his "little" Kendall Italian that's so "hidden" "you'll only find it if you get lost first"; a "limited staff" means it's "not fast food", but this "icon" has "been around forever", and for good reason.

Globe Cafe & Bar Ⓢ Ⓜ *Eclectic*

`18 | 18 | 15 | $30`

Coral Gables | 377 Alhambra Circle (SW 42nd Ave.) | 305-445-3555 | www.theglobecafe.com

"Music and martinis" join forces at this "lively" "lounge-and-listen" locus in Coral Gables whose "great happy hours" and "peoplewatching" add to a "Buenos Aires feel"; "bring patience" because "service could be better", but you may not care – even the "good" Eclectic fare, including "salads and sandwiches", seems secondary to the "happening" scene ("you mean they serve food here?").

Gordon Biersch ◑ *American*

`14 | 15 | 16 | $28`

Downtown | 1201 Brickell Ave. (12th St.) | Miami | 786-425-1130 | www.gordonbiersch.com

A sea of "fresh" suds, "juicy burgers" and outdoor seating steer "yuppies" into this Downtown "chain brewery" with an "upscale sports bar atmosphere"; however, "hit-and-miss service" and otherwise "mediocre" American grub have cynics snarling "go for the beer only" – and preferably during the "busy happy hour."

Gotham Steak *Steak*

`22 | 24 | 20 | $79`

Miami Beach | Fontainebleau Miami Beach | 4441 Collins Ave. (off Hwy. 195) | 305-674-4780 | www.fontainebleau.com

"Beautiful people and beautiful food" unite at this "sexy" spot from Alfred Portale (NYC's Gotham Bar & Grill), who brings Manhattan flair to the "extravagant" Fontainebleau Miami Beach; "melt-inyour-mouth steaks" and other chophouse standards vie for attention with a "gorgeous" space highlighted by a "showcase kitchen" and "dazzling" bi-level "wine reserve"; if "insane" tabs and service that can be "off" fire up some, more maintain it's "worth a special evening."

	FOOD	DECOR	SERVICE	COST

Grand Lux Cafe *Eclectic* | 19 | 21 | 19 | $31 |

Aventura | Aventura Mall | 19575 Biscayne Blvd. (NE 196nd St.) |
305-932-9113 | www.grandluxcafe.com

"Spun-off from the Cheesecake Factory", this somewhat "fancier" version, with branches dotted across South Florida, features an "everything-for-everybody" Eclectic menu that spans
the globe and arrives in "huge", "tasty" portions; if "beautiful",
vaguely Venetian decor and "speedy service" aren't enough, it's
"not too expensive" either.

☒ Graziano's Restaurant *Argentinean/Steak* | 26 | 21 | 23 | $47 |

NEW **Brickell Area** | 177 SW Seventh St. (bet. 1st & 2nd Aves.) |
Miami | 305-860-1426
Coral Gables | 394 Giralda Ave. (42nd Ave.) | 305-774-3599
Hialeah | 5993 W. 16th Ave. (60th St.) | 305-819-7461
Westchester | 9227 SW 40th St./Bird Rd. (92nd Ave.) |
305-225-0008
www.parrilla.com

"If you love a perfect steak" and "can't afford the flight to Argentina",
consider these "authentic" *parrillas* (grills) offering an "excellent" variety of the "juiciest meats" and a "fantastic selection" of
"reasonably priced" wines "on display along the dining room
walls"; "average Joes and culinary experts" alike appreciate the
"sharp, informed" service and "relaxed atmosphere" – just arrive
"hungry" and "don't tell your cardiologist"; P.S. the Brickell branch
opened post-Survey.

Grazie Italian Cuisine *Italian* | 24 | 22 | 24 | $57 |

South Beach | 701 Washington Ave. (7th St.) | Miami Beach |
305-673-1312 | www.grazieitaliancuisine.com

You'll "leave with a full stomach and a few new friends" at this "high-
quality" Italian whose "attentive, caring" staff "treats you like family"
as it dishes out "well-prepared" fare in an "elegant" setting; sure, it's
"pricey", but "it's South Beach – what do you expect?"

Green Street Cafe *French/Mediterranean* | 18 | 17 | 16 | $28 |

Coconut Grove | 3110 Commodore Plaza (Main Hwy.) | 305-444-0244 |
www.greenstreetcafe.net

"Waiting and dashing" for an outside perch (including "loungey
loveseats") are part of the "fun" at this "bustling" "corner staple"
where "Coconut Grove parades by your table"; while the kitchen
"pumps out" all manner of "solid" French-Med fare (some say "mediocre"), it's the "groaning-board breakfasts" and "happening"
brunches that really "draw the crowds."

Grillfish ❶ *Seafood* | 21 | 18 | 20 | $44 |

South Beach | 1444 Collins Ave. (Española Way) | Miami Beach |
305-538-9908 | www.grillfish.com

An "oldie but goodie", this "reasonably priced" seafooder delivers
"refreshingly simple" fin fare sans the South Beach "attitude";
throw in a "stylish setting", and its "loyal local following" fawns
it's a "real winner."

	FOOD	DECOR	SERVICE	COST

Grill on the Alley, The *American*
22 | 25 | 23 | $49

Aventura | Aventura Mall | 19501 Biscayne Blvd. (NE 195th St.) |
305-466-7195 | www.thegrill.com

With its "art deco decor" (e.g. "polished dark wood and chrome")
and "gourmet" American menu of "classic dishes" "done up nicely",
this Aventura chain link has such a "high-quality" sheen that even
boosters can't believe it's "in a mall"; "outside dining" and "terrific
service" add to the lure, as do "amazing" "happy-hour specials."

Grimpa Steakhouse *Brazilian/Steak*
23 | 24 | 23 | $56

Brickell Area | Mary Brickell Vlg. | 901 S. Miami Ave. (bet. 9th &
10th Sts.) | Miami | 305-371-5444 | www.grimpa.com

At this "sophisticated" "Brazilian-style churrascaria" in the Brickell
Area, "efficient" servers ensure that the "skewer food" - "delicious"
all-you-can-eat beef, chicken and fish - "just keeps on coming"
("until you request them to stop", that is); a "crazy good" salad bar,
"killer caipirinhas" and a "beautiful interior" with "colorful artwork"
add to the appeal, leading loyalists to decree you get a "big bang for
mucho bucks" here.

Guayacan Restaurant *Nicaraguan*
▽ 23 | 15 | 21 | $23

Little Havana | 1933 SW Eighth St. (19th Ave.) | Miami |
305-649-2015

Westchester | 9857 SW 40th St./Bird Rd. (97th Ave.) | 305-559-6655

"Generous portions" of "flavorful food" (e.g. "delicious churrasco" if
"you're in the mood for meat") attract fans to these "cozy", "casual"
Nicaraguans in Westchester and Little Havana; other lures include
moderate prices and "great service."

Guru International *Indian*
▽ 24 | 18 | 23 | $28

South Beach | 232 12th St. (bet. Collins & Washington Aves.) |
Miami Beach | 305-534-3996 | www.gurufood.com

"Reasonable prices" for "inventive" Indian fare attract admirers to
this "tastefully decorated" SoBe subcontinental with "friendly service"; unfortunately, it's a bit "out of the way", but that's a plus for
those who want to keep it "little-known" ("only recommend it to
your best friends").

Hakan Turkish Grill ◐ *Turkish*
▽ 20 | 12 | 18 | $29

South Beach | 1040 Alton Rd. (bet. 10th & 11th Sts.) | Miami Beach |
305-534-9557 | www.hakanturkishgrill.com

Owner Hakan Aksu "makes sure each guest has a great experience" at
this small but "reliable" South Beacher dishing up "yummy" Turkish
fare (including "awesome" lamb dishes) at midrange prices; expect to
rub elbows with lots of "locals", many with eyes glued on the "weekend
belly dancers" and "loud" "flat-screen TVs" broadcasting soccer.

ⓩ Hakkasan ◐ *Chinese*
26 | 26 | 23 | $80

Miami Beach | Fontainebleau Miami Beach | 4441 Collins Ave. (41st St.) |
786-276-1388 | www.fontainebleau.com

"Just like the one in London, but with a much hotter crowd", this
"contemporary" Cantonese by Britain's Alan Yau provides "top-of-

the-charts" fare in a "beautifully designed" space in the Fontainebleau Miami Beach, distinguished by "private" niches with ornately carved screens; "no question, it's expensive", but a "well-trained" crew enhances the "unique, transporting" experience.

Hanna's Gourmet Diner *French*   ▽ 26 | 14 | 22 | $39

North Miami Beach | 13951 Biscayne Blvd. (140th St.) |
305-947-2255

It's set in a "retro" "chrome diner", but the "delicious" "gourmet" French fare at this "unique" North Miami Beach bistro is "anything but diner food" (think "onion soup gratinée, escargot, etc."); "decent" prices and "friendly" staffers who "recognize repeat patrons" and "even entertain children" further its rep as a "local favorite."

Havana Harry's *Cuban*   21 | 15 | 18 | $27

Coral Gables | 4612 Le Jeune Rd. (Ponce de Leon Blvd.) | 305-661-2622
NEW **Kendall** | 9525 Kendall Dr. (bet. SW 94th & SW 97th Aves.) |
305-595-1116
www.hharrys.com

"Bring someone to share" the "huge portions and even bigger flavors" proffered by this Coral Gables eatery plating "simple", "well-prepared" "Cuban cuisine that tastes like Cubans make it"; critics complain the "decor isn't too special" and crow the food's "inconsistent", but "pleasant service", "reasonable prices" and "perfect" *vaca frita* (literally "fried cow") make it "worth a taste"; P.S. the Kendall locale opened post-Survey.

Here Comes the Sun 🈯 *Vegetarian*   22 | 7 | 18 | $18

North Miami | 2188 NE 123rd St. (bet. N. Bayshore Dr. & Sans Souci Blvd.) |
305-893-5711

"Healthy tastes great" at this "classic" in a North Miami natural-foods market, a "vegetarian's dream" where anything with the "special sun sauce" ("I'd use it as toothpaste if I could") leaves boosters beaming; there's "no decor", but that's "not the focus" anyhow – just "lots of delicious choices" for "little dollars"; P.S. "free frozen yogurt" leaves a "sweet impression."

Hiro Japanese ● *Japanese*   20 | 13 | 17 | $31

North Miami Beach | 3007 NE 163rd St. (Biscayne Blvd.) | 305-948-3687 |
www.hiro163.com

"After a hard night of clubbing", the "after-hours" crowd descends upon this "affordable" North Miami Beach strip-maller for "no-frills" sushi and other "consistently good" Japanese fare; while the unmoved mutter it's merely "run-of-the-mill" (the "tacky decor" doesn't help), an "easy" vibe and a 3:30 AM closing time make it a "must-go" for a "quick roll or a slow drink."

🄩 Hiro's Yakko San ● *Japanese*   26 | 12 | 21 | $33

North Miami Beach | 17040-46 W. Dixie Hwy. (bet. 170th & 171st Sts.) |
305-947-0064 | www.yakko-san.com

"All the chefs go to eat" at this "late-night" "foodies' paradise" in North Miami Beach, where the "out-of-this-world" (yet "reasonably priced") Japanese small plates and "rare" sashimi selections reward an "open mind"; though there's "no real decor", it's staffed by "helpful" servers and "always jammin'" – so "be prepared to wait."

Hosteria Romana ● *Italian* | 20 | 18 | 20 | $39 |

South Beach | 429 Española Way (bet. Drexel & Washington Aves.) | Miami Beach | 305-532-4299 | www.hosteriaromana.com

It's a "page right out of the Roman empire" swear devotees "full of *amore*" for this "entertaining" SoBe Italian where the "sexy" waiters "sing and dance" and the kitchen dishes "large portions" of "homestyle" fare; "pricey" tabs and a "touristy" feel irk a few, but even they admit "it's impossible to be in a bad mood" here.

House of India *Indian* | 18 | 14 | 16 | $31 |

Coral Gables | 22 Merrick Way (S. Douglas Rd.) | 305-444-2348 | www.houseofindiamiami.com

"Older than the Ganges", this Coral Gables Indian seems to "have upped the ante" in the kitchen, offering "solid" à la carte items and a lunch "buffet [that's] not bad for the price" (from $10.95); however, "dumpy" decor and "ok service" vex many, while a vocal minority still deems the subcontinental fare "substandard."

☑ Houston's *American* | 22 | 21 | 22 | $37 |

Coral Gables | 201 Miracle Mile (Ponce de Leon Blvd.) | 305-529-0141
North Miami Beach | 17355 Biscayne Blvd. (NE 172nd St.) | 305-947-2000
www.hillstone.com

See review in Ft. Lauderdale/Broward County Directory.

☑ Hy-Vong Ⓜ *Vietnamese* | 27 | 8 | 15 | $28 |

Little Havana | 3458 SW Eighth St. (bet. 34th & 35th Aves.) | Miami | 305-446-3674 | www.hyvong.com

"Be prepared to wait . . . and wait" (alas, no reservations) at this "crowded" Little Havana "hole-in-the-wall" where the Vietnamese food "made with pure love" is "so good it takes your breath away"; "don't expect fast service or stellar decor", but if you "go with patience", "heaven on a dish rewards your efforts", and it's an "excellent value" at that.

Icebox Café *Bakery/Eclectic* | 23 | 14 | 17 | $29 |

South Beach | 1657 Michigan Ave. (Lincoln Rd.) | Miami Beach | 305-538-8448 | www.iceboxcafe.com

The "decor may be boring as can be", but this "little" SoBe "bakery/restaurant" is "where locals in-the-know go" for "scrumptious, monumental desserts" and "attention-grabbing" Eclectic fare; service is "hit-or-miss" and the space "cramped", but for "homespun goodness" at "reasonable prices", it "can't be beat."

Ideas Restaurant ☒ *Spanish* | ▽ 20 | 17 | 22 | $55 |

Coconut Grove | 2833 Bird Ave. (Mary St.) | 305-567-9074 | www.ideasrestaurant.com

"Old-school traditional and new-school avant-garde" find middle ground at this "sophisticated" Coconut Grove Spanish whose "very good" fare pairs nicely with a "quirky" selection of Iberian wines; it's "expensive", but "big portions" and "attentive service" help compensate; P.S. "English is spoken but Spanish is preferable."

☑ Il Gabbiano ●☒ *Italian*

26 | 25 | 25 | $79

Downtown | One Miami Tower | 335 S. Biscayne Blvd. (SE 3rd St.) | Miami | 305-373-0063 | www.ilgabbianomia.com

A "slice of heaven" with "breathtaking" Biscayne Bay views, this "romantic" Downtowner from the owners of NYC's Il Mulino proffers "as good as it gets" Italian fare served in "giant portions" that "the smart will share"; waiters who "bend over backward" and a "superb" wine list help "make it the one place everyone's grateful to know about", and though budgeteers bemoan "outrageous" prices, most say "bring your appetite . . . and your wallet" and enjoy.

NEW Il Grissino *Italian*

- | - | - | M

Coral Gables | 127 Giralda Ave. (bet. Ponce de Leon Blvd. & SW 37th Ave.) | 305-461-3391

This rustic-elegant Coral Gables Italian featuring floor-to-ceiling windows and an onyx bar is named for the crunchy breadsticks that come with each meal; Milanese chef Simone Mua's moderately priced offerings include the likes of spaghetti with langoustine, zucchini and sun-dried tomatoes in white wine sauce.

☑ Il Mulino New York *Italian*

25 | 25 | 25 | $82

Sunny Isles Beach | Acqualina Hotel | 17875 Collins Ave. (bet. 178th & 183rd Sts.) | 305-466-9191 | www.ilmulino.com

"Why go to New York City?" ponder partisans of this "gorgeous" Big Apple import in Sunny Isles' oceanfront Acqualina Hotel, where it's a "real treat" to dine on "old-world" Italian fare served by "debonair" staffers; "it ain't New York" sneer some, but more say it's "outstanding" ("if you don't mind draining your wallet", that is); P.S. the "free appetizers" are a "meal in themselves", so "save room" for dinner.

Imlee *Indian*

23 | 16 | 17 | $31

Pinecrest | South Park Ctr. | 12663 S. Dixie Hwy. (bet. 124th & 128th Sts.) | 786-293-2223 | www.imleeindianbistro.com

A "lovely alchemy of fragrance and flavor" (e.g. "perfect curries") makes hearts flutter at this "cozy" Indian in a Pinecrest strip mall; "high prices" and a staff that's "efficient if not the friendliest" don't discourage adherents, who maintain they've "never been disappointed" – which explains why it can be "difficult to get a table."

Indochine ● *Asian*

21 | 16 | 18 | $31

Miami River | 638 S. Miami Ave. (SE 7th St.) | Miami | 305-379-1525

"All taste buds" (well, most of them at least) are "satisfied" at this midpriced, "cozy-hip meets retro-mod" Miami River Pan-Asian proffering "tasty" Thai fare and sushi; staffers "fall all over you trying to please", and though a few decry a "lackluster menu", more say "it's a solid choice" for "an easy dinner or drinks."

	FOOD	DECOR	SERVICE	COST

Islas Canarias *Cuban* | 20 | 11 | 17 | $21 |
Little Havana | 285 NW 27th Ave. (3rd St.) | Miami |
305-649-0440
Sweetwater | 13697 SW 26th St. (SW 137th Ave.) | Miami |
305-559-6666
www.islascanariasrestaurant.net

"Basic homestyle" Cuban cooking at "low prices" brings "customers out in droves" to these "reliable", "family-friendly" Little Havana and Sweetwater favorites; "language can be an issue" and picky sorts deem them "ordinary", but it's "worth a stop just for the tres leches" dessert.

Jaguar Restaurant *Pan-Latin* | 23 | 20 | 21 | $35 |
Coconut Grove | 3067 Grand Ave. (McFarlane Rd.) | 305-444-0216 |
www.jaguarspot.com

A "spicy atmosphere" matches the "innovative" cuisine at this "stylish" Pan-Latin where "there's always a crowd" sampling signature ceviche in giant spoons and "terrific cocktails"; "supernice servers" and "just-right" prices help it "earn its spot" as a Coco Grove "favorite."

Joe Allen *American* | 22 | 15 | 22 | $40 |
South Beach | 1787 Purdy Ave. (bet. 17th & 18th Sts.) | Miami Beach |
305-531-7007 | www.joeallenrestaurant.com

"When the glitz becomes overbearing" on South Beach, "locals" who "know best" head "off the beaten track" to this "relaxed but refined" NYC import and dig into "reasonably priced" American "comfort food with a gourmet touch"; yeah, noise levels can be "high", but you can "rely on" it for "no pretense, no b.s." dining and a "good bar scene."

☑ Joe's Stone Crab *Seafood* | 27 | 20 | 24 | $65 |
South Beach | 11 Washington Ave. (bet. 1st St. & S. Pointe Dr.) |
Miami Beach | 305-673-0365 | www.joesstonecrab.com

"Everybody should experience" this SoBe "stone crab mecca" "at least once" – and seemingly has, as it's voted Miami's Most Popular; the "killer claws", "sinful Key lime pie" and "even the fried chicken" – hauled through the "hectic" "cafeteria-type" space by "ruthlessly efficient" servers – "never disappoint", although the "top-dollar" tabs and no-res policy ("prepare for the wait of your life") do; still, the consensus is "go early, go late, but go", though "smart locals" get "takeout and eat on the beach."

Joey's Italian Café ☑ *Italian* | 22 | 22 | 21 | $35 |
Wynwood | 2506 NW Second Ave. (25th St.) | Miami | 305-438-0488 |
www.joeyswynwood.com

"Rub shoulders with artists, [art] dealers and police officers" as you down "affordable, authentic" fare at this "stylish" Italian (think "open kitchen", polished concrete floors, etc.) in the "up-and-coming" Wynwood arts district; service can be "spotty" and quiet sorts insist it'd "be better if it weren't so loud", but most maintain it's a "welcome addition" where "return visits are in order."

	FOOD	DECOR	SERVICE	COST

JohnMartin's ● *American/Irish*
17 | 18 | 17 | $28

Coral Gables | 253 Miracle Mile (bet. Ponce de Leon Blvd. & Salzedo St.) | 305-445-3777 | www.johnmartins.com

Aye, it's the "place to hang on St. Paddy's day", but habitués of this "old-school" Coral Gables pub ("it's like a cozy den") also dig its "basic", "fairly priced" American-Gaelic grub and "exciting beer selection"; add in "friendly service", and it feels "Irish to the bone."

Julio's *Vegetarian*
▽ 22 | 14 | 16 | $23

North Miami Beach | 1602 NE Miami Gardens Dr. (bet. 15th Ave. & NE 18th Rd.) | 305-947-4744 | www.juliosnaturalfoods.com

"If you want to eat healthy", surveyors suggest this frills-free North Miami Beacher dishing up "fresh" vegetarian fare and an "amazing selection of smoothies"; P.S. chef-owner Julio Balderman's departure may outdate the Food score; no longer serving wine.

Jumbo's ●⊅ *Diner*
▽ 22 | 9 | 21 | $19

Westernmost Dade | 7501 NW Seventh Ave. (NW 75th St.) | Miami | 305-751-1127

The "good home cooking", including "divine fried shrimp", comes with a "smile" at this 24/7 Westernmost Dade diner that's graced the "heart of Liberty City" for 50-plus years; it's decor deficient, but a "great bang for the buck" nonetheless.

Kampai *Japanese/Thai*
21 | 15 | 18 | $32

Aventura | Waterways Shopping Ctr. | 3575 NE 207th St. (NE 34th Ave.) | 305-931-6410
South Miami | 8745 Sunset Dr. (SW 87th Ave.) | 305-596-1551
www.kampaisunset.com

"Delicate, tasty" sushi and "amiable" service combine to hook seafoodies on this "casual" Japanese-Thai duo in Aventura and South Miami; some don't bite on merely "ok" fare and decor that "leaves something to be desired", but "consistency" and "reasonable prices" lure most to "return soon."

Kebab Indian ⓜ *Indian*
▽ 21 | 13 | 12 | $26

North Miami Beach | 514 NE 167th St. (NE 5th Ave.) | 305-940-6309 | www.kebabindia.com

There may be "fancier Indian restaurants", but both "vegetarians and meat eaters" can "satisfy their every craving" at this modest North Miami Beacher; bonus: it's a "real treat for the price."

Khoury's *Lebanese*
22 | 13 | 21 | $28

South Miami | 5887 SW 73rd St. (U.S. 1) | 305-662-7707

You "really have to look" for this "hidden" South Miami Lebanese, but "you'll be glad you did", especially when dining on "authentic, plentiful and tasty" fare "served by the nicest people"; it's "not much on decor", but then again, "you can't beat the prices with a stick."

Kon Chau *Chinese*
24 | 7 | 18 | $19

Westchester | 8376 Bird Rd. (SW 84th Ave.) | 305-553-7799

"The atmosphere is nothing to speak of", but that doesn't matter to acolytes of this "unpretentious" Westchester "hole-in-the-wall"

FOOD | DECOR | SERVICE | COST

with "outrageously delicious" dim sum and other Sino fare; it's "family-friendly" and "priced right" too – "just don't look around you."

La Casita *Cuban*　　　　21 | 14 | 19 | $22

Coral Gables | 3805 SW Eighth St. (Galiano St.) | 305-448-8224
Sweetwater | 7931 NW Second St. (bet. Flagler St. & 79th Ave.) |
Miami | 305-267-4444

These "casual" Coral Gables and Sweetwater "joints" "still bring the goods" when it comes to "authentic" "Cuban soul food", capped off by flan that's "better than my mother's – and that's saying quite a lot"; still, some guests advise gringos to "bring your English-Spanish dictionary", as the language barrier can be "challenging."

La Casona ● *Cuban*　　　19 | 11 | 17 | $20

West Sunset | 9606 Sunset Dr. (SW 97th Ave.) | Miami | 305-270-1017 |
www.lacasonarestaurantmiami.com

This no-frills West Sunset Cuban serves up all the island's traditional dishes, including the signature Cuban sandwich, at moderate prices; night owls take note: it stays open until midnight seven days a week; P.S. no reservations accepted.

La Cofradia 🅢🅜 *Peruvian*　　23 | 24 | 22 | $59

Coral Gables | 160 Andalusia Ave. (Ponce de Leon Blvd.) | 305-914-1300 |
www.lacofradia.com

Habitués are "happy" to frequent this Coral Gables Med-Peruvian that retooled itself to be a bit "more casual" and "not quite as expensive", while still providing "delicious, unusual" fare that packs "panache"; with a "beautiful", airy dining room and "good service", it adds up to a "very nice experience overall."

La Dorada ●🅩 *Seafood/Spanish*　　24 | 18 | 22 | $72

Coral Gables | 177 Giralda Ave. (Ponce de Leon Blvd.) | 305-446-2002 |
www.ladoradamiami.com

"Top-of-the-line Spanish seafood" "flown in daily" and prepared in the "traditional style" (such as "outstanding fish baked in sea salt") sets apart this "refined" Coral Gables space; largely "courteous" service is a plus, though some balk at "high prices."

La Goulue *French*　　　22 | 22 | 20 | $51

Bal Harbour | Bal Harbour Shops | 9700 Collins Ave. (96th St.) |
305-865-2181 | www.lagouluebalharbour.com

A "favorite when shopping at Bal Harbour", this "chic" French has a real "bistro feel", albeit with a somewhat "more attentive staff than one would find in a similar cafe in Paris"; most deem the dishes "consistently well prepared", if a bit "pricey", and the atmosphere "civilized" with outdoor seating that's a "plus."

La Locanda ● *Italian*　　▽ 23 | - | 21 | $35

South Beach | 419 Washington Ave. (bet. 4th & 5th Sts.) | Miami Beach |
305-538-6277 | www.lalocandasobe.com

"Small restaurant, big food" say boosters of this "excellent" SoBe Italian whose recent move to the space next door introduced a more modern vibe, a brick pizza oven and some new menu items into the mix; throw in "affordable" tabs and "handsome Italian waiters", and "mamma mia, that's a spicy combination."

La Loggia ⑆ Italian   21 | 18 | 19 | $32

Downtown | 68 W. Flagler St. (1st Ave.) | Miami | 305-373-4800 | www.laloggia.org

"Judges and lawyers rub elbows at lunch" at this Downtown Northern Italian "across from the courthouse", "chowing down" on "reasonably priced" dishes "prepared with flavor and love" and served amid columned "Pompeii-delic" decor; despite a "convivial" bar, it's otherwise "less busy" at night, creating a more "intimate" ambiance for dinner.

Lan Asian   23 | 12 | 20 | $26

South Miami | Dadeland Station | 8332 S. Dixie Hwy. (bet. N. Kendall Dr. & SW 67th Ave.) | 305-661-8141 | www.lanpanasian.com

"Delicious", "inventive" Pan-Asian cuisine ("from sushi to Korean beef to noodles") that "won't break the bank" makes this "unassuming" South Miami eatery one of the "best buys" around; it has a "strange mall setting" with "no ambiance", but the "high quality" and "warm service" help make up for it.

La Palma Ristorante ● Italian   21 | 23 | 22 | $53

Coral Gables | 116 Alhambra Circle (Galiano St.) | 305-445-8777 | www.lapalmaristorante.com

A "refreshing European atmosphere" bolstered by a "beautiful court-yard" makes this Coral Gables Tuscan set in a restored 1924 building "romantic to the max"; though many conclude the food is "very good but not excellent", most feel the "reasonable prices", "helpful" staff and "enjoyable" Sunday brunch buffet add to the "charm."

Lario's on the Beach ● Cuban   18 | 18 | 17 | $41

South Beach | 820 Ocean Dr. (bet. 8th & 9th Sts.) | Miami Beach | 305-532-9577 | www.bongoscubancafe.com

If you're hungry for "savory" "Cuban classics" and the "eye candy" passing by on Ocean Drive, pop star Gloria Estefan's "festive" South Beacher is one "you should definitely check out"; while critics call it "too touristy" with "inconsistent" service, most don't mind "once the mojitos start to flow"; P.S. reservations only taken for parties of six or more.

La Sandwicherie ● French/Sandwiches   23 | 10 | 17 | $13

South Beach | 229 14th St. (bet. Collins & Washington Aves.) | Miami Beach | 305-532-8934 | www.lasandwicherie.com

"Locals swear by" the "stellar sandwiches" and "addictive" smoothies at this "walk-up-to-the-window" French "pit stop" delivering a "fresh", "cheap bite on the go", "whether at 2 PM or 2 AM"; the "only seats are in an alley" (and there's "always a line"), but most maintain "you can't visit South Beach and not hang out here"; P.S. open till 5 AM on weekdays, 6 AM weekends.

Las Culebrinas Cuban/Spanish   22 | 16 | 20 | $31

Downtown | 4700 W. Flagler St. (47th Ave.) | Miami | 305-445-2337
Coconut Grove | 2890 SW 27th Ave. (Coconut Ave.) | 305-448-4090

(continued)

Las Culebrinas
Pinecrest | 12257 S. Dixie Hwy. (124th St.) | 305-969-3995
Hialeah | 4590 W. 12th Ave. (46th St.) | 305-823-5828
www.culebrinas.com

"Generous" plates of Cuban-Spanish "home cooking" (topped with "mojo that sends you straight to heaven") leave fans with "full tummies and smiling faces" at this "bargain" quartet where there's "not a lot of English spoken", but the staff is "willing"; some call Downtown's "hole-in-the-wall" the "best", while others prefer the "more upscale" Coconut Grover, with "live entertainment" Thursday–Saturday.

Las Vacas Gordas ● *Argentinean/Steak* | 21 | 12 | 15 | $38 |
Miami Beach | 933 Normandy Dr. (Bay Dr.) | 305-867-1717 |
www.lasvacasgordas.com

"Meat, meat and more meat" is the "hearty" specialty at this "popular" Miami Beach Argentine steakhouse, which shifted from "funky to modern" while maintaining its lively "alfresco" seating; though "spotty, sometimes brusque" service is a common beef, most applaud the "more than fair" prices, adding "unless your dinner guest is a lineman for the Dolphins, most steaks can be shared."

Las Vegas *Cuban* | 21 | 12 | 20 | $22 |
Little Havana | 6970 Collins Ave. (69th St.) | Miami | 305-864-1509 |
www.lasvegascubancuisine.com

See review in Ft. Lauderdale/Broward County Directory.

Le Bouchon du Grove *French* | 23 | 18 | 20 | $39 |
Coconut Grove | 3430 Main Hwy. (Grand Ave.) | 305-448-6060 |
www.lebouchondugrove.com

Guests savor "spot-on" French bistro cooking straight out of "Lyon" at this "casual" Coco Grove "go-to" that "still purrs" with an ambiance enhanced by its "amiable" staff; the space is a bit "cramped", and weekend dinners can be "hard to get into", but regulars recommend "walking in early" for weekend brunch that's a "treat."

Le Croisic *French* | ▽ 21 | 16 | 20 | $53 |
Key Biscayne | Arcade Shopping Ctr. | 180 Crandon Blvd. (bet. Harbor & Sonesta Drs.) | 305-361-5888

Visitors vouch for the "very good" French fare (with a Lebanese twist at lunch) at this "modest but pleasant" bistro on Key Biscayne; despite "friendly" service, however, dissenters say it's "too expensive for a restaurant in the parking lot of a small mall" and unless you live nearby "it's not worth the drive."

Le Provençal *French* | 22 | 19 | 21 | $44 |
Coral Gables | 266 Miracle Mile (Salzedo St.) | 305-448-8984 |
www.leprovencalrestaurant.com

Considered a Coral Gables "standard", this "enjoyable" bistro serves a "limited menu" of "delicious" "country French" fare "without much fuss"; the "personable" staff and "super value" (particularly for the prix fixe lunch) are a plus, but some feel the vibe just "misses"; P.S. the Decor score does not reflect a summer 2009 move.

FOOD | DECOR | SERVICE | COST

Lido at The Standard ● *Mediterranean* 21 | 25 | 16 | $45

South Beach | The Standard | 40 Island Ave. (Venetian Way) | Miami Beach | 305-673-1717 | www.standardhotel.com

The "spectacular setting" with "amazing" views of Biscayne Bay, plus "well-made, creative" Med dishes and a "stylish" atmosphere that encourages "kicking back", combine to make this "hidden jewel" at SoBe's Standard Hotel the "quintessential Miami restaurant"; the service is "extremely relaxed", but habitués say the "sunset and people-watching" help compensate.

Lime Fresh 21 | 14 | 17 | $15
Mexican Grill *Californian/Mexican*

Biscayne | The Shops at Midtown Miami | 3201 N. Miami Ave. (32nd St.) | Miami | 305-576-5463
North Miami Beach | Biscayne Commons | 14831 Biscayne Blvd. (bet. NE 146th & NE 151st Sts.) | 305-949-8800
South Beach | 1439 Alton Rd. (bet. 14th & 15th Sts.) | Miami Beach | 305-532-5463
NEW **Kendall** | 9005 SW 72nd Pl. (SW 10th Ave.) | 305-670-1022
www.limefreshmexicangrill.com

"Healthy Mexican" isn't an "oxymoron" at these "inexpensive", separately owned Cal-influenced "taquerias" whose "simple, fresh" eats (with an "array of hot sauces") are a "delicious" "alternative to fast food"; there's "always a line out the door", but service is "quick and efficient", and the "frozen sangria" packs a punch.

Linda B. Steakhouse *Steak* 19 | 17 | 20 | $63

Key Biscayne | 320 Crandon Blvd. (East Dr.) | 305-361-1111

Regulars "relax" at this "reliable" "meat-and-potatoes establishment" featuring "well-prepared" steaks and a "nice neighborhood bar"; still, others feel it "hasn't aged gracefully", with "dowdy" decor, "inconsistent" service and an "overpriced" menu, calling it just "ok if you don't want to leave Key Biscayne."

Little Havana *Cuban* 21 | 15 | 21 | $27

North Miami | 12727 Biscayne Blvd. (NE 127th St.) | 305-899-9069 | www.littlehavanarestaurant.com

You'll "need to be rolled out the door" after dinner thanks to the "large portions" of "well-prepared" Cuban food ("even the bread is good") at this "pleasant" North Miami and Deerfield Beach duo; "fast service" and "super-reasonable" prices make it a "great choice for lunch" as well.

Little Saigon ●♥ *Vietnamese* ∇ 24 | 10 | 18 | $26

North Miami Beach | 16752 N. Miami Ave. (bet. NW 167th & 168th Sts.) | 305-653-3377

Pho fans fill up for a "budget" price ("try the rice noodle dishes if you're ravenous") at this "amazing" Vietnamese "joint" in North Miami Beach that's "open late" (till 1 AM most nights); even aesthetes ignore the "storefront ambiance", because "food is the focus here"; P.S. cash only.

	FOOD	DECOR	SERVICE	COST

Los Ranchos   *S. American/Steak* | 21 | 17 | 19 | $32 |

Biscayne | Bayside Mktpl. | 401 Biscayne Blvd. (bet. NE 4th & 5th Sts.) | Miami | 305-375-8188
Kendall | The Falls Shopping Ctr. | 8888 SW 136th St. (U.S. 1) | 305-238-6867
Sweetwater | Holiday Plaza | 125 SW 107th Ave. (W. Flagler St.) | Miami | 305-552-6767
www.beststeakinmiami.com

"Juicy, flavorful" steaks sizzle at these Latin American meateries known for "Nicaraguan-style churrasco", "great" chimichurri and "jalapeño sauce to die for", along with "abundant" sides; though it's "not fancy" and many say the "service needs improvement", most consider it an "excellent value" nonetheless.

Lost & Found Saloon   *Southwestern*   ▽ | 20 | 18 | 19 | $22 |

Design District | 185 NW 36th St. (NW 2nd Ave.) | Miami | 305-576-1008 | www.thelostandfoundsaloon-miami.com

Those who've stumbled in "savor the unique menu" and microbrews at this "little" Southwestern saloon "off the beaten path" in the Design District; it even has a "Wild West" look, complete with wagon wheel chandeliers and steel cacti, "but it's not cheesy" praise pardners, and the meals are "reasonably priced."

NEW Lou's Beer Garden ☀ *American* | – | – | – | M |

Miami Beach | New Hotel | 7337 Harding Ave. (bet. 73rd & 74th Sts.) | 305-704-7879 | www.lousbeergarden.com

Chef-owner Luis 'Lou' Ramirez's way-casual American plunked poolside in Miami Beach's New Hotel spills out plenty of craft beers and puts the 'gastro' in 'gastropub' with dishes like Iberico squid stuffed with chorizo and Manchego cheese; if you just want a burger with your brew, you can get that too, along with other pub-grub crowd-pleasers like Buffalo wings and quesadillas.

Macaluso's ☀Ⓜ *Italian* | 23 | 17 | 18 | $54 |

South Beach | 1747 Alton Rd. (bet. Abe Resnick Blvd. & 17th St.) | Miami Beach | 305-604-1811 | www.macalusosmiami.com

"Suddenly it's 1955 with Sinatra, big Cadillacs and red sauce" at this "upscale" strip-mall "hideaway" with an "attitude" that dishes up "Staten Island Italian food SoBe-style" (including some of the "best meatballs ever"); just remember the "rules": "no reservations" (for parties of seven or fewer), no written menu and "no substitutions", so "don't ever, ever ask" – at least if you want to "get out of there alive."

Magnum Ⓜ *American/Eclectic*   ▽ | 21 | 17 | 24 | $39 |

Upper East Side | 709 NE 79th St. (Biscayne Blvd.) | Miami | 305-757-3368 | www.magnumlounge.com

With a "bon vivant" atmosphere like a "piano lounge from the 1940s" and a clientele "almost evenly divided between gays and bluehairs", this "festive" Upper East Side New American is the place to go for "good food, loud music and just enjoying life"; "don't be scared" by the "hole-in-the-wall" facade, as the interior is "quite nice" and the "personable" owners and staff encourage "great vibes."

	FOOD	DECOR	SERVICE	COST

Mahogany Grill, The Ⓜ *Soul Food*   ∇ 23 | 21 | 18 | $39

Miami Gardens | 2190 183rd St. NW (NW 22nd Ave.) | 305-626-8100 |
www.tmgmiami.com

Hearty helpings of "terrific" "upscale soul food", including such classics as chicken 'n' waffles and mac 'n' cheese, ensure that even "big folks" won't "leave hungry" from this Miami Gardens eatery featuring live jazz on weekends; on the downside, service can "take forever", but most agree "it's worth the wait"; P.S. also closed Tuesdays.

Maiko ● *Japanese*   ∇ 20 | 13 | 17 | $37

South Beach | 1255 Washington Ave. (bet. 12th & 13th Sts.) |
Miami Beach | 305-531-6369 | www.maikosushi.com

"For takeout or a quick lunch", this "casual" SoBe standby provides "generous" portions of "good" sushi and "standard" Japanese dishes; despite somewhat "tight quarters", diners say the "price is right."

NEW Maitardi Ⓢ *Italian*   - | - | - | M

Design District | 163 NE 39th St. (bet. NE 1st & NE 2nd Aves.) |
Miami | 305-572-1400 | www.maitardimiami.com

Alfresco dining on a spacious, oak-shaded patio is a highlight of this affordable and stylish (read: colorful mosaic-tiled walls and pizza oven) but tiny Design District Northern Italian; Friday and Saturday night DJs rock the house while the kitchen dishes its signature seafood lasagna – shrimp, scallops, crab, squid, fresh fish in dill lobster sauce – and mango and quinoa salad.

NEW Mandolin Ⓢ *Greek*   - | - | - | M

Design District | 4312 NE Second Ave. (bet. NE 43rd & NE 44th Sts.) |
Miami | 305-576-6066 | www.mandolinmiami.com

One of Miami's newest little dreamboats, this Design District destination set in a 1940s house features an Aegean blue-and-white paint job and a lovely ancient tree in the garden that brings to mind a Greek fishing village; friendly young owners and staffers make everyone feel right at home, as does the simple Turkish and Hellenic fare (grilled fish and greens are tops) served at moderate prices.

Mango's Tropical Cafe ● *Eclectic*   15 | 20 | 16 | $34

South Beach | 900 Ocean Dr. (9th St.) | Miami Beach | 305-673-4422 |
www.mangostropicalcafe.com

"Watch the wackiness happen" on South Beach at this "high-octane" "party" place where "half-naked girls and buff guys dance on the bar" to the delight of "happy" "out-of-towners"; so what if the tropical-inspired Eclectic fare is "pretty average" – fans are willing to shell out for the "hot" scene anyway; P.S. no caps, bandanas, flip-flops or tank tops for men; cover charge after 10 PM.

Marhaba
Mediterranean Cuisine *Lebanese*   ∇ 21 | 16 | 21 | $26

South Miami | The Shops at Sunset Pl. | 5701 Sunset Dr. (SW 57th Ave.) |
305-740-5880

Medheads make tracks for the "fresh", "flavorful" Lebanese specialties at this "reasonably priced" South Miamian where weekend belly dancing enhances the "pleasant" Middle Eastern ambiance; still, many prefer to smoke hookahs outside and escape the "cacophony."

Mario the Baker   *Italian/Pizza* | 19 | 9 | 17 | $19 |

Downtown | 43 W. Flagler St. (NW Miami Ct.) | Miami | 786-316-0166
Coral Gables | Red Bird | 5755 SW 40th St. (bet. 58th Ave. & Red Rd.) | 305-665-0941
Upper East Side | 250 NE 25th St. (Biscayne Blvd.) | Miami | 305-438-0228
North Miami | 13695 W. Dixie Hwy. (NE 137th St.) | 305-891-7641
www.mariothebakerpizza.com

Dubbed the "garlic capital of the world" by devotees, these separately owned "neighborhood" Italians turn out "solid pizza" and other "inexpensive" "comfort food" that's "perfect for families and large groups"; even if the decor "doesn't exist" and "service could be better", it's still the kind of "joint" where you can "come as you are and feel right at home."

Maroosh Ⓜ *Mediterranean/Mideastern* | 24 | 22 | 23 | $36 |

Coral Gables | 223 Valencia Ave. (bet. Ponce de Leon Blvd. & Salzedo St.) | 305-476-9800 | www.maroosh.com

Diners find a "different", "exotic" experience at this "wonderful" Coral Gables Med–Middle Eastern cooking up "delicious" dishes that go "beyond the typical hummus and gyros", complemented by an "affordable" wine selection; weekend belly dancing "livens up" the "nicely lit and decorated" space, making for a "most entertaining" meal.

🆉 Matsuri Ⓜ *Japanese* | 27 | 20 | 20 | $37 |

South Miami | 5759 Bird Rd. (bet. Red Rd. & SW 58th Ave.) | 305-663-1615

Yes, it's in a "nondescript strip mall", but this South Miami "institution" even has "sushi snobs" raving it's one of the "best Japanese" options in town; with a "sleek" makeover that's "improved the ambiance" (if not the "spotty service") and "reasonably priced" fin fare so "fresh it's still flapping", it's no wonder devotees demand you "put this one on your A-list."

Meat Market ➊ *Steak* | 24 | 25 | 22 | $72 |

South Beach | 915 Lincoln Rd. (bet. Jefferson & Michigan Aves.) | Miami Beach | 305-532-0088 | www.meatmarketmiami.com

"Sexy and chic", this "loungey" New American "meat heaven" (from the Touch team) catering to a "beautiful" SoBe clientele is "not your standard steakhouse"; "excellent" beef (with "creative sauces"), "exquisite" fish and an "incredible" wine selection served by a "delightful" staff attract "big spenders" who keep the room "always busy" and "noisy", so "get your lungs ready"; P.S. "Friday happy-hour specials are an added bonus."

Melting Pot   *Fondue* | 20 | 19 | 21 | $43 |

North Miami Beach | 15700 Biscayne Blvd. (157th St.) | 305-947-2228
West Sunset | 11520 Sunset Dr. (SW 117th Ave.) | Miami | 305-279-8816
www.meltingpot.com
See review in Palm Beach County Directory.

	FOOD	DECOR	SERVICE	COST

NEW Mercadito ● Mexican

| - | - | - | M |

Downtown | 3252 NE First Ave. (bet. 36th & 38th Sts.) | Miami | 786-369-0430 | www.mercaditorestaurants.com

The sister of the New York taco shop that could, this tortilla-sized Downtown Mexican keeps a hipster vibe going with its funky bar scene that spills out onto the sidewalk dining room; it serves ceviche, tacos and guac platters meant for sharing, plus plenty of tequila cocktails and sangria to wash it all down.

Mia ● Eclectic

| - | - | - | E |

Downtown | 20 Biscayne Blvd. (Flagler St.) | Miami | 305-642-0032 | www.miabiscayne.com

This swanky restaurant and ultra-lounge brings outsized SoBe chic to Downtown, with a plush, clublike design by Isaac Valdes that boasts multiple LED-equipped bars, a state-of-the-art sound system and a giant interactive electronic wall; meanwhile, chef Gerdy Rodriguez's chic Eclectic fare is ultranational, ranging from classic and nouveau tapas and sushi to ceviche and meat and seafood mixed grills; P.S. it's across from American Airlines Arena.

Miami's Chophouse Steak

| 21 | 21 | 22 | $69 |

Downtown | Metropolitan One | 300 S. Biscayne Blvd. (SE 2nd Ave.) | Miami | 305-938-9000 | www.miamichophouse.com

Formerly Manny's Steakhouse, this "high-end" Downtown carnivorium still turns out "mammoth steaks and sides for sharing", so be sure to "bring an appetite"; "excellent" service helps make it "great for power lunches" (hence the clubby decor), even if prices are as "oversized" as the portions.

☑ Michael's Genuine Food & Drink American

| 26 | 21 | 24 | $54 |

Design District | Atlas Plaza | 130 NE 40th St. (bet. NE 1st & 2nd Aves.) | Miami | 305-573-5550 | www.michaelsgenuine.com

"Everything rocks" at chef-owner Michael Schwartz's "justly popular" New American, a "genuine delight" where fans "ooh and ahh" over the "locally sourced and creatively cooked" concoctions from the "homey open kitchen"; "attentive service without condescension", "pleasant" if "understated" decor, "lovely patio" seating and "affordable prices" add to the appeal, making this "Design District dining at its best."

☑ Michy's M American/French

| 27 | 20 | 25 | $62 |

Upper East Side | 6927 Biscayne Blvd. (bet. Biscayne Blvd. & 69th St.) | Miami | 305-759-2001 | www.michysmiami.com

Chef Michelle Bernstein "continues to reign over Miami's culinary scene" at her "always innovative" Upper East Sider whose "constantly changing menu" allows diners to order "full or half portions" of "melt-in-your-mouth" New American–French "comfort food with Latin and Southern twists"; service is predictably "attentive and knowledgeable", and while some dis "funky decor" and "high prices" for a neighborhood that's a "tad seedy", the majority proclaims this a "true gem in a field of rocks."

	FOOD	DECOR	SERVICE	COST

Mike's Italian New York Style Pizza & Restaurant *Pizza*
▽ 21 | 15 | 18 | $21

Kendall | 13712 84th St. SW (SW 137th Ave.) | 305-382-6200
"Traditional Italian dishes" and thin-crust pies are the draw at this "local joint" bringing a bit of "NYC" to Kendall; the service and space could both use "improvement", but loyalists still "love eating here."

Mint Leaf Indian Brasserie *Indian*
23 | 19 | 16 | $40

Coral Gables | 276 Alhambra Circle (bet. Ponce de Leon Blvd. & Salzedo St.) | 305-443-3739 | www.mintleafib.com
Setting "a new standard for Indian fare" in the area, this Coral Gables eatery (with cousins in London) "rates high" with its "intriguing" apps, "tender, flavorful meats" and "excellent vegetarian options" served in an "elegant" room; "fair to poor" service is a sore point, though, and portions are "on the small side", leading some to feel it's "too expensive"; P.S. a second location is planned for Brickell.

Miss Saigon Bistro *Vietnamese*
23 | 15 | 21 | $31

Coral Gables | 148 Giralda Ave. (Ponce de Leon Blvd.) | 305-446-8006
NEW **South Beach** | 540 Washington Ave. (6th St.) | Miami | 305-531-4200
Pinecrest | 9503 S. Dixie Hwy. (bet. Datran Blvd. & SW 95th St.) | 305-661-2911
www.misssaigonbistro.com
"Delectable" noodles and other Vietnamese staples in "good-sized portions" attract admirers to these "friendly", family-owned Coral Gables and Pinecrest "favorites" that also offer "excellent value"; they're "not trendy" or "fancy", but that's all the more reason most find them "enjoyable" all around; P.S. the SoBe branch opened post-Survey.

Miss Yip Chinese Cafe *Chinese*
19 | 18 | 18 | $32

South Beach | 1661 Meridian Ave. (bet. Lincoln Rd. & 17th St.) | Miami Beach | 305-534-5488 | www.missyipchinesecafe.com
"Gourmet Chinese" featuring dim sum "galore" "does the trick" at this "stylish" SoBe lair; some assess it's "cool, but no big whoop", though others "totally recommend" it to visitors, since "you can stroll down Lincoln Road" afterward; P.S. a Miss Yip Downtown is in the works.

Molina's ● *Cuban*
▽ 22 | 14 | 18 | $24

Hialeah | 4100 E. Eighth Ave. (E. 41st St.) | 305-687-0008
A "great place to get your Cuban food fix", this "no-frills" Hialeah haven serves "abundant quantities" of fried pork and other dishes that are "underpriced for the quality"; service is "fast" too – the "only con" is that "the staff speaks limited English."

Monty's *Seafood*
15 | 18 | 16 | $33

South Beach | Miami Beach Marina | 300 Alton Rd. (3rd St.) | Miami Beach | 305-672-1148 | www.montyssouthbeach.com
Monty's Raw Bar *Seafood*
Coconut Grove | Monty's Marina | 2550 S. Bayshore Dr. (Aviation Ave.) | 305-856-3992
"Dynamite" marina views set the stage for "breezy", "happening" happy hours at these SoBe and Coconut Grove seafooders delivering

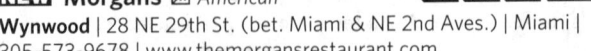

"decent" stone crab claws and "lots of fried" morsels to go with the drinks; "you pay for the atmosphere, not the food", but the "tropical" (and "touristy") ambiance with live calypso music practically "dares you not to have fun."

Moon Thai Restaurant *Japanese/Thai* | 23 | 15 | 19 | $26 |

Coral Gables | 1118 S. Dixie Hwy. (Augusto St.) | 305-668-9890
Kendall | Kendall Plaza | 16311 SW 88th St. (SW 167th Ave.) | 305-388-5901
www.moonthai.com

"A favorite for sushi and Thai", this "expanding" chainlet offers a wide range of "fresh" eats in a "bustling atmosphere" that's "popular with the University of Miami kids"; "efficient" service and "affordable" prices (particularly for "lunch specials") add to the appeal.

NEW Morgans Ⓜ *American* | - | - | - | I |

Wynwood | 28 NE 29th St. (bet. Miami & NE 2nd Aves.) | Miami | 305-573-9678 | www.themorgansrestaurant.com

It may be just what the edgy Wynwood neighborhood needs: an unpretentious family-style restaurant proffering fantastically laid-back breakfasts and weekend brunches; the simple American comfort food includes such savories as meatloaf sandwiches, chicken pot pie and pulled pork, plus pizza, salads and lots of homey soups, all served by a crew of welcoming hipsters who make you feel happy (ditto the recession-era prices).

⚡ Morton's The Steakhouse *Steak* | 25 | 23 | 24 | $69 |

Brickell Area | 1200 Brickell Ave. (SW 13th St.) | Miami | 305-400-9990
Coral Gables | 2333 Ponce de Leon Blvd. (bet. Aragon Ave. & Miracle Mile) | 305-442-1662
Miami Beach | The Crown at Miami Beach | 4041 Collins Ave. (bet. 40th & 41st Sts.) | 786-454-4022
North Miami Beach | 17399 Biscayne Blvd. (NE 173rd St.) | 305-945-3131
www.mortons.com
See review in Palm Beach County Directory.

Mr. Chow ⚫ *Chinese* | - | - | - | E |

South Beach | W South Beach | 2201 Collins Ave. (bet. 22nd & 23rd Sts.) | Miami Beach | 305-695-1695 | www.mrchow.com

In SoBe's hip W Hotel, a dramatic two-story space dominated by a gigantic Swarovski crystal chandelier provides a glittery showcase for Michael Chow's pricey regional Chinese fare; chowhounds salivate over the signature Beijing duck and other specialties, including gold-leaf shumai, served in the ornate dining room or on the spacious patio.

Mykonos *Greek* | 18 | 12 | 16 | $24 |

Coral Way | 1201 SW 22nd St./Coral Way (SW 12th Ave.) | Miami | 305-856-3140 | www.mykonosmiami.com

"Bring your belly" to the "big happy party" at this "mom-and-pop Greek" in Coral Way serving a "solid" (some say "stereotypical") menu; the "dated" decor "won't make you feel like you're in Santorini", but the "huge portions", "right" prices and festive atmosphere make it a hoot "if you're with the right crowd."

	FOOD	DECOR	SERVICE	COST

Naoe ☑ *Japanese*

| | - | - | - | M |

Sunny Isles Beach | 175 Sunny Isles Blvd. (bet. Collins Ave. & Intercoastal Waterways Bridge) | 305-947-6263 | www.naoemiami.com

Local piscivores are flipping over this omakase-only Japanese in Sunny Isles, a sleek and sublime jewel box of a spot where chef Kevin Cory serves pristine fin fare at affordable prices; P.S. it shares the name of the brewery that provides the sake, which is also the chef's Japanese family name.

☑ Nemo ● *American*

| | 24 | 22 | 22 | $60 |

South Beach | 100 Collins Ave. (1st St.) | Miami Beach | 305-532-4550 | www.nemorestaurant.com

Droves of diners "love" this "still hot" SoBe New American offering "innovative", "inspiring" seafood, a "thoughtful" wine list and "awesome" Sunday brunch amid a "fabulous" ambiance, complete with lots of French doors, a patio "under the tree-framed sky" and a "scene that's caught up" to its locale; "it's not for the faint of wallet", but most agree it's a "pleasure" from "beginning to end"; P.S. numerous changes, including menu and decor tweaks, are in the works.

Neomi's Grill *American*

| | - | - | - | VE |

Sunny Isles Beach | Trump Int'l Sonesta Beach | 18001 Collins Ave., 2nd fl. (bet. 178th & 183rd Sts.) | 305-692-5770 | www.trumpmiami.com

"Cutting-edge culinary techniques" produce "extravagant flavor combinations" at this New American "hidden gem" in a Sunny Isles Beach hotel; true, "small portions" and "high prices" are part of the package, but the "creative, challenging and often quite delicious" fare is "worth it if you're looking for something out of the ordinary."

New Chinatown *Chinese*

| | 18 | 13 | 17 | $31 |

South Miami | 5958 S. Dixie Hwy. (SW 73rd St.) | 305-662-5650

"Well-done" "Chinese food for the American palate" paired with an "up-to-date" wine list make this South Miami longtimer a "reliable" choice; however, doubters decry "upscale" prices for fairly "unremarkable" fare and "brusque" service.

News Cafe ● *Diner*

| | 17 | 16 | 16 | $26 |

South Beach | 800 Ocean Dr. (8th St.) | Miami Beach | 305-538-6397 | www.newscafe.com

Dubbed a "mandatory part of any South Beach trip", this "always busy" 24/7 diner (with a newsstand inside) is a "delightful place to take in the Ocean Drive scene" and watch the crowds "walking, strolling and strutting by" over a "lazy outdoor brunch" (that's "much better" than dinner); "old news but the tourists still like it" jeer some, but the rest ask "what's not to love?"

Nexxt Cafe *Eclectic*

| | 18 | 14 | 14 | $28 |

South Beach | 700 Lincoln Rd. (Euclid Ave.) | Miami Beach | 305-532-6643 | www.thenexxtcafe.com

"I thought people in SoBe didn't eat – I was wrong" admit visitors to this Eclectic "Cheesecake Factory knockoff" delivering "gigantic portions" of food from a "huge menu with pretty much something for everyone"; "fairly decent" prices and "ample outdoor seating" that's "amazing for people-watching" help keep it "swamped with crowds" despite complaints about "haphazard" service "with attitude."

Nikki Beach *Eclectic*

| 17 | 24 | 16 | $54 |

South Beach | Penrod's | 1 Ocean Dr. (1st St.) | Miami Beach | 305-538-1111 | www.nikkibeach.com

"Mingle" with the "young", "hot crowd" at this "exotic" SoBe "trendsetter" "right on the beach", where the "simple but stylish" Eclectic fare comes with a "beautiful view" and "dancing after the sun goes down" on weekends; critics are cool on "so-so" food and service for "expensive" tabs, but others reason "when you have South Beach as your decor, everything tastes, looks and seems better."

⦿ Nobu Miami Beach ☻ *Japanese*

| 27 | 22 | 22 | $85 |

South Beach | Shore Club | 1901 Collins Ave. (20th St.) | Miami Beach | 305-695-3232 | www.noburestaurants.com

"Fantastic, inventive, fresh, expensive": that pretty much sums up this "sizzling" SoBe spot from Nobu Matsuhisa that attracts the "biggest movers and shakers of Miami, NYC and Hollywood" for "exceptional" Japanese-Peruvian fare, including "imaginative" sushi of "unparalleled quality"; detractors dis "crowded, noisy" quarters and a "fashion mag"–ready staff that can be a bit "pretentious", but most say "rob a bank" and go – it's "an experience you'll never forget."

NEW Norman's 180 *Eclectic*

| – | – | – | M |

Coral Gables | Westin Colonnade | 180 Aragon Ave. (Ponce de Leon Blvd.) | 305-529-5180 | www.normans180.com

Mango Gangster Norman Van Aken – along with son/partner/co-chef Justin Van Aken – does a 180 from his original über-posh namesake with this more casual, less pricey Eclectic in Coral Gables' Westin Colonnade Hotel; the menu embraces the farm-to-table philosophy, applied to dishes as disparate as Vietnamese pho, fried chicken and an ever-changing array of small plates.

Novecento *Argentinean*

| 20 | 19 | 18 | $40 |

Brickell Area | 1414 Brickell Ave. (SE 14th St.) | Miami | 305-403-0900 ☻
NEW **Key Biscayne** | 620 Crandon Blvd. (bet. W. Enid & Westwood Drs.) | 305-362-0900
Coconut Grove | 121 Alhambra Plaza (bet. Galiano St. & Merrick Way) | 305-557-0900 ☻ ⊠
www.bistronovecento.com

With a "solid" menu of Med-influenced Argentine cuisine, a "sexy bar scene full of well-heeled young professionals" and a "Buenos Aires" ambiance, this trio of "social gathering places" has found the "recipe for success"; while critics cite "just ok" food and "impossible noise levels", most find it "comfortable inside and out."

Oasis ⊠ *Mediterranean*

| ∇ 19 | 13 | 18 | $27 |

Miami Beach | 976 Arthur Godfrey Rd. (Alton Rd.) | 305-674-9005

"Healthy Mediterranean comes to Miami Beach" say those who savor the "refreshing" salads and other "tasty" eats in "good-sized" portions at this "casual neighborhood spot" with sidewalk seating; it's "great for lunch after the gym" and "perfect when you don't want to pay a fortune for a night out", leaving some to wonder "why it isn't more popular."

◪ Oceanaire Seafood Room *Seafood*   24 | 23 | 23 | $64

Downtown | Mary Brickell Vlg. | 900 S. Miami Ave. (10th St.) | Miami | 305-372-8862 | www.theoceanaire.com

"For fresher fish you'd have to drop a line yourself" gush fin fans about the "simply but expertly prepared" seafood and "wonderful raw bar" at this "elegant", "ocean liner"–like Downtowner, part of a "high-end chain"; "exceptional" service is another asset, and while some cite "expense-account" prices and a "corporate" feel, that doesn't deter the "high-rolling" "older crowd."

Ocean Prime *Seafood/Steak*   24 | 25 | 23 | $57

Aventura | Aventura Mall | 19501 Biscayne Blvd. (William Lehman Cswy.) | 305-931-5400 | www.ocean-prime.com

Surf 'n' turf fans tout this "mall surprise" in Aventura for its "top-notch seafood", "fabulous steaks" and "elegant, nightclublike setting" enhanced by a "charming" staff; though some are peeved by the "pricey" menu, a "fun bar scene" with "live music" (in-season) adds to the "boisterous" atmosphere and helps keep it "packed at all times."

Off the Grille Bistro *Caribbean*   - | - | - | I

Kendall | 12578 SW 88th St. (bet. SW 125th & 127th Aves.) | 305-274-2300 | www.offthegrille.com

All the Caribbean curry and jerk dishes are "a notch above the usual strip-mall fast food" at this small, "ultracasual" "bargain" choice in Kendall, a "great lunch spot" where the plates are so generous "you can eat two meals from one"; regulars "prefer sitting on the side-walk" to eating inside and rejoice that it's now got a liquor license for beer and wine (you can still BYO for a $10 corkage).

Oggi Caffe *Italian*   21 | 19 | 22 | $37

North Bay Village | 1666 79th St. Cswy. (Hispañola Ave.) | 305-866-1238 | www.oggicaffe.com

Satisfied surveyors say you "simply cannot go wrong" with the "con-sistently good" Italian fare served in a "homey atmosphere" at this "neighborhood" North Bay Villager; though a few cite "unexcep-tional" cooking, the generally "moderate" tabs and "excellent" ser-vice have kept local guests "going there for years."

Oishi Thai *Japanese/Thai*   25 | 22 | 24 | $48

North Miami | 14841 Biscayne Blvd. (146th St.) | 305-947-4338 | www.oishithai.com

The "secret is out" about this "marvelous" North Miami "find" where the "exciting" Japanese-Thai creations by a Nobu alum in-clude "out-of-this-world" sushi, "rocking" pad Thai and "fresh sea-sonal specials" (not to mention a few "copycat" dishes); "chic" surroundings with a "South Beachy feel", "warm, welcoming" ser-vice and "fair" tabs complete the "Zen experience."

	FOOD	DECOR	SERVICE	COST

☒ OLA *Pan-Latin* | 27 | 22 | 24 | $64 |

South Beach | Sanctuary Hotel | 1745 James Ave. (bet. 17th & 18th Sts.) | Miami Beach | 305-695-9125 | www.olamiami.com

Even "locals feel like they're on vacation" at toque Douglas Rodriguez's "fantastic" "find" in South Beach's Sanctuary Hotel, where the "modern" mood mirrors the "innovative, playful Pan-Latin" fare (particularly the "spectacular ceviche"); "exceptional" servers "guide you through the many choices", and while the "small plates" can "add up", it's a small price to pay for a "gastronomic experience."

Old Lisbon *Portuguese* | 24 | 16 | 22 | $38 |

Coral Way | 1698 SW 22nd St./Coral Way (17th Ave.) | Miami | 305-854-0039

NEW **South Miami** | 5837 Sunset Dr. (SW 58th Ct.) | 305-662-7435
www.oldlisbon.com

Codfish prepared "every which way imaginable" is the "excellent" "house specialty" at this "friendly" and "unpretentious" Coral Way Portuguese; though the decor is "totally outdated" and it's "not inexpensive", it's "fantastic for a late afternoon lunch with *vinho verde*"; P.S. the South Miami branch opened post-Survey.

Old San Juan *Puerto Rican* | ▽ 19 | 13 | 18 | $28 |

West Miami | 1200 SW 57th Ave. (12th St.) | 305-263-9911 | www.oldsanjuanmiami.com

Avid islanders "go for the mofongo" (mashed plantains with a choice of additions) at this "hole-in-the-wall" in West Miami serving a "good rendition of Puerto Rican cuisine"; "warm service", "great music" and value-packed lunch buffets (pricier for weekend brunch) override the "divey" digs.

OneBurger ☒ *Burgers* | 18 | 10 | 12 | $15 |

Coral Gables | 367 Alhambra Circle (SW 42nd Ave.) | 305-529-5555 | www.oneburger.com

"Open-minded" patty lovers praise the 30-plus varieties of "innovative gourmet burgers" (from Kobe to Cuban-style) at this Coral Gables "upscale fast-food joint" that causes serious "cravings"; the "minimalist" dining room smacks of "school cafeteria" to some, and others lament "tiny food" and no alcohol, but savvy burgeristas say go "next door" to Globe Cafe (owned by the same folks) for your liquid refreshment.

Original Daily Bread Marketplace *Mideastern* | ▽ 22 | 12 | 18 | $16 |

Coconut Grove | 2400 SW 27th St. (S. Dixie Hwy.) | 305-856-0363 | www.dailybreadmarketplace.com

Picky patrons approve of the "legitimate" homemade hummus, "properly sauced" specialties and the "best pita" around at this Coconut Grover delivering Middle Eastern fare that's "always fresh" and "cheap"; since it's "in a marketplace" the surroundings are "nothing fancy", but regulars "love" the place anyway.

	FOOD	DECOR	SERVICE	COST

Original Pancake House, The *American*

| | 20 | 11 | 17 | $17 |

Aventura | 21215 Biscayne Blvd. (NE 213th St.) | 305-933-1966
Kendall | Total Sunset Plaza | 11510 SW 72nd St. (SW 115th Ct.) |
305-274-9215
Doral | 9901 NW 41st St. (bet. NW 97th & 102nd Aves.) | Miami |
786-507-0564
www.originalpancakehouse.com

"Killer" pancakes ("try the apple") and "fluffy" "baked omelets" the
"size of a small tricycle tire" please "families", "late-risers" and
other folks who "bring an appetite" to these "popular" American
chain links; though an "airplane hangar atmosphere" and "long
waits" bedevil some, many agree "for good old-fashioned breakfasts, this is the place to go."

Origin Asian Bistro *Asian*

| | 22 | 18 | 20 | $32 |

South Miami | 5850B Sunset Dr. (SW 58th Ct.) | 305-668-8205

Origin Asian Bistro & Sushi *Asian*

Key Biscayne | 200 Crandon Blvd. (bet. Harbor & Sonesta Drs.) |
305-365-1260
www.originbistro.com

An "extensive", "surprising" menu of "super-fresh" fare, from "fantastic" Malaysian dishes to sushi, brings out the "love" for these
"breezy", "dependable" Pan-Asians; the "hospitable" staff is a plus
too, as are the "decent prices"; P.S. the South Miami branch moved
to Sunset Drive post-Survey.

☑ Ortanique
on the Mile *Caribbean/New World*

| | 26 | 22 | 23 | $54 |

Coral Gables | 278 Miracle Mile (Salzedo St.) | 305-446-7710 |
www.cindyhutsoncuisine.com

There's a "fabulous" "island feel" in the air at this "creative" Coral
Gables eatery, where "beautiful aromas" waft from the "flavorful"
Caribbean-New World cuisine starring "fresh seafood" and the
"cabanalike decor" evokes a "porch along the beach"; true, it's
"pricey" and often "crowded", but servers "who love what they do"
plus the "best mojitos in town" work their own magic.

☑ Osteria del Teatro ☒ *Italian*

| | 26 | 17 | 25 | $65 |

South Beach | 1443 Washington Ave. (Española Way) | Miami Beach |
305-538-7850 | www.osteriadelteatromiami.com

The "cooked-to-perfection" Northern Italian "food is the star" of
this "small gem on South Beach" that offers "so many specials you'll
need to take notes"; luckily, "super-friendly" servers who "really
know the menu" are there to assist in the "loud, close quarters"
(some suggest a "renovation" is in order), and if it's "not cheap",
partisans remind you're paying for a "step above the rest."

NEW Otentic ● *French*

| | - | - | - | M |

South Beach | 710 Washington Ave. (7th St.) | Miami Beach |
305-531-1464 | www.otentic-restaurant.com

Tiny (18 seats), laid-back and ooh-la-la French, this modestly decorated (and priced) South Beach bistro makes freshness a priority;

expect a flurry of flavor in everything from its signature 'farmer' steak with blue cheese or pepper sauce to its roster of savory crêpes, filled with Francophile favorites like Provençal vegetables.

Outback Steakhouse *Steak*
| 17 | 15 | 18 | $30 |

Coral Way | Flagler Park Plaza | 8255 W. Flagler St. (82nd Ave.) | Miami | 305-262-9766
North Miami Beach | 3161 NE 163rd St. (bet. Biscayne & Interama Blvds.) | 305-944-4329
Kendall | Town & Country Ctr. | 11800 Sherry Ln. (bet. Mills Dr. & SW 117th Ave.) | 305-596-6771
Miami Lakes | 15490 NW 77th Ct. (Miami Lakes Dr.) | 305-558-6868
Westchester | Briar Bay Shopping Ctr. | 13145 SW 89th Pl. (SW 136th St.) | 305-254-4456
www.outback.com

"Meat lovers on a budget" report that this "midtier", Aussie-themed chain chophouse provides terrific "bang for the buck", not to mention "basic" steaks and "hefty sides" (the famed bloomin' onion supplies "a week's worth of calories" in a single serving); it's "not known for subtlety" – starting with the "overly friendly, chat 'n' squat" service – but when you "don't want to splurge", it's a "decent" enough option.

☑ Palm, The *Steak*
| 26 | 19 | 24 | $70 |

Bay Harbor Islands | 9650 E. Bay Harbor Dr. (96th St.) | 305-868-7256 | www.thepalm.com

"Old-school dining" is alive and well in Bay Harbor Islands at this "distinguished" chain carnivorium, born in NYC in 1926 and drawing "movers and shakers" ever since with its "enormous" steaks and lobsters plated in "distinguished" settings adorned with celebrity "caricatures"; sure, the tabs are reminiscent of "mortgage payments" and service can career from "top-notch" to "surly", but ultimately it's "consistently good."

☑ Palme d'Or ☒ Ⓜ *French*
| 28 | 28 | 28 | $80 |

Coral Gables | Biltmore Hotel | 1200 Anastasia Ave. (Columbus Blvd.) | 305-913-3201 | www.biltmorehotel.com

Rated No. 1 in the Miami Survey for Food, Decor and Service, this "exquisite" New French is "as close to perfection as you can get", an "inviting, unintimidating" bastion of "old-world elegance" in the "magnificent" Biltmore Hotel; chef Philippe Ruiz's "innovative" small plates are "beautifully presented" "gastronomic delights" complemented by an "excellent wine list" and "tuxedoed servers" who "set the stage for an outstanding dining experience"; it's "pricey" for sure, but have no doubt: "you will be thrilled."

Panya Thai *Thai*
| - | - | - | M |

North Miami Beach | 520 NE 167th St. (bet. NE 5th & 6th Aves.) | 305-945-8566 | www.panyathai.com

"When they say spicy they mean it" at this North Miami Beach strip-maller serving "carefully prepared", "authentic" Thai food that's "Bangkok"-caliber and "not for the faint of heart"; plus, admirers appreciate that the "extensive" menu goes "a bit beyond the standard."

	FOOD	DECOR	SERVICE	COST

Papichi *Italian* ▽ 20 | 15 | 21 | $36

Pinecrest | 9619 S. Dixie Hwy./U.S. 1 (Datran Blvd.) | 305-668-1848 | www.papichirestaurant.com

"Big plates of pasta", "wood-oven pizza" and chicken are the headliners of the Brazilian-influenced Italian menu at this Pinecrest eatery; some deem it "ordinary", however, and find it "a bit frustrating that a place that's always full of families" is short on "kids' portions."

Paquito's *Mexican* 22 | 20 | 20 | $27

North Miami Beach | RK 162nd Biscayne Plaza | 16265 Biscayne Blvd. (Sunny Isles Blvd.) | 305-947-5027 | www.paquitosmiami.com

"Every day feels like Cinco de Mayo" at this "colorful" cantina in North Miami Beach where the "worthy" fare "tastes as if a real Mexican grandma is in the kitchen"; a "caring, competent" staff, "strong" margaritas and "inexpensive" tabs seal the deal for a range of fans: "Latino families, couples on dates, local workers and singles who party at the active bar."

Z Pascal's on Ponce Z *French* 27 | 20 | 25 | $63

Coral Gables | 2611 Ponce de Leon Blvd. (bet. Almeria & Valencia Aves.) | 305-444-2024 | www.pascalmiami.com

"You can always expect creative dishes" from chef-owner Pascal Oudin, whose "intimate" Coral Gables bistro features "exquisitely prepared" New French fare paired with "gracious", "civilized" service; it can be "costly", "cramped" and "noisy", but *amis* aver this "little piece of Paris" is nonetheless *"très magnifique."*

Pasha's *Mediterranean* 20 | 14 | 16 | $19

Brickell Area | 1414 Brickell Ave. (SE 14th St.) | Miami | 305-416-5116
Brickell Area | Four Seasons | 1441 Brickell Ave. (14th Ln.) | Miami | 305-381-3938
Coral Gables | 130 Miracle Mile (bet. Galiano St. & Ponce De Leon Blvd.) | 305-764-3040
Design District | 3801 N. Miami Ave. (I-195) | Miami | 305-572-1150 Z
Aventura | Aventura Mall | 19501 Biscayne Blvd. (NE 195th St.) | 305-917-4007
South Beach | 900 Lincoln Rd. (Jefferson Ave.) | Miami Beach | 305-673-3919 ☽
www.pashas.com

"Get your Med on" at these "stylish" "standbys" offering "healthy, upscale fast food" that's "delicious, refreshing" and served by an "energetic" counter staff; the SoBe branch wins compliments as the "best budget buy for alfresco Lincoln Road dining", plus the "people-watching is great" too.

Paul Bakery *Bakery/Sandwiches* 18 | 16 | 13 | $20

Miami Beach | 450 Lincoln Rd. (bet. Drexel & Washington Aves.) | 305-531-1200 ☽
Aventura | Aventura Mall | 19575 Biscayne Blvd. (195th St.) | 305-682-8012
www.paulusa.com

Oh, just "start your diet tomorrow" and hit these "French cafe"-style bakeries where you can "sit outside with a newspaper" and nosh on "delicious" desserts and sandwiches; there's a "snooty", "sour" staff to contend with and some say the spots are "overhyped", but "crowds do know *something,* after all."

Pei Wei Asian Diner Asian
19 | 14 | 16 | $16

Kendall | 13616 N. Kendall Dr. (SW 137th Ave.) | 305-386-8510 | www.peiwei.com

"Filling the gap between budget Chinese takeout" and higher-priced parent P.F. Chang's, this "affordable", "order-at-the-counter" chain delivers "enjoyable", "modernized" Asian chow at a "fast pace"; maybe the dishes could use more "pizzazz" and the "rushed" service irks some, but families keep it "crowded" since the "kids love it."

Pelican Café ❶ American
23 | 22 | 21 | $43

South Beach | Pelican Hotel | 826 Ocean Dr. (bet. 8th & 9th Sts.) | Miami Beach | 305-673-1000 | www.pelicanhotel.com

The "watermelon mojitos" alone keep "die-hard fans" returning to this "funky but not over the top" American in the Diesel-owned Pelican Hotel, though the "excellent food" and "good service" certainly don't hurt; add in an "alfresco beachfront" setting with "great people-watching", and you've got a "perfect place for lunch in SoBe."

Peppy's in the Gables Italian
▽ 20 | 20 | 22 | $42

Coral Gables | 216 Palermo Ave. (Ponce de Leon Blvd.) | 305-448-1240

Northern Italian "home cooking the way mom used to make" wins over *paesani* at this "pleasant" Coral Gables "favorite" staffed by a "friendly", "attentive" crew; though a few find the decor "dated", more appreciate the "cozy", candlelit ambiance, recommending it for both "family dinners" and "romantic meals."

Perricone's Marketplace & Cafe Italian
20 | 20 | 20 | $35

Brickell Area | 15 SE 10th St. (S. Miami Ave.) | Miami | 305-374-9449 | www.perricones.com

"Fresh, flavorful" and "inexpensive" Italian "delicacies" prove "addictive" to admirers at this "laid-back" Brickell cafe set in a "relocated farmhouse"; even better, "relaxing" in the "enchanting backyard" under the "big banyan tree" is "like eating in the Garden of Eden", plus the "on-site gourmet market" offers lots of take-home "favorites."

☑ P.F. Chang's China Bistro Chinese
21 | 21 | 20 | $33

Downtown | Mary Brickell Vlg. | 901 S. Miami Ave. (SE 9th St.) | Miami | 305-358-0732
North Miami Beach | 17455 Biscayne Blvd. (bet. NE 172nd St. & Point East Dr.) | 305-957-1966
Pinecrest | The Falls | 8888 SW 136th St. (U.S. 1) | 305-234-2338
www.pfchangs.com

"It may be a chain", but it's a "well-oiled" one and "always busy" thanks to its "tasty", "reliable", "modern" Chinese fare ("check out the lettuce wraps") served in a relatively "upscale" environment that's "loud" but "fun"; just be aware that service "varies", and the wise advise "make reservations or you'll wait."

	FOOD	DECOR	SERVICE	COST

Philippe ● *Chinese*
`21` `24` `20` `$79`

South Beach | Gansevoort South Beach Hotel | 2305 Collins Ave. (23rd St.) | Miami Beach | 305-674-0250 | www.philippechow.com
"See-and-be-seen" Sinophiles flock to this SoBe Chinese, the local outpost of New York–based Philippe Chow, flaunting a "stunning", "modern-chic" setting and "imaginative" fare (including "expertly carved" Peking duck); while critics contend it's "absurdly expensive" and "lacks the oomph" of other "trendy" types, game guests find it's "fun every once in a while" for a "splurge."

Pilar *American/Seafood*
`24` `18` `22` `$36`

Aventura | 20475 Biscayne Blvd. (NE 203rd St.) | 305-937-2777 | www.pilarrestaurant.com
"Cooked-just-right" New American seafood dishes lure Aventurans to this "sophisticated" "surprise" in an "otherwise mundane" strip mall; though the "comfortable" but "noisy" surroundings get mixed reviews, "fair prices" and "amicable" service keep it a "good value."

Piola ● *Pizza*
`22` `17` `19` `$23`

Brickell Area | 1250 S. Miami Ave. (SW 13th St.) | Miami | 305-374-0031
South Beach | 1625 Alton Rd. (bet. Lincoln Rd. & 16th St.) | Miami Beach | 305-674-1660
www.piola.it
"Delicious thin-crust pizzas and pasta" with a touch of "Brazilian style" have people "lining up" to get into these "local hipster" pie parlors in SoBe and Brickell (part of an international chain) that offer an "astounding variety of toppings" along with "terrific" drinks; what's more, the Alton Road locale is "perfect for a dinner-and-a-movie date" since it's "next to the multiplex"; P.S. "don't miss unlimited gnocchi nights on the 29th of each month."

Pita Hut *Israeli*
`17` `9` `14` `$19`

Miami Beach | 530 Arthur Godfrey Rd. (bet. Prairie & Royal Palm Aves.) | 305-531-6090 | www.pita-hut.com
"All the Israeli staples" – and sushi too – can be found at this Miami Beach kosher nook known for "feel-good" falafel, shawarma and other inexpensive bites; some assess it's "acceptable but unexciting" and say there's "no atmosphere whatsoever", but at least it's convenient for "picking up something to bring to the beach."

Pit Bar-B-Q, The *BBQ*
`20` `8` `14` `$18`

Westernmost Dade | 16400 SW Eighth St. (Krome Ave.) | Miami | 305-226-2272 | www.thepitbarbq.com
"Savory, finger-licking barbecue" "done with the right amount of smoke and spice" compels 'cue-lovers to "travel a way" to this "spartan" yet "folksy" Westernmost Dade "institution"; true, the "loud Spanish music" isn't for everyone, but many relish sitting outside for the "real Everglades effect."

Pizza Rustica *Pizza*
`21` `8` `14` `$14`

South Beach | 1447 Washington Ave. (Española Way) | Miami Beach | 305-538-6009 ●

(continued)

(continued)

Pizza Rustica

South Beach | 667 Lincoln Rd. (bet. Euclid & Meridian Aves.) | Miami Beach | 305-672-2334 ●

South Beach | 863 Washington Ave. (bet. 8th & 9th Sts.) | Miami Beach | 305-674-8244 ●

NEW **South Miami** | 6800 SW 57th Ave. (Ponce De Leon Blvd.) | 305-740-6464 ▨

www.pizza-rustica.com

The "fantastic selection of unusual pizzas" with "gourmet toppings" makes for a "rewarding experience" at these separately owned Roman-style eateries dishing up "large" rectangular slices with a "thick, crisp and buttery" crust; though you may have to "fight your way to the counter and scream your order", most agree it's "great for late-night food on a budget" or a "speedy take-out" meal.

Pizza Volante *Pizza*

- | - | - | I

Design District | 3918 N. Miami Ave. (bet. 39th & 40th Sts.) | Miami | 305-573-5325 | www.pizzavolantemiami.com

Jonathan Eismann's industrial-chic pizzeria and mozzarella bar lures locals to the Design District for relatively inexpensive designer pies and panini, gorgeous salads and terrific wine values; but it's not just the crowd that's coming from nearby – lots of toppings are sourced from area farms, pleasing locavores and vegetarians alike.

Por Fin *Mediterranean/Spanish*

22 | 23 | 21 | $51

Coral Gables | 2500 Ponce de Leon Blvd. (Andalusia Ave.) | 305-441-0107 | www.porfinrestaurant.com

"Catalan comes to Coral Gables" at this "happening" Spanish-Med "surprise" offering "unusual twists on traditional dishes" (with a "decadent" touch) by an alum of Spain's El Bulli; a few feel the kitchen is "overreaching" and the execution sometimes "falls short", but compensations include a "beautiful" setting amped up by a "sexy" upstairs bar scene and service that's "right on the mark."

Prelude by Barton G. ● *American*

- | - | - | M

Downtown | Adrienne Arsht Ctr. | 1300 Biscayne Blvd. (NE 14th St.) | Miami | 305-576-8888 | www.preludebybartong.com

South Beach's most theatrical restaurateur brings his latest offering Downtown to the Arsht Center for the Performing Arts; the show-stopping space (bright colors, high ceilings) features prix fixe–only American meals, with two-course lunches and brunches ($29) and three-course dinners ($49) that can include everything from mini-burgers and goat cheese tortellini to tuna-and-roasted-beet salad and duck confit.

Prime Italian ● *Italian/Steak*

24 | 22 | 21 | $75

South Beach | Hilton Bentley Miami/South Beach | 101 Ocean Dr. (1st St.) | Miami Beach | 305-695-8484 | www.mylesrestaurantgroup.com

"Family-style meets SoBe-style" at this "hopping" Italian steakhouse that puts a "modern twist" on cooking from The Boot, offering "big portions to share" (with "hungry friends"), accented by "truffle oil and Kobe beef for all"; a "professional" staff tends to the "trendy" room, and while it's a "wallet-buster", fans assure the "scene" is "worth it"; P.S. walk-ins sometimes hop over here "if the wait at [sister restaurant] Prime One Twelve across the street is too long."

☑ Prime One Twelve ◐ *Seafood/Steak* | 26 | 23 | 23 | $85 |

South Beach | 112 Ocean Dr. (1st St.) | Miami Beach | 305-532-8112 | www.prime112.com

"Nothing exceeds like excess" at this "vibrant", even "frenzied" SoBe "steakhouse to end all steakhouses" serving up *Flintstones*-size portions of "extraordinary seafood and meat" amid an "eye candy"–crammed "scene" that lures "power brokers, celebs and pro athletes alike"; service ranges from "fast and friendly" to "rushed" and "rude" and "reservations are somewhat irrelevant", while even admirers admit the place is "too everything" ("too expensive, too crowded, too noisy"); in the end, though, it's "still the one to beat."

Provence Grill *French* | ▽ 18 | 14 | 17 | $37 |

Brickell Area | 1223 Lincoln Road (bet. Alton Rd. & West Ave.) | Miami | 305-531-1600 | www.provencegrill.com

Surveyors "satisfy" a "steak and pommes frites craving" or have a "light lunch" on the porch at this "welcoming", "country-style" Brickell Area bistro; the "casual" feel, "well-priced" menu and parking lot ("highly desirable in this area") are pluses, though a few are "disappointed" by an "unambitious" kitchen.

Puerto Sagua ◐ *Cuban* | 20 | 9 | 16 | $19 |

South Beach | 700 Collins Ave. (7th St.) | Miami Beach | 305-673-1115

"Cheap, delicious and close to the beach", this "quality standby" on SoBe (since 1962) "thankfully never changes" its "ample portions" of "authentic Cuban luncheonette food" served from morning to late-night; though it "looks like an old cafeteria", it's "beloved by locals and tourists alike" who "don't have to break the law by flying to Havana."

Q American Barbeque ☒ *American* | - | - | - | M |

Design District | 4029 N. Miami Ave. (NW 41st St.) | Miami | 305-227-2378 | www.qamericanbarbeque.com

No need to get directions to this good ol' American BBQ joint from Jonathan Eismann (Pacific Time, Pizza Volante), where live music, an in-house smoker and a pot-bellied pit turn out finger-lickin' ribs, chicken and wings served alongside slaw, beans and cornbread; just follow the smoke to find this nicely priced Design District newcomer that seems more down-home than Downtown.

Quattro Gastronomia Italiana ◐ *Italian* | 22 | 23 | 19 | $63 |

South Beach | 1014 Lincoln Rd. (bet. Lenox & Michigan Aves.) | Miami Beach | 305-531-4833 | www.quattromiami.com

"Classic" Northern Italian fare served in a "stylish" Lincoln Road locale with a "beautiful" bar keeps this South Beacher "full all the time"; it's "nice to eat outside" and take in the "scene", and while critics contend it's "pretentious" and "way overpriced", others feel it's a "decent" choice for the "touristy strip."

FOOD | DECOR | SERVICE | COST

Quinn's Restaurant *Seafood*

25 | 23 | 23 | $60

South Beach | Park Central Hotel | 640 Ocean Dr. (bet. 6th & 7th Sts.) | Miami Beach | 305-673-6400 | www.quinnsmiami.com

"Exquisitely prepared" seafood (including "amazing" signature Bam!Bam! shrimp) by chef-owner Gerry Quinn draws fish fanciers to this SoBe "favorite" with a "relaxed" "tropical" ambiance, "delightful sea breezes" and "endless people-watching"; "engaging" service and a nightly guitarist enhance the atmosphere, though some pout it's "pricey" with a "touristy" bent.

Racks Italian Bistro & Market ● *Italian*

- | - | - | M

North Miami Beach | Intracoastal Mall | 3933 NE 163rd St. (36th Ave.) | 305-917-7225 | www.grrestaurant.com

Though this eatery on the North Miami Beach waterfront prides itself on its puffy pizza with charred crusts (the result of a blistering coal-burning oven), waitresses in eye-popping bustiers also serve up a full menu of Italian classics and a fine selection of vino; cozy booths, exposed-brick walls and moderate prices complete the picture, as does the ongoing loop of gangster films.

Randazzo's Little Italy *Italian*

23 | 20 | 19 | $39

Coral Gables | 385 Miracle Mile (SW 42nd Ave.) | 305-448-7002 | www.randazzoslittleitaly.com

"It's gravy, not sauce, *capiche*?" at this Coral Gables Italian, co-owned by "personable" former boxer Marc Randazzo, serving "knockout" Chicago-style dishes that are big enough for "three people"; its large space, with retro photos and movies like *Goodfellas* in the background, is a "hoot", though the "loud", "crowded" atmosphere and "more expensive" tabs are drawbacks for some.

RA Sushi *Japanese*

19 | 22 | 17 | $32

South Miami | 5829 SW 72nd St. (bet. SW 58th Ave. & SW 58th Ct.) | 305-341-0092 | www.rasushi.com

See review in Palm Beach County Directory.

Red Fish Grill ◨ *Seafood*

20 | 25 | 21 | $44

Coral Gables | 9610 Old Cutler Rd. (96th St.) | 305-668-8788 | www.redfishgrill.net

A "sublime" setting "overlooking Biscayne Bay" in a "historic" beachfront building in Matheson Hammock Park makes this "hard-to-find" Coral Gables "hideaway" "unbeatable for watching a Miami sunset" and stirring up some "romance"; the seafood is "well executed", and while some say it "doesn't quite match up" to the surroundings, most find the meal "magical" nonetheless; P.S. "make sure it's not mosquito season" when you go.

◪ Red Light ●◨ *American*

26 | 16 | 18 | $36

Upper East Side | Motel Blu | 7700 Biscayne Blvd. (77th St.) | Miami | 305-757-7773 | www.redlightmiami.com

You won't find "better food for prices like these" declare disciples of chef Kris Wessel, whose "oh-so-cool" Upper East Sider in a riverside "1950s hotel" turns out "local, seasonal, sustainable" New

American fare with a "bit of New Orleans flavor" (the "BBQ shrimp alone is worth a visit"); that helps make up for "haphazard" service and a somewhat "dicey" location, though for some that's just "part of the charm."

Red the Steakhouse *Steak*
25 | 25 | 25 | $70

South Beach | 119 Washington Ave. (1st St.) | Miami Beach | 305-534-3688 | www.redthesteakhouse.com

"Cooked-to-perfection" steaks, a "sophisticated" setting and "warm, wonderful" service by a "delightful" staff keep carnivores cooing over this "posh" South Beach "standout"; despite an "approachable wine list", though, a few beef about the "red ink you'll face when the check arrives."

⊠ Restaurant at the Setai, The *Asian*
22 | 27 | 23 | $87

South Beach | The Setai | 2001 Collins Ave. (20th St.) | Miami Beach | 305-520-6000 | www.setai.com

SoBe sojourners round out their "culinary CV" at this "mind-blowing" Pan-Asian, savoring a "decadent" meal of "creative", "palate-pleasing" (some say "pretentious") dishes accompanied by "personal" service amid "gorgeous", "Zen-like" surroundings; while "stratospheric" prices come with the territory, most affirm it's "worth the splurge", whether you "save it for a special occasion", "just won the lottery or came by private yacht."

Rice House of Kabob *Persian*
∇ 21 | 10 | 16 | $19

South Beach | 1318 Alton Rd. (bet. 13th & 14th Sts.) | Miami Beach | 305-531-0332
Kendall | 13742 SW 56th St. (SW. 137th Ave.) | 305-387-6815
Doral | 1450 NW 87th Ave. (15th St.) | Miami | 305-418-9464
www.ricehouseofkabob.com

"Flavorful" kebabs and other "aromatic" eats offer a fine "introduction to Persia's delights" at this "quick, reliable" mini-chain; the counter service is "friendly" enough, though there's little to "no decor" apart from "big-screen TVs"; P.S. a North Miami venue is due.

River Oyster Bar, The ⊠ *Seafood*
24 | 19 | 21 | $46

Miami River | 650 S. Miami Ave. (SW 7th St.) | Miami | 305-530-1915 | www.therivermiami.com

A "grand array of oysters" greets guests who go for a taste of the town's "freshest" bivalves and other "fabulous" dishes at this "lively" seafooder near the Miami River; the decor's "nothing special", but a "cool wine list", "personable" service and a "local" vibe make it a "special place" anyway.

Rock Fish Grill ⓜ *American/Seafood*
∇ 21 | 19 | 19 | $32

Kendall | Kendall Gates Shopping Ctr. | 12042 SW 88th St. (SW 122nd Ave.) | 305-271-1251 | www.rockfishmiami.com

Diners who dub it a "local favorite" say this Traditional American decorated with rock 'n' roll memorabilia is the "best little neighborhood restaurant in Kendall" for its "homemade" seafood-focused fare, "attentive" service and "great" prices; it's "somewhat out of the way", but most "would go back."

	FOOD	DECOR	SERVICE	COST

☒ Romeo's Cafe ☒Ⓜ *Italian*　27 | 19 | 28 | $87

Coral Way | 2257 SW 22nd St./Coral Way (bet. 22nd & 23rd Aves.) | Miami | 305-859-2228 | www.romeoscafe.com

There's "no menu", "little" space and many "surprises" at this "foodie's dream" in Coral Way, where chef-owner Romeo Majano "comes out to see what you like", then "takes you on a culinary journey" with "outstanding" multicourse Northern Italian meals "customized to each diner's preference"; it's "exquisite" and "expensive", with a staff "working like a precision timepiece" to ensure a "memorable experience" whether you're there to "celebrate, impress a date or propose."

Rosalia's *Italian*　18 | 14 | 18 | $29

Aventura | Aventura Mall | 19501 Biscayne Blvd. (195th St.) | 305-792-2006

Shoppers "in a hurry" at the bustling Aventura Mall dig into the "good" Italian "classics" at this "small", often "crowded" bistro, a "great alternative" if "you can't get into the Cheesecake Factory next door"; however, even "super-reasonable prices" and "efficient service" can't tempt a few naysayers, who deem it just "ok."

Rosa Mexicano *Mexican*　21 | 22 | 20 | $43

Downtown | Mary Brickell Vlg. | 900 S. Miami Ave. (bet. 9th & 10th Sts.) | Miami | 786-425-1001 | www.rosamexicano.com

Fans find "tasty", "fresh Mex without the Tex" along with "don't-miss" pomegranate margaritas at this "hopping" Downtown link in a slightly "upper-end" NYC-based chain; the decor, complete with a blue water wall, is "fantastic", and even if it's "a little more expensive than your traditional Mexican place", "at least there are no mariachis" and the "guacamole made tableside" is "killer."

Rosinella *Italian*　19 | 12 | 16 | $31

Brickell Area | 1040 S. Miami Ave. (bet. 10th & 11th Sts.) | Miami | 305-372-5756

South Beach | 525 Lincoln Rd. (bet. Drexel & Pennsylvania Aves.) | Miami Beach | 305-672-8777 ◑
www.rosinella.net

"You'd bet your mother was in the kitchen" of these "cozy", "always busy" SoBe and Brickell Italians dishing up "good basic pastas and pizza", plus "excellent" specials; though crusty types call them "ho-hum" and cite "hit-or-miss" service, steady customers claim the "consistent" cooking for a "reasonable price" keeps them a "winner."

Royal Bavarian Schnitzel Haus *German*　▽ 19 | 17 | 20 | $33

Upper East Side | 1085 NE 79th St. (10th Ave.) | Miami | 305-754-8002 | www.schnitzelhausmiami.com

"Good wursts, fine schnitzels and all the other classic fixings" with imported brews to "wash them all down" are on the menu of this Upper East Side German with "crazy" decor and a "wonderful beer garden"; some say the fare is only "so-so" and are put off by the "boisterous" crowd, but others bellow Bavaria, "here I come."

	FOOD	DECOR	SERVICE	COST

Rusty Pelican *Seafood*

| | 16 | 22 | 18 | $44 |

Key Biscayne | 3201 Rickenbacker Cswy. (Arthur Lamb Jr. Rd.) |
305-361-3818 | www.therustypelican.com

The "fabulous" Miami vista draws "out-of-towners" and other skyline
seekers to this somewhat "dated" seafooder that's a "waterfront institution" on Key Biscayne; the brunch bunch "loves" the Sunday
buffet, though otherwise most agree "you can't beat the view, but
you can beat the food."

☑ Ruth's Chris Steak House *Steak*

| | 25 | 22 | 24 | $65 |

Coral Gables | 2320 Salzedo St. (Aragon Ave.) | 305-461-8360 |
www.ruthschris.com

"Nothing beats a steak sizzling in butter" at this "special-occasion",
New Orleans–based chain where the "melt-in-your-mouth" chops
are "cooked to perfection" and presented on "hot plates"; even if the
"decor varies" (from "blah" to "old-fashioned in a good way"), service is "attentive" and the "off-the-charts" pricing manageable "so
long as your boss doesn't care how much you spend."

NEW Sakaya *Korean*

| | - | - | - | I |

Downtown | Midtown Shops | 3401 N. Miami Ave.
(entrance on Buena Vista Ave., bet. 34th & 36th Sts.) | Miami |
305-576-8096 | www.sakayakitchen.com

Check the chalkboard for the daily specials at this new Korean fast-
fooder where Downtowners grab a tray and order at the counter
(the early word is nothing beats the sweet honey-orange short ribs);
there's also an impressive wine, sake and beer collection, but no
surprise there – the owner was the sommelier at the Mandarin
Oriental before opening his own cheap and cheerful storefront.

Sakura *Japanese*

| | 22 | 13 | 20 | $37 |

Coral Gables | 440 S. Dixie Hwy. (SW 42nd Ave.) | 305-665-7020 |
www.sakuragables.com

Admirers admit there's "no ambiance, no decor, no nothing . . . except sushi" that's "done very well" at this "reasonable" Coral Gables
Japanese, which has "been around so long for a reason"; the staff
"treats you like family", and Korean dishes are on the menu too, so
you can "take a non-sushi eater and they'll be very happy."

Salmon & Salmon *Peruvian*

| | ▽ 23 | 6 | 18 | $35 |

Westernmost Dade | 2907 NW Seventh St. (bet. 29th & 30th Aves.) |
Miami | 305-649-5924

"Fresh seafood at decent prices" is why this "tiny" joint in Westernmost Dade "fills up" with fans hungry for "authentic", "delicious"
ceviche and other Peruvian fare; "don't be discouraged" by the location "in a not-so-nice neighborhood" – it's a real "find."

☑ S&S Restaurant ⊟ *Diner*

| | 21 | 10 | 21 | $13 |

Downtown | 1757 NE Second Ave. (NE 17th St.) | Miami | 305-373-4291

Eaters embark on a "pleasant trip back to Miami in the '50s" at this
"old-fashioned" Downtown diner that dishes up "good homestyle"
American cooking and sandwiches, and takes "unhealthy breakfasts

	FOOD	DECOR	SERVICE	COST

to the highest (and tastiest) level"; it may be a "dump", but "wait-resses who still call you 'hon'" make it "throwback dining at its best", and "cheap prices" make it Dade's No. 1 Bang for the Buck; P.S. open till 6 PM weekdays, 2 PM weekends.

Sardinia ● *Italian* | 23 | 21 | 20 | $53 |

South Beach | 1801 Purdy Ave. (18th St.) | Miami Beach | 305-531-2228 | www.sardinia-ristorante.com

"Tucked away" on South Beach, this "out-of-the-ordinary" "gem" is "frequented mostly by locals" who appreciate its "inventive" Sardinian fare (including "fantastic wood-burning oven dishes") and "excep-tional wine list" with choices that "won't cost you an arm and a leg"; the atmosphere is "chic" and "comfortable" with "cosmopolitan" service, and though a few detect a "pretentious" air, overall it's a "popular trysting place."

NEW Sawa *Japanese/Mediterranean* | - | - | - | M |

Coral Gables | Village of Merrick Park | 360 San Lorenzo Ave. (SW 42nd Ave.) | 305-447-6555 | www.sawarestaurant.com

With its mix of Med, Middle Eastern and Japanese cuisines and de-cor that blends a curvaceous backlit bar, an elegant dining room and a cabana-style lounge, this Coral Gables Eclectic certainly lives up to its name ('togetherness'); smokers can puff away on hookahs filled with a variety of flavored tobaccos or even spiked with alcohol.

☒ Scarpetta *Italian* | 25 | 27 | 25 | $83 |

Miami Beach | Fontainebleau Miami Beach | 4441 Collins Ave. (41st St.) | 305-674-4660 | www.fontainebleau.com

Chef Scott Conant brings this NYC-bred Italian to the Fontainebleau Miami Beach, "impressing" guests with "unconventional", "incredi-ble" dinners provided by a "spectacular" staff; the "intoxicatingly lovely" setting with a "seaside" ambiance enhances the "totally Miami vibe", and though the bill is a "shocker", fans affirm it's "100% worth it."

Scorch Grillhouse & Wine Bar *Steak* | ▽ 18 | 15 | 21 | $33 |

North Miami | 13750A Biscayne Blvd. (135th St.) | 305-949-5588

This "friendly" American steakhouse in North Miami "won't scorch your wallet" with its "plentiful" portions of "tasty grilled meats", "huge wine list" and "interesting drink specials"; so what if the room is "noisy" and the menu "limited" – "what they do, they do very well."

Scotty's Landing *American* | 14 | 19 | 14 | $22 |

Coconut Grove | 3381 Pan American Dr. (S. Bayshore Dr.) | 305-854-2626

"Flip-flops are required" at this "super-casual" American "hangout" "on the water in Coconut Grove", where the "not–South Beach" crowd goes to "drink a beer and eat a fish sandwich" or burger while "listening to a band"; "if you venture much further" on the menu, "you're asking for it", but it "transports you to the Keys like no other place in town"; P.S. live music Friday–Sunday.

	FOOD	DECOR	SERVICE	COST

Sergio's ● *Cuban*

20 | 13 | 17 | $19

Coral Way | 3252 SW 22nd St./Coral Way (32nd Ave.) | Miami | 305-529-0047
Kendall | 13550 SW 120th St. (137th Ave.) | 305-278-2024
Westchester | 9330 SW 40th St./Bird Rd. (bet. 93rd & 94th Aves.) | 305-552-9626
www.sergios.com

"Well-cooked, well-priced" Cuban food is "*muy bueno*" at this "not fancy" chainlet where "portions big enough for the largest appetites" mean plenty of patrons "bring home doggy bags"; though a few cite a language barrier, the "servers take care of you with that great Latin lovin'", plus most branches stay "open late."

NEW Shake Shack ● *Burgers*

South Beach | 1111 Lincoln Rd. (Lenox Ave.) | Miami Beach | 305-434-7787 | www.shakeshack.com

The Big Apple comes to the Magic City in the form of New York restaurateur Danny Meyer's SoBe outpost of his chain of upscale burger joints, where the contemporary decor makes a stylish backdrop for black Angus beef patties ground fresh daily; it *is* Florida after all, so there's also umbrella-shaded sidewalk seating, people-watching aplenty and Key lime shakes.

☑ Shibui ● *Japanese*

26 | 16 | 22 | $31

Kendall | 10141 SW 72nd St. (102nd Ave.) | 305-274-5578 | www.shibuimiami.com

"Outstanding", "creative" and "exotic" sushi "in the suburbs" distinguishes this "wonderful" Kendall Japanese that's the "real deal"; the "small", "run-down" setting is a drawback, but "reasonable prices and terrific service" ensure high "demand", so "get your reservation" since it's "always packed."

Shoji ● *Japanese*

24 | 19 | 20 | $56

South Beach | 100 Collins Ave. (1st St.) | Miami Beach | 305-532-4245 | www.shojisushi.com

Regulars roll in for "exquisite sushi with prices to match" at this "understated" but "amazing" SoBe Japanese; it "may not have the flash of some of its competitors", but "generous" portions, "attentive" service and a "nice atmosphere" ("inside or alfresco") all work to "keep the crowds flowing" from lunch to "late-night."

Shorty's Bar-B-Q *BBQ*

19 | 12 | 18 | $20

South Miami | 9200 S. Dixie Hwy. (S. Dadeland Blvd.) | 305-670-7732
Doral | 2255 NW 87th Ave. (bet. NW 21st Terr. & 25th St.) | Miami | 305-471-5554
Westchester | 11575 SW 40th St./Bird Rd. (117th Ave.) | 305-227-3196
www.shortys.com

"It's not pretty and it's kinda messy, but it's good eatin'" affirm fans of the "fall-off-the-bone" ribs, "creamy coleslaw" and the "sweetest" corn turned out by this "venerable" BBQ chain founded in the '50s; "people of all stripes" sit down at the "long picnic-style tables", relishing the "relaxed", "rustic" atmosphere along with the "rockin'" grub.

	FOOD	DECOR	SERVICE	COST

Shula's Steak House   *Steak*

Miami Beach | Alexander Hotel | 5225 Collins Ave. (north of Beach View Park) | 305-341-6565

Miami Lakes | 6842 Main St. (Ludlam Rd.) | 305-820-8047 ●

Miami Lakes | Don Shula's Golf Club | 7601 NW Miami Lakes Dr. (east of Palmetto Expwy.) | 305-820-8102 ⑤ Ⓜ

www.donshula.com

| 21 | 20 | 21 | $62 |

"He's no longer coaching the Dolphins, but Don Shula can broil a mean steak" say fans of this "fun, casual" chophouse chain featuring "unobtrusive service" and "giant" portions; the "kitschy" "football theme" loses points with some opponents, however, who also chide "expensive" prices for meals that aren't quite "inspiring."

Siam Palace   *Thai*

South Miami | 9999 Sunset Dr. (SW 102nd Ave.) | 305-279-6906

| ▽ 25 | 19 | 23 | $34 |

A "caring" owner sets the tone for this South Miami Thai providing "standout" dishes and "excellent" service for those in-the-know; while not quite palatial, it's "fair for business lunches" and "one of the more reliable restaurants in town."

☑ Smith & Wollensky ● *Steak*

South Beach | 1 Washington Ave. (S. Pointe Pk.) | Miami Beach | 305-673-2800 | www.smithandwollensky.com

| 23 | 24 | 23 | $68 |

"If you're looking for cow cooked correctly", "stake out" this SoBe steakhouse that "stays true" to the NYC "original" with its "amazing aged meat", "attentive service" and "men's club" decor; you may need to "bring your mortgage broker" to cover the tab, but a "huge wine list" helps "wash away the sting of sticker shock"; bonus: the "stunning" waterfront digs offer a "spectacular" view of "cruise ships sailing by."

Solea   *Spanish*

South Beach | W South Beach | 2201 Collins Ave. (22nd St.) | Miami Beach | 305-938-3111 | www.whotels.com

| - | - | - | E |

This Spaniard dishing up a savory selection of tapas in the W South Beach may play the shy older sister to the glitzier Mr. Chow next door, but that doesn't make it any less enticing (or less expensive); low lighting, cozy banquettes and a meandering patio with a pool view are geared toward those seeking a quiet evening, and not a scene.

Soya & Pomodoro ☒ *Italian*

Downtown | 120 NE First St. (bet. 1st & 2nd Aves.) | Miami | 305-381-9511 | www.soyapomodoro.com

| ▽ 21 | 23 | 18 | $23 |

"An unexpected haven in Downtown Miami", this "quirky", "bohemian" Italian dishes up "excellent homemade pastas" and "decent, friendly" service at an "affordable" price; "glowing" guests say the live music Thursday–Saturday is the "icing on the cake."

Soyka   *American*

Upper East Side | 5556 NE Fourth Ct. (Biscayne Blvd.) | Miami | 305-759-3117 | www.soykarestaurant.com

| 20 | 19 | 21 | $35 |

"Gallery-hopping" gadabouts and the "business crowd" pop into this "hip, casual" Upper East Sider for "comforting" New American fare that's "two notches up from a diner"; the group-friendly, "warehouse"-like space tends to get "noisy", and some feel there's "nothing spectacular" here, but the "cool vibe" and "good value" keep it a "mainstay."

NEW Sparky's Roadside BBQ ☒ *BBQ* — — — I

Downtown | 204 NE First St. (NE 2nd Ave.) | Miami | 305-377-2877 | www.sparkysroadsidebarbecue.com

There's nothing fancy at this ultracasual Downtown paean to smoked meats (unless you include birdhouses on the walls), but serious Q-balls roll right in for barbecued ribs, brisket, pork and chicken 'cooked low and slow'; if you're not into BBQ, there's also a burger and grilled chicken and fried catfish sammies, all at affordable tabs; P.S. closed weekends.

Z Spiga *Italian* 26 24 25 $49

South Beach | 1228 Collins Ave. (bet. 12th & 13th Sts.) | Miami Beach | 305-534-0079 | www.spigarestaurant.com

For a "quiet retreat" in a "frenetic, youth-obsessed zip code", SoBe solace-seekers saunter "off the beaten path" (well, a "few blocks from the beach") to this "reliable", "romantic" Northern Italian; with "reasonable prices", "professional service" and "cozy" outdoor seating, no wonder it's "lasted a long time."

Spris *Pizza* 21 15 17 $27

Coral Gables | 2305 Ponce de Leon Blvd. (Giralda Ave.) | 305-444-3388
South Beach | 731 Lincoln Rd. (bet. Euclid & Meridian Aves.) | Miami Beach | 305-673-2020 ☽
www.spris.cc

"Everyone needs a pizza hangout", and these "inexpensive" South Beach and Coral Gables options "fit the bill" with "fresh, simple, thin-crust" pies; though there's often a "scramble" for seating in SoBe, the Lincoln Road "people-watching" helps keep the crowds more bearable.

Sra. Martinez ☒ *Spanish* 24 25 25 $53

Design District | 4000 NE Second Ave. (40th St. & 2nd ave) | Miami | 305-573-5474 | www.sramartinez.com

Chef Michelle Bernstein (aka Señora Martinez) "has outdone herself" at this "happening" Design District Spaniard whose "insanely delicious" – and "adventurous" – "tapas with a twist" have diners "almost licking the plates"; "outstanding" service, "delicious cocktails" at the "upstairs bar" and "beautiful modern" decor (you'll forget you're in an "old post office") dull the pain of prices that "add up quickly", leaving the overall impression that "Miami could use more of this."

NEW STK Miami *American/Steak* — — — VE

Miami Beach | Gansevoort South Beach Hotel | 2377 Collins Ave. (24th St.) | 305-604-6988 | www.stkhouse.com

Loud and loungey is what you expect in Miami Beach – and that's just what you get at this sexy American meat emporium in the Ganesvoort Hotel, where the waiters and servers are as hot as the sizzling

Parmesan truffle fries; even with reservations, you'll wait in the bar sipping designer cocktails with other eager guests, but it's worth the price of admission for the cool tunes and peerless people-watching; P.S. *Hell's Kitchen* alum Ralph Pagano is now helming the kitchen.

NEW Sugarcane Raw Bar Grill ● *Eclectic* | – | – | – | E |

Downtown | 3250 NE First Ave. (bet. 36th & 38th Sts.) | Miami | 786-369-0353 | www.sugarcanerawbargrill.com

The Eclectic little sister of the ever-popular SushiSamba, this sweet spot north of Downtown offers a vast array of Pan-Asian small plates, including items from a raw bar, robata grill and sushi bar, as well as a few curveballs like buttery roast chicken and cheese and charcuterie plates; accommodating staffers and a funky industrial warehouse space with soaring ceilings and a vast outdoor patio complete the package, but beware: prices that seem cheap add up faster than you can say 'oh, sugar.'

Sushi House ●Ⓜ *Asian/Japanese* | ▽ 25 | 24 | 19 | $51 |

North Miami Beach | Avanti Shopping Ctr. | 15911 Biscayne Blvd. (Sunny Isles Blvd.) | 305-947-6002 | www.sushihousenmb.com

Designed with a "chic, whispery" white-on-white look, this North Miami Beach spot seems to "belong on South Beach, and so does the crowd"; its "huge", "creative sushi rolls" and Pan-Asian dishes make an impression too, and if the occasional holdout finds them "overpriced", early-bird specials are a plus.

Sushi Maki *Japanese/Thai* | 20 | 17 | 18 | $30 |

NEW Brickell Area | 1000 S. Miami Ave. (SW 10th St.) | Miami | 305-415-9779

Coral Gables | 2334 Ponce de Leon Blvd. (Aragon Ave.) | 305-443-1884

NEW Kendall | 11531 N. Kendall Dr. (SW 113th Place Circle W.) | 305-595-2332

Palmetto Bay | King's Bay Shopping Ctr. | 14491 S. Dixie Hwy. (Mitchell Dr.) | 305-232-6636

South Miami | 5812 Sunset Dr. (SW 58th Ave.) | 305-667-7677 www.sushimakirestaurants.com

"Decent food at a decent price" ("especially during lunch") satisfies diners at this growing Japanese-Thai chainlet delivering "fresh" sushi with "many combos to choose from"; the decor "needs work" and the cuisine is "not terribly creative", but "don't expect it to sing a song and dance at the price you're paying."

Su Shin *Japanese* | ▽ 25 | 16 | 21 | $29 |

Kendall | 10501 N Kendall Dr./SW 88th St. (107th Ave.) | 305-271-3235

Su Shin Izakaya Ⓩ *Japanese*

Coral Gables | 159 Aragon Ave. (bet. Coral Way & Giralda Ave.) | 305-445-2584 | www.izakayarestaurant.com

"Tasty, creative small dishes" and "top-notch sushi" are served "efficiently and with character" at these separately owned Japanese joints in Coral Gables and Kendall; they're "not fancy", but fans observe "if they served this food in a fancy room, they could get $40 a roll!"

	FOOD	DECOR	SERVICE	COST

Sushi Rock Cafe ● *Japanese*
21 | **13** | **18** | **$31**

South Beach | 1351 Collins Ave. (bet. 13th & 14th Sts.) | Miami Beach | 305-532-2133 | www.sushirockcafe.com

"Solid" sushi and a "rocking" vibe add up to an "always fun" time at this "informal" SoBe Japanese whose "reasonable" prices help ensure it's "always full"; while a few feel it's "more about style than quality", you can't beat the "location" to "watch all the beautiful people."

⏹ SushiSamba
23 | **23** | **18** | **$51**

dromo ● *Japanese/S American*

South Beach | 600 Lincoln Rd. (Pennsylvania Ave.) | Miami Beach | 305-673-5337 | www.sushisamba.com

"It's cool, it's hot", it's a "sexy, loud and exciting" scene that "just screams South Beach", with "fab", "inventive" sushi and other Japanese-Brazilian-Peruvian dishes "served by a trendy staff to flashy customers"; sure, it's "expensive" and service can be "iffy", but given all the "up-to-the-minute cocktails" and "tasty morsels", it's the "perfect spot" to "start the party."

Sushi Siam *Japanese/Thai*
21 | **15** | **18** | **$35**

Key Biscayne | 632 Crandon Blvd. (bet. Enid & Sunrise Drs.) | 305-361-7768
South Beach | 647-649 Lincoln Rd. (Pennsylvania Ave.) | Miami Beach | 305-672-7112
South Miami | 5582 NE Fourth Ct. (54th St.) | 305-751-7818

"Delightful Thai and sushi" served by a "pleasant staff" for a "fair price" please patrons who "love the attention and the food" at this mini-chain; though the setting can feel "cramped" and some deem the fare "predictable", most are satisfied with its "high quality" overall.

Sylvano's ● *Italian*
20 | **13** | **19** | **$33**

South Beach | 820 Alton Rd. (bet. 8th & 9th Sts.) | Miami Beach | 305-673-3959 | www.sylvanos.com

"Italians and locals" know that for "reliable red sauce at gentle prices", this "busy" SoBe Italian sports cafe is a "great groove any time of day"; servers with "no attitude" and a "low-key" ambiance are groovy too, and while some gripe they "could do without all the sports channels on flat-screen TVs", most appreciate that "you get what you expect – nothing more, nothing less."

Taco Rico Tex-Mex *Tex-Mex*
21 | **8** | **15** | **$15**

Coral Gables | 473 S. Dixie Hwy. (Le Jeune Rd.) | 305-663-3200

It may be a "dive" with decor that's "the pits", but everyone from "University of Miami students" to "families" frequents this "fun, cramped" Coral Gables eatery for "cheap" Tex-Mex that tastes as if "mamacita's in the kitchen"; "humongous" portions are a plus, as long as you "don't let yourself get overstuffed."

NEW Talavera *Mexican*
– | **–** | **–** | **I**

Coral Gables | 2299 Ponce de Leon Blvd. (Giralda Ave.) | 305-444-2955 | www.talaveraspot.com

Named for the pottery made since the 16th century in the city of Puebla, this colorful, casual Coral Gables Mexican adorns its bar with paintings of south-of-the-border celebs and its budget-friendly menu with regional specialties from around the country; those in-the-know suggest checking out the signature 'huarache grill', a choice of grilled proteins and accompaniments piled atop a fried corn masa cake.

Tantra ● *Eclectic* | 20 | 23 | 18 | $61 |

South Beach | 1445 Pennsylvania Ave. (bet. Española Way & 15th St.) | Miami Beach | 305-672-4765 | www.tantra-restaurant.com

"Visually stunning" decor ("indoor tents and a real-grass floor") and "tantalizing" Eclectic fare really "spice things up" at this "sexy" South Beach eatery/club where "loud, pulsating music sets the mood"; "too loud" moan some, who suggest you "pass on this attempt at arousal" unless you savor service "with a little attitude" and prices that make "your libido drop to the floor."

Tapas & Tintos ● *Mediterranean/Spanish* | 20 | 17 | 17 | $32 |

South Beach | 448 Espanola Way (bet. Drexel & Washington Aves.) | Miami Beach | 305-538-8272 | www.tapasytintos.com

"Relax, drink and be merry" at this "lively" SoBe Spanish-Med that attracts a "mostly young crowd" looking for "fun times" and "no-frills, no-gimmicks tapas"; surveyors split on service ("friendly" vs. "unfriendly"), but there's general agreement it's "worth putting on your short list"; P.S. the free "Monday tango lessons are not to be missed."

Tap Tap Haitian *Haitian* | 22 | 23 | 21 | $28 |

South Beach | 819 Fifth St. (bet. Jefferson & Meridian Aves.) | Miami Beach | 305-672-2898 | www.taptaprestaurant.com

For a "cultural experience" that's "more than a meal", this "festive" Haitian "hangout" with a "creative islands menu", "genuine service" and "wonderful" murals offers a "break from the usual" on South Beach; it helps to have an "adventurous palate", but the combination of "music, art, yummy food, killer cocktails" and "good prices" means "it's always a party."

Tarpon Bend *Seafood* | 18 | 17 | 17 | $29 |

Coral Gables | 65 Miracle Mile (bet. Douglas Rd. & Galiano St.) | 305-444-3210 | www.tarponbend.com

At this "lively" Coral Gables "haunt" in a "barlike setting", a "boisterous young crowd" and "killer martinis" lead to "happy hours that can get crazy"; there's also "decent" seafood on offer, though the "noisy" setting is disquieting for some chowhounds; P.S. the Ft. Lauderdale branch is a handy place for Broward Center showgoers to "grab a bite."

Taverna Opa ● *Greek* | 19 | 16 | 17 | $37 |

South Beach | 36-40 Ocean Dr. (bet. Biscayne & 1st Sts.) | Miami Beach | 305-673-6730 | www.tavernaoparestaurant.com

See review in Ft. Lauderdale/Broward County Directory.

Thai & Sushi Bistro *Thai* | ∇ 22 | 19 | 20 | $29 |

West Sunset | 9565 SW 72nd St. (bet. SW 94th Pl. & SW 97th Ave.) | Miami | 305-279-8583

Surveyors smitten by this "attractive little neighborhood place" (ex Thai Orchid) head to West Sunset for midpriced grub "prepared as

FOOD | DECOR | SERVICE | COST

it would be in Thailand", plus "good" service and a "nice beer selection"; detractors aren't so flowery, insisting it's "hit-or-miss"; P.S. there's a DJ Wednesdays, Fridays and Saturdays.

Thai House South Beach ● *Thai*   ▽ 23 | 16 | 20 | $27

South Beach | 1137 Washington Ave. (11th St.) | Miami Beach | 305-531-4841 | www.thaihousesobe.com

The "yum" lunch specials and "huge portions" of "very good" Siamese fare rich in "fresh and lively flavors" go down easily at this moderately priced South Beacher; if a few fret about an "unexciting menu", even they admit "spicy here isn't gringo spicy, it's Thai native spicy."

Thai House II *Thai*   24 | 20 | 20 | $33

North Miami Beach | 2250 NE 163rd St. (bet. Biscayne Blvd. & W. Dixie Hwy.) | 305-940-6075

"Fresh, nicely presented sushi" and "excellent" Thai fare are why this "beautiful" North Miami Beach Siamese-Japanese has "been around forever" (or at least since 1986); "attentive" service, "not-bad prices" and a "calming" ambiance mean diners "will go again."

Timo *Italian/Mediterranean*   25 | 21 | 23 | $51

Sunny Isles Beach | 17624 Collins Ave. (bet. 175th Terr. & 178th St.) | 305-936-1008 | www.timorestaurant.com

"You forget the strip-mall surroundings with the first bite" of "seasonal", "imaginative" Italian-Med fare (including "superb" wood-fired pizza) at this "sophisticated", "bustling and convivial" "favorite" by chef/co-owner Tim Andriola in "up-and-coming" Sunny Isles Beach; with its "excellent" service, "expertly mixed" drinks and "fair prices", guests agree it's "doing everything right."

Tiramesu ● *Italian*   21 | 17 | 19 | $36

South Beach | 721 Lincoln Rd. (Meridian Ave.) | Miami Beach | 305-532-4538 | www.tiramesu.com

"There's a reason why" this Italian – "tucked among the tourist traps" on South Beach – has been around since 1988: "generous portions" of "consistently good" fare served by an "attentive" staff; there's also an "awesome beat-the-clock special" and "outdoor seating" for "people-watching"; P.S. "don't leave" without trying its namesake dessert.

Titanic Brewery ● *American*   16 | 15 | 17 | $24

Coral Gables | 5813 Ponce de Leon Blvd. (San Amaro Dr.) | 305-667-2537 | www.titanicbrewery.com

"Solid", affordable pub grub is just the tip of the iceberg at this "chill-axed" Coral Gables American where "live bands" and "microbrews galore" make it a "U. of Miami hangout"; some snip it's "too loud" and the fare is "nothing special", but "get the sampler" of suds and you'll leave "lightheaded with delight" anyway.

T-Mex Cantina ● *Mexican*   ▽ 23 | 13 | 19 | $15

South Beach | 235 14th St. (bet. Collins & Washington Aves.) | Miami Beach | 305-538-3009 | www.t-mex.net

Diners get "plenty of food for the price" (plus "two-for-one tacos on Tuesdays") at these "little" SoBe and Ft. Lauderdale Mexicans that'll

FOOD | DECOR | SERVICE | COST

"knock your flavor socks off"; there's not much decor, but patrons are too busy "snarfing down" the "down-and-dirty burritos" to notice – particularly in the wee hours "after a late night out partying."

Toni's Sushi Bar ● *Japanese* | 25 | 16 | 21 | $48 |

South Beach | 1208 Washington Ave. (12th St.) | Miami Beach | 305-673-9368 | www.tonisushi.com

It's "not the most glamorous" eatery on South Beach (read: no "velvet rope"), but the "ultrafresh sashimi", "excellent" sushi and "imaginative" rolls served at this "intimate" Japanese "institution" make it a star nonetheless; add in "attentive" service, a "soothing atmosphere" and "decent sake selection", and you'd better "be sure to make a reservation."

Tony Chan's Water Club *Chinese* | 22 | 20 | 22 | $42 |

Downtown | Grand Doubletree Hotel | 1717 N. Bayshore Dr. (NE 17th Terr.) | Miami | 305-374-8888 | www.tonychans.com

The "amiable" waiters "actually seem to envy your dinner" (especially the "fabulous Peking duck") at this "upscale" Chinese venue in a Downtown Doubletree that proffers "beautifully presented" "designer" fare fresh from an "open kitchen"; "somewhat pricey" tabs trouble wallet-watchers, but the majority "would definitely return", if only for that "nice view of Biscayne Bay"; P.S. there's sushi for raw-fin fans too.

Town Kitchen & Bar *Eclectic* | 18 | 19 | 16 | $32 |

South Miami | Plaza 57 Bldg. | 7301 SW 57th Ct. (bet. SW 73rd & 74th Sts.) | 305-740-8118 | www.townkitchenbar.com

"Those unwilling to trek to South Beach" make tracks to this industrial-"chic" South Miami Eclectic for its "solid comfort cuisine" (some say merely "decent"), "affordable" tariffs and "must" happy hour; indoors it's "loud" and "crowded" so "prepare to yell", though "you can hear yourself think" on the "great" patio; wherever you perch, "service can be spotty."

Trattoria Luna *Italian* | 24 | 19 | 25 | $40 |

Pinecrest | Dadeland Plaza | 9477 S. Dixie Hwy. (S. Datran Blvd.) | 305-669-9448 | www.trattorialuna.com

"All the old standbys" make an appearance at this "enjoyable" Pinecrest Italian – including the "truly professional" waiters who've "been there a long time"; it's "tiny", so "you have to fight to get a table" and the "noise can be overwhelming", but "reasonable prices" and "wonderful" food "make up for that."

Trattoria Sole *Italian* | 21 | 19 | 19 | $36 |

South Miami | 5894 Sunset Dr. (U.S. 1) | 305-666-9392 | www.blurestaurantsgroup.com

"Impress a date with your good taste" by making "recommended" reservations at this "solid" South Miami Italian, where "well-prepared" dishes are "delicious any day, any time" and "tolerably" priced; though it can be "noisy" ("gives me a headache") and service "iffy at times", *amici* aver that dining here is "always a pleasure"; P.S. recent tweaks to the dining room may outdate the Decor score.

	FOOD	DECOR	SERVICE	COST

Tropical Chinese *Chinese*
25 | 17 | 20 | $33

Westchester | Tropical Park Plaza | 7991 SW 40th St. (SW 79th Ave.) | 305-262-7576

"No one does dim sum better" proclaim partisans of this "midrange" Chinese "institution" whose "professional (if not exactly warm and cuddly)" servers deliver "amazing" chow on carts "fresh" from an "open kitchen"; toss in "unbelievable Peking duck", and it's little wonder most gladly "travel a long way" to Westchester for a meal, though some say it's actually the "shortest flight to Hong Kong."

Tutto Pasta 🗷 *Italian*
23 | 14 | 22 | $31

Brickell Area | 1751 SW Third Ave. (bet. SW 17th & 18th Rds.) | Miami | 305-857-0709 | www.tuttopasta.com

"Everything comes from the market" at this "economical" Brickell Italian where a "well-trained staff" serves "consistently delicious" fare, including "fresh-made pastas" and "great" daily specials; it's "hard to find" and "compact", but "patrons just keep coming" anyway.

Tutto Pizza *Pizza*
23 | 14 | 21 | $22

Brickell Area | 1753 SW Third Ave. (bet. SW 17th & 18th Rds.) | Miami | 305-858-0909 | www.tuttopizza.org

"Innovative thin-crust pizzas" made with the "freshest ingredients" get huzzahs from those pie-eyed over this casual Brickell "keeper" whose chef puts a Brazilian spin on his brick-oven creations; it's also affordable, and sidewalk tables allow you to "sit outside, get a cold one and enjoy life"; P.S. sib Tutto Pasta is next door.

Two Chefs 🗷 *American*
24 | 17 | 22 | $51

South Miami | 8287 S. Dixie Hwy. (SW 67th Ave.) | 305-663-2100 | www.twochefsrestaurant.com

Whatever you do, "save room" for the "off-the-chart soufflés" at this "long-established" – and "expensive" – South Miami New American, though the rest of the "wonderful" menu is also "deserving of your attention" ("try the meatloaf!"); a "warm" staff helps compensate for "bland" decor in a room that's a "bit noisy for intimate conversation", but overall, it gives a "strip mall" a "gourmet" vibe that gourmands appreciate; P.S. cooking classes offered.

Uva 69 *Cuban/French*
21 | 18 | 19 | $30

Upper East Side | 6900 Biscayne Blvd. (NE 69th St.) | Miami | 305-754-9022 | www.uva-69.com

A "neighborhood feel" and "savory" fare (mostly sandwiches, soups and "fresh" salads) has made this "funky" Cuban-French bistro and its attached sculpture garden "mainstays" of the Upper East Side; meanwhile, reasonable tabs, "nice outdoor seating" and an "excellent" Sunday brunch help make it "worth the drive over from the beach."

Van Dyke Cafe, The ● *American*
17 | 19 | 16 | $31

South Beach | 846 Lincoln Rd. (bet. Jefferson & Meridian Aves.) | Miami Beach | 305-534-3600 | www.thevandykecafe.com

"Listen to music" in the upstairs lounge or sit outdoors and "watch the Lincoln Road scene" at this "lively" SoBe "sister of News Cafe" proffering a "tasty" array of New American grub at "moderate prices"; "ok" is more like it shrug the less enthralled, but fans insist "varied menu, varied people" is "what Miami Beach is all about."

☑ Versailles ◐ *Cuban*

21	14	18	$26

Little Havana | 3555 SW Eighth St. (SW 35th Ave.) | Miami | 305-444-0240
This "doyen of Cuban restaurants in Little Havana" offers the "ultimate Miami experience", with "large portions of tasty", "authentic" fare and a clientele dressed in everything from "flip-flips to furs" that includes "movie stars, politicians, even defeated dictators"; if the "tacky", "diner"-esque decor and "uneven" service elicit a few ver-sighs, the "affordable" prices, "history" and "endless energy" lead most to "feel like they're in Cuba without the communism."

NEW Villa By Barton G. ◐ *Continental*

-	-	-	VE

South Beach | Former Versace Mansion | 1116 Ocean Dr. (bet. 11th & 12th Sts.) | Miami Beach | 305-576-8003 | www.thevillabybartong.com
Showstopping gastropreneur Barton G. has taken over the South Beach mansion of the late Gianni Versace, now home to this mosaic-studded, blue-and-gold restaurant and ultraluxe 10-room hotel (flashes popping each evening outside the ornate iron gates signal celebs in the midst); the modern Continental cuisine served on – what else? – Versace china includes molecular touches like nitrogenized Caesar salad dressing and features, predictably, prices that might be able to pay for a night at a hotel . . . just not this one.

Villagio Restaurant *Italian*

20	20	20	$39

Coral Gables | Village of Merrick Park | 358 San Lorenzo Ave. (Ponce De Leon Blvd.) | 305-447-8144
"After a round of shopping" at the Village of Merrick Park (or at its newer sib at Colonnade Outlets), canny consumers "keep coming back" to this "always crowded" Italian for its "dependable" if "basic" fare at "value" prices; inside can be "loud and chaotic" and servers "distracted", so admirers advise "sit outside" and enjoy the "park-like setting"; P.S. it's a sib of Luna Cafe.

NEW Water Club ◐ *American*

-	-	-	M

North Miami Beach | Intracoastal Mall | 3969 NE 163rd St. (NE 36th Ave.) | 305-944-8411 | www.thewaterclubmiami.com
A prime Intracoastal location, 500 feet of boat dockage and a celebrity toque – former *Top Chef*-testant Andrea Curto-Randazzo – come together at this stylish, relatively affordable North Miami Beach behemoth with 500 seats for indoor-outdoor dining (plus 600 more in the bar/lounge); the Traditional American menu includes everything from burgers and bivalves to steaks and seafood, washed down with selections from the extensive wine list.

NEW Waxy O'Connor's ◐ *Pub Food*

-	-	-	I

Brickell Area | 690 SW First Ct. (SW 7th St.) | Miami | 786-871-7660 | www.waxys.com
This Brickell Area pub looks and tastes the part with digs adorned with dark wood and stained glass and an affordable menu packed with

comfort fare like shepherd's pie; however, its location on the Miami River and its versions of regional goodies like conch fritters and grouper ceviche mean its South Florida roots aren't forgotten.

White Lion Cafe 🅢🅜 *American* ▽ 19 | 20 | 23 | $32

Homestead | 146 NW Seventh St. (bet. 1st & 2nd Aves.) | 305-248-1076 | www.whitelioncafe.com

It's "worth the drive from Miami" purr partisans of this "little secret in Homestead", a "quaint old cottage" turned "civilized and comfortable" American serving "country cooking from another era"; "warm" service, "live music" on Fridays and "enormous "homemade desserts" sweeten the deal.

☒ Wish *American* 25 | 26 | 25 | $63

South Beach | The Hotel | 801 Collins Ave. (8th St.) | Miami Beach | 305-674-9474 | www.wishrestaurant.com

If you're pining for "palate-tingling" New American fare served by an "attentive", "unsnooty" staff, "your wish comes true" at this "hideaway" in SoBe's The Hotel – just "sit outdoors" by the "fountain" in the "romantic" palm garden; naturally, it's a "little pricey", but converts coo "if this isn't a tropical paradise, I don't know what is"; P.S. be sure to "have drinks on the roof" at the "open-air" Spire Bar.

World Resources *Japanese/Thai* 20 | 16 | 18 | $37

South Beach | 719 Lincoln Rd. (Meridian Ave.) | Miami Beach | 305-535-8987 | www.worldresourcecafe.com

Its "odd name" stumps some, but after a "yummy martini" most concentrate instead on this "pleasant" SoBe Asian's "extensive menu" of "reliable" cuisine, including "terrific" Thai dishes and a "wonderful array of sushi"; "absolutely average" counter critics, but they're rebuffed by those who say "you can't beat the cost", especially when "eating outside watching the pretty people pass"; P.S. changes in the kitchen may outdate the Food score.

W Wine Bistro 🅢 *French* ▽ - | 18 | 20 | $32

Design District | 3622 NE Second Ave. (NE 36th St.) | Miami | 305-576-7775 | www.wwinebistro.com

With its "great" vino selection, tastings and "fun" choices "by the glass", this "neighborhood" Design District French is "like hanging out in your friend's wine cellar, if your friend has a wine cellar the size of a small restaurant"; new owners have expanded the midpriced menu (including entrees like tuna tartare), while a retail side and no-corkage Wednesdays add to the appeal.

Xixón Cafe 🅢 *Spanish* 24 | 16 | 19 | $29

Coral Way | 2101 Coral Way (SW 21th Ave.) | Miami | 305-854-9350 | www.xixoncafe.com

"Olé!" cry connoisseurs of this "unpretentious" Coral Way "joint" whose "amazing" tapas and "awesome *bocadillos*" (sandwiches) showcase a "true taste of Spain"; it's "small" and you'll have to "jostle for a table", but it's "not about the decor", particularly considering the "courteous" service, "well-stocked" retail market and "impressive wine selection" (and "affordable" to boot).

FOOD | DECOR | SERVICE | COST

Yard House ● *American*
19 | 19 | 19 | $28

Coral Gables | Village of Merrick Park | 320 San Lorenzo Ave. (bet. Ponce De Leon Blvd. & SW 42nd St.) | 305-447-9273 | www.yardhouse.com
See review in Palm Beach County Directory.

Yuca *Nuevo Latino*
20 | 20 | 19 | $50

South Beach | 501 Lincoln Rd. (Drexel Ave.) | Miami Beach | 305-532-9822 | www.yuca.com
"Go for the food, stay for the dancing" suggest salsa-loving survey-ors smitten by this "cool-as-ever" Nuevo Latino "icon" on "trendy Lincoln Road" that's still turning out "creative" fare with an "eloquent twist" ("goes beyond any on South Beach"); still, even "great mojitos" and "friendly service" can't sway dissidents who find the place "pricey" and "past its prime."

Yuga ⊠ *Asian*
24 | 15 | 23 | $33

Coral Gables | 357 Alcazar Ave. (bet. SW 42nd Ave. & Salzedo St.) | 305-442-8600 | www.yugarestaurant.com
"Just a couple of blocks off Miracle Mile", this "intimate" Coral Gables cousin of Lan presents a "similar" menu of "innovative, healthy" Pan-Asian fare replete with "fine-dining flourishes"; a "speedy" staff and "reasonable prices" are other reasons regulars say "go eat there so it'll stick around."

NEW Zuma ● *Japanese*
- | - | - | E

Downtown | Epic Hotel | 270 Biscayne Boulevard Way (Brickell Ave.) | Miami | 305-577-0277 | www.zumarestaurant.com
The contemporary Japanese cuisine inspired by the casual, tapas-oriented style of dining called izakaya is as chic and fashionable as the earth-toned, wood-and-steel dining room of this Downtown scenester overlooking the Miami River; among its amenities are a sushi bar and robata grill, sake bar and lounge, outdoor terrace and boat access.

Zuperpollo ● *S American*
21 | 12 | 19 | $22

Brickell Area | 1247 SW 22nd St./Coral Way (bet. 12th & 13th Aves.) | Miami | 305-856-9494 | www.zuperpollo.com
"Transport yourself to South America" for "grilled meats done right", "tasty" rotisserie chicken and "live music" (Thursday-Sunday) at this "charming little" Brickell Area "sleeper"; it "helps if you speak Spanish" and the setting is "simple", but portions "so large you can't finish" and "inexpensive" tabs explain why the "parking lot is always full."

KEY WEST & THE KEYS RESTAURANT DIRECTORY

FOOD DECOR SERVICE COST

MOST POPULAR
1. Louie's Backyard | *Amer./Carib.*
2. Blue Heaven | *Floribbean*
3. Seven Fish | *Seafood*
4. Michaels | *American*
5. Cafe Marquesa | *American*

TOP FOOD
28 Pisces | *Amer./Seafood*
     Santiago's Bodega | *Eclectic*
     Michaels | *American*
27 Pierre's | *Eclectic*
     Cafe Marquesa | *American*

TOP DECOR
28 Din. Rm. at Little Palm
27 Louie's Backyard
     Pierre's
     Morada Bay Beach
25 Cafe Marquesa

TOP SERVICE
27 Michaels
26 Din. Rm. at Little Palm
25 Cafe Marquesa
24 Pisces
     Seven Fish

A&B Lobster House   *Seafood* | 23 | 21 | 22 | $47 |

Key West | 700 Front St. (Simonton St.) | 305-294-5880 |
www.aandblobsterhouse.com

A "refined place in a crazy town", this seafooder combines a "breath-taking waterfront view of Key West's marina" with "traditional", "excellent" fare and "accommodating" service that's all "worth paying extra for"; the "come-as-you-are" ambiance sets the right tone for "sitting out on the covered porch" and soaking in the scene; P.S. there's a cigar bar, as well as the less-expensive Alonzo's eatery downstairs.

Abbondanza   *Italian* | 19 | 17 | 18 | $31 |

Key West | 1208 Simonton St. (Louisa St.) | 305-292-1199 |
www.abbondanzakeywest.com

"Hearty", "not fancy" Italian cuisine served "family-style" attracts "locals and tourists alike" to this "cute" locale with "old Key West atmospherics"; though critics feel that "quantity" wins out over "quality", it's an "economical" choice that's "great" for groups.

Alabama Jacks   *Seafood* | 18 | 17 | 18 | $20 |

Key Largo | 58000 Card Sound Rd. (west of the toll bridge) | 305-248-8741

"Bikers", "beachgoers" and "square dancers" love to "hang out" at this "gritty" Key Largo seafood shack that's "perched over the water in the middle of nowhere"; you can "fill your belly for a good price" with "delicious" conch fritters and "ice-cold beer" to the tune of "honky-tonk" bands (on weekends), and enjoy "what the Keys used to be."

Ambrosia   *Japanese* | 24 | 23 | 21 | $41 |

Key West | Santa Maria Suites Resort | 1401 Simonton St. (South St.) |
305-293-0304 | www.keywestambrosia.com

"Innovative" sushi and "top-shelf" sakes "delight" the senses at this "swank" Japanese whose "glitzy" location in the Santa Maria Suites is "almost too cool for Key West"; indeed, visitors savor the tantalizing "touch of South Beach" (and are grateful to find a place that "doesn't have cream cheese in all of its rolls"), dubbing it a "winner."

Antonia's   *Italian* | 25 | 23 | 24 | $50 |

Key West | 615 Duval St. (bet. Angela & Southard Sts.) | 305-294-6565 |
www.antoniaskeywest.com

This "classy", "comfortable" Duval Street "fixture" – a "Key West landmark for decades" – still delivers upscale, "outstanding Italian specialties" and "first-class" service under "owners who go out of their way to maintain tradition"; it's "more grown-up" than others in the area, so "reserve ahead of time" and "leave the hubbub" behind.

Azur *Mediterranean*
| 26 | 22 | 24 | $44 |

Key West | 425 Grinnell St. (corner Eaton & Fleming Sts) | 305-292-2987 | www.azurkeywest.com

This "inviting" Key West retreat is a bit "off the beaten path" but worth finding for its "accomplished" coastal Med cuisine, "excellent" wine list and "friendly" service; the "lovely" patio with a waterfall is a "cool place to dine", especially during the "fabulous" Sunday brunch.

Bad Boy Burrito ⊠⊄ *Mexican*
| ▽ 22 | 12 | 18 | $14 |

Key West | 1220½ Simonton St. (bet. Front & Greene Sts.) | 305-292-2697 | www.badboyburrito.com

What may be some of the "best burritos on the East Coast" can be found at this "great little" Key West Mexican, where you can "make your own combo" with "fresh, delicious ingredients" ranging from Kobe beef to tofu, and take it out in biodegradable packaging; while there's "not much room to sit", "after the bars, what's better?"

Bagatelle *Caribbean/Seafood*
| 23 | 22 | 20 | $42 |

Key West | 115 Duval St. (bet. Front & Greene Sts.) | 305-296-6609 | www.bagatellekeywest.com

"Tasty" fare that's "not too expensive", an "accommodating" staff and a "romantic" setting in a "lovely, historic" 1884 house are the components of the "whole package" offered at this Caribbean seafooder; for a "magical Key West atmosphere", "sit on the wrap-around porch" or balcony and "watch the parade along Duval"; P.S. a recent refurb may not be reflected in the Decor score.

Banana Cafe *French*
| 26 | 20 | 21 | $27 |

Key West | 1215 Duval St. (Louisa St.) | 305-294-7227 | www.bananacafekw.com

For "melt-in-your-mouth crêpes" that fans call the "best this side of the Seine", this "cute" French bistro is "like Paris in Key West, only the weather is better"; regulars are generally pleased by the "warm" service and roomy digs and recommend arriving early to sit on the "outdoor balcony" and "watch the Duval Street crawlers."

Barracuda Grill *Eclectic*
| 23 | 16 | 19 | $38 |

Marathon | 4290 Overseas Hwy. (43rd St.) | 305-743-3314

Beyond its "unimposing storefront", this Marathon Eclectic turns out "excellent" fare that's "definitely upscale for the Keys"; since it "fills up quick" there may be "a bit of a wait", but the staff's "hospitality" helps the time pass, and who knows, "there's a good chance the guy next to you caught what's on your plate."

◪ Blue Heaven *Floribbean*
| 24 | 22 | 21 | $31 |

Key West | 729 Thomas St. (Petronia St.) | 305-296-8666 | www.blueheavenkw.com

You just might find "chickens walking between your legs" in the outdoor dining room of this "amazing", "island"-style Bahama Village

FOOD | DECOR | SERVICE | COST

"legend" where the "gourmet eclectic" Floribbean fare is "absolutely delicious" and the Bloody Marys "just what the doctor ordered"; true, "there's often a wait" and it is a "destination for some of the cruise ships", but the "carefree setting" makes for a "unique experience" that "defines Key West."

B.O.'s Fish Wagon ⊘ *Seafood*
24 | 15 | 18 | $18

Key West | 801 Caroline St. (William St.) | 305-294-9272 | www.bosfishwagon.com

"No shirt, no shoes, no problem" say fans of this "refreshingly" "ramshackle" Key West seafood "hut" that "keeps rockin' the conch fritters and fish sandwiches year after year"; though some might be "tempted to walk the other way" at first sight, it's "usually packed with people" drinking "ice-cold beer."

Braza Lena *Brazilian*
- | - | - | E

Key West | 421 Caroline St. (bet. Duval & Whitehead Sts.) | 305-432-9440
Islamorada | 83413 Overseas Hwy. (mi. marker 83.5) | 305-664-4940 Ⓜ
www.brazalena.com

"You won't leave hungry" from this pair of Brazilian steakhouses in Key West and Islamorada, where waiters proffer more than a dozen different cuts of meat and poultry from giant skewers; the "excellent" buffet items and "hard-to-find wines" are added enticements.

Cafe, The Ⓢ *Vegetarian*
- | - | - | M

Key West | 509 Southard St. (bet. Bahama & Duval Sts.) | 305-296-5515

"Creative", "yummy" vegetarian fare plus a "few seafood choices" are the stock in trade of this "small", "easygoing" Key Wester whose "cute" environs feature a rotating display of local artwork; "large portions" bolster its affordability, and a "good selection of wine and beer rounds out the experience."

Ⓩ Cafe Marquesa *American*
27 | 25 | 25 | $61

Key West | Marquesa Hotel | 600 Fleming St. (Simonton St.) | 305-292-1244 | www.marquesa.com

"Upscale and cosmopolitan", this Key West "jewel" known for its "imaginative", "memorable" New American dinners served by a "gracious", "spot-on" staff hits a "home run from first to last"; while some feel it's a little "too formal" for the area, many admire the "elegant", "intimate" setting and call it the "class of the Keys."

Café Solé *Caribbean/French*
24 | 20 | 23 | $48

Key West | 1029 Southard St. (Frances St.) | 305-294-0230 | www.cafesole.com

Just "relax and forget everything else" at this "little" French-Caribbean "hideaway" in Key West, "where the locals go" for "inspired" seafood, particularly the "incredible" hog snapper, enhanced by a "tropical" ambiance and "charming" service; it's slightly "pricey" and the location "away from the noise of Downtown" can make it "a bit difficult to find", but wayfarers assure it's "worth the search."

	FOOD	DECOR	SERVICE	COST

Calypso's Seafood Grille ⊄ *Seafood* ▽ 23 | 14 | 19 | $33

Key Largo | Ocean Bay Marina | 1 Seagate Blvd. (Ocean Bay Dr.) | 305-451-0600

This "off-the-beaten-track" Key Largo "hangout" that's "basically outside but under a roof" channels the "Keys' vibe to the max" as it cooks up "extremely fresh, well-prepared fish"; you "gotta love the plastic forks and knives", and if service is not "the fastest", well, just groove with the "laid-back" atmosphere; P.S. closed Tuesdays.

Camille's *American* 22 | 17 | 21 | $28

Key West | 1202 Simonton St. (Catherine St.) | 305-296-4811 | www.camilleskeywest.com

"Known for its acclaimed breakfasts", brunches and lunches that often generate "long lines", this Key West American turns out plates that can be "over-the-top creative or simple and tasty", set down by "seasoned servers" who "lend personality" to a meal; it's "a little more expensive than the typical diner, but heck, you're on vacation so you deserve it"; P.S. dinner also served.

Chanticleer South Ⓜ *French* ▽ 24 | 20 | 20 | $61

Islamorada | 81671 Old Hwy. (Johnston Rd.) | 305-664-0640 | www.chanticleer-south.com

"Not the type of restaurant you'd expect to find in the Keys", this Islamorada "respite" for "haute cuisine" by former Nantucket chef-restaurateur Jean-Charles Berruet leaves Francophiles exclaiming "superb"; it is "expensive" and "not much attention is given" to the "intimate" room's decor, but the "cooking compensates" for a lack of designer flourishes.

Chico's Cantina *Mexican* ▽ 24 | 18 | 25 | $27

Key West | 5230 U.S. 1 (Cross St.) | 305-296-4714 | www.chicoscantina.com

"Generous" plates of "reliable and frequently outstanding Mexican specialties" together with "excellent" service and a lively atmosphere keep this "family-owned" Key Westy a "locals' favorite"; for the full effect, skip the "dark" interior and "shoot for the patio."

Commodore
Waterfront Restaurant *Seafood/Steak* ▽ 22 | 23 | 21 | $52

Key West | A & B Marina | 700 Front St. (Simonton St.) | 305-294-9191 | www.commodorekeywest.com

Have a "pleasant Papa Hemingway dining experience" "overlooking the harbor" while enjoying the "lovely views" and ordering off a "great steak and seafood menu" at this Key Wester; it can be "pricey" and "service tends to be laid-back", so "hold onto your shorts" and "relax."

Conch Republic Seafood Co. *Seafood* 19 | 20 | 20 | $34

Key West | 631 Greene St. (bet. Elizabeth & Simonton Sts.) | 305-294-4403 | www.conchrepublicseafood.com

Revelers relish the "evening ruckus" at this "crazy" Key West seafood "warehouse" boasting "fantastic" water views, nightly "live music" and an 80-ft. bar; servers who are "friendly but not officious" fit the bill, and while some call the "simple", "decent" seafood "expensive for what you get" and the atmosphere "touristy", most admit it's a "fun place to eat and drink."

Croissants de France *Bakery/French* | 25 | 16 | 19 | $19 |

Key West | 816 Duval St. (bet. Olivia & Petronia Sts.) | 305-294-2624 | www.croissantsdefrance.com

"*Mais oui*, it's more" than the "best croissants you can imagine" at this Key West French bakery and bistro offering "authentic" pastries and "light breakfasts", plus full lunches and dinners (including "great" sandwiches and soups); set outdoors with a backdrop of lush "tropical vegetation", it's a "fabulous" way to "start the day."

Ⓩ Dining Room at Little Palm Island Resort *French/Pan-Latin* | 26 | 28 | 26 | $87 |

Little Torch Key | Little Palm Island Resort | 28500 Overseas Hwy. (Hwy. 1, mi. marker 28.5) | 305-872-2551 | www.littlepalmisland.com

Lovers laud this "exquisite oasis" at a "private island resort" off Little Torch Key (reachable only by "private launch") as a piece of "absolute paradise", voting it Top Decor in the Keys; "words cannot do justice" either to the French–Pan-Latin fare, and while you may have to "take out a loan to pay the tab", the "gracious" staff and "marvelous" setting (where you can "dine alfresco with your feet in the sand") make it "well worth the cost."

Duffy's Steak & Lobster House *Seafood/Steak* | 19 | 16 | 19 | $36 |

Key West | 1007 Simonton St. (Truman Ave.) | 305-296-4900

"The name says it all" about this "casual, basic" Key Wester where "steak and Florida lobster are what they do best"; it draws both "families" and "young" folks, and while some merely allow it's "better than Outback", it's convenient for those who want to be "close to the action."

El Meson de Pepe *Cuban* | 21 | 21 | 19 | $33 |

Key West | 410 Wall St. (Front St.) | 305-295-2620 | www.elmesondepepe.com

It's "next to the famous sunset celebration" on Mallory Square, but this Key West Cuban "in the middle of tourista-ville" nevertheless "surprises" with "delicious" dishes and mojitos for relatively "cheap" tabs; "terrific" live salsa and a staff with a "great attitude" add to the "festive" atmosphere, leading fans to wonder "why go to Havana?"

El Siboney *Cuban* | 26 | 12 | 20 | $22 |

Key West | 900 Catherine St. (Margaret St.) | 305-296-4184 | www.elsiboneyrestaurant.com

"Many locals recommend" this "real" Key West "favorite" for "large", "low-priced" plates of "blow-your-mind" Cuban fare that'll leave you "smiling"; though the room is "not particularly attractive", it's "always bustling", so "be prepared for a wait."

	FOOD	DECOR	SERVICE	COST

Finnegan's Wake Irish Pub ❶ *Irish* — 18 | 18 | 19 | $24

Key West | 320 Grinnell St. (bet. Eaton & James Sts.) | 305-293-0222 | www.keywestirish.com

"Get a pint, bangers and mash" and other "generous" servings of "Irish grub" at this "picturesque" (and recently refurbed) Key West pub with a "wonderful" staff; the "outstanding beer selection", "live music on weekends" and "good-sized TVs for sports nuts" lure fans to its slightly "out-of-the-way" locale, though some feel it's a "better choice for entertainment than it is for food."

Grand Café Key West, The ❷ *Eclectic* — ▽ 22 | 21 | 21 | $43

Key West | 314 Duval St. (bet. Caroline & Eaton Sts.) | 305-292-4740 | www.grandcafekeywest.com

"Eat, see and be seen" at this Key West Eclectic sought out for its "sensational" cooking, a "romantic" setting with a "tropical" court-yard and plenty of "local color"; though it's a bit "expensive", "you're under the stars in your shirt sleeves in January, watching the people on Duval Street, so who cares?"

Green Turtle Inn Ⓜ *Seafood* — - | - | - | M

Islamorada | 81219 Overseas Hwy. (Parker Dr.) | 305-664-2006 | www.greenturtleinn.com

Opened 64 years ago as a modest roadside cafe, this midpriced Islamorada seafooder is now one of the Keys' best-known dining destinations (even landmarks need some help, though, so it closed a few years back for a complete refurb); today, the all-day menu covers all the local bases, from cracked conch and smoked fish dip to fish sandwiches and diver scallops over pappardelle.

Half Shell Raw Bar *Seafood* — 23 | 18 | 19 | $29

Key West | 231 Margaret St. (Caroline St.) | 305-294-7496 | www.halfshellrawbar.com

"If you like it raw", this "iconic" Key West "shack" is the place to go for "fresh", "amazingly cheap" oysters and other "right-off-the-boat" seafood, washed down with a cold beer; it's undeniably "di-vey", with "benchlike" seating, but "grab a table by the water" and you'll get a "taste of old Florida that's not to be missed."

Hot Tin Roof *Caribbean/Eclectic* — 23 | 24 | 21 | $50

Key West | Ocean Key Resort | 0 Duval St. (Front St.) | 305-295-7057 | www.oceankey.com

A "unique blend" of "fine dining with a water view" that's "literally and figuratively a level above the chaos of Mallory Square" sets apart this "terrific" Caribbean-Eclectic at the Ocean Key Resort; "nice" servers add to the charm, while a "grand view of the sunset" makes it a natural for "date night."

Island Grill *Asian/Seafood* — 22 | 22 | 21 | $33

Islamorada | 85501 Overseas Hwy. (after Snake Creek Bridge) | 305-664-8400 | www.keysislandgrill.com

To get in the Islamorada "mood", "chill on the outdoor deck" of this "laid-back" Asian-fusion seafooder and sip a "nice cold beer by the water" while scarfing down "surprisingly creative", "not too expensive" dishes like "tuna nachos"; "you'll wait if you're not early" for dinner, but "friendly" service, "live music" and "purple sunsets" help make it a "must-stop."

Jimmy Buffett's
Margaritaville Cafe ● *American*

| 15 | 19 | 17 | $29 |

Key West | 500 Duval St. (bet. Fleming & Southard Sts.) | 305-292-1435 | www.margaritaville.com

Chow down on a "cheeseburger in paradise" at this "busy", "touristy" Key West American, a "mecca" for "partying" Parrot Heads, with "decent" margaritas, live music Tuesday–Sunday and signature "island vibe"; "give me a break" squawk cynics who caw "Jimmy wouldn't eat here if he didn't own the place."

Kaiyó ⊠ *American/Asian*

| - | - | - | M |

Islamorada | 81701 Old Hwy. (mile marker 82) | 305-664-5556 | www.kaiyokeys.com

When you tire of fried grouper sandwiches and Key lime pie, this is the place to go for all things Asian, with a touch of Florida to keep it real; a perky, quirky Islamorada hot spot (and midpriced at that), it's set in a colorful clapboard house decorated with watery murals and lots of funky water-themed artwork and draws a crowd year-round.

Kelly's Caribbean Bar,
Grill & Brewery *American/Caribbean*

| 21 | 23 | 21 | $35 |

Key West | 301 Whitehead St. (Caroline St.) | 305-293-8484 | www.kellyskeywest.com

Guests "sit in the garden under the trees" at this "quiet" Key West Caribbean-American, co-owned by actress Kelly McGillis, and enjoy the "tasty fare with a variety of house-brewed beers on tap"; set in the former offices of Pan Am, the space is chock-full of "aviation history", and its "hangout bar" and "hip" staff help make it "one of the island's best happy hours"; P.S. it offers a daily brunch until 4 PM.

Keys Fisheries *Seafood*

| 24 | 16 | 17 | $23 |

Marathon | 3502 Gulfview Ave. (Louisa St.) | 305-743-4353 | www.keysfisheries.com

"A modest joint with picnic tables right on the water", this "hidden treasure" in Marathon is known for its "extremely fresh fish", stone crabs and an "awesome" lobster Reuben; as it's largely "self-serve", "locals" and tourists alike "line up early to order at the window" and grab "cheap drinks" before tucking into one of "the best casual meals between Miami and Key West."

La Trattoria *Italian*

| 24 | 21 | 22 | $40 |

Key West | 524 Duval St. (Applerouth Ln.) | 305-296-1075 | www.latrattoria.us

This "wildly popular" Key West Italian will make you an "evening you can't refuse", dishing up "fabulous" (if somewhat "high-priced") fare "with a touch of class", served by an "exceptional" staff; for well-mixed cocktails and live music, Virgilio's Martini Bar at the back of the restaurant is an "oasis off Duval."

	FOOD	DECOR	SERVICE	COST

☑ Louie's Backyard *American/Caribbean*   25 | 27 | 23 | $57

Key West | 700 Waddell Ave. (Vernon St.) | 305-294-1061 |
www.louiesbackyard.com

"It doesn't get any better" than "the sea, the sun, the food" at this "classy, romantic" "longtime winner" in Key West, voted Most Popular in the Keys for its "magnificent" ocean view, "superb" Caribbean-American cuisine and "informed" service; dinner can be a "wallet-bust" and a few cite "snooty" treatment, but to its legion of champions there's just "no other place like it"; P.S. "make reservations well in advance."

Mangia Mangia *Italian*   20 | 17 | 18 | $33

Key West | 900 Southard St. (Margaret St.) | 305-294-2469 |
www.mangia-mangia.com

"Classic Italian comfort food" (featuring "fresh pasta") is the calling card of this "quaint little" family-owned Key Wester whose "reasonable" prices and "pleasant outdoor garden" ensure it's "coveted by locals"; be advised that it's "off the beaten track" and doesn't take reservations, so there's often a "line outside."

Mangoes *Seafood*   19 | 19 | 18 | $35

Key West | 700 Duval St. (Angela St.) | 305-292-4606 |
www.mangoskeywest.com

Though "smack in the middle of Duval Street", this hugely "popular", "full-of-energy" Key West seafooder is "still quite civilized", with "affordable" "Florida-licious" fare (capped off by "fantastic" Key lime pie) served by staffers who ably navigate the "hustle and bustle"; true, it gets "loud" inside, but the "delightful" outdoor patio is a "must for people-watching."

Marker 88 *American*   22 | 22 | 21 | $43

Islamorada | 88000 Overseas Hwy. (mi. marker 88) | 305-852-9315 |
www.marker88.info

Providing "elegant" dining on "classic" seafood dishes amid "spectacular" "water and sunset views", this enduring New American in Islamorada remains a "favorite" of many; some say it would "benefit from some updating" (the "scenery doesn't help the food or service"), but others counter "it's the Keys – relax and it's fine."

Martin's *Caribbean/European*   ▽ 24 | 23 | 23 | $46

Key West | 917 Duval St. (Truman St.) | 305-295-0111 |
www.martinskeywest.com

The "über"-European cuisine always comes with a "hint of Key West" at this "chic, upscale" eatery that's perfect for those who say "enough already with the seafood – bring on the spaetzle"; the "refreshing" ambiance and "lovely" garden get an enthusiastic thumbs-up too.

☑ Michaels *American*   28 | 23 | 27 | $54

Key West | 532 Margaret St. (bet. Fleming & Southard Sts.) |
305-295-1300 | www.michaelskeywest.com

"One of the best and most intimate places to dine in Key West" is chef Michael Wilson's high-end "culinary gem" of an American, where the steaks are "superb", the desserts "fabulous" and the martinis "to die for"; further elevated by an "outstanding" staff (it's rated No. 1 for Service in the Keys), a "gorgeous" garden and "delectable" fondue at the outdoor bar, it's "in a class by itself"; P.S. wallet-watchers can opt for the less-expensive 'Light Side' menu 5:30–7:30 PM.

Morada Bay Beach Café *New World* | 23 | 27 | 22 | $45 |

Islamorada | 81600 Overseas Hwy. (Palm Ave.) | 305-664-0604 | www.moradabay-restaurant.com

"Sitting at tables in the sand and watching the sunset" over "beautifully prepared" seafood and other New World dishes "will leave you feelin' good, mon" at this "quintessential Keys restaurant" in Islamorada; vets advise dressing "formal" – meaning "your best flip-flops and a clean pair of shorts" – and catching the "classic" monthly Full Moon party; P.S. no reservations.

Mo's ⍁ *French* | 21 | 11 | 19 | $24 |

Key West | 1116 White St. (Eliza St.) | 305-296-8955

A "wonderful", "simple" and "inexpensive" French menu (with a few Creole items at lunch) draws a following to this "friendly" little Key West "storefront" "off the beaten path"; while it gets so "busy" it can be a "nut house", satisfied fans say "anytime is time" for a visit.

nine one five bistro & | 25 | 23 | 23 | $46 |
wine bar *American/Mediterranean*

Key West | 915 Duval St. (Truman Ave.) | 305-296-0669 | www.915duval.com

This "charming" Key West "gem" is a "must for foodies" offering "fabulous" small and large Med–New American plates, including "unbelievable" devils on horseback, matched by a "wine drinker's wine list"; service is "excellent" too, and the "lovely" porch means "people-watching" is a bonus; P.S. late-night noshers can hit the upstairs tapas bar until 2 AM.

Origami *Japanese* | ∇ 25 | 19 | 22 | $33 |

Key West | Searstown Shopping Plaza | 1075 Duval St. (Virginia St.) | 305-294-0092

"Excellent" sushi is the star of this "unpretentious" Key West Japanese where customers like to "sit outside" on the patio; though it strikes some as "unimaginative", it ranks high among devotees as "the place" to go.

Outback Steakhouse *Steak* | 17 | 15 | 18 | $30 |

Key West | Searstown Shopping Plaza | 3230 N. Roosevelt Blvd. (Glynn R. Archer Jr. Dr.) | 305-292-0667 | www.outback.com

See review in Miami/Dade County Directory.

Pepe's Cafe & Steakhouse *Seafood/Steak* | 24 | 18 | 23 | $32 |

Key West | 806 Caroline St. (bet. Margaret & William Sts.) | 305-294-7192 | www.pepescafe.net

The "rustic", even "shabby", looks of this century-old surf 'n' turfer in Key West could "fool you", but it dishes up "terrific" breakfasts with "freshly baked breads" that "remind you of home cooking" (the dinners are a bit more "ordinary"); "funky and unique" with a "warm" atmosphere, it attracts "plenty of tourists" but is also a "great place to meet the locals."

☑ Pierre's *Eclectic*   27 | 27 | 24 | $63

Islamorada | 81600 Overseas Hwy. (Palm Ave.) | 305-664-3225 | www.pierres-restaurant.com

"Memorable" meals are made at this Islamorada Eclectic (a higher-end sister to Morada Bay Beach Café next door) whose "fabulous" food, "unbelievable" water views and "plantation-style" setting leave diners "blown away"; indeed, it's an "expensive" "one-of-a-kind experience", but smitten surveyors "could do this every day"; P.S. "sit upstairs away from the families" for a "romantic evening."

☑ Pisces *American/Seafood*   28 | 25 | 24 | $71

Key West | 1007 Simonton St. (Truman Ave.) | 305-294-7100 | www.pisceskeywest.com

Fans find "foodie heaven in a funky town" at this "superlative" Key West New American with a fish focus, voted No. 1 for Food in the Keys; the "unexpectedly" "arty" interior is decorated with signed Warhol prints and the service is "top-drawer", so while you could certainly "spend all your conch shells here", most are happy to splurge for a "special occasion."

Rusty Anchor ⌧ *Seafood*   21 | 16 | 19 | $31

Stock Island | 5510 Third Ave. (5th St.) | 305-294-5369

"Always fresh" seafood served by "seasoned veterans" for "reasonable" prices keeps this "quaint, nautical" Stock Islander "filled with locals"; it's a bit "hard to find" and dining at "peak times" means you'll probably "wait a bit", but after all, it's a "classic"; P.S. reservations for groups of six or more only.

Salute! On The Beach *Italian/Seafood*   ▽ 22 | 20 | 21 | $39

Key West | 1000 Atlantic Blvd. (bet. Reynolds & White Sts.) | 305-292-1117 | www.saluteonthebeach.com

Now that this "cozy", "on-the-beach" Italian is owned by the proprietors of Blue Heaven, there's "more than one heaven" in Key West; a menu that's "strong on seafood" offers "out-of-the-ordinary" dishes, while the "reasonable" prices and "Riviera"-like feel help keep it "jammed at lunch and dinner with locals."

☑ Santiago's Bodega *Eclectic*   28 | 18 | 23 | $37

Key West | 207 Petronia St. (Emma St.) | 305-296-7691 | www.santiagosbodega.com

"Splendid" tapas that "explode with flavor" make this "charming", "friendly" Key West Eclectic a "treat", as do the "outstanding wines" and prices that seem "cheaper" than others of its ilk; the setting's as "small" as the plates, so "make reservations" ("especially if you want to eat outside"), and don't be "deterred" by its "questionable" Bahama Village location – you're just a few blocks from Duval.

	FOOD	DECOR	SERVICE	COST

Sarabeth's Ⓜ *American* | 25 | 20 | 24 | $32 |

Key West | 530 Simonton St. (bet. Fleming & Southard Sts.) | 305-293-8181 | www.sarabethskeywest.com

"Way to go Sarabeth!" exclaim aficionados of "terrific" American breakfasts and brunches featuring "delicious" "homemade breads and jams", the main attractions at this "Key West outpost of the famed NYC cafe" that's "equally appealing" for lunch and dinner; ensconced in a "renovated" Old Town space, the "quaint", "comfortable" setting features a "wonderful" patio and "friendly" service.

Schooner Wharf *Seafood* | 15 | 18 | 19 | $23 |

Key West | 202 William St. (Elizabeth St.) | 305-292-3302 | www.schoonerwharf.com

"Old Florida" lives at this "gritty" "hangout" on Key West Harbor with "tables on the sand", "laid-back" vibes and "can't-go-wrong" prices; the seafood-heavy grub is "ok", but you really "go there for" the two "insanely busy" happy hours (beginning daily at 7 AM and 5 PM) fueled by "strong drinks" and "great" live music.

Seven Fish *Seafood* | 26 | 16 | 24 | $43 |

Key West | 632 Olivia St. (Elizabeth & Simonton Sts.) | 305-296-2777 | www.7fish.com

It may look "like a converted Laundromat", but inside this Key West "treasure" in an "offbeat area of Old Town", "hospitable" servers ferry "fabulous", "fresh" seafood with Asian influences that's "well priced" for the quality; "book way ahead", because there are "not many tables" in the "cramped" space, and "both locals and tourists beat a path to the door"; P.S. closed Tuesdays.

SHOR American Seafood Grill *Seafood* | - | - | - | E |

Key West | Hyatt Key West Resort & Marina | 601 Front St. (Simonton St.) | 305-809-4000 | www.hyattkeywest.com

This Hyatt Key West Resort & Marina venue has "stylish", modern decor to go along with its Americanized seafood preparations; expect "premium" pricing to go along with the "amazing" harbor view.

Sloppy Joe's Bar *American* | 14 | 18 | 17 | $25 |

Key West | 201 Duval St. (Greene St.) | 305-294-5717 | www.sloppyjoes.com

"As much of a Key West fixture as Buffett, Hemingway and six-toed cats", this 1933 hangout's "cheap" drinks, "loud" live music and "anything-goes" vibe earn its rep as a "frat party for the 30-plus crowd"; as for the "standard" American bar grub, it's "just there to fill the stomach" until the next meal "back on the cruise ship", or to delay the inevitable "fall off the stool."

Snapper's Waterfront Restaurant *Seafood* | 22 | 20 | 22 | $34 |

Key Largo | 139 Seaside Ave. (Ocean View Blvd.) | 305-852-5956 | www.snapperskeylargo.com

"Wonderful outdoor dining" with a view of the "mangroves and ocean", a "varied seafood menu" and "value" prices are why this "casual" Key Largo "staple" is a "must-stop"; there are also "inside and outside bars" manned by "pleasant" folks, plus "live music" Monday–Saturday.

Spanish Gardens Café Ⓜ Spanish

| - | - | - | M |

Islamorada | Galleria Plaza | 80925 Overseas Hwy. (bet. Old Sr-905 & Parker Dr.) | 305-664-3999 | www.spanishgardenscafe.com

After chef-restaurateur Jose Palomino won a local following with a small cafe in Islamorada's Rain Barrel Village artisan center, he opened this rustic, art-filled Spanish/tapas bar and market in nearby Galleria Plaza; fish-ophiles may find their gills watering over classic seafood paella, Galician-style octopus and clams with salsa verde, all at relatively moderate prices and featuring mostly organic ingredients.

Square One American

| 22 | 22 | 24 | $50 |

Key West | Duval Sq. | 1075 Duval St. (bet. Truman Ave. & Virginia St.) | 305-296-4300 | www.squareonerestaurant.com

Though it "condones flip-flops", this "oasis" on the "quiet end" of Key West's Duval Street is regarded as a "touch of class", serving up "fine", "pricey" New American fare to the strains of live piano; adventure-seekers, however, wish it would "update" the "predictable" menu.

Tasters Grille & Market Eclectic

| - | - | - | M |

Tavernier | Tavernier Towne Ctr. | 91252 Overseas Hwy. (MM 91.2) | 305-853-1177 | www.tastersgrille.com

The Tavernier space once occupied by old-timer Anthony's has found favor as a midpriced twofer whose Eclectic cafe doles out casual daytime eats like panini, salads, wraps, burgers and ceviche, augmented by more complex small and large plates at dinner and an extensive wine selection; the market side is a convenient stop for wine, cheese and specialty foods; P.S. waterside deck seating is due.

Thai Cuisine Thai

| ▽ 15 | 13 | 16 | $30 |

Key West | 513 Greene St. (Ann St.) | 305-294-9424 | www.keywestthaicuisine.com

Ok, the Thai fare served up at this Key West "convenience-store" look-alike is "nothing special", but it's "good" enough to quell a craving; there's a sushi bar too, and though the maki and sashimi are likewise merely "passable", the moderate prices keep the entire endeavor a standby, "year in, year out."

Turtle Kraals BBQ/Seafood

| 19 | 18 | 19 | $31 |

Key West | Land's End Marina | 231 Margaret St. (Caroline St.) | 305-294-2640 | www.turtlekraals.com

With a "fine location" at "touristy" Land's End Marina, this "roomy", "nothing-fancy" indoor/outdoor Key Wester specializes in "fresh-off-the-docks seafood", "memorable" views and "great specials" at happy hour; beware that "highs" as well as "lows" abound on the menu, which includes "decent" BBQ; P.S. hotheads can now chill thanks to the recent addition of air-conditioning.

	FOOD	DECOR	SERVICE	COST

Two Friends Patio ● *American*

| 19 | 18 | 19 | $26 |

Key West | 512 Front St. (bet. Ann & Duval Sts.) | 305-296-3124 |
www.twofriendskeywest.com

Locals remain faithful to this Key West American because its "always breezy" "open-air" setting and "fun" servers "seem to bring out the 'nice' in everyone"; other reasons include breakfasts, lunches and dinners that are as "reliable" as they are affordable, plus entertainment in the form of "great people-watching."

Upper Deck at Louie's ⬛Ⓜ *Eclectic*

| ▽ 23 | 23 | 20 | $45 |

Key West | 700 Waddell Ave. (Vernon St.) | 305-294-1061 |
www.louiesbackyard.com

"Gorgeous ocean views", "great" vini and "bold, flavorful" Eclectic tapas make for a "winning combo" at this "casual" wine bar; it's the upstairs sibling of Louie's Backyard, and be advised that "both the prices and the staircase" are "steep."

Ziggie & Mad Dog's *Seafood/Steak*

| 24 | 20 | 21 | $52 |

Islamorada | 83000 Overseas Hwy. (mi. marker 83) | 305-664-3391 |
www.ziggieandmaddogs.com

A "diamond" in a field of "tiki bars", this "cozy" Islamorada venture offers a "South Beach dining experience" by way of "wonderful seafood" and steaks, an "extensive wine list" and "expensive" tabs; the "decor is just average", but that doesn't deter "locals, tourists" and the occasional "famous athlete" (former Dolphin Jim 'Mad Dog' Mandich is a co-owner) from "rubbing elbows" at the "great bar"; P.S. now serves lunch.

FT. LAUDERDALE/ BROWARD COUNTY

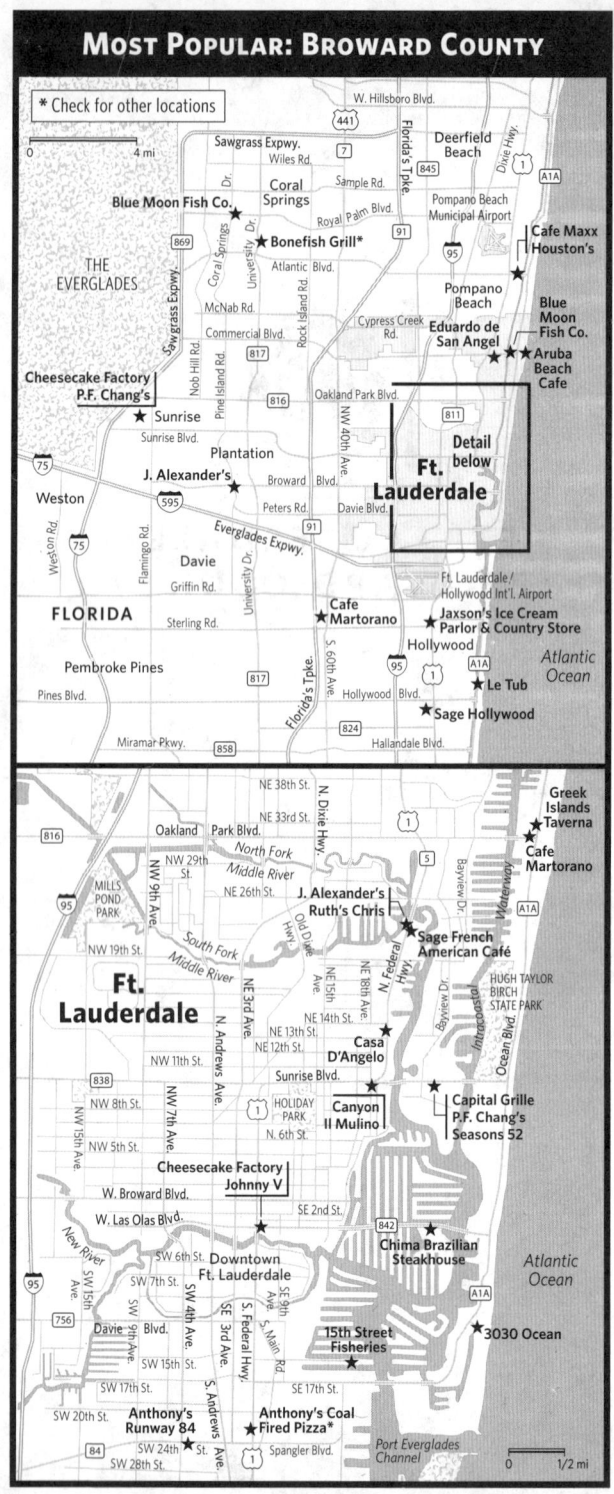

MOST POPULAR: BROWARD COUNTY

* Check for other locations

0   4 mi

W. Hillsboro Blvd.

441

7

845

Dixie Hwy.

1

A1A

Deerfield Beach

Sawgrass Expwy. Wiles Rd.

Sample Rd.

Coral Springs

Royal Palm Blvd.

Pompano Beach Municipal Airport

Blue Moon Fish Co.

869

★ Bonefish Grill*

Coral Springs Dr.

University Dr.

Atlantic Blvd.

91

95

Cafe Maxx ★ Houston's

THE EVERGLADES

McNab Rd.

Commercial Blvd.

Rock Island Rd.

Cypress Creek Rd.

Pine Island Rd.

Nob Hill Rd.

817

Pompano Beach

Eduardo de San Angel

★ ★ ★

Blue Moon Fish Co.

Aruba Beach Cafe

Cheesecake Factory
P.F. Chang's

816

Oakland Park Blvd.

811

★ Sunrise

Sunrise Blvd.

NW 40th Ave.

Detail below

Ft. Lauderdale

Plantation

J. Alexander's ★

Broward Blvd.

75

Weston

595

Peters Rd.

91

Davie Blvd.

Weston Rd.

75

Everglades Expwy.

Ft. Lauderdale / Hollywood Int'l. Airport

Flamingo Rd.

Davie

University Dr.

Griffin Rd.

FLORIDA

Sterling Rd.

Cafe Martorano ★

Jaxson's Ice Cream Parlor & Country Store

817

S. 60th Ave.

95

1

A1A

Hollywood

Atlantic Ocean

Pembroke Pines

Pines Blvd.

Hollywood Blvd.

★ Le Tub

Florida's Tpke.

824

★ Sage Hollywood

Miramar Pkwy.

858

Hallandale Blvd.

NE 38th St.

NE 33rd St.

N. Dixie Hwy.

1

Greek Islands Taverna ★

816

Oakland Park Blvd.

North Fork

NW 29th St.

Middle River

5

Bayview Dr.

Cafe Martorano ★

MILLS POND PARK

NW 19th St.

NE 26th St.

J. Alexander's
Ruth's Chris

A1A

NW 9th Ave.

South Fork

Old Dixie Hwy.

★ Sage French American Café

Ft. Lauderdale

Middle River

NE 15th Ave.

NE 18th Ave.

N. Federal Hwy.

HUGH TAYLOR BIRCH STATE PARK

N. Andrews Ave.

N. 3rd Ave.

NE 14th St.

NE 13th St.

NE 12th St.

Ocean Blvd.

838

NW 11th St.

Casa D'Angelo ★

Bayview Dr.

Intracoastal Waterway

1

Sunrise Blvd.

NW 8th St.

HOLIDAY PARK

Canyon
Il Mulino

Capital Grille
P.F. Chang's
Seasons 52

NW 7th Ave.

N. 6th Ave.

★

NW 5th St.

NW 15th Ave.

Cheesecake Factory
Johnny V

95

W. Broward Blvd.

SE 2nd St.

New River

W. Las Olas Blvd.

842

Chima Brazilian ★ Steakhouse

SW 6th St.

SW 7th St.

Downtown Ft. Lauderdale

Atlantic Ocean

756

Davie Blvd.

SW 9th Ave.

SW 4th Ave.

SE 3rd Ave.

S. Federal Hwy.

S. 9th Ave.

S. Main St.

A1A

SW 15th St.

15th Street Fisheries

★ 3030 Ocean

N. 15th Ave.

SW 17th St.

SE 17th St.

SW 20th St.

Anthony's Runway 84

Anthony's Coal
Fired Pizza*

Port Everglades Channel

84

SW 24th St.

S. Andrews Ave.

1

Spangler Blvd.

SW 28th St.

0   1/2 mi

Most Popular: Broward County

1. Blue Moon Fish | *Seafood*
2. Casa D'Angelo | *Italian*
3. Capital Grille | *Steak*
4. Bonefish Grill | *Seafood*
5. Anthony's Pizza | *Pizza*
6. Cafe Maxx | *American/Eclectic*
7. Seasons 52 | *American*
8. Cheesecake Factory | *Amer.*
9. Greek Islands Taverna | *Greek*
10. 3030 Ocean | *American/Seafood*
11. Canyon | *Southwestern*
12. Chima | *Brazilian/Steak*
13. Eduardo | *Eclectic/Mex.*
14. P.F. Chang's | *Chinese*
15. 15th St. Fisheries | *Seafood*
16. Il Mulino | *Italian*
17. Ruth's Chris | *Steak*
18. Anthony's Runway | *Italian*
19. Houston's | *American*
20. Cafe Martorano | *Italian*
21. Sage* | *French*
22. Aruba Beach | *Amer./Carib.*
23. Johnny V* | *Floribbean*
24. J. Alexander's | *Amer.*
25. Jaxson's Ice Cream* | *Ice Cream*
26. Le Tub | *Burgers*

Many of the above restaurants are among the Broward area's most expensive, but if popularity were calibrated to price, a number of other restaurants would surely join their ranks. To illustrate this, we have added two lists comprising 80 Best Buys on page 111.

* Indicates a tie with restaurant above

Top Food

27 LaSpada's Hoagies | Deli
   Eduardo | Eclectic/Mexican
   Casa D'Angelo | Italian
   La Brochette | Mediterranean

26 Canyon | Southwestern
   Valentino's Cucina | Italian
   Cafe Maxx | American/Eclectic
   Rainbow Palace | Chinese
   Cheese Course | Eclectic
   Capital Grille | Steak
   Thai Spice | Thai

25 Silver Pond | Chinese
   Grille 66 | Seafood/Steak
   Tom Jenkins' | BBQ
   3030 Ocean | Amer./Seafood
   Acquolina Ristorante | Italian
   By Word of Mouth | American
   Cafe Martorano | Italian
   Ruth's Chris | Steak
   Bluefin Sushi | Japanese/Thai

   Cafe Seville | Spanish
   Bistro Mezza. | Amer./Italian
   Josef's | Italian
   Greek Islands Taverna | Greek
   Hi-Life Café | American
   Morton's | Steak
   Blue Moon Fish | Seafood
   Gianni's | Italian

24 Lola's | American
   Council Oak Steaks | Steak
   Galanga | Japanese/Thai
   Chima | Brazilian/Steak
   Da Campo Osteria | Italian
   Truluck's | Seafood
   Runyon's | Continental
   Johnny V's | Floribbean
   Sunfish | American/Seafood
   Jasmine Thai | Thai
   Tuscan Grille* | Italian
   Capriccio | Italian

BY CUISINE

AMERICAN (NEW)

26 Canyon
   Cafe Maxx
25 3030 Ocean
   By Word of Mouth
   Bistro Mezzaluna

AMERICAN (TRAD.)

22 Houston's
   Gold Coast Grill
   Jaxson's Ice Cream
21 Le Tub
   J. Mark's

CARIBBEAN/CUBAN

24 Calypso
22 Sugar Reef
21 Little Havana
   Las Vegas
20 Padrino's

CHINESE

26 Rainbow Palace
25 Silver Pond
23 Christine Lee's
22 Christina Wan's
21 P.F. Chang's

CONTINENTAL

24 Runyon's
23 Vienna Café
   Brooks
19 Wine Cellar
‒ Tatiana Cabaret Restaurant

ECLECTIC

27 Eduardo de San Angel
26 Cafe Maxx
   Cheese Course
23 Sushi Blues Cafe
   Himmarshee B&G

FRENCH

22 Le Bistro
   Café La Bonne Crepe
   Sage
18 Paul Bakery
‒ Saint Tropez

ITALIAN

27 Casa D'Angelo
26 Valentino's Cucina
25 Acquolina Ristorante
   Cafe Martorano
   Bistro Mezzaluna

Excludes places with low votes, unless otherwise indicated

Menus, photos, voting and more – free at ZAGAT.com

MEDITERRANEAN

27	La Brochette
21	Casablanca Cafe
20	Giorgio's Grill
19	H2O
–	Ilios

SEAFOOD

25	Grille 66
	3030 Ocean
	Blue Moon Fish
24	Council Oak Steaks
	Truluck's

STEAKHOUSES

26	Capital Grille
25	Grille 66
	Ruth's Chris
	Morton's
24	Council Oak Steaks

THAI

26	Thai Spice
25	Bluefin Sushi
24	Galanga
	Jasmine Thai
23	Sukhothai

BY SPECIAL FEATURE

BREAKFAST

22	Café La Bonne Crepe
	Bin 595
	Sugar Reef
21	Shula's
20	Original Pancake House

BRUNCH

25	Blue Moon Fish
22	Sage
	Sugar Reef
20	Giorgio's Grill
17	Aruba Beach

BUSINESS DINING

27	Eduardo de San Angel
	Casa D'Angelo
26	Cafe Maxx
	Rainbow Palace
	Capital Grille

CHILD-FRIENDLY

27	LaSpada's Hoagies
26	Tokyo Sushi∇
23	Anthony's Pizza
22	Roasted Pepper
	Jaxson's Ice Cream

DOCK & DINE

25	Grille 66
	Blue Moon Fish
24	Da Campo Osteria
22	Houston's
	Rustic Inn

EARLY-BIRD

24	Sunfish
22	Christina Wan's

	Primavera
21	Old Florida
19	15th St. Fisheries

PEOPLE-WATCHING

26	Cheese Course
25	Cafe Martorano
	Bistro Mezzaluna
24	Council Oak Steaks
	Da Campo Osteria

QUICK BITES

27	LaSpada's Hoagies
26	Tokyo Sushi∇
	Cheese Course
25	Tom Jenkins'
23	kitchenetta

QUIET CONVERSATION

27	Eduardo de San Angel
26	Valentino's Cucina
	Rainbow Palace
25	Cafe Seville
	Josef's

SINGLES SCENES

25	Cafe Martorano
24	Truluck's
	Johnny V
23	Sushi Blues Cafe
	Himmarshee

TRENDY

26	Canyon
	Capital Grille
25	Cafe Martorano
	Bistro Mezzaluna
	Hi-Life Café

BY LOCATION

GREATER FT. LAUDERDALE

27 | LaSpada's Hoagies
25 | Blue Moon Fish
24 | Galanga
23 | Village Grille
22 | Primavera

NE BROWARD

26 | Cafe Maxx
25 | Gianni's
24 | Calypso
23 | Anthony's Pizza
Brooks

NW BROWARD

27 | LaSpada's Hoagies
25 | Bluefin Sushi
Blue Moon Fish
24 | Runyon's
Jasmine Thai

SE BROWARD

25 | Acquolina Ristorante
Cafe Martorano
24 | Lola's
Council Oak Steaks
Hollywood Prime

SW BROWARD

27 | La Brochette
24 | Capriccio
23 | Anthony's Pizza
22 | Roasted Pepper
Brio Tuscan Grille

WEST/W. CENTRAL BROWARD

27 | LaSpada's Hoagies
26 | Cheese Course
25 | Silver Pond
25 | Acquolina Ristorante
Josef's

Top Decor

26 Via Luna
Council Oak Steaks

25 Grille 66
Capital Grille
Trina

24 YOLO
Chima
Da Campo Osteria
Mai-Kai
Sublime
Seasons 52
Truluck's
Hollywood Prime

23 III Forks
Blue Moon Fish
Galanga
China Grill
Rainbow Palace
Morton's
Casablanca Cafe

22 Eduardo de San Angel
3030 Ocean
Acquolina Ristorante
Timpano Chophouse
Cap's Place
Ruth's Chris
Canyon
Christine Lee's
Il Toscano
Bin 595
RA Sushi
Capriccio
Casa D'Angelo
Brio Tuscan Grille

21 Lola's
JB's on the Beach
Houston's
Brooks
Grand Lux Cafe
Tuscan Grille

OUTDOORS

Acquolina Ristorante
Blue Moon Fish
Grille 66
JB's on the Beach
Oceans 234
Pelican Landing
Steak 954
Trina
Via Luna
Wild E. Asian Bistro
YOLO

ROMANCE

Blue Moon Fish
Café Sharaku
Casablanca Cafe
Casa D'Angelo
Eduardo de San Angel
Grille 66
La Brochette
Saint Tropez
Serafina
Sugar Reef
3030 Ocean
Valentino's Cucina

ROOMS

Brooks
Council Oak Steaks
Mai-Kai
Melting Pot
Morton's
Pier Top Restaurant
Ruth's Chris
Sage Hollywood
Sublime
Timpano Chophouse
Truluck's
Via Luna

VIEWS

Brooks
Council Oak Steaks
Mai-Kai
Melting Pot
Morton's
Pier Top Restaurant
Ruth's Chris
Sage Hollywood
Steak 954
Sublime
Timpano Chophouse
Truluck's

Top Service

<u>26</u> La Brochette
Eduardo de San Angel
Rainbow Palace
Capital Grille

<u>25</u> Casa D'Angelo
Council Oak Steaks

<u>24</u> Cafe Maxx
Hi-Life Café
Morton's
Cafe Vico
Ruth's Chris
Valentino's Cucina
Lola's
Grille 66
Capriccio
Chima
Cafe Seville
Thai Spice
3030 Ocean
Sukhothai

Vienna Café

<u>23</u> Bistro Mezzaluna
Seasons 52
Acquolina Ristorante
Truluck's
Brooks
Hollywood Prime*
Via Luna*
La Veranda
Runyon's
Canyon
Bin 595
Josef's
J. Mark's
Fulvio's 1900
Tuscan Grille*
Village Grille
Galanga
Da Campo Osteria
Blue Moon Fish

Best Buys

In order of Bang for the Buck rating.

1. LaSpada's Hoagies
2. Jaxson's Ice Cream
3. Lime Fresh Mexican
4. Cheese Course
5. Pizza Rustica
6. Original Pancake House
7. Anthony's Pizza
8. Tom Jenkins'
9. Floridian
10. Lucille's American Café
11. El Tamarindo
12. Shorty's Bar-B-Q
13. Las Vegas
14. Mario the Baker
15. Jasmine Thai
16. Paul Bakery
17. Sukhothai
18. Christina Wan's
19. Moon Thai Restaurant
20. Southport Raw Bar
21. Village Grille
22. Stir Crazy
23. TooJay's Deli
24. Le Tub
25. Little Havana
26. Calypso
27. Padrino's
28. Brio Tuscan Grille
29. Roasted Pepper
30. Café La Bonne Crepe
31. Cheesecake Factory
32. Whale's Rib
33. Eddie Hills Sushi & Thai
34. Vigneto's Italian Grill
35. My Big Fat Greek Rest.
36. Caspian Persian
37. Mama Mia Restaurant
38. Thai Spice
39. Grand Lux Cafe
40. India House

OTHER GOOD VALUES

Basilic Vietnamese Grill
Big City Tavern
Bonefish Grill
Cafe Seville
Cafe Vico
Galanga
Gianni's
Giovanni's
Gold Coast Grill
Greek Islands Taverna
Hi-Life Café
Houston's
Il Mulino
Indian Chiillies
La Veranda
Le Bistro
Lemongrass Asian Bistro
Lola's
Madras Café
Marumi Sushi

Noodles Panini
Old Florida
Outback Steakhouse
P.F. Chang's
Pho Hoa
Sage
Saigon Cuisine
Saito's Japanese
Saxsay
Seafood World
Seasons 52
Sorella Ristorante
Sugar Reef
Trattoria Bella Cibo
Udipi
Vienna Café
Village Tavern
Viva Chile
Wine Cellar
Woodlands

FT. LAUDERDALE/
BROWARD COUNTY
RESTAURANT
DIRECTORY

	FOOD	DECOR	SERVICE	COST

Acquolina Ristorante Italiano *Italian* | 25 | 22 | 23 | $46 |

Hallandale | 124 S. Federal Hwy. (SE 2nd St.) | 954-454-2410
Weston | 2320 Weston Rd. (Royal Palm Blvd.) | 954-389-1880
www.acquolinaweston.com

"New York Italian food" has "finally come" to Weston with the arrival of this "simple yet elegant" eatery, bringing "generous portions" of *eccellente* individual or family-style dishes served by "professional" staffers who make diners "feel like royalty"; quiet types caution "it can get loud", so sit outside "weather permitting" – "it is Florida, after all"; P.S. the Hallandale branch opened post-Survey.

Aizia *Asian*   ▽ | 24 | 23 | 20 | $52 |

Hallandale | Diplomat Landing | 3660 S. Ocean Dr.
(E. Hallandale Beach Blvd.) | 954-602-8393 | www.aiziahollywood.com

"Seductive lighting" adds to the "sexy Zen" atmosphere when dining at this pricey Asian in Hallandale's Diplomat Landing; the "modest sake selection" and "well-chosen wine list" complement exotic fare with Thai, Japanese, Indonesian and Korean accents.

A La Turca *Turkish*   ▽ | 20 | 14 | 18 | $27 |

Hollywood | 2027 Hollywood Blvd. (N. 21st Ave.) | 954-925-5900

You "must try" the "homemade gyro" at this "authentic" Turkish spot in a small, casual storefront in Downtown Hollywood; the "varied", midpriced menu includes numerous "interesting" dishes ("as well as some pedestrian ones"), so adventurous diners may want to "run with the staff's recommendation"; P.S. a recent renovation may not be reflected in the Decor score.

Ambry German &
American Restaurant 🗷 *American/German* | – | – | – | M |

Ft. Lauderdale | 3016 E. Commercial Blvd. (Bayview Dr.) | 954-771-7342 |
www.ambryrestaurant.com

The atmosphere may be more casual steakhouse than Bavarian nook, but no matter: this Ft. Lauderdale German gem where everyone feels *willkommen* has been drawing fans of schnitzels, sauerbraten and other Teutonic treats for 50 years; a salad bar, American standards and, natch, imported brews round out the midpriced menu.

🆉 Anthony's Coal Fired Pizza *Pizza* | 23 | 16 | 20 | $21 |

Ft. Lauderdale | 2203 S. Federal Hwy. (SE 22nd St.) |
954-462-5555
Pompano Beach | 1203 S. Federal Hwy. (SE 12th St.) | 954-942-5550
Coral Springs | Magnolia Shops | 9521 Westview Dr. (University Dr.) |
954-340-2625
Cooper City | Home Depot Shopping Ctr. | 11037 Pines Blvd. (Hiatus Rd.) |
954-443-6610
Weston | Weston Commons | 4527 Weston Rd. (Griffin Rd.) |
954-358-2625
Plantation | 512 N. Pine Island Rd. (bet. Broward & Cleary Blvds.) |
954-474-3311
www.anthonyscoalfiredpizza.com

"It's smokin'!" declare devotees of the "tasty" coal-fired pizza at this "no-frills" chain whose "limited menu" also features "wings with pizzazz" and "salads big enough for two"; even if the "well-done" pies are deemed "burnt" by some, most salute the "crispest crusts imaginable" and happily brave "daunting waits" to savor them.

Anthony's Runway 84 Ⓜ *Italian* | 23 | 19 | 21 | $49 |

Ft. Lauderdale | 330 State Rd. 84 (bet SW 3rd & SW 4th Ave) | 954-467-8484 | www.facebook.com

You feel "like you're on a flight with the Sopranos" at this "old-style" Italian, a Ft. Lauderdale "landmark" whose "airplane-themed decor" provides a "kitschy" backdrop for a "Jersey-type" "dining experi-ence" (read: "oversized portions" of "tasty" red-sauce favorites served "family-style"); be advised that getting a table "can take hours", "even with a reservation", but it's "worth the wait" for one of the "best shows in town."

Argentango Grill ● *Argentinean* | 21 | 18 | 19 | $35 |

Hollywood | 1822 Young Circle (Harrison St.) | 954-920-9233 | www.argentangogrill.com

Carnivores take note: the "enormous" skirt steaks alone can "feed a family of four" at this Hollywood "standby" offering "*delicioso*" "beef with an Argentinean flair"; if critics fret it's "not what it used to be" and dis "uneven service" and decor that needs "sprucing", "reasonable prices" and the "yummy sangria made at your table" soothe most.

Aruba Beach Cafe *American/Caribbean* | 17 | 19 | 18 | $29 |

Lauderdale-by-the-Sea | 1 E. Commercial Blvd. (Andrews Ave.) | 954-776-0001 | www.arubabeachcafe.com

It's "Ft. Lauderdale's answer to Margaritaville", so no wonder "ev-eryone is having fun, fun, fun" at this "funky" Lauderdale-by-the-Sea getaway "right on the beach" with a "spectacular view" (plus plenty of "eye candy"); true, the "location is better" than the American-Caribbean chow, but the "yummy" Bimini bread, "busy bar scene" and "steel drummer pounding out beats" on weekends makes it easy to imagine "you're really in Aruba."

Basilic Vietnamese Grill *Vietnamese* | - | - | - | I |

Lauderdale-by-the-Sea | 218 E. Commercial Blvd. (bet. Bougainvilla & Sea Grape Drs.) | 954-771-5798

With pho in the forefront, this family-owned Lauderdale-by-the-Sea spot, a rare Vietnamese destination east of U.S. 441, has found its place in the sun with its exotic menu, contemporary dining room and inexpensive beer (with Asian brews) and wine list; P.S. banh mi sandwiches are available at lunchtime.

Beach Watch Ⓜ *American/Seafood* | ▽ 13 | 15 | 14 | $34 |

Dania Beach | Dania Beach Pier | 300 N. Beach Rd. (Dania Beach Blvd.) | Dania | 954-929-4887 | www.beach-watch.com

When it comes to "superb" ocean views in a "magical location", this Dania Beach pier eatery "right over the ocean" has few peers; still, even though the owners buy fresh fish from local anglers, foes fume the New American fare "doesn't live up to the location", so just "go for a drink and watch the waves."

	FOOD	DECOR	SERVICE	COST

NEW Bellini's Coal Fired Pizza *Pizza*

| - | - | - | I |

Ft. Lauderdale | 1535 N. Federal Hwy. (Sunrise Blvd.) | 954-235-5464 |
www.bellinispizza.com

Stylish decor (e.g. glimmering sconces, dark-wood furniture) and a
separate bar area help make this Ft. Lauderdale pizza palace a date-
night destination as well as a haven for kids who want to make their
own pies (with pre-stretched dough); panini, pasta and salads are
also on the menu, but it's the crispy coal-fired specialties that star
here, as well as the wallet-friendly prices.

Big City Tavern *American*

| 19 | 19 | 19 | $34 |

Ft. Lauderdale | 609 E. Las Olas Blvd. (Federal Hwy.) | 954-727-0307 |
www.bigtimerestaurants.com

"There's something to please everyone" at this "lively" Ft. Lauderdale
"hot spot", from the "rockin' bar scene" powered by "young professionals" sipping "well-mixed libations" to the "tasty" New American
fare ("just ok" to some) and "people-watching" from "covered outdoor seating"; it can be as "noisy" as "Grand Central Station" with
service that's "hit-or-miss", but "reasonable prices" and a "hip vibe"
make it a "standby" for many.

Billy's Stone Crab
Restaurant & Market *Seafood*

| 22 | 15 | 18 | $51 |

Hollywood | 400 N. Ocean Dr. (Arizona St.) | 954-923-2300 |
www.crabs.com

"Ask for a table by the dock" so you can enjoy the "incomparable"
Intracoastal view while cracking "super-fresh" stone crabs (in season) or devouring other "select seafood" at this Hollywood "original" without the "hoopla" – or "long waits" – of Joe's Stone Crab in
Miami Beach; if modernists maintain it's a bit "old-fashioned",
afishionados vow "it makes for a lovely evening"; P.S. the Decor
score may not reflect post-Survey renovations.

Bimini Boatyard
Bar & Grill *American*

| 17 | - | 18 | $32 |

Ft. Lauderdale | 1555 SE 17th St. (bet. Eisenhower Blvd. & 15th Ave.) |
954-525-7400 | www.biminiboatyard.com

Patrons "arrive by yacht" to savor the "million-dollar" marina view
(and "ridiculously good" Bimini bread) at this "longtime"
Ft. Lauderdale American with a "casual" but "upscale" "tropical atmosphere" and "lively bar scene"; some sigh "it's been years" since
it's been "on top of its game", but recent renovations and a menu up-
grade aim to rectify that.

Bin 595 *American*

| 22 | 22 | 23 | $43 |

Plantation | Renaissance Hotel | 1230 S. Pine Island Rd. (State Rd. 84) |
954-308-4595 | www.bin595.com

Diners are happily "surprised" when they find this "elegant" eatery
in Plantation's Renaissance Hotel, featuring "creative" (and
"pricey") New American fare with a "Caribbean flair" that's
enhanced by "excellent service"; judging by the "quiet" green-and-
burgundy space, however, it's still largely "undiscovered."

	FOOD	DECOR	SERVICE	COST

Bistro 555 *Italian* ▽ 23 | 21 | 25 | $32

Davie | Muvico Shoppes | 15651 Sheridan St. (Dykes Rd.) | 954-358-0808 | www.bistro555.com

The "owner checks on every table" and "says hello" at this "ultra-friendly" Italian in Davie's Paradise Park, a "delicious neighborhood place" whose "value-priced" menu is popular with moviegoers; expect simple but "nice decor", outdoor seating on an enclosed patio and an "attentive staff" that'll "treat you like family."

Bistro Mezzaluna *American/Italian* 25 | 20 | 23 | $51

Ft. Lauderdale | 741 SE 17th St. (S. Federal Hwy.) | 954-522-6620 | www.bistromezzaluna.com

"Tucked away" in a "nondescript" Ft. Lauderdale strip mall, this "forever popular" Italian–New American "classic" is "still turning out" fare "you can count on", including "outstanding beef and seafood dishes served with flair"; the place is "always crowded", with a "loud", "active bar scene" and "expensive" tabs, but devotees deem it a "pleasure" nonetheless; P.S. "make reservations!"

Bistro 17 *American* ▽ 24 | 19 | 23 | $42

Ft. Lauderdale | Renaissance Hotel | 1617 SE 17th St. (Eisenhower Blvd.) | 954-626-1700 | www.renaissancehotels.com

A "well-kept secret", this New American inside Ft. Lauderdale's Renaissance Hotel offers "delicious" fare complemented by "outstanding service" and "nice decor" (e.g. bamboo floors and color-splashed walls); while it can be "pricey", it's "convenient for after boat or beach."

☑ Bluefin Sushi *Japanese/Thai* 25 | 18 | 21 | $36

Parkland | Parkland Town Ctr. | 6694 Parkside Dr. (bet. Holmberg Rd. & NW 70th Pl.) | 954-755-0120 | www.bluefinsushi.com

See review in Palm Beach Directory.

☑ Blue Moon Fish Co. *Seafood* 25 | 23 | 23 | $48

Lauderdale-by-the-Sea | 4405 W. Tradewinds Ave. (Commercial Blvd.) | 954-267-9888

Coral Springs | 10317 Royal Palm Blvd. (Coral Springs Dr.) | 954-755-0002 Ⓜ

www.bluemoonfishco.com

Voted Broward's Most Popular, this "romantic" Lauderdale-by-the-Sea fish house on the Intracoastal (with a "quieter", view-free, separately owned sib in Coral Springs) continues to hook patrons with its "fabu seafood", "outstanding Sunday brunch" and "service with a smile"; it's "pricey", for sure, but "get a seat outside" and "you'll have a piece of heaven" – as well as a "gorgeous" vista of the "über-rich motoring by" on "mega-yachts."

Bluepoint Ocean Grill *Seafood* ▽ 17 | 18 | 18 | $36

Hollywood | Seminole Paradise at Hard Rock Hotel & Casino | 5730 Seminole Way (Rte. 441) | 954-327-8911 | www.bluepointamerica.com

Odds are, customers can count on "consistent" fin fare, "strong drinks" and a "spectacular" lakeside view (if you nab one of the "lovely cafe tables" outside) at this high-rollin' seafooder at Seminole Hard Rock Hotel & Casino; "attentive" servers up the ante, making it a "great place to meet before heading to the clubs."

☑ Bonefish Grill Seafood   22 | 20 | 21 | $35

Ft. Lauderdale | 6282 N. Federal Hwy. (NE 62nd St.) | 954-492-3266
Coral Springs | 1455 N. University Dr. (Shadow Wood Blvd.) | 954-509-0405
Davie | Weston Commons | 4545 Weston Rd. (Griffin Rd.) | 954-389-9273
Plantation | 10197 W. Sunrise Blvd. (Nob Hill Rd.) | 954-472-3592
www.bonefishgrill.com

You can almost "feel the sea breeze" at these "upscale yet casual" chain seafooders whose "broad selection" of "consistently delicious", "always-fresh" fish ("if it swims, they have it") has habitués "hooked"; "fair prices" and "courteous", "well-trained" servers help explain why they're usually "jam-packed "with a "loud" crowd, so "be prepared to wait"; P.S. "the bang-bang shrimp is to die-die for."

Bongusto! Ristorante ☒ Italian   ▽ 23 | 16 | 24 | $42

Ft. Lauderdale | 5640 N. Federal Hwy. (NE 56th St.) | 954-771-9635 | www.bongustoitalian.com

For 20-plus years, this Ft. Lauderdale "red-sauce" Italian has been cooking up "tasty" food like "grandma used to make"; it's "nothing fancy", with an "old-world–style" setting ("read: needs some sprucing") and "great waiters", but supporters sigh "we like it that way."

Brazaviva Churrascaria Brazilian   18 | 18 | 19 | $55
(fka Fuegovivo Churrascaria)

Sunrise | 14301 W. Sunrise Blvd. (144th Ave.) | 954-514-5851 | www.brazaviva.com

Just "keep the food coming" command carnivores at this Sunrise Brazilian, where "accommodating" servers whisk towering skewers of "all-you-can-eat" grilled meat ("some excellent, some fair") to tables set amid dark-wood beams and stucco arches; disgruntled diners dis an "anemic" salad bar and "pricey" tabs, though the "awesome" caipirinhas compensate.

Brio Tuscan Grille Italian   22 | 22 | 20 | $31

NEW **Hallandale** | Village at Gulfstream Park | 600 Silks Run (bet. Hallandale Beach Blvd. & U.S. 1) | 954-362-1600
Pembroke Pines | The Shops at Pembroke Gardens | 14576 SW Fifth St. (Hwy. 75) | 954-431-1341
www.brioitalian.com

Serving up "a little taste of Italy", these South Florida outposts of a "popular" national outfit offer "excellent food for a chain", including "tasty pastas", "zesty pizzas" and other "flavorful fare"; while a few suggest they're "so loud you should go there only with someone you don't really want to talk to", most consider them "great for a casual night out", with a "bustling neighborhood bistro" ambiance and "delightful" outdoor dining.

Brooks ⓜ Continental
23 | 21 | 23 | $48

Deerfield Beach | 500 S. Federal Hwy. (¼ mi. south of Hillsboro Blvd.) | 954-427-9302 | www.brooks-restaurant.com

"They really know what they're doing" at this "tried-and-true" Continental classic in Deerfield Beach, a "special-occasion" choice for nearly three decades that draws an "older clientele" impressed by the "impeccable" service, "extensive menu" and discounted "opera lunches" in season; though it may be "getting a bit long in the tooth", nostalgists insist it's still a "wonderful experience."

Bubba Gump Shrimp Co. Seafood
15 | 16 | 17 | $27

Ft. Lauderdale | 429 S. Ft. Lauderdale Beach Blvd. (bet. Las Olas Blvd. & SE 5th St.) | 954-463-0777 | www.bubbagump.com

See review in Miami/Dade County Directory.

By Word of Mouth ⓢ American
25 | 15 | 22 | $46

Ft. Lauderdale | 3200 NE 12th Ave. (E. Oakland Park Blvd.) | 954-564-3663 | www.bywordofmouthfoods.com

The "name says it all" confide connoisseurs of this "quirky" "treasure" in Northeast Ft. Lauderdale where "wonderful" servers take you to "deli-like display cases" showcasing "gourmet" New American fare and you "pick what looks good" (that's just about "everything", including "incredible desserts"); it's "hard to find" and the "small", "simple" space can be "noisy", but most agree it's "worth the inconvenience" – and the "pricey" tabs.

Café Emunah Seafood
▽ 23 | 20 | 24 | $36

Ft. Lauderdale | 3558 N. Ocean Blvd. (bet. 35th & 36th Sts.) | 954-561-6411 | www.myemunah.com

"It's not your typical kosher" rave regulars who find refuge in the "tranquil environment" at this Ft. Lauderdale cafe, complete with tea bar and WiFi-equipped lounge; the menu may be "limited", but "innovative" seafood and sushi that's "artfully prepared" and presented leave admirers admonishing "try it, you'll like it!"

NEW Café Europa Italian
- | - | - | M

Ft. Lauderdale | 910 E. Las Olas Blvd. (bet. SE 9th & 10th Aves.) | 954-763-6600

After closing its doors a few years ago because of an expansion at the Riverside Hotel, this Ft. Lauderdale favorite is back in stylish new digs on Las Olas; diners can dig into the midpriced menu of casual Italian entrees and desserts in the warm-hued, high-ceilinged space complete with wine bar or opt for a seat on the patio.

Café La Bonne Crepe French
22 | 17 | 20 | $29

Ft. Lauderdale | 815 E. Las Olas Blvd. (bet. SE 8th & 9th Aves.) | 954-761-1515 | www.labonnecrepe.com

"Even the staff speaks French" at this "little piece of Paris on Las Olas", a "cozy" bistro that's "been around forever and with good reason": you "can't beat" its "awesome crêpes", plus it's a "great spot for breakfast"; *alors*, some fuss that it's "cramped" and "noisy" inside, but patio seating (well, a "few tables") and modest prices are *très* welcome.

Cafe Martorano *Italian*

25 | 17 | 19 | $68

Ft. Lauderdale | 3343 E. Oakland Park Blvd. (N. Ocean Blvd.) | 954-561-2554

NEW **Hollywood** | Seminole Paradise at Hard Rock Hotel & Casino | 6751 Seminole Way (bet. Griffin & Stirling Rds.) | 954-584-4450 www.cafemartorano.com

"Always a scene", this Ft. Lauderdale "destination" "where you can wait for hours" ("no reservations") is a "mix of [mobster] movies, disco balls and great food" courtesy of "larger than life" chef-owner Steve Martorano, who turns out "old-school South Philly" Italian dishes like "baseball-size meatballs that melt in your mouth"; it's a "real love-it-or-hate-it experience", with fans raving it's "fun, fun, fun" while foes rant it's "crowded, noisy" and "crazy expensive" – in any event, it's "not to be forgotten"; P.S. the Hollywood branch opened post-Survey.

☑ Cafe Maxx *American/Eclectic*

26 | 20 | 24 | $58

Pompano Beach | 2601 E. Atlantic Blvd. (NE 26th Ave.) | 954-782-0606 | www.cafemaxx.com

After more than 25 years, this "sophisticated" New American–Eclectic in Pompano Beach is "still wonderful" thanks to chef Oliver Saucy's "creative" menu, an "outstanding" wine list and "polished but not stuffy" service; nitpickers nag that the decor "needs updating" (the "dumpy strip-mall" locale doesn't help) and bemoan "out-of-sight prices", but aficionados contend it delivers "Maxx-a-yum enjoyment" that's "worth every penny."

Cafe Seville ☒ *Spanish*

25 | 19 | 24 | $44

Ft. Lauderdale | 2768 E. Oakland Park Blvd. (Bayview Dr.) | 954-565-1148 | www.cafeseville.com

The owners "welcome you as if you eat every day" at this "little Spanish jewel", and you may wish to after sampling its "wonderful" Iberian fare, including tapas and seafood "cooked with care and love"; it's "hidden" in a "pedestrian" Ft. Lauderdale strip mall, but "moderate prices", "terrific" wines and "delightful" servers help you forget that.

Café Sharaku ☒ *Asian*

▽ 27 | 15 | 22 | $41

Ft. Lauderdale | 2736 N. Federal Hwy. (bet. E. Oakland Park Blvd. & NE 26th St.) | 954-563-2888 | www.cafesharaku.com

Anyone "who appreciates subtlety of flavor and a flair for presentation" will enjoy this 18-seat "little jewel box" in Ft. Lauderdale that's home to chef-owner Iwao Kaita's "sophisticated" Asian fusion fare; it's "not a place for a rushed dinner", but with its "refined service", "midrange prices" and "intimate" (some say "sterile") setting, it's an "oasis of calm" you may not want to leave anyway.

Cafe Vico *Italian*

24 | 20 | 24 | $43

Ft. Lauderdale | IHOP Plaza | 1125 N. Federal Hwy. (Sunrise Blvd.) | 954-565-9681 | www.cafevicorestaurant.com

"Bravo!" cheer celebrants of this "romantic" Ft. Lauderdale Italian, where the "delicious" (and "well-priced") Northern Italian fare comes with a "warm greeting" from "enthusiastic" owner Marcos Vico Rodrigues; add in "personable service" and "cute" decor, and it's no surprise admirers gush it "just keeps getting better."

Calypso ⊠ Caribbean/Seafood
| 24 | 14 | 20 | $28 |

Pompano Beach | 460 S. Cypress Rd. (5th St.) | 954-942-1633 | www.calypsorestaurant.com

"Don't miss the flying-fish cakes" at this Pompano Beach Caribbean, a "tropical getaway" that's so "relaxed" it "feels like the Keys"; just "ignore" the "iffy" storefront locale and "have a good time" – after all, the "beer's cold", the prices are "cheap" and the "flavorful" fare "can't be beat"; P.S. closed Saturday–Sunday except for private events.

Cantina Laredo Mexican
| 19 | 20 | 19 | $32 |

NEW Hallandale | Village at Gulfstream Park | 501 Silks Run (bet. Hallandale Beach Blvd. & U.S. 1) | 954-457-7662 | www.cantinalaredo.com
See review in Palm Beach Directory.

☑ Canyon American/Southwestern
| 26 | 22 | 23 | $52 |

Ft. Lauderdale | 1818 E. Sunrise Blvd. (N. Federal Hwy.) | 954-765-1950 | www.canyonfl.com

A "hip vibe" pervades this "sophisticated" Southwestern in Ft. Lauderdale, a "relatively small", often "crowded" nook featuring "killer" cuisine with "unique flavor combos", "helpful" staffers and "intimate" booths with "drawn curtains"; the "no-reservations policy is a pain", but "sublime prickly pear margaritas" ("in a class by themselves") from the "shwanky bar" ease "long waits."

☑ Capital Grille Steak
| 26 | 25 | 26 | $65 |

Ft. Lauderdale | 2430 E. Sunrise Blvd. (Bayview Dr.) | 954-446-2000 | www.thecapitalgrille.com
See review in Miami/Dade County Directory.

Capriccio ● Italian
| 24 | 22 | 24 | $41 |

Pembroke Pines | 2424 N. University Dr. (Sheridan St.) | 954-432-7001 | www.capriccios.net

"Long live romantic restaurants" purr poetic patrons who rhapsodize over the "nightly music" ("singers, a pianist, strolling violinists"), "attentive servers" and "delicious" if "pricey" Italian fare at this Pembroke Pines "standby", an *isola bella* in a sea of chains"; all that entertainment makes it "a bit loud", but no matter: it's still an "excellent choice" for a "special occasion."

Cap's Place Island Seafood
| 19 | 22 | 20 | $43 |

Lighthouse Point | 2765 NE 28th Ct. (take ferry from dock) | 954-941-0418 | www.capsplace.com

Visitors ferry over to this "unique" seafooder open since 1928 off Lighthouse Point, a "cool piece" of history that once served as Al Capone's hideaway; critics who call it a "tourist trap" with "unmemorable" fare suggest "go for the boat ride" and the "quaintitude", while more forgiving fans insist it's "worth the effort" ("what more could a visitor to South Florida want?").

FOOD | DECOR | SERVICE | COST

Casa Bella *Italian*
▽ 24 | 22 | 22 | $41

Dania Beach | 129 N. Federal Hwy. (bet. NE 1st & 2nd Sts.) | Dania | 954-923-1000 | www.casabellaofdania.com

Set in a circa-1912 home, this "charming" Dania Beach "blast from the past" proffers "very good" Southern Italian fare served with "style" in nine themed spaces awash in "whimsical" decorations (indeed, it's "over-the-top at Christmas"); tip: "pick a different room each time you visit" to mix things up.

Casablanca Cafe *American/Mediterranean*
21 | 23 | 20 | $38

Ft. Lauderdale | 3049 Alhambra St. (Seabreeze Blvd.) | 954-764-3500 | www.casablancacafeonline.com

"Bogie would have liked" the "perfect blend" of "romance and Bohemia" at this "picturesque" Med-American, set in a 1927 home with a "fabulous view" of Ft. Lauderdale beach; while the location tends to "trump" the "good, basic food and service", overall it's a "delightful" place "to watch the world – and time – "go by.""

☑ Casa D'Angelo *Italian*
27 | 22 | 25 | $59

Ft. Lauderdale | Sunrise Square Plaza | 1201 N. Federal Hwy. (bet. E. Sunrise Blvd. & NE 13th St.) | 954-564-1234 | www.casa-d-angelo.com

"*Magnifico*" rave regulars who say "master chef" Angelo Elia turns out some of the "best" and most "authentic" Italian cuisine in Ft. Lauderdale; "generous servings" of "homemade pasta" star in "dishes so out of this world it's hard to choose", all paired with "world-class" wines and "ready-to-please" service; securing a seat can be a "challenge" and it's "expensive", "crowded and loud", but "go anyway"; P.S. the Boca sib is a bit "more stylish" and "quieter."

Casa Maya Grill *Mexican*
- | - | - | I

Deerfield Beach | Cove Shopping Ctr. | 301 SE 15th Terr. (E. Hillsboro Blvd.) | 954-570-6101 | www.casamayagrill.com

Sunny dishes from owner Emilio Dominguez's Yucatán homeland are the highlight at this colorful, inexpensive Deerfield Beach nook; the extensive menu includes roasted pork marinated in sour oranges and mole rojo poblano burritos along with Mexican favorites.

Caspian Persian Grill *Persian*
21 | 10 | 18 | $25

Plantation | Plantation Crossroads | 7821 W. Sunrise Blvd. (N. University Dr.) | 954-236-9955

"It's worth the trouble" finding this Plantation storefront to savor "real Persian food", from standard kebabs to Moroccan stews, plus an "excellent lunch buffet" (just ignore the "dinerlike decor"); there's no alcohol, but with an "inexpensive" menu offering "something for everybody", few seem to mind.

Checkers Old Munchen *German*
- | - | - | I

Pompano Beach | 2209 E. Atlantic Blvd. (bet. 22nd & 23rd Aves.) | 954-785-7565

Pompano Beachers satisfy their cravings for Wiener schnitzel and sauerkraut at this cozy, affordable German storefront lined with decorative steins and beer bottles; stop by for the monthly brew parties and sample hoppy pilsners, lagers or whatever's on tap.

� Cheesecake Factory ● *American* | 20 | 19 | 19 | $29 |

Ft. Lauderdale | 600 E. Las Olas Blvd. (S. Federal Hwy.) | 954-463-1999
Sunrise | Sawgrass Mills Oasis | 2612 Sawgrass Mills Circle (Flamingo Rd.) | 954-835-0966
www.thecheesecakefactory.com
See review in Miami/Dade County Directory.

🔳 Cheese Course *Eclectic* | 26 | 15 | 18 | $18 |

NEW **Hallandale** | Village at Gulfstream Park | 601 Silks Run (U.S. 1) | 954-458-4670
Weston | Weston Town Ctr. | 1679 Market St. (Town Center Circle) | 954-384-8183
www.thecheesecourse.com
Whether you "say cheese" or not, you'll be smiling at the "amazing" selection of fromage (150 varities), "wonderful" "gourmet sandwiches" and "quality wines" at this counter-service Eclectic in Weston Town Center; granted, "limited seating" means it's "cramped inside" and "getting an outside table can be a hassle", but that only adds to the "European cafe" vibe; P.S. the other branches opened post-Survey.

🔳 Chima Brazilian Steakhouse *Brazilian/Steak* | 24 | 24 | 24 | $59 |

Ft. Lauderdale | 2400 E. Las Olas Blvd. (SE 25th Ave.) | 954-712-0580 | www.chima.cc
It's "Valhalla for carnivores" at this "high-end" Ft. Lauderdale rodizio where gaucho-garbed waiters "waltz around" a "gorgeous space" (Brazilian pottery, "cool lighting", courtyard with waterfalls, etc.) delivering a "never-ending" parade of "well-prepared" meat and seafood; it's easy to "overeat", so "pace yourself" – starting with the "overwhelming salad bar" that's a "meal in itself."

🔳 China Grill *Asian* | 23 | 23 | 20 | $60 |

Ft. Lauderdale | Hilton Ft. Lauderdale Marina | 1881 17th St. SE (bet. Eisenhower Blvd. & 23rd Ave. SE) | 954-759-9950 | www.chinagrillmgt.com
See review in Miami/Dade County Directory.

Christina Wan's *Chinese* | 22 | 17 | 22 | $27 |

Ft. Lauderdale | Victoria Park Shoppes | 664 N. Federal Hwy. (bet. NE 6th & 7th Sts.) | 954-527-0228 | www.christinawans.com
Fans say you'll "be a regular after your first visit" to owner Christina Wan's Ft. Lauderdale "treat", where the "fresh, tasty" Chinese fare is "just plain good eats"; it's a "bit more upscale" than its competitors, but "cheerful" servers who "cater to every whim", "understated decor" and its proximity to theaters "make up for it."

Christine Lee's ● *Chinese* | 23 | 22 | 20 | $46 |

Hallandale | Gulfstream Park Racing & Casino | 901 S. Federal Hwy. (SE 9th St.) | 954-457-6255 | www.christinelees.com
"You can't beat the view" of the track at this "elegant" Chinese entry at Gulfstream Park, where patrons dine on "delicious" if "pricey"

steaks, stir-fries and sushi; natch, some "miss" the old Sunny Isles digs ("they should stop horsing around") and wager that service can be "inconsistent", but it's generally a safe bet for a "fun" time.

☑ Council Oak Steaks & Seafood *Steak*   24 | 26 | 25 | $67

Hollywood | Seminole Paradise at Hard Rock Hotel & Casino | 1 Seminole Way (Rte. 441) | 954-327-7501 | www.seminolehardrockhollywood.com

Hungry high rollers head to this "classy" chophouse, a "plush" refuge from the "smoke" in the Seminole Hard Rock Hotel & Casino; the "excellent" steaks and "family-style" sides are predictably "pricey", but it's "worth it" to loyalists, who say Sunday brunch (a "glorious excess") is a good gamble too; P.S. an extensive post-Survey refurb added more terrace dining and updated the interior.

Creolina's Dixie Takeout *Cajun/Creole*   ▽ 23 | 7 | 23 | $20

Davie | Randall Square | 13150 W. State Rd. 84 (SW 130th Ave.) | 954-524-2003 | www.dixietakeout.com

It may be in a "tiny", newish home in a "strip mall", but habitués have followed "one of Broward's best-kept secrets" to Davie nonetheless; chef-owner Mark Sulzinski whips up the same "wonderful", "down-home" Cajun-Creole creations at "inexpensive" prices, and what's more, "irreverent" waitress Rosie O'Neal still "puts on a great show."

Da Campo Osteria *Italian*   24 | 24 | 23 | $62

Ft. Lauderdale | Il Lugano Hotel | 3333 NE 32nd Ave. (bet. Oakland Park Blvd. & NE 34th Ave.) | 954-226-5002 | www.dacampofl.com

"Todd [English] has done it again" sigh fans of the celeb chef's "terrific" Ft. Lauderdale debut in a "comfortable" if "small" space in the Il Lugano Hotel, where the "true gourmet" Northern Italian fare "can be as stunning as the Intracoastal view"; if a few fret it "doesn't live up to the hype", most agree it's a "welcome addition" – particularly when "friendly" servers "make mozzarella at your table" ("showtime!").

NEW D'Angelo Pizza *Pizza*   - | - | - | M

Oakland Park | 4215 N. Federal Hwy. (bet. 38th & 43rd Sts.) | 954-561-7300 | www.pizzadangelo.com

Chef-owner Angelo Elia spent eight years getting the details right for this new Oakland Park pizza palace three miles north of Casa D'Angelo, his pricier fine-dining destination; pie-eyed patrons settle into a sleek, urban space (lots of mirrors, wine bottles, a patio) for a wide choice of 'za from a wood-burning oven, plus calzones, cheese boards, small plates and daily specials best enjoyed with a selection from the extensive wine list.

East City Grill *American*   21 | 20 | 20 | $45

Weston | Weston Town Ctr. | 1800 Bell Tower Ln. (Bonaventure Blvd) | 954-659-3339 | www.eastcitygrill.com

"Eat outside by the water" and enjoy a "sunset cocktail" paired with "well-prepared" New American fare, including truffle-crusted sea

	FOOD	DECOR	SERVICE	COST

scallops, at this "upscale" "neighborhood favorite" in Weston; while fans dig the "friendly service", "active bar scene" and "lovely atmosphere", a few loyalists lament it's "become hit-or-miss", with "over-the-top prices" to boot.

Eddie Hills Sushi & Thai *Japanese/Thai* | 22 | 9 | 18 | $24 |

Hallandale | 134 N. Federal Hwy. (NE 2nd St.) | 954-454-0023 | www.eddiehills.com

With a "huge menu covering everything Asian", this Hallandale staple sates surveyors seeking "super-wow sushi and Thai" at "prices that keep you coming back for more"; the decor may be "lacking" in the "old-time diner" setting ("you can never be underdressed"), but the "long lines say it all."

Ƶ Eduardo | 27 | 22 | 26 | $56 |
de San Angel ⓩ *Eclectic/Mexican*

Ft. Lauderdale | 2822 E. Commercial Blvd. (bet. Bayview Dr. & NE 28th Ave.) | 954-772-4731 | www.eduardodesanangel.com

Don't expect the "typical tacos and tamales" at this "high-end" hacienda in Ft. Lauderdale, but rather "divine" Eclectic-Mexican fare; chef-owner Eduardo Pria's "commitment to excellence" extends to his "gracious" staffers, who are "helpful but not obtrusive" as they navigate the "cozy", "romantic" quarters; all in all, it's a "rare find" that's "always at the top of its game."

NEW Elle's Ⓜ *Asian/Caribbean* | - | - | - | M |

Miramar | 12312 Miramar Pkwy. (off S. Flamingo Rd.) | 954-437-0071 | www.ellesrestaurant.com

Set in an unassuming Miramar suburban plaza, this casual, contemporary multitasker features sophisticated (and affordable) cuisine – bar bites to large plates – with Latin, Asian and Caribbean influences; there's a thoughtful wine list sans big markups, and the bottles are also available from the owners' market next door.

El Tamarindo *Salvadoran* | 22 | 14 | 22 | $23 |

Ft. Lauderdale | 233 State Rd. 84 (SW 3rd Ave.) | 954-467-5114
El Tamarindo Coal Fired Pizza *Salvadoran/Pizza*
Hallandale | 712 Atlantic Shores Blvd. (N. Federal Hwy.) | 954-456-4447

Be sure to sample the "homemade hot sauce" at this family-owned "gem" near Ft. Lauderdale/Hollywood International Airport, where "warm service" complements the "solid" Salvadoran cuisine (plus "excellent pizza" at the Hallandale spin-off); even better, "prices are unbelievably low", so "once you've found it, you'll be back."

Ferdo's Grill ⓩ *Mideastern* | ∇ 21 | 15 | 21 | $28 |

Ft. Lauderdale | 4300 N. Federal Hwy. (NE 43rd St.) | 954-492-5552 | www.ferdosgrill.net

The "weekend belly dancing" really shakes things up at this "friendly" Ft. Lauderdale "neighborhood stop" known for its "generous portions" of "well-spiced" Middle Eastern fare, including "delicious" Syrian-inspired specialties; if some call the decor "uninspired", "reasonable prices" are reason enough to overlook it.

	FOOD	DECOR	SERVICE	COST

☑ 15th Street Fisheries *Seafood* | 19 | 18 | 19 | $39 |

Ft. Lauderdale | Lauderdale Marina | 1900 SE 15th St. (Cordova Rd.) | 954-763-2777 | www.15streetfisheries.com

"Delightful" Intracoastal views and tarpon feedings make patrons "feel like they're on vacation" at this "longtime" seafooder in Ft. Lauderdale, with "upscale" dining upstairs and a "casual Bahamian" vibe dockside; while new ownership resulted in higher scores, critics still carp it's "past its prime", citing "outdated decor" and "steep" prices for "ordinary" grub, though the "lovely" setting tends to "make up for any shortcomings."

Fin & Claw *Austrian/Seafood*   ∇ | 17 | 12 | 19 | $41 |

Lighthouse Point | 2476 N. Federal Hwy. (Copans Rd.) | 954-782-1060

"Bring me the cornbread straight from the oven" demand diners at this seafood-heavy Lighthouse Point Austrian, where owners Willie and Donna Schlager "make you feel like part of the family"; still, some say the place is "nothing special", and "in need of an update" at that.

Floridian, The ● *Diner* | 18 | 12 | 18 | $18 |

Ft. Lauderdale | 1410 E. Las Olas Blvd. (SE 15th Ave.) | 954-463-4041

"Breakfast at the Flo is a Ft. Lauderdale tradition", hence the cast of "characters" "from all walks of life" who descend on this 24/7 "institution" for "decent", "well-priced" diner fare; even if servers can be "cranky" and the place "could use a rehab" (it's been around since 1937 after all), "go for the experience" anyway.

Fulvio's 1900 *Italian* | 23 | 20 | 23 | $48 |

Hollywood | 1900 Harrison St. (19th Ave.) | 954-927-1900 | www.fulvios1900.com

Don't expect "your typical lasagna and meatballs" – though the "meatballs *are* heavenly" – at this "elegant" Downtown Hollywood red-saucer offering a "wonderful menu" of "upscale" Italian fare; though surveyors split on cost ("fair" vs. "overpriced"), few deny that "service is excellent", and oenophiles toast the "great wine list" with 300 labels, 25 by the glass.

Galanga *Japanese/Thai* | 24 | 23 | 23 | $39 |

Wilton Manors | 2389 Wilton Dr. (NE 8th Terr.) | 954-202-0000 | www.galangarestaurant.com

"Waiters double as eye candy" at this "cool" Wilton Manors mainstay dishing out "inventive and palate-pleasing" Thai and Japanese fare in an "exotic" space incorporating a "huge" 700-gallon fish tank (a "tongue-in-cheek distraction at the sushi bar"), "soft lighting" and a "delightful" garden; the only thing missing is a full liquor license ("beer and wine only"), but "it's all good" regardless.

Gianni's *Italian* | 25 | 16 | 22 | $36 |

Pompano Beach | 1601 E. Atlantic Blvd. (NE 16th Ave.) | 954-942-1733 | www.giannisofpompano.com

You'll be in "garlic heaven" at this "traditional" Pompano Beach Italian, a "consistent pleaser" whose "unbelievable portions" of "excellent" (and "moderately priced") fare have been "drawing crowds" for two decades; it's "almost impossibly loud", but that's just the sound of a "friendly, fun environment."

Giorgio's Grill *Mediterranean* | 20 | 18 | 18 | $36 |

Hollywood | 606 N. Ocean Dr. (New York St.) | 954-929-7030 | www.giorgiosgrill.com

Frugalistas suggest you arrive "before sunset" to take advantage of the "value"-priced "twilight dinners" and "fabulous Intracoastal views" (particularly from the new patio) at this "romantic" and "reliable" Hollywood Med, or stop by for the "nice Sunday brunch"; "so-so" service can be a distraction, however.

NEW Giovanni's *Italian/Peruvian* | - | - | - | M |

Pembroke Pines | Pines Professional Campus | 17864 NW Second St. (Pines Blvd.) | 954-441-3474

This inviting newcomer hidden in a Pembroke Pines medical complex is garnering locals' attention, as much for its traditional Peruvian and Italian dishes (churrasco, chicken Parmesan, flan) as the whimsical decor (gold angels and bronze, wood and brick accents); modest prices and jazz on Wednesday and Sunday evenings sweeten the deal.

Gold Coast Grill *Seafood* | 22 | 20 | 21 | $35 |

Coral Springs | The Walk at University | 2752 N. University Dr. (Royal Palm Blvd.) | 954-255-3474 | www.goldcoastseafoodgrill.com

"The fish is always fresh" and the "outside dining always good" at this "reliable" American seafooder in Coral Springs serving "sizable portions" of "tasty" fin fare and steaks; a "lovely bar" and "great happy hour" keep imbibers bubbly, and even a few critics concede that while the place may not "wow you" (though its new owners may change that), you'll likely leave "pleased"; P.S. wine dinners held monthly.

Grand Lux Cafe *Eclectic* | 19 | 21 | 19 | $31 |

Sunrise | Colonnade Outlets | 1780 Sawgrass Mills Circle (Sunrise Blvd.) | 954-838-9711 | www.grandluxcafe.com

See review in Miami/Dade County Directory.

Z Greek Islands Taverna *Greek* | 25 | 15 | 22 | $35 |

Ft. Lauderdale | 3300 N. Ocean Blvd. (Oakland Park Blvd.) | 954-565-5505 | www.greekislandstaverna.com

"Why go to Greece?" ponder partisans "wowed" by this "hard-to-beat", "no-gimmick" Ft. Lauderdale taverna where diners dig into "grilled-to-perfection lamb chops" and "drink ouzo"; given its "fair prices" and "efficient" service, it's "always mobbed" – with tables "close together" and a "line out the door" (it "moves rather quickly") – so "get here early" and don't be shocked if it becomes a "regular dining spot."

Z Grille 66 *Seafood/Steak* | 25 | 25 | 24 | $63 |

Ft. Lauderdale | Hyatt Regency Pier 66 | 2301 SE 17th St. (23rd Ave.) | 954-728-3500 | www.grille66andbar.com

Sit on the "heavenly terrace" and "watch the yachts" float by on Ft. Lauderdale's Intracoastal at this "elegant" Hyatt complex eatery where "out-of-town visitors will be wowed" by the "outstanding" surf 'n' turf, "superb" 800-label wine list and "high-end service"; "arm-and-a-leg" prices startle some, but the majority "keeps going back."

NEW Havana's Cuban Cuisine *Cuban*   — | — | — | I

Cooper City | Timberlake Plaza | 8600 Griffin Rd. (S. Pine Island Rd.) | 954-230-1400 | www.havanasrestaurants.com

Crowds clamoring for inexpensive Cuban classics, along with a few Argentinean and Mexican choices, are packing this 90-seat Cooper City newcomer; the bright, airy dining room and inviting bar belie its location in a strip mall.

Helen Huang's Mandarin House *Chinese* ▽ 18 | 13 | 22 | $23

Hollywood | 2031 Hollywood Blvd. (Dixie Hwy.) | 954-923-1688

A "popular" pick for "reliable" Chinese-vegetarian fare, this Hollywood family business provides "efficient service" amid "decor that hasn't changed" in years; so the food "may not be novel", but it's "fresh and tasty" and comes with a "personal hello" from Helen herself.

Hi-Life Café M *American*   25 | 19 | 24 | $45

Ft. Lauderdale | Plaza 3000 | 3000 N. Federal Hwy. (south of Oakland Park Blvd.) | 954-563-1395 | www.hilifecafe.com

This "tucked-away" Ft. Lauderdale spot is no longer owned by Chuck Smith and toque Carlos Fernandez, but the *Top Chef* also-ran continues to win a "well-deserved following" for his "creative" Southern-accented American fare ("you must have the Coca-Cola cake") with the help of "up-to-snuff" servers; the space is "dark" to some, "cozy" to others, but either way, it's a "sweet little" place.

Himmarshee Bar & Grille *American/Eclectic*   23 | 18 | 22 | $42

Ft. Lauderdale | 210 SW Second St. (bet. 2nd & 3rd Aves.) | 954-524-1818 | www.himmarshee.com

With its "deep menu" of "innovative" Eclectic–New American fare, "well-chosen wine list" and "sharp staff", this "upscale" yet "unpretentious" eatery near the Broward Center for the Performing Arts has become a "pre- or post-theater" "hot spot"; while outdoorsy types eschew the "loftlike" interior for "people-watching" on the patio, there's no avoiding the "jumping bar scene" – and few wish to.

Hollywood Prime M *Steak*   24 | 24 | 23 | $75

Hollywood | Westin Diplomat Resort | 3555 S. Ocean Dr. (E. Hallandale Beach Blvd.) | 954-602-6000 | www.hollywoodprime.com

Carnivores mete out kind words for the "ginormous" steaks and "generous, tasty sides" at this "special-occasion" chophouse in Hollywood's Westin Diplomat; no doubt "it'll cost an arm and a leg", but considering the "friendly" service and "beautiful setting" (rich woods, classic artwork, etc.), even pragmatists say it's "worth it."

Z Houston's *American*   22 | 21 | 22 | $37

Pompano Beach | 2821 E. Atlantic Blvd. (NE 28th Ave.) | 954-783-9499 | www.hillstone.com

A "chain that doesn't feel like one", these "reliable" Miami-area outposts "click" thanks to a "pretty darn good" menu of "all-American comfort" items and a "modern metropolitan" ambiance that brings in "mingling singles" after work; despite debate on the cost – "inexpensive" vs. "overpriced" – most report "solid quality" here; P.S. the Pompano Beach branch has "great views."

H2O *Italian/Mediterranean*

| 19 | 21 | 17 | $41 |

Ft. Lauderdale | 101 S. Ft. Lauderdale Beach Blvd./A1A (Cortez St.) | 954-414-1024

Some surveyors are "surprised" to come across this "beautifully appointed" yet "casual" cafe on Ft. Lauderdale's famed beach strip whose "large" oceanfront patio offers a "beautiful" panorama of surf, sand and sun-worshiper; indeed, the Italian-Med cuisine gets mixed notices ("tasty" vs. "passable") and a few fuss over "non-professional" service, but that location just "can't be beat."

Ichiban *Japanese*

| 20 | 17 | 20 | $33 |

Davie | Shoppes of Arrowhead | 2411 S. University Dr. (Nova Dr.) | 954-370-0767 | www.ichibanatdavie.com

It may be "nothing exceptional", but when Davie denizens desire "fresh" sushi and other "dependable" Japanese fare, this strip-mall mainstay beckons; the fact that it's a "good value" to boot cause most to overlook the "minimal" decor.

Ilios *Mediterranean/Spanish*

| - | - | - | E |

Ft. Lauderdale | Hilton Ft. Lauderdale Beach Resort | 505 N. Ft. Lauderdale Beach Blvd. (bet. Las Olas & Sunrise Blvds.) | 954-414-2630 | www.hilton.com

"Hidden" near the sixth-floor pool deck of the Ft. Lauderdale Hilton, this "relative newcomer" serves "imaginative" tapas and other Spanish-Med cuisine with "fresh" flavors; patrons can perch on the oceanfront terrace, in the wall-carving–adorned dining room or at the "active" illuminated bar.

NEW Il Mercato Café & Wine Shop ⓜ *Eclectic*

| - | - | - | M |

Hallandale | 1454 E. Hallandale Beach Blvd. (NE 14th Ave.) | 954-457-3700 | www.ilmercatocafe.com

Sporting the look of a European bistro, this twofer tucked in a Hallandale Beach strip mall presents well-priced Eclectic menus from the husband-and-wife team of Michael and Emily Lynch, including a few dishes reflective of her Nordic heritage; oenophiles will appreciate the various vintages on hand, plus there are wine tastings on Monday nights.

Il Mulino *Italian*

| 22 | 16 | 20 | $39 |

Ft. Lauderdale | 1800 E. Sunrise Blvd. (U.S. 1) | 954-524-1800 | www.ilmulinofl.com

A "garlic lover's paradise", this "affordable", "no-frills" Italian in Ft. Lauderdale is a popular place to "grab a bite" before catching a flick at the nearby Gateway Cinema; inasmuch as there's "nothing special about the decor", fans focus instead on the "monster portions" of "surprisingly good" red-sauce fare delivered by "congenial" servers who'll "roll you out" to your car afterward.

	FOOD	DECOR	SERVICE	COST

Il Toscano *Italian*

22 | 22 | 20 | $41

Weston | Waterway Shoppes | 2282 Weston Rd. (Royal Palm Blvd.) | 954-385-5883 | www.iltoscanoweston.net

Solace-seekers "love sitting out back" to take in the "romantic" lakeside view at this "casual but classy" Italian in a Weston shopping center ("of all places!"); while some say it's "nothing out of the ordinary", supporters salute "well-prepared" fare and "attentive" staffers.

India House *Indian*

20 | 13 | 17 | $26

Plantation | Quality Inn | 1711 N. University Dr. (Sunrise Blvd.) | 954-565-5701 | www.indiahouserestaurant.com

You might not expect "authentic Indian cuisine" in the lobby of a Plantation Quality Inn, but the "tasty", "perfectly seasoned" fare "belies the location"; there's "no ambiance" and "slower than usual service" at times, but it's a "great value" (particularly the popular lunch buffet), another reason most say "give it a shot."

NEW Indian Chillies *Chinese/Indian*

- | - | - | I

Pembroke Pines | 2092 N. University Dr. (bet. Sheridan & Taft Sts.) | 954-392-0999 | www.indianchillies.com

This small, cheery subcontinental in a Pembroke Pines storefront is known for its chaats (street snacks), Indian-style Chinese fare, weekend brunch and tandoori specialties; indeed, there's a lot to choose from, but the budget-friendly pricing means you can try a lot of dishes, plus there's family-style dining.

Ireland's 🅂Ⓜ *Seafood/Steak*

▽ 22 | 24 | 23 | $54

Weston | Hyatt Regency Bonaventure Conference Center & Spa | 250 Racquet Club Rd. (bet. E. Mall & W. Mall Rds.) | 954-349-5656 | www.bonaventure.hyatt.com

"Finally", there's a "high-end" surf 'n' turfer in Weston, though it's "hidden" inside the Hyatt Regency Bonaventure; while meat-and-potatoheads praise the "traditional" fare (e.g. "exceptional lambchops"), service and decor (hardwood floors, red-and-yellow banquettes), the "high tabs" are harder to swallow.

J. Alexander's *American*

20 | 20 | 21 | $33

Ft. Lauderdale | 2415 N. Federal Hwy. (26th St.) | 954-563-9077
Plantation | 8550 W. Broward Blvd. (Pine Island Rd.) | 954-916-8837
www.jalexanders.com

See review in Palm Beach County Directory.

Jasmine Thai *Thai*

24 | 18 | 21 | $26

Margate | Cocogate Plaza | 5103 Coconut Creek Pkwy. (State Rd. 7) | 954-979-5530 | www.jasminethai-sushi.com

Curry connoisseurs commend the "delectable" Thai treats at this Margate "go-to", a fixture for more than two decades with an "extensive menu" that includes local favorites like volcano chicken ("explodes with flavor") and sushi; some dis the booth-packed space as a "bit drab", but "reasonable prices" and "sweet service" compensate.

	FOOD	DECOR	SERVICE	COST

Jaxson's Ice Cream Parlor & Country Store *Ice Cream*

22 | 19 | 19 | $16

Dania Beach | Jaxon's Dania Plaza | 128 S. Federal Hwy. (Stirling Rd.) | Dania | 954-923-4445 | www.jaxsonsicecream.com

For 50-plus years, this Dania Beach "blast from the past" has been dishing up "huge portions" of "awesome" homemade ice cream ("sugar coma in 5, 4, 3, 2 ,1 . . .") and "standard" American vittles in an "old-fashioned" country store setting; there's often a "long line", so consider the outdoor "take-out window", but you'll miss the barrels of "penny candy" – "not a penny anymore", alas – and weekend acts.

JB's on the Beach *Seafood/Steak*

17 | 21 | 17 | $36

Deerfield Beach | 300 N. Ocean Blvd. (Hillsboro Blvd.) | 954-571-5220 | www.jbsonthebeach.com

"One of the few" area restaurants "right on the beach", this "happening" surf 'n' turfer near the Deerfield Beach pier is "all about the location" and "being seen" at the "rockin' bar"; the grub and service are "ok", but when you can "watch the volleyballers" and listen to live "island music" just "inches" from the ocean, "does the food really matter that much?"

J. Mark's *American*

21 | 20 | 23 | $34

NEW **Ft. Lauderdale** | Sunrise Square | 1245 N. Federal Hwy. (NE 13th St.) | 954-390-0770
Pompano Beach | 1490 NE 23rd St. (N. Federal Hwy.) | 954-782-7000
www.jmarksrestaurant.com

"Friendly" staffers strive to "make you feel welcome" at this mid-priced Pompano Beacher, a "charming" "neighborhood place" with "solid" American fare (e.g. "wings that'll set your mouth on fire") and a "handy" location near "shopping and movies"; quiet types warn the "upscale" wood-and-brick interior can get "loud", so "sit outside" or at the bar if the noise annoys; P.S. the Ft. Lauderdale branch opened post-Survey.

Johnny V *Floribbean*

24 | 21 | 22 | $58

Ft. Lauderdale | 625 E. Las Olas Blvd. (Federal Hwy.) | 954-761-7920 | www.johnnyvlasolas.com

From the "amazing cheese selection" to the "interesting menu" of "scrumptious" Floribbean cuisine, chef-owner Johnny Vinczencz continues to "tantalize taste buds" at his "hip" eatery "in the heart of Las Olas"; if a few grumble about "inconsistent" service and cooking, the majority maintain it's still a "first-rate choice for top-tier dining."

Josef's ☒Ⓜ *Italian*

25 | 20 | 23 | $54

Plantation | Central Park Pl. | 9763 W. Broward Blvd. (Nob Hill Rd.) | 954-473-0000 | www.josefsplantation.com

"Those who find this wonderful place" "hidden" in a Plantation strip mall "return time and again" say surveyors smitten by chef-owner Josef Schibanetz's "hearty", "consistently interesting" Northern

Italian dishes reflecting his Austrian heritage; it's all bolstered by a "fascinating (and reasonable) wine list" and service so "warm" "you'll really feel like a guest."

Kiko *Japanese/Thai*

- | **-** | **-** | **M**

Plantation | Fountains Shoppes of Distinction | 801 S. University Dr. (SW 78th Ave.) | 954-473-0077 | www.kikorestaurant.com

A new location on University Drive, sleek decor and contemporary sushi and saketini bars have turned this handsome haven into one of the hippest spots in Plantation; then again, the moderately priced Japanese and Thai fare has done its part, as well as the knowledgeable servers who help patrons navigate the huge menu.

Kingshead Pub, Restaurant & British Market ● *British*

- | **-** | **-** | **I**

Sunrise | 2692 N. University Dr. (NW 26th St.) | 954-572-5933 | www.kingsheadpubsunrise.com

Sports fans pack into this classic British pub set in a Sunrise shopping center as much for the games on the telly as for the well-priced grub, including fish 'n' chips and cottage pie (with a splash of Guinness); the stout-hearted go right for the bevy of brews on tap, plus there's live music several nights a week; P.S. on-the-go noshers can get housemade dishes and imported groceries in the next-door market.

kitchenetta trattoria tipica italiana Ⓜ *Italian*

23 | **16** | **21** | **$43**

Ft. Lauderdale | 2850 N. Federal Hwy. (bet. E. Oakland Park Blvd. & NE 26th St.) | 954-567-3333

The "airplane hangar"-like interior and "stark glass front" of this Ft. Lauderdale trattoria encourages so much "noise" that "all you can do is eat", but that's a given since plates arrive with "gargantuan portions" of "wonderful" Italian fare; pile on "reasonable prices" and "spot-on service", and supporters say it's no wonder it's "always packed."

Kuluck Ⓜ *Persian*

- | **-** | **-** | **M**

Tamarac | Midway Plaza | 5879 N. University Dr. (Commercial Blvd.) | 954-720-6980 | www.kuluck.com

Adventurous diners decree it's "worth the trip" to Tamarac for the "tasty" fare at this upscale Persian; an outdoor hookah lounge adds to the "nice club atmosphere", though it's the weekend "belly dancers" and DJ that really keep patrons on their toes.

La Barraca Ⓜ *Spanish*

22 | **20** | **21** | **$34**

Hollywood | 115 S. 20th Ave. (Hollywood Blvd.) | 954-925-0050 | www.paellas.com

"Don't fill up" on the "tasty tapas" or "potent sangria" at this "charming" Hollywood Spaniard, because chef-owner Jorge Luis Fernandez also churns out "paellas that should not be missed"; "reasonable prices" and "phantomlike" servers are other "crowd"-pleasers, but it's the Thursday–Saturday flamenco shows that really "add to the fun."

	FOOD	DECOR	SERVICE	COST

☒ La Brochette Bistro Ⓜ *Mediterranean*   27 | 20 | 26 | $46

Cooper City | Embassy Lakes Plaza | 2635 N. Hiatus Rd. (Sheridan St.) |
954-435-9090 | www.labrochettebistro.com

"You'll be blown away" by this "tiny" Med in Cooper City predict partisans who implore "don't even look at the menu" until you hear chef-owner Aboud Kobaitri's "wonderful specials" (including "amazing fresh fish"); add in a "top-notch staff" that's voted No. 1 for Service in Broward County, "reasonable prices" and a "lovely", "romantic" space, and you've got a "local find" where "reservations are a must."

La Creperie Ⓜ *French*   ▽ 23 | 16 | 24 | $31

Lauderhill | Sun Village Plaza | 4589 N. University Dr. (NW 44th St.) |
954-741-9035 | www.lacrepierieinternational.com

It's in an "off-the-beaten-path" Lauderhill strip mall, but Francophiles flock to this "delightful" French bistro anyway for "excellent" crêpes and other Gallic goodies, all served "piping hot" by a "friendly staff"; *mais oui,* the "tables are close together" and it gets "crowded", but overall it's a "charming" "treat" that's "not to be forgotten."

☒ LaSpada's Original Hoagies *Deli*   27 | 8 | 22 | $11

Lauderdale-by-the-Sea | 4346 Seagrape Dr. (Commercial Blvd.) |
954-776-7893
Coral Springs | 7893 W. Sample Rd. (bet. Riverside & Woodside Drs.) |
954-345-8833
Davie | Shoppes of Arrowhead | 2645 S. University Dr. (Nova Dr.) |
954-476-1099
www.laspadashoagies.com

"Meat goes flying through the air" and "lands on fresh-cut rolls" as "pros" "put on a show" at this veteran sandwich trio, voted Broward's No. 1 for Food *and* Bang for the Buck by economical enthusiasts who exclaim "these are the best, biggest, baddest subs in town" (just "try eating a whole Monster yourself"); sure, they're "short on decor" and "out-the-door lines" are the norm, but "service is fast" and the "wait is worth it" for the "holy grail of hoagies"; P.S. a Boca Raton branch was added post-Survey, and others are due.

Las Vegas *Cuban*   21 | 12 | 20 | $22

Ft. Lauderdale | 2807 E. Oakland Park Blvd. (Bayview Dr.) | 954-564-1370
Hollywood | 1212 N. State Rd. 7 (bet. Arthur & Garfield Sts.) |
954-961-1001
Pembroke Pines | Westfork Plaza | 15941 Pines Blvd. (160th Ave.) |
954-443-7440
Pembroke Pines | 9905 Pines Blvd. (bet. NW 98th & Palm Aves.) |
954-431-6883
Plantation | 7015 W. Broward Blvd. (NW 70th Ave.) | 954-584-4400
www.lasvegascubancuisine.com

After nearly 30 years, Antonia Vilariño's "family business" has become a "no-nonsense" chainlet specializing in "authentic" Cuban cuisine that reminds amigos of "going to lunch at grandma's"; the decor at early locations may be "uninspiring", but "there's a reason" these spots are "always crowded" – a "caring staff", "affordable prices" and "simple", "delicious" "home-cooked food."

	FOOD	DECOR	SERVICE	COST

Latitudes ● *Floribbean* | ▽ 18 | 21 | 17 | $38

Hollywood | Hollywood Beach Marriott | 2501 N. Ocean Dr. (Carolina St.) | 954-924-2202 | www.hollywoodbeachmarriott.com
"Sitting outside and watching the waves" may be the "best thing" about this "romantic" space at the Hollywood Beach Marriott, where the sun-weary can also enjoy the "lovely view" from inside; alas, "mediocre" Floribbean fare and service don't entice many, though the "wonderful vibe" is enough for some.

La Veranda *Italian* | 22 | 21 | 23 | $38

Pompano Beach | 2121 E. Atlantic Blvd. (N. Federal Hwy.) | 954-943-7390
"For a little old-world charm", "you can't beat" sitting "under the stars" in the "lovely garden" of this "romantic" Pompano Beacher, which dishes up "large portions" of "yummy" Italian fare to go with all that "atmosphere"; "friendly service" and "reasonable prices" are other reasons why locals "have loved" the place for 30-plus years.

Le Bistro Ⓜ *French* | 22 | 18 | 23 | $44

Lighthouse Point | Main Street Plaza | 4626 N. Federal Hwy. (bet. NE 44th & 48th Sts.) | 954-946-9240 | www.lebistrorestaurant.com
"These folks love what they do" say Lighthouse Pointers of this "sleeper in a strip mall", where chef Andy Trousdale uses only the "freshest seasonal ingredients" to create his "scrumptious" French fare (including a "lot of healthful options") and wife/co-owner Elin promotes a "friendly" atmosphere, abetted by "charming" decor and staffers; P.S. a post-Survey revamp added a wine and tapas bar.

ⓩ Lemongrass Asian Bistro *Asian* | 23 | 17 | 19 | $34

Ft. Lauderdale | 3811 N. Federal Hwy. (bet. 38th & 39th Sts.) | 954-564-4422 | www.lemongrassasianbistro.com
See review in Palm Beach Directory.

Le Tub ●⊟ *Burgers* | 21 | 14 | 11 | $22

Hollywood | 1100 N. Ocean Dr. (A1A) | 954-921-9425 | www.theletub.com
For "food with 'tude" (*GQ* and Oprah calling it the USA's best burger joint "a few years back" didn't help), Hollywooders head to this "funky" former gas station with a "sketchy tub and toilet decor" for what truly *are* "awesome" hamburgers; "don't go hungry", though: service is "surly" and "brutally slow" ("you can wait in excess of an hour" for your grub), so enjoy the "million-dollar view" of the Intracoastal while your appetite builds.

Lime Fresh Mexican Grill *Californian/Mexican* | 21 | 14 | 17 | $15

Coconut Creek | Promenade at Coconut Creek | 4425 Lyons Road (Wiles Rd.) | 954-586-2999
Pembroke Pines | The Shops at Pembroke Gardens | 601 SW 145th Terr. (Pines Blvd.) | 954-436-4700
www.limefreshmexicangrill.com
See review in Miami/Dade County Directory.

	FOOD	DECOR	SERVICE	COST

Little Havana *Cuban*
21 | 15 | 21 | $27

Deerfield Beach | 721 S. Federal Hwy. (SE 7th Ct.) | 954-427-6000 | www.littlehavanarestaurant.com
See review in Miami/Dade County Directory.

Lola's 🅜 *American*
24 | 21 | 24 | $43

Hollywood | 2032 Harrison St. (bet. S. 20th Ave. & Dixie Hwy) | 954-927-9851 | www.lolasonharrison.com
"Full bellies, big smiles and lots of praise" is often the end result at this "culinary star of Harrison Street" – chef-owner Michael Wagner's "sleek" but "unpretentious" Hollywood "destination", where "exquisitely fun" New American "comfort food" (e.g. "breathtaking" Coca-Cola BBQ ribs) and creative cocktails have diners "doing a happy dance"; an "outstanding" staff is rewarded by a much-improved Service score, and pragmatists take note: the place is "good for all kinds of budgets."

Lucille's American Café *American*
19 | 16 | 20 | $22

Weston | 2250 Weston Rd. (Commerce Pkwy.) | 954-384-9007 | www.lucillescafe.com
"Who can resist a classic meatloaf?" declare diner denizens who find this "upscale" version of a 1940s luncheonette the "perfect place" for American "comfort food" in Weston; "solid" and "affordable", it's a "good choice for families", and the "tiny muffins" that "come with the bill" are a "nice touch."

Madras Café *Indian*
20 | 11 | 16 | $26

Pompano Beach | Palm Plaza | 1434 S. Powerline Rd. (W. McNab Rd.) | 954-977-5434 | www.madrascafe.net
Few "wudda thought" you'd find "imaginative dishes from the subcontinent" in a "nowhere" Pompano Beach strip mall, but that's where the "local Indian population" heads when it wants "authentic", "delicious" fare (especially during the "great" lunch buffet); if some cynics snap the place is "totally lacking in atmosphere" and has "gotten pricey", more give it a "thumbs-up."

Mai-Kai *Chinese*
15 | 24 | 19 | $48

Ft. Lauderdale | 3599 N. Federal Hwy. (NE 37th St.) | 954-563-3272 | www.maikai.com
You'll want to "put on a grass skirt and jump into a volcano (in a good way)" at this Ft. Lauderdale "tiki haven", a '50s-era "kick" with "tropical kitsch" trappings, "campy cocktails" and an "awesome" "Polynesian floor show"; some pupu the "expensive" Cantonese-American chow, but even doubters admit it's the "ultimate tourist experience", so "go anyway" – well, "at least once."

Mama Mia Restaurant ❶ *Italian*
20 | 15 | 19 | $28

Hollywood | 1818 S. Young Circle (Harrison St.) | 954-923-0555 | www.miagrill.com
"Be prepared to share" the "huge portions" of "good, wholesome" Italian food at this "popular" eatery on Hollywood's Young Circle where you'll see the "whole neighborhood" noshing; though detrac-

FOOD DECOR SERVICE COST

tors dismiss it as just "ok", citing "inconsistent" fare and decor that "needs updating", few debate that prices are "reasonable."

Mancini's Ristorante Italiano *Italian*   22 | 19 | 21 | $51

Ft. Lauderdale | 1017 E. Las Olas Blvd. (SE 10th Terr.) | 954-764-5510 | www.mancinis1.com

Pastafarians get "hungry just thinking about" the "authentic" Northern Italian specialties at this "upscale" Ft. Lauderdale cafe, where scene-seekers "sit outside" and "watch the action on Las Olas"; if some contend it's "too costly", the "live music" hits all the right notes.

Mario the Baker *Italian/Pizza*   19 | 9 | 17 | $19

Hollywood | 7996 Pines Blvd. (S. University Dr.) | 954-983-8150

Sunrise | 2220 N. University Dr. (bet. Sunset Strip & W. Sunrise Blvd.) | 954-742-3333

www.mariothebakerpizza.com

See review in Miami/Dade County Directory.

Marumi Sushi ● *Japanese*   - | - | - | I

Plantation | 8271 W. Sunrise Blvd. (bet. Pine Island Rd. & University Dr.) | 954-318-4455 | www.marumisushi.com

Set in a simple Plantation storefront, this Japanese destination is known for authentic, adventurous, affordable cuisine; there's a full menu of sushi, sashimi and cooked dishes, of course, but check the specials board and don't miss the daily fresh catch, inasmuch as whole fish can be divided and prepared in various ways (including steamed, fried and grilled); P.S. open till 1:30 AM.

NEW Mason Jar *American*   - | - | - | M

Ft. Lauderdale | 2980 N. Federal Hwy. (bet. E. Oakland Park Blvd. & Federal Hwy.) | 954-568-4100 | www.themasonjarcafe.com

Fans saddened by the spring 2010 closing of Las Olas Café will be happy to that hear co-owner Paula Pace has moved to a new Ft. Lauderdale location, where she, business partner Scott Kraft and chef Ernesto Rado are offering upscale American comfort food (e.g. chicken pot pie, meatloaf) in a small storefront; P.S. beverages are served in mason jars, hence the name.

Mazza Mediterranean   ∇ 23 | 20 | 20 | $32
Cuisine *Greek/Lebanese*

Pembroke Pines | 15749 Pines Blvd. (bet. NE 155th Ave. & Westfork Plaza Way) | 954-436-9997 | www.mazzarestaurant.net

Spanakopita-seekers in Pembroke Pines head to this "neighborhood favorite" for "excellent" Greek-Lebanese fare in a modest storefront; "friendly service" seals the deal.

Melting Pot *Fondue*   20 | 19 | 21 | $43

Ft. Lauderdale | 1135 N. Federal Hwy. (E. Sunrise Blvd.) | 954-568-1581

Coral Springs | 10374 W. Sample Rd. (bet. Coral Springs & NW 101st Ave.) | 954-755-6368

Cooper City | Countryside Shops | 5834 S. Flamingo Rd. (bet. Stirling Rd. & SW 55th St.) | 954-880-0808

www.meltingpot.com

See review in Palm Beach County Directory.

	FOOD	DECOR	SERVICE	COST

Moon Thai Restaurant *Thai* | 23 | 15 | 19 | $26 |

Coral Springs | 9637 Westview Dr. (bet. NW 98th Ln. &
N. University Dr.) | 954-752-4899
Weston | 2818 Weston Rd. (S. Commerce Pkwy.) | 954-384-7275
www.moonthai.com
See review in Miami/Dade County Directory.

☑ Morton's The Steakhouse *Steak* | 25 | 23 | 24 | $69 |

Ft. Lauderdale | 500 E. Broward Blvd. (bet. SE 3rd Ave. & S. Federal Hwy.) |
954-467-9720 | www.mortons.com
See review in Palm Beach Directory.

Mustard Seed ☑ *American/Eclectic* | – | – | – | M |

Cooper City | 8616 Griffin Rd. (Pine Island Rd.) | 954-252-0002
NEW **Plantation** | 256 S. University Dr. (W. Broward Blvd.) |
954-533-9326
www.mustardseedbistro.com
Fans are following Timothy and Lara Boyd to their third dining venture, a cozy Cooper City nook with whimsical decor, a midpriced Eclectic-American menu that changes weekly and a boutique-heavy wine list; despite a humble location in a strip mall, it's a hot reservation; P.S. a Plantation outpost with a small market opened post-Survey.

My Big Fat Greek Restaurant *Greek* | 20 | 13 | 19 | $26 |

Dania Beach | 3445 Griffin Rd. (SW 34th Terr.) | Dania | 954-961-5030 |
www.mbfgr.com
"Waiters dance and sing" and "iguanas bask in the trees" of this waterfront Greek in Dania Beach with "huge portions" of "reliable" chow, "quick service" and "low prices"; all in all, it's a "fun" "escape", as long as you "don't go for the decor" and ignore the "cheesy name."

Myung Ga Tofu & BBQ *Korean*   ▽ | 21 | 12 | 20 | $24 |

Weston | Shoppes of Weston | 1944 Weston Rd.
(N. Corporate Lakes Blvd.) | 954-349-7337
To truly "enjoy the authentic Korean cuisine" at this Westonite, "order a little bit of everything", including tofu casseroles and "lots of sides"; the place "needs atmosphere", but since the fare comes courtesy of "attentive" staffers, the biggest gripe is its far-off locale.

Noodles Panini *Italian* | 23 | 17 | 19 | $32 |

Ft. Lauderdale | 821 E. Las Olas Blvd. (bet. SE 8th & 9th Aves.) |
954-462-1514 | www.noodlespaninirestaurant.com
Get the "pasta with red sauce" and "huge meatballs" when you join the "ladies who lunch" at this "small but charming" Italian "in the heart" of Las Olas; pragmatists warn the "limited menu" is a "little pricey", but most overlook that and enjoy the "happening" scene from the patio – even if it's "hard to avoid the tourists."

North Ocean Grill *Seafood/Steak*   ▽ | 18 | 19 | 18 | $39 |

Ft. Lauderdale | Pelican Beach Resort | 2000 N. Ocean Blvd.
(N. Atlantic Blvd.) | 954-568-9431 | www.pelicanbeach.com
"Eat outside" on the old-fashioned "country porch" and soak in the ocean views at this surf 'n' turfer in Ft. Lauderdale's Pelican Beach

	FOOD	DECOR	SERVICE	COST

Resort that's popular for its "early-bird dinner" and family-friendly amenities (kids' menu, crayons, etc.); alas, dissatisfied surveyors say "boring food" and "pricey" tabs trump the "convenient" digs.

Oceans 234 *Seafood*

18	20	18	$37

Deerfield Beach | 234 N. Ocean Blvd. (NE 2nd St.) | 954-428-2539 | www.oceans234.com

"It's on the beach, baby", so "sit out back" and "watch the bikinis walk by" while you "chow down" on "surprisingly good" seafood; throw in a "cold mojito", though, and even critics concede "you can't help but enjoy yourself" at this "relaxing" Deerfield Beacher; P.S. there's now sushi to savor as well.

Old Florida Seafood House *Seafood*

21	12	21	$36

Wilton Manors | 1414 NE 26th St. (bet. Dixie Hwy. & NE 16th Ave.) | 954-566-1044 | www.oldflaseafood.com

Ok, it's a "little worn", but "that's alright" declare devotees of this Wilton Manors "classic" that's been serving up "hearty portions" of "fresh" fin fare (including "lots of fried seafood") for more than 30 years; while young 'uns yap about an "older crowd" amassing for the "great early-bird specials", "reasonable prices" and "first-rate service" reel in fans who sigh it "doesn't get more traditional than this."

Old Heidelberg *German*

-	-	-	M

Ft. Lauderdale | 900 State Rd. 84 (SW 9th Ave.) | 954-463-6747 | www.oldheidelbergdeli.com

Put some oomph in your oompah-pah at this Ft. Lauderdale German where it's always Oktoberfest, particularly since dishes like schnitzel, veal shank and knockwurst fill the affordable menu; throw in imported beer, traditional decor (beer steins, wood accents), weekend music and an affable staff, and you've got a real party.

Original Pancake House, The *American*

20	11	17	$17

Ft. Lauderdale | 2851 N. Federal Hwy. (bet. NE 26th St. & Oakland Park Blvd.) | 954-564-8881
Coral Springs | 10599 W. Atlantic Blvd. (bet. Coral Springs & University Dr.) | 954-255-8080
Davie | 6650 Dykes Rd. (bet. Sheridan St. & Stirling Rd.) | 954-272-0825
Plantation | 8460 W. Broward Blvd. (bet. N. Pine Island Rd. & NW 84th Ave.) | 954-473-2771
www.originalpancakehouse.com
See review in Miami/Dade County Directory.

Outback Steakhouse *Steak*

17	15	18	$30

Ft. Lauderdale | 1801 SE 10th Ave. (SE 17th St.) | 954-523-5600
Ft. Lauderdale | 6201 N. Federal Hwy. (NE 62nd St.) | 954-771-4390
Coral Springs | 650 Riverside Dr. (bet. W. Atlantic Blvd. & Ramblewood Dr.) | 954-345-5965
Pembroke Pines | 7841 Pines Blvd. (N. University Dr.) | 954-981-5300
Plantation | 1823B N. Pine Island Rd. (Sunrise Blvd.) | 954-370-9956
www.outback.com
See review in Miami/Dade County Directory.

	FOOD	DECOR	SERVICE	COST

Padrino's *Cuban*

20	14	19	$25

Hallandale | 2500 E. Hallandale Beach Blvd. (S. Ocean Dr.) | 954-456-4550

Plantation | Fountains Shoppes of Distinction | 801 S. University Dr. (SW 78th Ave.) | 954-476-5777

www.padrinos.com

See review in Palm Beach County Directory.

Paul Bakery *Bakery/Sandwiches*

18	16	13	$20

Sunrise | Colonnade Outlets | 1800 Sawgrass Mills Circle (Sunrise Blvd.) | 954-846-0344 | www.paulusa.com

See review in Miami/Dade County Directory.

Pelican Landing *Eclectic*

∇ 18	19	18	$33

Ft. Lauderdale | Hyatt Regency Pier 66 | 2301 SE 17th St. (23rd Ave.) | 954-525-6666 | www.pier66.com

Simply "watching the yachts go by on the Intracoastal" floats many a boat at this midpriced Eclectic at the Hyatt Regency Pier, and even the waterfront ramble to get there "adds to the fun"; there's a "limited menu" of "sandwiches, salads" and some of the "best fish tacos around", but most "go for the view."

☑ P.F. Chang's China Bistro *Chinese*

21	21	20	$33

Ft. Lauderdale | The Galleria | 2418 E. Sunrise Blvd. (NE 24th Ave.) | 954-565-5877

Sunrise | Sawgrass Mills | 1740 Sawgrass Mills Circle (W. Sunrise Blvd.) | 954-845-1113

www.pfchangs.com

See review in Miami/Dade County Directory.

Pho Hoa *Vietnamese*

∇ 23	11	16	$18

Tamarac | 5435 N. State Rd. 7 (W. 53rd St.) | 954-739-9888 | www.phohoa.com

Fans of Vietnam's famed noodle soup will find "big bowls" of "every kind of regional pho" and a "huge menu" of other specialties at this Tamarac chain link whose "quick" servers are always "happy to have you as a guest"; "don't be put off by the decor", though – just "sit, eat and enjoy" the "fresh, delicious" fare.

Pho 78 *Vietnamese*

∇ 17	9	15	$15

Pembroke Pines | 7849 Pines Blvd. (bet. N. University Dr. & 78th Terr.) | 954-989-6770

It's basically decor-free, but pho-natics say go for the "filling" portions of "traditional beef soup" and other "exotic" Vietnamese fare at this Pembroke Pines strip-maller; maybe some have "had better", but the fact that it's "easy on the wallet" pulls in penny-pinchers.

Pier Top Restaurant Ⓜ *American*

-	-	-	VE

Ft. Lauderdale | Hyatt Regency Pier 66 | 2301 SE 17th St. (23rd Ave.) | 954-728-3530 | www.piertop.com

For more than four decades, visitors have been taking a spin around the "fun" glass-enclosed lounge atop the Hyatt Regency Pier 66, where "nothing beats the 360-degree view" of Ft. Lauderdale "from up high"; but now that Sunday brunch is part of the picture, the ever-changing panorama can be enjoyed with an all-you-can-eat "gourmet" American spread and bottomless mimosas.

Pizza Rustica ⚫ *Pizza* 21 | 8 | 14 | $14

Ft. Lauderdale | 3327 E. Oakland Park Blvd. (Ocean Blvd.) | 954-567-2992
Hollywood | 1928 Hollywood Blvd. (bet. S. 19th & 20th Aves.) | 954-923-3878
www.pizza-rustica.com
See review in Miami/Dade County Directory.

Primavera *Italian* 22 | 16 | 20 | $44

Oakland Park | Primavera Plaza | 830 E. Oakland Park Blvd. (NE 8th Terr.) | 954-564-6363 | www.trueitalian.com
Chef-owner Giacomo Dresseno "cares about his customers", which may explain why this "small" Northern Italian has prospered for more than 25 years "hidden" in an Oakland Park strip mall; though a few suggest its "glory days" are behind it, *paesani* praise the "reasonable prices" and insist "you'll never leave hungry or disappointed"; P.S. recent renovations may outdate the Decor score.

Z Rainbow Palace *Chinese* 26 | 23 | 26 | $57

Ft. Lauderdale | 2787 E. Oakland Park Blvd. (Bayview Dr.) | 954-565-5652 | www.rainbowpalace.com
"Make no mistake", this "elegant" Ft. Lauderdale "splurge" "is no ordinary Chinese restaurant", as evident by the "mouthwatering" cuisine (including "out-of-this-world dumplings"), "tuxedo-clad servers" who are "as professional as they come" and extensive wine list; natch, the "terrific-all-around" experience may give you "sticker shock", but loyalists agree it's "worth" the "big bucks."

RA Sushi *Japanese* 19 | 22 | 17 | $32

Pembroke Pines | 201 SW 145th Terr. (142nd Ave.) | 954-342-5454 | www.rasushi.com
See review in Palm Beach County Directory.

Rivals Waterfront Sports Grille *American* ∇ 16 | 16 | 14 | $32

Hollywood | Westin Diplomat Resort | 3460 S. Ocean Dr. (E. Hallandale Beach Blvd.) | 954-602-8760 | www.rivalshollywood.com
"If you want to watch sports" within eyeshot of "perfect" Intracoastal views, there are "more TVs than you can imagine" at this upscale Hollywood haven in the Westin Diplomat Resort; though some cry foul over "average" American grub and "slow service", the "amazing Kobe sliders" and truffle fries are a hit on game days.

Roasted Pepper, The M *Italian* 22 | 17 | 22 | $30

Pembroke Pines | 9893 Pines Blvd. (N. Palm Ave.) | 954-450-8800 | www.theroastedpepper.com
Good news: the garlic rolls "are guaranteed to keep the vampires away" at this "noisy" Pembroke Pines perennial that "gives you that old Italian family feel"; then again, 10-ounce martinis, "good prices" and "huge portions" of "delicious" dishes bathed in "red sauce" attract everyone else; P.S. there's "live entertainment" on weekends.

	FOOD	DECOR	SERVICE	COST

Runyon's *Continental*

24 | 18 | 23 | $52

Coral Springs | 9810 W. Sample Rd. (bet. Coral Hills Dr. & NW 99th Way) | 954-752-2333 | www.runyonsofcoralsprings.com

The "Old Faithful of Coral Springs", this "pricey" Continental snags praise for its "ample portions" of beef "done just right", "knowledge-able" staff and nightly shows in the piano bar; if it's "showing its age", the "same old, same old is probably what makes regulars return."

Rustic Inn Crabhouse *Seafood*

22 | 14 | 18 | $36

Ft. Lauderdale | 4331 Anglers Ave. (bet. Griffin Rd. & SW 42nd St.) | 954-584-1637 | www.rusticinn.com

Get crackin' squeal surveyors who "put on bibs" and "hammer away" at the "succulent" garlic crabs at this "ticky-tacky rustic" seafooder; sure, it "can be pricey", but after 55 years, it's still a Ft. Lauderdale "must" – as long as you "don't go with a headache", "wear good clothes" or mind dining on tables covered with white butcher paper.

⚡ Ruth's Chris Steak House *Steak*

25 | 22 | 24 | $65

Ft. Lauderdale | 2525 N. Federal Hwy. (bet. Oakland Park & Sunrise Blvds.) | 954-565-2338 | www.ruthschris.com
See review in Miami/Dade County Directory.

Sage French American Café *French*

22 | 18 | 21 | $38

Ft. Lauderdale | Regions Shopping Plaza | 2378 N. Federal Hwy. (NE 21th St.) | 954-565-2299

Sage Hollywood *French*

Hollywood | 2000 Harrison St. (20th Ave.) | 954-391-9466
www.sagecafe.net

After more than two decades as a Ft. Lauderdale Francophile "favor-ite", this "cozy" cafe now shares the spotlight with an "attractive" Hollywood sib sporting "updated" decor, an "upscale raw bar" and a louder din; happily, both feature chef-owner Laurent Tasic's "comfort-ing" "country French" fare, "efficient service" and "reasonable" tabs.

Saigon Cuisine *Vietnamese*

– | – | – | I

Margate | 1394 N. State Rd. 7 (Coconut Creek Pkwy.) | 954-975-2426 | www.saigoncuisineflorida.com

Dine amid colorful works created by a Vietnamese artist at this Margate spot whose extensive menu features affordable banh mi (Vietnamese sandwiches), pho and an array of regional specialties; bonus: there's live jazz Saturday nights.

Saint Tropez *French*

– | – | – | M

Ft. Lauderdale | 1010 E. Las Olas Blvd. (SE 10th Terr.) | 954-767-1073
Listen to Edith Piaf while you savor "truly French" dishes at this "lit-tle gem" on Las Olas; the menu is "limited", but "generous portions" and "fine service" make most "happy."

Saito's Japanese Steakhouse *Japanese/Steak*

21 | 18 | 21 | $32

Coconut Creek | Promenade at Coconut Creek | 4443 Lyons Rd. (Wiles Rd.) | 954-582-9888 | www.saitosteakhouse.com
See review in Palm Beach County Directory.

Saxsay *Peruvian*

| | - | - | - | I |

Sunrise | 9160 W. Commercial Blvd. (bet. 91st & 94th Aves.) | 954-746-5099

Tile floors and wood-topped tables set the stage for well-priced Peruvian cuisine at this Sunriser, where you can watch cooks prepare authentic dishes like ceviche, tripe stew and *lomo saltado* (salted tenderloin); end your meal with such delicacies as *suspiro a la limeña*, a creamy confection "as soft and sweet as a Lima woman's sigh."

Seafood World Ⓜ *Seafood*

| | 22 | 13 | 20 | $36 |

Lighthouse Point | Main Street Plaza | 4602 N. Federal Hwy. (¾ mi. north of Sample Rd.) | 954-942-0740 | www.seafood-world.com

"You gotta love the chowdah" (both New England and conch) at this "unassuming" Lighthouse Pointer known for its "well-prepared" Bahamian-style specialties; there's "no real atmosphere", but the attached "take-out market" means you "can be assured" of getting some of the "freshest seafood in Broward."

🅉 Seasons 52 *American*

| | 23 | 24 | 23 | $41 |

Ft. Lauderdale | Galleria Mall | 2428 E. Sunrise Blvd. (Bayview Dr.) | 954-537-1052 | www.seasons52.com

It "feels so virtuous" eating at this "wholesome" chain ("all items under 475 calories, no butter or trans fats"), the "perfect marriage" of "healthful dining, fine service" and a "beautiful", "Frank Lloyd Wright"-ish setting; the "seasonal" New American fare uses "only the freshest ingredients", while a "top-shelf wine selection" and "way cool" desserts that come in "shot glasses" seal its rep as a "real winner"; P.S. the waterside seating at the Palm Beach Gardens locale is "gorgeous."

Serafina *Italian*

| | ▽ 21 | 21 | 21 | $48 |

Ft. Lauderdale | 926 NE 20th Ave. (Sunrise Blvd.) | 954-463-2566 | www.serabythewater.com

The "excellent" cuisine, "charming" staff and "fabulous surroundings" at this "small", candlelit trattoria "make you feel as if you're in Italy", though it's actually "one of the most romantic settings" in Ft. Lauderdale; beware, however, if you snag a table on the "intimate" terrace overlooking the Middle River: "you may not want to leave."

Sette Bello *Italian*

| | ▽ 27 | 23 | 27 | $45 |

Ft. Lauderdale | 6241 N. Federal Hwy. (NE 62nd St.) | 954-351-0505 | www.settebellofla.com

"*Magnifico!*" exclaim enthusiasts of this casual Ft. Lauderdale Italian with a 200-label wine list, a bevy of Roman arches and a "friendly" chef-owner, Franco Filippone (ex Casa D'Angelo), who "cooks like he's cooking for his own family"; it's a "new favorite" of supporters who sigh "these folks are really trying . . . and it's working."

Shorty's Bar-B-Q *BBQ*

| | 19 | 12 | 18 | $20 |

Deerfield Beach | 120 S. Powerline Rd. (W. Hillsboro Blvd.) | 954-596-2448
Davie | 5989 S. University Dr. (Stirling Rd.) | 954-680-9900
www.shortys.com

See review in Miami/Dade County Directory.

	FOOD	DECOR	SERVICE	COST

Shula's on the Beach *Steak*

| | 21 | 20 | 21 | $62 |

Ft. Lauderdale | Westin Beach Resort | 321 N. Ft. Lauderdale Beach Blvd. (A1A) | 954-355-4000 | www.donshula.com
See review in Miami/Dade County Directory.

Siam Cuisine *Thai*

| | ▽ 20 | 19 | 21 | $31 |

Wilton Manors | 2010 Wilton Dr. (NE 20th St.) | 954-564-3411 | www.siamcuisineflorida.com

A "pioneer" of "authentic" Siamese in Broward, this "comfortable" Wilton Manors space continues to churn out "some of the best Thai food in the area", plus a full menu of sushi and sashimi options; it's "not much on atmosphere", but "value" pricing and a "fun" staff keep it "hopping."

☑ Silver Pond ◑ *Chinese*

| | 25 | 10 | 16 | $31 |

Lauderdale Lakes | 4285 N. State Rd. 7 (south of Commercial Blvd.) | 954-486-8885

It's the "real deal" – "just look at the Asian clientele" dining at this "always packed" Lauderdale Lakes strip-maller with an "extensive" selection of "authentic Hong Kong–style Chinese food" that's "not for the faint of heart" (i.e. "no chow mein here"); "indifferent service" and "remodel"-ready digs aside, admirers agree "there isn't a bad dish on the menu"; P.S. "go with a group" so you can share.

NEW SoLita *Italian*

| | - | - | - | M |

Ft. Lauderdale | 1032 E. Las Olas Blvd. (SE 11th Ave.) | 954-357-2616 | www.solitalasolas.com

A black-granite bar with a glowing violet wall, crystal chandeliers and cozy couches signal that patrons are in for a mix of traditional and contemporary at this see-and-be-seen Italian set in the former home of Mark's Las Olas; sweet-pepper poppers, chicken parm and housemade meatballs are highlights, while live jazz on Tuesdays adds to the buzzy vibe.

Sorella Ristorante *Italian*

| | - | - | - | I |

Pembroke Pines | 15933 Pines Blvd. (160th Ave.) | 954-620-1125 | www.sorellaristorante.com

The Vilariños, the family behind the popular Las Vegas and Vila chainlets, have moved beyond their usual Cuban and Mexican menus to launch their first Italian entry; located in a Pembroke Pines storefront, the casual, family-friendly space offers a wide range of traditional fare (including pizza) at prices that won't break the bank.

Southport Raw Bar ◑ *Seafood*

| | 19 | 13 | 17 | $22 |

Ft. Lauderdale | 1536 Cordova Rd. (bet. SE 15th & 16th Sts.) | 954-525-2526 | www.southportrawbar.com

"Come with the kids, the grandkids, the neighbors" and "don't bother to change" into fancy duds for this "friendly" Ft. Lauderdale "dive" luring locals for 38 years; it's "no-frills", natch, but it's "fun" watching "boats come in from the Intracoastal", and the "inexpensive" seafood includes some of the "best clam chowder south of Cape Cod."

	FOOD	DECOR	SERVICE	COST

Steak 954 *Steak*
▽ 24 | 28 | 20 | $76

Ft. Lauderdale | W Ft. Lauderdale | 401 N. Ft. Lauderdale Beach Blvd. (Bayshore Dr.) | 954-414-8333 | www.steak954.com

If you "want to impress your date", grab the "gold Amex" and head to this "romantic" spot in the oceanfront W Ft. Lauderdale for steak and seafood; it's part of Stephen Starr's empire (Buddakan and Morimoto in Philly and NYC, et al.), so expect memorable decor inside and out, including a "15-ft.-long jellyfish tank that's pretty wicked."

Stir Crazy *Asian*
20 | 18 | 18 | $26

Pembroke Pines | The Shops at Pembroke Gardens | 14571 SW Fifth St. (off Pines Blvd.) | 954-919-4900 | www.stircrazy.com

Kids flip for these "gimmicky but tasty" Pan-Asian chain links in Pembroke Pines and Boca – "order off the menu" or "create your own" meal by picking from a lineup of "fresh ingredients" that are then "stir-fried up"; detractors deride the "noisy" setting and sniff "what's the big deal?", but "good prices" make this a wok star for the thrifty.

Sublime Ⓜ *Vegan*
22 | 24 | 22 | $36

Ft. Lauderdale | 1431 N. Federal Hwy. (bet. 13th St. & 14th Ct.) | 954-615-1431 | www.sublimerestaurant.com

"Who knew vegan food could be so sexy?" say satisfied surveyors who dine amid the 10-ft. waterfalls and Peter Max artwork at this "beautiful" Ft. Lauderdale destination where "even carnivores" enjoy the "fresh, well-seasoned" "meatless eats"; some skeptics scowl it's "pricey" and "a bit pretentious", but all in all, it's *the* place to eat your vegetables"; P.S. proceeds go "directly to an animal welfare society."

Sugar Reef *Caribbean*
22 | 21 | 21 | $37

Hollywood | 600 N. Surf Rd. (bet. Fillmore & New York Sts.) | 954-922-1119 | www.sugarreefgrill.com

"You'd never guess" that this "funky" "fish shack" "smack dab on the Boardwalk" in Hollywood is a "temple of fine dining" – that is, until you dig into chef/co-owner Patrick Farnault's "fresh, tasty and attractively prepared" French-themed Caribbean cuisine; "friendly service", "fun" people-watching and the "ocean view make it even better."

Sukhothai *Thai*
23 | 18 | 24 | $28

Ft. Lauderdale | Gateway Shopping Ctr. | 1930 E. Sunrise Blvd. (Federal Hwy.) | 954-764-0148 | www.sukhothaiflorida.com

"Am I in Bangkok?" query connoisseurs of this "neighborhood favorite" where "charming" owner Susie Komolsane and son Eddie Watana provide a "comfortable" atmosphere and "consistently tasty" Thai fare; despite its location in Ft. Lauderdale's "unassuming" Gateway Shopping Center, "big portions, low prices and great service" give it "staying power."

Sunfish Grill Ⓢ Ⓜ *American/Seafood*
24 | 20 | 22 | $56

Ft. Lauderdale | 2761 E. Oakland Park Blvd. (bet. Bayview Dr. & NE 27th Ave.) | 954-564-6464 | www.sunfishgrill.com

Though longtime toque Anthony Sindaco is gone, fans insist chef-owner Erika Di Battista's "innovative" New American seafooder in

| | FOOD | DECOR | SERVICE | COST |

Ft. Lauderdale is still "terrific", citing "outstanding fish" that's "creatively presented", "desserts like no other" and "friendly service"; still, a few nostalgists prefer its "quainter" former home, suggesting it "may have grown too big for its britches", with prices to match.

Sushi Blues Cafe *Eclectic*

| 23 | 19 | 21 | $34 |

Hollywood | 2009 Harrison St. (bet. Dixie Hwy. & 20th Ave.) | 954-929-9560 | www.sushiblues.com

At this "funky" Downtown Hollywood "mainstay", weekend blues and jazz duet with "inventive" raw-fin fare ("combining papaya and eel in a sushi roll gets an A+ in my book"); add in "tasty" Asian-inflected Eclectic cuisine, "out-of-this-world drinks" and a "welcoming staff", and no wonder it "hasn't lost a beat" after 20 years.

Su Shin Thai *Japanese/Thai*

| ∇ 23 | 17 | 20 | $32 |

Lauderhill | 4595 N. University Dr. (44th St.) | 954-741-2569 | www.sushinthai.net

"Consistently good" sushi is still the big fish at this "pleasant" Lauderhill Japanese, though its owners have "added Thai food" to the mix; while some say the changes mean the place "doesn't have the personality" it once did, fans avow they're "never disappointed."

Tarantella Ristorante *Italian*

| ∇ 24 | 21 | 23 | $33 |

Weston | Weston Town Ctr. | 1755 Bell Tower Ln. (Main St.) | 954-349-3004 | www.tarantellas.net

Named for the lively folk dance of Southern Italy, this "straightforward" Weston Town Center trattoria wins plaudits for its "large portions" of "consistently good" chow; it's also "family-friendly", so beware: the dining room – awash in Sicilian furniture and hand-painted tiles – can be a "zoo" on busy weekend nights.

Tarpon Bend *Seafood*

| 18 | 17 | 17 | $29 |

Ft. Lauderdale | 200 SW Second St. (SE 2nd Ave.) | 954-523-3233 | www.tarponbend.com

See review in Miami/Dade County Directory.

Tatiana Cabaret
Restaurant ● *Continental/Russian*

| - | - | - | E |

Hallandale | 1710 E. Hallandale Beach Blvd. (bet. Layne Blvd. & 16th Ave.) | 954-454-1222 | www.fltatianarestaurant.com

One look at the well-heeled patrons, Murano glass chandeliers and gold-leaf ceilings at this "pricey" Hallandale supper club, and you'll think "you've walked into a wedding" (indeed, many are held here); beyond nuptials, though, there's a large menu of "good" Continental-Russian fare, dancing into the wee hours and weekend cabaret.

Taverna Opa ● *Greek*

| 19 | 16 | 17 | $37 |

Hollywood | 410 N. Ocean Dr. (bet. Arizona & Taylor Sts.) | 954-929-4010 | www.tavernaopa.com

"Dance on the table", "throw napkins", "sing" and "drink ouzo" – you're in for a "fun night" at these "wild and crazy" Greeks; sure, "it's a party every time you go", but don't forget about the "decent" Hellenic fare, and arrive "early" if you "don't want all that noise."

	FOOD	DECOR	SERVICE	COST

Taverna Yiamas *Mediterranean* ▽ 15 | 13 | 16 | $26

Hollywood | 1948 Hollywood Blvd. (bet. 19th & 20th Aves.) |
954-925-1001

"Nightly belly dancing" and hookahs have been added to the mix at
this Downtown Hollywooder, a former Greek eatery now dishing out
"hearty portions" of "tasty" Med fare; just "allow time to enjoy the
food", because service can be "slow"; P.S. outside seating available.

☑ Thai Spice *Thai* 26 | 21 | 24 | $36

Ft. Lauderdale | 1514 E. Commercial Blvd. (bet. NE 13th Ave. &
NE 15th Terr.) | 954-771-4535 | www.thaispicefla.com

"When they say hot, they mean hot" at this "upscale" Ft. Lauderdale
strip-maller that heat-seekers turn to for some of the "best Thai
food in town"; patrons choose from a "varied menu" or a "long list of
daily specials", whisked to tables by "attentive" staffers who dart
among three "pretty" dining rooms and "colorful fish tanks."

☒ 3030 Ocean *American/Seafood* 25 | 22 | 24 | $55

Ft. Lauderdale | Harbor Beach Marriott Resort & Spa | 3030 Holiday Dr.
(Seabreeze Blvd.) | 954-765-3030 | www.3030ocean.com

"In a sea of generic hotel restaurants", this "elegant" New American
in the Marriott on Ft. Lauderdale beach "stands out" with its "inventive", "consistently excellent" seafood from chef Dean Max and
"professional service"; if a few aesthetes aver its "lobby" locale
"leaves a lot to be desired", most deem it a "good catch."

III Forks *Seafood/Steak* 23 | 23 | 22 | $63

NEW **Hallandale** | Village at Gulfstream Park | 501 Silks Run
(bet. Hallandale Beach Blvd. & U.S. 1) | 954-457-3920 | www.iiiforks.com
See review in Palm Beach County Directory.

Timpano Chophouse *Italian/Steak* 21 | 22 | 21 | $49

Ft. Lauderdale | 450 E. Las Olas Blvd. (SE 3rd Ave.) | 954-462-9119 |
www.timpanochophouse.net

"Try to get a booth" and "don't miss the mussels" at this "lively" Italian
chophouse in Ft. Lauderdale, a "home away from home" for "snowbirds who miss their favorite steak and martini" meccas; it can be
"expensive" and "noisy", but the "signature drinks", "friendly service" and "Sinatra-era ambiance" usually "make for a fun night."

T-Mex Cantina ● *Mexican* ▽ 23 | 13 | 19 | $15

Ft. Lauderdale | 204 SW Second St. (SW 2nd Ave.) | 954-463-2003 |
www.t-mex.net
See review in Miami/Dade County Directory.

Toa Toa Chinese Restaurant & Authentic Dim Sum *Chinese* - | - | - | I

Sunrise | Pine Plaza | 4145 NW 88th Ave. (Pine Island Rd.) |
954-746-8833

Devotees searching for dim sum inevitably find their way to this
Sunrise spot that features more than 50 handmade buns, potstick-
ers and other bites; for heartier appetites, there's a full Chinese
menu; P.S. closed Wednesdays.

| | FOOD | DECOR | SERVICE | COST |

Continental with "yummy" fare; it's "popular", so it can get too "cozy", but a "staff that couldn't be sweeter" and "wonderful" wines take the edge off.

Vigneto's Italian Grill *Italian*   22 | 16 | 22 | $30

Weston | 1342 SW 160th Ave. (Indian Terr.) | 954-660-0470
Plantation | 1663 S. University Dr. (bet. Peters Rd. & Rte. 84) | 954-915-0806
www.vignetos.com

A "step up from most neighborhood pasta joints", this "popular" midpriced duo provides "large portions" of "consistent, simple" Italian fare that tastes like *"nonna* is in the back"; if surveyors give Plantation's food and service a slight edge over Weston's, even *paesani* say both would do well to "improve decor."

Village Grille *American*   23 | 20 | 23 | $30

Lauderdale-by-the-Sea | 4404 El Mar Dr. (Commercial Blvd.) | 954-776-5092 | www.villagegrille.com

Lauderdale-by-the-Sea locals "pack" this airy spot near the beach, and the "consistently good" American eats – including "wonderful breakfasts" (a "deal") – are only part of the reason; there's also live music, "friendly service" and a choice of seating: "outside for a view of the action or inside in comfortable booths."

Village Tavern *American*   20 | 20 | 20 | $32

Pembroke Pines | 14555 SW Second St. (SW 145th Ave.) | 954-874-1001 | www.villagetavern.com

"Surprisingly good for a chain", these Pembroke Pines and Boynton Americans are pleasing wallet-watchers with an "expansive" menu that "covers a full range of price points", plus a "half-priced wine night" (Wednesday); it can get "noisy", but "spacious dining areas, comfortable seating" and "enthusiastic" service make the clatter "bearable."

Villagio *Italian*   20 | 20 | 20 | $39

NEW **Sunrise** | Colonnade Outlets | 1760 Sawgrass Mills Circle (Sunrise Blvd.) | 954-846-2176
See review in Miami/Dade County Directory.

Viva Chile *Chilean*   - | - | - | I

Davie | 6013 Stirling Rd. (bet. 58th & 61st Aves.) | 954-581-8138
Chileans – and fans searching for the country's flavorful fare – head to this Davie nook for homey dishes like pastel de choclo (similar to shepherd's pie) and empanadas; the small, simply decorated restaurant ratchets things up on Saturday nights, when it offers music.

Whale Raw Bar & Fish House *New England*   16 | 14 | 16 | $26

Parkland | 7619 N. State Rd. 7 (bet. Marina Blvds. & W. Hillsboro) | 954-345-9190 | www.thewhalerawbar.com
It's no fluke fans flip over the "outdoor tables" at this Parkland seafooder, as they provide a "pleasant place" to dig into New England–style fin fare; but thar be many a dissident who blubber about "average food and service", "poor decor" (including a suspended orca) and an overall feeling that there's "nothing really distinguishing" here.

	FOOD	DECOR	SERVICE	COST

Whale's Rib, The *Seafood*

| | 21 | 14 | 20 | $27 |

Deerfield Beach | 2031 NE Second St. (A1A) | 954-421-8880

"Tourists feel like locals" at this "divey" Deerfield Beach "seafood shack" where the "inexpensive" "fresh fish", "cold beer" and "excellent whale fries" (i.e. "homemade potato chips") snare sun-lovers who arrive "straight from the beach"; indeed, "no place is less casual or noisier", so "come in your T-shirt and sandals" to truly fit in; P.S. it was featured on the Food Network's *Diners, Drive-ins and Dives.*

Wild East Asian Bistro *Asian*

| | 22 | 20 | 20 | $37 |

Ft. Lauderdale | 1200 E. Las Olas Blvd. (SE 12th Ave.) | 954-828-1888 | www.wildeastbistro.com

It's a "bit hidden", but that's one reason loyalists "love" this "classy" Las Olas Pan-Asian on the Himmarshee Canal; while a few fuss it's "not as good as it was", "creative" eats that come in a "feast of flavors" and "flights of sake" satisfy most, and the "gondolas passing by" make the serene setting even more "delightful"; P.S. check out the new Asian tapas menu.

Wine Cellar Ⓜ *Continental*

| | 19 | 18 | 19 | $31 |

Ft. Lauderdale | LA Shops Plaza | 199 E. Oakland Park Blvd. (N. Andrews Ave.) | 954-565-9021

Lola the cockatoo greets guests at this '70s-era Ft. Lauderdale Continental known for its "tasty" German and Hungarian cuisine and "campy" decor (including an on-site "aviary"); "early birds" hunting for "great deals" can also be found here, though they're often shooed out "so the next wave of bargain-eaters can come in"; P.S. also closed Tuesdays.

Woodlands *Indian*

| | ▽ 23 | 15 | 20 | $23 |

Lauderhill | Blvd. | 4816 N. University Dr. (47th St.) | 954-749-3221 | www.woodlandsus.com

"Excellent dosas" and other "traditional" South Indian cuisine sate heat-seekers and the meat-averse alike at this no-frills Lauderhill "vegetarian paradise"; service that's "better than fancier joints" and "affordable" prices make it a "good choice" for "casual dining."

YOLO *American*

| | 21 | 24 | 21 | $43 |

Ft. Lauderdale | 333 E. Las Olas Blvd. (3rd Ave.) | 954-523-1000 | www.yolorestaurant.com

With a "fab scene" as scorching "hot" as the "outdoor fire pits" on its "exquisite" patio lounge, this "handsome", "newish" creation from the Tarpon Bend team is "drawing Ferraris" – and the "beautiful people" who drive them – "like ants to sugar"; the midpriced American fare and "attractive" staff get mixed marks, however, with a fair share claiming both "aren't on par with the cool surroundings"; P.^ its name is short for 'You Only Live Once.'

STEAKHOUSES

26 Chops Lobster
Capital Grille

Abe & Louie's
25 New York Prime
Ruth's Chris

BY SPECIAL FEATURE

BRUNCH

27 Café Boulud
26 Abe & Louie's
23 Sundy House
21 Ta-boo
Charley's Crab

BUSINESS DINING

27 Café Boulud
26 Chops Lobster
32 East
L'Escalier
Capital Grille

CHILD-FRIENDLY

26 Little Moir's
23 John G's
Lemongrass Asian Bistro
Sloan's
Mellow Mushroom

DOCK & DINE

23 Seasons 52
River House
22 Jetty's
21 Prime Catch
19 Old Calypso

EARLY-BIRD

26 Captain Charlie's
25 Entre Nous

24 Kee Grill
Uncle Tai's
23 Bistro

HOTEL DINING

27 Café Boulud (Brazilian Court)
26 Four Seasons
L'Escalier (Breakers)
25 Flagler Steak (Breakers)
23 Sundy House

PEOPLE-WATCHING

26 Chops Lobster
32 East
25 Café L'Europe
Kathy's Gazebo
Palm Beach Grill

QUICK BITES

24 Brass Ring Pub
23 John G's
Sushi Jo's
Café Centro
22 Pizza Girls

SINGLES SCENES

26 32 East
23 Cabana
Mellow Mushroom
21 Ta-boo
Dada

BY LOCATION

CENTRAL COUNTY

27 Marcello's La Sirena
Chez Jean-Pierre
Café Boulud
26 Four Seasons
L'Escalier

NORTH CENTRAL COUNTY

26 Capital Grille
25 Café Chardonnay
Ruth's Chris
Entre Nous
24 Brass Ring Pub

NORTH COUNTY

26 Little Moir's
Captain Charlie's
24 Kee Grill
Buonasera
23 Lazy Loggerhead

SOUTH COUNTY

27 LaSpada's Hoagies
Casa D'Angelo
26 Chops Lobster
32 East
Capital Grille

Top Decor

27	Sundy House		Jetty's
	L'Escalier		Bizaare Ave. Cafe
	Café Boulud		Ta-boo
	Four Seasons		Café Chardonnay
26	Café L'Europe		Palm Beach Grill
25	Chops Lobster		Sloan's Ice Cream
	Flagler Steak		Absinthe
	Capital Grille		Echo
	Renato's		Uncle Tai's
24	Seasons 52		RA Sushi Bar
	Truluck's		Sailfish Marina
	Abe & Louie's		Casa D'Angelo
	Leopard Lounge		Old Calypso
23	Ill Forks	21	Kee Grill
	River House		Coco
	11 Maple St.		Rocco's Tacos*
	Too Bizaare		New York Prime
	Chez Jean-Pierre		Arturo's
	Morton's		Houston's
22	Ruth's Chris		Marcello's La Sirena

OUTDOORS

Bice	Prime Catch
Cafe Sapori	Renato's
Dune Deck Café	Sailfish Marina
Max's Grille	Sundy House

ROMANCE

Arturo's	Four Seasons
Buonasera	Kathy's Gazebo
Café Boulud	L'Escalier
Café L'Europe	Renato's
Casa D'Angelo	Sundy House

ROOMS

Café Boulud	Four Seasons
Café L'Europe	Leopard Lounge
Capital Grille	L'Escalier
Chez Jean-Pierre	Trevini

VIEWS

P⋯a Boat	Old Calypso
⋯a Rosa	Prime Catch
⋯rab	River House
⋯ Sea.	Sailfish Marina
	Sundy House
	Two Georges

Top Service

26 | Four Seasons
11 Maple St.
Café Boulud
Chez Jean-Pierre
L'Escalier
Marcello's La Sirena
Capital Grille

25 | Flagler Steak
Café L'Europe
Chops Lobster
Casa D'Angelo
Flagler Grill
Abe & Louie's

24 | Morton's
Ruth's Chris
Entre Nous
Café Chardonnay
Kathy's Gazebo

23 | Renato's
Seasons 52

Truluck's
Palm Beach Grill
Arturo's
Leopard Lounge
River House
32 East
La Cigale
Sundy House
Il Girasole
Ziree Thai

22 | Captain Charlie's
Sapori
Trattoria Romana
LaSpada's Hoagies
Bistro
III Forks
Dolce de Palma
Kee Grill
Uncle Tai's
Ta-boo

Best Buys

In order of Bang for the Buck rating.

1. Sloan's Ice Cream
2. LaSpada's Hoagies
3. Pizza Girls
4. Five Guys
5. Cheese Course
6. Brass Ring Pub
7. Pizza Rustica
8. Original Pancake House
9. Anthony's Pizza
10. Tin Muffin Café
11. John G's
12. Mellow Mushroom
13. Hamburger Heaven
14. Lazy Loggerhead
15. Howley's
16. Dune Deck Café
17. Ziree Thai
18. Ben's Kosher Restaurant
19. Dave's Last Resort
20. Blue Anchor
21. Rocco's Tacos
22. Stir Crazy
23. TooJay's Deli
24. Park Avenue BBQ
25. Havana
26. Padrino's
27. Mississippi Sweets BBQ
28. Taso's Greek Taverna
29. Cheesecake Factory
30. Yard House
31. China Dumpling
32. Cay Da
33. Hurricane Café
34. Don Ramon's
35. Brewzzi
36. Cuban Cafe
37. Grand Lux Cafe
38. Saito's Steak
39. Uncle Julio's
40. Village Tavern

OTHER GOOD VALUES

Bimini Twist
Bizaare Ave. Cafe
Brogues
Cantina Laredo
Carmine's Pizza
Flakowitz
Grease Burger Bar
Grille on Congress
Harry & the Natives
Hot Pie Pizza
Lemongrass Asian Bistro
Mondo's
Paddy Mac's
Relish
Snappers
Two Georges

PALM BEACH/
PALM BEACH COUNTY
RESTAURANT
DIRECTORY

	FOOD	DECOR	SERVICE	COST

☑ Abe & Louie's Steak
26 | 24 | 25 | $64

Boca Raton | 2200 W. Glades Rd. (NW Sheraton Way) | 561-447-0024 | www.abeandlouies.com

Carnivores converge on this Boston-based "real men's steakhouse" – a Boca Raton "classic" voted the Palm Beach area's Most Popular – where diners gush over "amazing" "bone-in filets", "wonderful seafood" and "quality sides" that can be "shared"; though some grumble about "noise levels that'll give you nightmares" and "expensive" tabs, an "ultraprofessional" staff with "deep knowledge" of the "diverse, fairly priced wine list" and "elegant, clubby surroundings" help make it a "winner."

Absinthe American
19 | 22 | 20 | $39

Boca Raton | Boca Raton Marriott | 5150 Town Center Circle (Military Trail) | 561-620-3754 | www.absintheboca.com

"Absinthe makes the heart grow fonder" riff fans of this New American in the Boca Raton Marriott who "can't understand why" its "creative" cuisine and "swanky" decor have "not caught on" – maybe it's because tougher customers feel "it just doesn't have the panache" they're looking for, and the fare is "only so-so, especially for the price."

☑ Anthony's Coal Fired Pizza Pizza
23 | 16 | 20 | $21

Stuart | Stuart Centre | 2343 SE Federal Hwy. (Hwy. 714) | 772-287-7741

Palm Beach Gardens | Marshall's Plaza | 2680 PGA Blvd. (Prosperity Farms Rd.) | 561-804-7777

Boca Raton | 21065 Powerline Rd. (bet. Glades Rd. & W. Palmetto Park Rd.) | 561-208-6600

Delray Beach | 115 NE Sixth Ave. (bet. 1st & 2nd Sts.) | 561-278-7911

Wellington | Shops of Isla Verde | 1000 State Rd. 7 (Victoria Groves Blvd.) | 561-615-1255

www.anthonyscoalfiredpizza.com

See review in Ft. Lauderdale/Broward County Directory.

NEW Apicius Continental/Italian
- | - | - | E

Lantana | 210 E. Ocean Ave. (Dixie Hwy.) | 561-533-5998

You'll be dining in style at this pricey Lantana newcomer, whose all-outdoor – but weather-protected – dining room is complemented by an indoor bar/lounge; expect an ambitious menu melding modern Italian and more traditional dishes (like the signature 14-ounce filet mignon with foie gras), all paired with wines from a huge cellar.

Arturo's Ristorante Italian
23 | 21 | 23 | $55

Boca Raton | 6750 N. Federal Hwy. (Berkeley St.) | 561-997-7373 | www.arturosrestaurant.com

"Old world" to the nth degree, this "high-society" Boca Italian is "well known" for employing "impeccable" "jacketed waiters", who roll antipasto and dessert carts stocked with "traditional", "fabulous" selections and prepare "tasty" "homemade pasta" dishes tableside; live piano provides an appropriately "throwback" soundtrack for the "formal" setting – which, no surprise, youngsters think "needs a face-lift."

	FOOD	DECOR	SERVICE	COST

Banana Boat ● *Seafood* — 16 | 17 | 17 | $28

Boynton Beach | 739 E. Ocean Ave. (SE 6th St.) | 561-732-9400 |
www.bananaboatboynton.com

"Essentially a watering hole" where the "young and old" come for "strong drinks" and "incredible views" of yachts on the Intracoastal, this "been-around-forever" alfresco Boynton Beacher also serves "acceptable" "basic" seafood for "reasonable prices"; it's "fun" for a "lazy lunch", while at night, it really "jumps", so expect "long, long waits – and short, short skirts"; P.S. live music Thursday–Sunday.

Bar Louie ● *American* — 17 | 18 | 17 | $28

Boynton Beach | 1500 Gateway Blvd. (N. Congress Ave.) | 561-853-0090 |
www.barlouieamerica.com

"Frugal friends" meet to "watch the game" at this Boynton Beach branch of the Chicago-based sports pub whipping up a "large variety" of "simple, satisfying" American grub and "good drinks"; service is "spotty" and the place is often "noisy", but the "outside bar is fun", and on Tuesday evenings, "you can get burgers for a buck."

Ben's Kosher Restaurant & Caterers *Deli/Jewish* — 20 | 16 | 17 | $24

Boca Raton | The Reserve | 9942 Clint Moore Rd. (Rte. 7) | 561-470-9963 |
www.bensdeli.net

"The Lower East Side" comes to West Boca via this incarnation of the "not-fancy" kosher eatery doling out "deli-cious" "Jewish soul food" such as sandwiches "stacked a mile high" ("a little pricey", but "not too bad"); though some sensitive types kvetch about the servers' "NY attitude", for the "homesick", it's "as comforting as the pastrami."

Bice Ristorante *Italian* — 21 | 21 | 20 | $54

Palm Beach | 313½ Worth Ave. (bet. Cocoanut Row & Hibiscus Ave.) |
561-835-1600 | www.bicegroup.com

"See-and-be-seen" "snowbirds" nest in this "chichi" Palm Beach iteration of the "popular" Italian mini-chain whose "beautiful, breezy" patio is a "delight"; service can swing from "helpful" to "snooty" depending on how "rich and famous" you are, and though many deem the food "authentic and zesty", some calculate that it's "way too pricey" for being "not that special."

Bimini Twist *Seafood* — 22 | 21 | 22 | $35

West Palm Beach | 8480 Okeechobee Blvd. (Sansbury Way) |
561-784-2660 | www.mybiminitwist.com

This "reliable" West Palm Beach seafooder reels 'em in with "fresh", "not fancy" fare in a "tropical" setting; an "attentive" staff works the "lively" space, which can get "noisy when crowded" with "early birds" packing in for "sunset specials"; P.S. it now takes reservations.

Bistro, The *Continental* — 23 | 20 | 22 | $48

Jupiter | Driftwood Plaza | 2133 S. U.S. 1 (Olympus Circle) | 561-744-5054 |
www.thebistrojupiter.com

At this "upbeat" "little hideaway" in a Jupiter shopping plaza, the "friendly" staff's "knowledge of the varied Continental menu" pleases a "sophisticated" crowd; it's "not inexpensive", but the "tasty, gourmet" fare "lives up to the ambiance."

Bizaare Avenue Cafe *Eclectic*   21 | 22 | 21 | $35

Lake Worth | 921 Lake Ave. (S. H St.) | 561-588-4488 | www.bizaareavecafe.com

It's "like eating in your living room" at this "young, happening", "unusual" Lake Worth Eclectic – that is, if your living room is packed with a "hodgepodge" of "unmatched furniture, funky antiques" and "quirky" art, and "pretty much everything is for sale"; as far as victuals go, there's an "interesting" slate of tapas and entrees, all "well prepared" and affordably priced; P.S. the dinner-only upstairs bistro is a bit more formal.

Blue Anchor, The *Pub Food*   19 | 19 | 18 | $26

Delray Beach | 804 E. Atlantic Ave. (Palm Sq.) | 561-272-7272 | www.theblueanchor.com

Expect "Britain in Delray" at this "near-authentic English pub" (the exterior's "real decor" was shipped over "piece by piece") pouring a "huge selection of draft beers" to pair with "fantastic fish 'n' chips" and other "classic", "inexpensive" grub; "if you don't care for loud rock" (which is live Thursday–Saturday), "bring your earplugs."

☑ Bluefin Sushi *Japanese/Thai*   25 | 18 | 21 | $36

Boca Raton | VPC Ctr. | 861 Yamato Rd. (Congress Ave.) | 561-981-8986 | www.bluefinthaisushi.com

"Fun for your mouth" and relatively easy on your wallet, this Boca eatery prepares a "great variety" of "tasty" Thai and "terrific" sushi (including "interesting rolls" like a lobster bomb that's "truly the bomb"); it's in an "average-looking strip mall", but you're "lucky to get a table in season" – good thing staffers "serve you quickly", and "with a smile" too; P.S. the Parkland branch feels like a trip to the "beach without the attitude."

☑ Bonefish Grill *Seafood*   22 | 20 | 21 | $35

Stuart | Stuart Ctr. | 2283 S. Federal Hwy. (SE Monterey Rd.) | 772-288-4388
Palm Beach Gardens | 11658 Hwy. 1 (PGA Blvd.) | 561-799-2965
Boca Raton | Shops at Boca Grove | 21069 Powerline Rd. (Boca Grove Blvd.) | 561-483-4949
Boynton Beach | 1880 N. Congress Ave. (Gateway Blvd.) | 561-732-1310
www.bonefishgrill.com

See review in Ft. Lauderdale/Broward County Directory.

Brass Ring Pub ◑ *Pub Food*   24 | 10 | 18 | $16

North Palm Beach | 200 U.S. 1 (Northlake Blvd.) | 561-848-4748
Royal Palm Beach | 10998 Okeechobee Blvd. (bet. Sparrow Dr. & Wildcat Way) | 561-296-4563
www.brassringpub.net

"Diverse" folks, whether in "boots or flip-flops", gather at this "honky-tonk" bar in North Palm Beach for what may be the "best burger" around, other "cheap" grub and "icy cold pitchers of beer" served "quick"; the Royal Palm Beach version is more family-friendly, as it has a larger "restaurant part" and a "game room."

	FOOD	DECOR	SERVICE	COST

Brewzzi *American/Italian*

	18	17	18	$27

West Palm Beach | CityPlace | 700 S. Rosemary Ave. (Okeechobee Blvd.) |
561-366-9753
Boca Raton | Glades Plaza | 2222 Glades Rd. (NW Executive Center Dr.) |
561-392-2739
www.brewzzi.com

"Mile-high meatloaf", "big" burgers, "oversized" salads, "giant desserts", "huge booths", "spread-out" digs – yes, everything is "oversized" at these "raucous" American mall brewpubs in Boca and West Palm, where the tastes may be "simple" but the prices are "reasonable"; there's also a "large variety of beers", some of them "homemade", and occasionally "long waits" for a table.

Brogues *Pub Food*

	▽ 16	17	20	$20

Lake Worth | 621 Lake Ave. (bet. K & L Sts.) | 561-585-1885
This "cozy", "semi-authentic" Lake Worth Irish pub doles out "average" grub – but "who's here to eat?" wonder the "entertaining characters" who are skilled in ordering their cheap pints "by hand-signal only" (the nightly live music and other entertainment is "really loud").

Buonasera *Italian*

	24	21	22	$58

Jupiter | Driftwood Plaza | 2145 S. U.S. 1 (1½ mi. south of Indiantown Rd.) |
561-744-0543 | www.buonaserajupiter.com
Advocates advise "don't be misled by the storefront in a strip-mall location", because the Italian fare prepared at this Jupiter ristorante is "elegant" and "wonderful", just like the "impressive wine list"; while many agree that it's "expensive", a vocal minority deems it "astronomically overpriced" for being merely "so-so."

Cabana *Nuevo Latino*

	23	20	20	$39

NEW **West Palm Beach** | 533 Clematis St. (Rosemary Ave.) |
561-833-4773
Delray Beach | 105 E. Atlantic Ave. (1st Ave.) | 561-274-9090
www.cabanarestaurant.com
"No need to go to South Beach" for "fantastic" Nuevo Latino cuisine, "awesome mojitos" and a "hot", "always buzzing" scene – this "colorful" Delray Beacher "has it all", plus prices and portions that equal "value" in these "tight times"; "for great people-watching, sit outside if weather permits"; P.S. its West Palm Beach sib reopened in a new location post-Survey.

NEW Cabo Flats ● *Mexican*

	–	–	–	M

Palm Beach Gardens | Downtown at the Gdns. |
11701 Lake Victoria Gardens Ave. (PGA Blvd.) | 561-624-0024 |
www.caboflats.com
It's a fiesta every night at this Palm Beach Gardens Mexican (with Californian influences) whose indoor/outdoor bar and sidewalk lounge draw tequila and 'rita lovers; inside, the party continues with piñata-bright dining rooms and friendly servers dishing up house-special guacs and salsas with moderately priced traditional fare.

	FOOD	DECOR	SERVICE	COST

☑ Café Boulud *French*

| 27 | 27 | 26 | $76 |

Palm Beach | Brazilian Court Hotel | 301 Australian Ave. (Hibiscus Ave.) | 561-655-6060 | www.danielnyc.com

"A little slice of New York heaven", this "magical" Daniel Boulud outpost in the Brazilian Court Hotel is "*the* big deal in Palm Beach", where the "beautiful people" say *oui* to "fab chef" Zach Bell's "sublime" "French cuisine without the French attitude" and an "exemplary" wine list overseen by "class-act" sommeliers; you'll need to "open your pocketbook" and hand over the "black card", but after being pampered by a "superior" staff in a "gorgeous tropical setting", many sigh "it doesn't get better than this."

Cafe Cellini *Continental*

| ▽ 25 | 23 | 26 | $48 |

Palm Beach | Palm Beach President | 2505 S. Ocean Blvd. (north of Lake Worth Bridge) | 561-588-1871 | www.cafecellini.com

Like much of its clientele, this Continental is an "oldie but goodie", and "one of Palm Beach's loveliest places", what with all the "fresh flowers" and "elegant" murals; its "formally dressed" fans also cheer the "delightful menu", the near "perfect service" and, yes, the "early-bird bargains."

Café Centro *Italian*

| 23 | 20 | 22 | $39 |

West Palm Beach | 2409 N. Dixie Hwy. (Northwood Rd.) | 561-514-4070 | www.mycafecentro.com

There's "not much" in West Palm's Northwood neighborhood, but this "warm", "pretty" spot would be a "gift" wherever, as it serves thoroughly "enjoyable" Italian fare, featuring "outstanding pizzas" and seafood, at "lower-than-expected prices" ("even the wines are reasonable"); there are two interior dining spaces, a back bar where a "fabulous piano player" serenades and sidewalk seating, all patrolled by "friendly, professional" staffers.

☑ Café Chardonnay *American*

| 25 | 22 | 24 | $56 |

Palm Beach Gardens | Garden Square Shoppes | 4533 PGA Blvd. (Military Trail) | 561-627-2662 | www.cafechardonnay.com

"It may not look like much from the outside", but this "inventive" American in a Palm Beach Gardens "strip mall" ("so Florida") is "still living up to its fabulous reputation" after "more than 20 years"; "well-educated" waiters help diners decipher an "outstanding" selection of "wines by the glass" and bottle, and if a few fret it's all too "pricey", devotees decree it's "the best thing" for a "special occasion" "next to child care."

Café des Artistes ⊠Ⓜ *French*

| - | - | - | M |

Jupiter | Riverwalk | 318 S. US Hwy. 1 (Indiantown Rd.) | 561-747-0998

You'll crow like the roosters on display at this midpriced cafe at the Jupiter Yacht Club complex where Francophiles order up quiche, tarte Tatin, soups and sandwiches, plus daily specials; set in a cozy alcove overlooking the marina, it's got a take-out case for cheeses, just-baked pastries and more, along with special-order foods for the galley at home or on the yacht.

	FOOD	DECOR	SERVICE	COST

☑ Café L'Europe ☒ Continental
| 25 | 26 | 25 | $72 |

Palm Beach | 331 S. County Rd. (Brazilian Ave.) | 561-655-4020 |
www.cafeleurope.com

You'll "feel like you've made it" at this "exquisite", "flower-filled"
"landmark" whose owners "stay on top of all details", from the "extraordinary" Continental cuisine and "comprehensive" wine list to
the "impeccable" service; while a few tsk "the grande dame is getting old" and rip into "expensive" tabs, the majority maintains it's
"Palm Beach with a capital P" – so "wear your good jewelry" and
"see how the other half lives."

Cafe Sapori Italian
| 24 | 20 | 22 | $56 |

West Palm Beach | 205 Southern Blvd. (Washington Rd.) |
561-805-7313 | www.cafesapori.com

"Insiders" aged "22 to 72" "flock across the bridge" for this "swinging"
West Palm scene, not to mention its "amazing selection" of "expertly prepared" Italian; the "swank" digs may be "loud", but add in
"well-selected wines", "friendly, efficient service" and a "terrific patio", and you've got "a sure winner – if you're not on a budget."

Caffe Luna Rosa Italian
| 20 | 18 | 19 | $39 |

Delray Beach | 34 S. Ocean Blvd. (bet. E. Atlantic Ave. & Miramar Dr.) |
561-274-9404 | www.caffelunarosa.com

"Across the street from the beach" sits this Delray Italian where
both "natives and tourists" say it's "worth the wait" to perch outside
for "reliable", "traditional" breakfasts, brunches, lunches and dinners ("lots of specials" ensure there's "something for everyone");
"warm service" and real "bar action" add to its appeal.

NEW Caliente Kitchen Mexican
| - | - | - | M |

Delray Beach | 8 E. Atlantic Ave. (Swinton Ave.) | 561-450-6940 |
www.calientekitchen.net

More lounge than restaurant, this terra-cotta–hued Mexican newcomer in Delray is known for its party vibe, so don't be surprised to
see the many tequilas it stocks tossed back by young night owls; go
earlier for a meal of tacos, burritos, guac and other standards, but
bring a wallet – even chips and salsa cost.

Callaro's Prime Steak & Seafood Steak
| 21 | 18 | 20 | $43 |

Manalapan | Plaza Del Mar | 264 S. Ocean Blvd. (Ocean Ave.) |
561-493-2622 | www.callarosprime.com

This "reliable" Manalapan meatery across from the Ritz is an "easy
place to dine", what with its "pleasant" atmosphere, live entertainment Thursday–Saturday and "efficient" staff; tabs can be a "bit
pricey", but when you consider that the "delicious steaks" "come
with sides", it's actually a "value."

Cantina Laredo Mexican
| 19 | 20 | 19 | $32 |

Palm Beach Gardens | Midtown | 4635 PGA Blvd. (Military Trail) |
561-622-1223 | www.cantinalaredo.com

The "energy of a fiesta" pulsates within this Palm Beach Gardens
Mexican (and its newer Hallandale sib) where guests applaud the

"great guacamole" "made tableside", "good selection of traditional and unusual dishes" and myriad tequilas; the fare "incorporates a bit of the gourmet", but still, quite a few "uninspired" surveyors assess it's "not worth the price."

Z Capital Grille *Steak* 26 | 25 | 26 | $65

Palm Beach Gardens | Legacy Pl. | 11365 Legacy Ave. (PGA Blvd.) | 561-630-4994
Boca Raton | Town Center Mall | 6000 Glades Rd. (St. Andrews Blvd.) | 561-368-1077
www.thecapitalgrille.com
See review in Miami/Dade County Directory.

NEW Capri Ristorante Italiano 🛇 *Italian* - | - | - | M

Boca Raton | 39 SE First Ave. (Federal Hwy.) | 561-391-8044 | www.capriristorante.com
This Chicago import brings traditional Italian favorites (e.g. linguine and clams) to Boca courtesy of its moderately priced menu, which is accompanied by a similarly reasonable wine list; the upscale, dark-wood interior is comfortable for neighborhood types in suits or shorts, though you may have to shout to the servers during peak hours to place your order in the open, lively space.

Z Captain Charlie's Reef Grill *Seafood* 26 | 12 | 22 | $36

Juno Beach | Beach Plaza | 12846 U.S. 1 (bet. Juno Isles Blvd. & Olympus Dr.) | 561-624-9924
"The freshest fish" is served in "imaginative, delicious" preparations – or "however you want it" – at this "informal" Juno Beach strip-mall seafooder whose "incomparable value" extends to the "awesome wine list" (possibly the "lowest markups" around); just "don't be put off" by the "dumpy" "Old Florida" "bar setting", the "noise" or a no-reservations policy that leads to "long waits in season."

NEW Carmine's Coal Fired Pizza *Italian/Pizza* - | - | - | M

Jupiter | Abacoa | 4575 Military Trail (Indian Creek Pkwy.) | 561-340-3930 | www.carminescfp.com
Conjoined with CG Burgers, this Jupiter pizzeria awash in booths and tables is casual, family-friendly and a font of crispy pies and midpriced Italian comfort food – spaghetti and meatballs is a signature – geared toward red-sauce fare; a full bar along the back with TVs sates the sports-minded, while a refrigerator case up front offers take-out foods prepped by Carmine's Gourmet Market in the Gardens.

NEW Caruso's *Italian* - | - | - | E

Boca Raton | Royal Palm Plaza | 187 SE Mizner Blvd. (Federal Hwy.) | 561-367-7488 | www.carusoristorante.net
At this small, family-owned Italian in Boca's Royal Palm Plaza, a selection of unusual regional Romano dishes (e.g. faro and truffles) vies for appetites alongside pastas and meat entrees; patrons can sit on the sidewalk by the fountain or sip grappa in the adjacent Rouge Bar, enjoying an altogether classy vibe that's accompanied by predictably upscale prices.

	FOOD	DECOR	SERVICE	COST

☑ Casa D'Angelo *Italian*

27 | 22 | 25 | $59

Boca Raton | 171 E. Palmetto Park Rd. (bet. Federal Hwy. & Mizner Blvd.) | 561-996-1234 | www.casa-d-angelo.com
See review in Ft. Lauderdale/Broward County Directory.

Cay Da Ⓜ *Vietnamese*

22 | 12 | 22 | $28

Boca Raton | Colony Plaza | 7400 N. Federal Hwy. (NE 74th St.) | 561-998-0278
"If you're after atmosphere", this "plain" "storefront in a nondescript North Boca shopping center" is "not for you"; however, if you want "authentic, delicious" Vietnamese fare that offers "good value", stop by – you'll be "treated like an appreciated guest" by a family that "takes enormous pride" in its endeavor.

NEW CG Burgers *Burgers*

- | - | - | I

Jupiter | Abacoa | 4575 Military Trail (Indian Creek Pkwy.) | 561-340-3940 | www.cgburgers.com
Connected to Carmine's Coal Fired Pizza by a dining room/bar, this affordable counter-order burger boutique in Jupiter is all about the stuff between the buns; they're handfuls of prime beef with all the fixin's, best enjoyed with a craft brew at an outdoor table or inside while nestled in one of the booths.

Charley's Crab *Seafood*

21 | 20 | 21 | $47

Palm Beach | 456 S. Ocean Blvd. (Hammon Ave.) | 561-659-1500 | www.muer.com
Ogle the "gorgeous water views" at this "upscale" Palm Beach "classic" serving "consistently good" seafood; foes fuss it's "nothing special", citing "hit-or-miss service" and "cookie-cutter" fare, but more say it's a "must for tourists and locals alike."

☑ Cheesecake Factory *American*

20 | 19 | 19 | $29

West Palm Beach | CityPlace | 701 S. Rosemary Ave. (Okeechobee Blvd.) | 561-802-3838 ●
Palm Beach Gardens | Downtown at the Gdns. | 11800 Lake Victoria Gardens Ave. (Gardens Blvd.) | 561-776-3711
Boca Raton | 5530 Glades Rd. (Butts Rd.) | 561-393-0344 ●
www.thecheesecakefactory.com
See review in Miami/Dade County Directory.

☑ Cheese Course *Eclectic*

26 | 15 | 18 | $18

NEW **Boca Raton** | Mizner Park | 305 Plaza Real (NE 3rd St.) | 561-395-4354 | www.thecheesecourse.com
See review in Ft. Lauderdale/Broward County Directory.

☑ Chez Jean-Pierre Bistro ⓢ *French*

27 | 23 | 26 | $73

Palm Beach | 132 N. County Rd. (bet. Sunrise & Sunset Aves.) | 561-833-1171
"Observe the social rituals of the Palm Beach elite" while indulging in chef-owner Jean-Pierre Leverrier's "fantastic" French fare ("makes you feel like you can fly") at this "sparkling" bistro that's "always packed"; "perfect" Dover sole and "knowledgeable" staffers wow a crowd that includes some regulars "older than the vintage

wines", while aesthetes appreciate the "funky, Magritte-like art"; if a few *non*-sayers sniff it's "not all that", for most it's a "breath of fresh country air."

China Dumpling *Chinese*
22 | 12 | 18 | $25

Boynton Beach | 1899 N. Congress Ave. (Gateway Blvd.) | 561-737-2612 | www.chinadumplings.com

Devotees "dream about" the "delicious" dumplings (sometimes "circulated on carts" by "efficient" staffers) and other "mouth-watering goodies" prepped in this "casual" Chinese eatery's "open kitchen"; a few frown upon "unremarkable" decor and pan the place as "nothing special", but to most it's a "little bit of Chinatown" in Boynton Beach; P.S. there's "great dim sum" on weekends.

🅉 Chops Lobster Bar *Seafood/Steak*
26 | 25 | 25 | $71

Boca Raton | Royal Palm Pl. | 101 Plaza Real S. (1st St.) | 561-395-2675 | www.chopslobsterbar.com

While claw-noisseurs commend the "flash-fried lobster" ("so much better than it sounds"), it's the "fantastic steaks" and "delicious sides" that have turned this "high-quality" "Atlanta import" into a "major Boca scene"; add in "gorgeous" surroundings with an open kitchen, a "happening" bar with live entertainment and "telepathic" staffers, and you've got "dining bliss" – which explains the "long waits" even "with a reservation"; of course, it's "expensive" "unless you own (not lease) a Bentley", but a "satisfying" "splurge" nonetheless.

City Cellar
Wine Bar & Grill *Mediterranean*
20 | – | 19 | $39

West Palm Beach | CityPlace | 700 S. Rosemary Ave. (Okeechobee Blvd.) | 561-366-0071 | www.bigtimerestaurants.com

The "huge tower of wine behind glass" is "heaven" for oenophiles who pour into this "upscale" CityPlace Med for "after-movie and - theater dining"; though some contend it "might try to do too much", "consistent food and service", a "vibrant", recently refurbed "barn of a space" and, yes, an "excellent" selection of vino by the glass explains why it's "always packed."

City Oyster & Sushi Bar *Seafood*
21 | 19 | 19 | $42

Delray Beach | 213 E. Atlantic Ave. (2nd Ave.) | 561-272-0220 | www.cityoysterdelray.com

The "name says it all" at this "lively" – and "not inexpensive" – Downtown Delray "see-and-be-seen" seafooder, where a "hip bar" and "large selection of regional oysters", "tasty" fish entrees and sushi draw a "young, spiffy crowd"; it can get quite "noisy", though, so "go when the batteries in your hearing aid are dead" or "sit outside."

Coco *Asian*
22 | 21 | 20 | $46

Palm Beach | Bradley Park Hotel | 290 Sunset Ave. (Bradley Pl.) | 561-832-3734 | www.cocopalmbeach.com

Partisans of this Palm Beach Pan-Asian have come to expect "fire-works in the kitchen" from a chef who "knows his stuff and tries to be different"; not different enough for some, who deem the fare "ordinary", but they're outnumbered by those enamored by the "unbelievable flavors", "quick" service and "beautiful" Bradley Park Hotel setting (especially the "pleasant" courtyard).

Conchy Joe's Seafood *Seafood*

| 19 | 20 | 19 | $32 |

Jensen Beach | 3945 NE Indian River Dr. (Jensen Beach Blvd.) | 772-334-1130 | www.conchyjoes.com

"What a setting!" shriek seafoodistas upon discovering this "casual" Jensen Beach "must-see" on the Intracoastal dishing up some of the "best conch chowder" around; while the fare's "fine", it's "not the focus" here, but if "good drinks", "laid-back service" and "grooving to an island beat" (live reggae Thursday–Sunday) appeal, "this is the one."

COOL'A FISHBAR *Seafood*

| 22 | 19 | 21 | $35 |

Palm Beach Gardens | Legacy Pl. | 11340 Legacy Ave. (PGA Blvd.) | 561-622-2227

The surf's always up at this "cool" Kee Grill cousin in Palm Beach Gardens where "you feel like you're in a shack on the beach", albeit one with "excellent" seafood that's "priced right"; add in "pleasant" service, and no wonder most agree you're in for "plenty of fun."

Copper Canyon Grill *American*

| - | - | - | M |

Boca Raton | 2006 NW Executive Center Circle (Glades Rd.) | 561-893-8838 | www.ccgrill.com

This Maryland-based chain link has made its mark in Boca Raton with a subtle round-up theme and a horseshoe-shaped bar stocked with liquor, craft beers and wines; a moderate, meat-heavy menu – including the signature spit-roasted chicken, steaks and Big John's Meatloaf Stack – pleases business crowds and families alike, who can watch chefs roll sushi or sizzle the steers over the grill.

Cottage, The ● Ⓜ *Eclectic*

| ▽ 16 | 20 | 14 | $26 |

Lake Worth | 522 Lucerne Ave. (bet. L & M Sts.) | 561-586-0080 | www.thecottagelw.com

Sipping "martinis" in this "charming" Eclectic's outside lounge is "like having drinks on your own patio", instead of a "nice, quiet" spot in Downtown Lake Worth; but those who "want to love" the place chide "slow service", and the "large variety" of small plates gets mixed marks ("tasty" to just "ok"); still, there's always that "wonderful bar."

Couco Pazzo *Italian*

| 22 | 16 | 21 | $40 |

Lake Worth | 915-917 Lake Ave. (S. Dixie Hwy.) | 561-585-0320 | www.coucopazzo.com

"Plentiful portions" of "above-average" Italian fare satisfy surveyors at this Downtown Lake Worth two-fer (the "main dining room has the ambiance", the adjacent cafe "has the crowd"); it may need a little "updating", but "friendly service" and "moderate prices" help make it a "favorite."

Crazy Buffet *Asian*

| 15 | 12 | 14 | $26 |

West Palm Beach | 2030 Palm Beach Lakes Blvd. (I-95) | 561-616-9288 | www.gocrazybuffet.com

The "all-you-can-eat sushi" is a "crazy value" at this West Palm Beach buffet, but those not into "squishy fish" can "overfill their plates" with "decent" Asian fusion and kid-friendly fare like pizza; it's "somewhat more expensive" than its rivals and a tad "tired", but "if you leave here hungry you were just too lazy to get up."

Cuban Cafe *Cuban*
20 | **13** | **21** | **$27**

Boca Raton | Plumtree Ctr. | 3350 NW Boca Raton Blvd. (bet. 40th St. & Glades Rd.) | 561-750-8860
Delray Beach | Shoppes at Delray | 14400 S. Military Trail (W. Atlantic Ave.) | 561-450-8470
www.cubancafe.com

Expect a "fun trip to old Havana" at these "real-deal" Cuban cafes where diners almost expect "Ricky Ricardo to do 'Babalu'" as they chow on "generous portions" of "authentic" specialties brought by "playful" servers; the decor is "simple" but the "price is right", thus perfect for "super-casual nights out" with the "whole family."

Cucina Dell' Arte ● *Italian*
21 | **18** | **20** | **$50**

Palm Beach | 257 Royal Poinciana Way (bet. Bradley Pl. & N. County Rd.) | 561-655-0770 | www.cucinadellarte.com

This Palm Beacher wears two hats, making it a "hot spot any time of day": diners dig its "consistent" Italian fare, including "good pizza, pasta and panini", while the "young, single set" amasses when it becomes a "mini nightclub" after 10 PM, with music till the wee hours; in any event, "prices lean to the high side", so bring dough.

Cugini Grille & Martini Bar *Seafood/Steak*
▽ **20** | **19** | **18** | **$51**

Delray Beach | 270 E. Atlantic Ave. (SE 2nd Ave.) | 561-274-6244 | www.cuginigrilledelray.com

A "great early-hour" dinner draws guests to this wood-and-brick-bedecked surf 'n' turfer in Downtown Delray Beach that works a few Italian dishes (including chicken Gorgonzola fettuccine) into the mix; all in all, it's a "standard Atlantic Avenue venue", though some "expect better for the price"; P.S. there's a DJ Friday–Saturday.

☒ Dada ● *American/Eclectic*
21 | **20** | **19** | **$37**

Delray Beach | 52 N. Swinton Ave. (bet. E. Atlantic Ave. & 1st St.) | 561-330-3232 | www.dadaofdelray.com

Every room in this Delray Beach "hipster hangout" set in an "old house" has "its own funky feel and charm", so go with an "open mind" and a craving for "creative", "carefully prepared" Eclectic-American dishes; the "young", "noisy" crowd may "not know Dada from doo-doo" and service "can be flaky", but live entertainment, "seating under the stars" and a "hopping bar" make it "worth the adventure."

Dave's Last Resort & Raw Bar ● *American*
19 | **16** | **18** | **$24**

Lake Worth | 632 Lake Ave. (bet. K & L Sts.) | 561-588-5208 | www.daveslastresort.com

Sports lovers "mingle, drink" and down "decent" pub grub at this "lively", "no-frills" American that's become a "favorite" Downtown Lake Worth "destination", especially on game days when the 15 TVs are blaring; even if "service can be slow", the "funky old Florida atmosphere" makes it a "pleasant" place to "hang out."

Dockside Sea Grille *Seafood*
▽ 19 | 16 | 18 | $31

Lake Park | 766 Northlake Blvd. (Flagler Blvd.) | 561-842-2180 |
www.docksideseagrille.com

It "feels like a huge tiki hut" on the waterfront deck at this Lake Park
"hole-in-the-wall" where it's "fun to sit outside" and chill;
otherwise, the consensus is there's "nothing to rave about" here,
though a few patrons profess that the "reasonably priced" seafood
is "surprisingly good."

Dolce de Palma 🅂 *Italian*
26 | 15 | 22 | $43

West Palm Beach | 1000 Okeechobee Rd. (Parker Ave.) |
561-833-6460 | www.dolcedepalma.com

"Amazing food comes out of the tiny kitchen" at this "pricey" West
Palm place that's praised for its "sense, style and substance", as
well as its "well-presented" Italian fare that's "interesting without
scaring off the retirees"; even with a recent refurb that expanded the
dining room, "reservations may be hard to come by", leaving loyalists lamenting "too bad it's no longer a secret."

Don Ramon's *Cuban*
18 | 11 | 16 | $23

NEW West Palm Beach | 300 Clematis St. (Federal Hwy.) |
561-832-5418
West Palm Beach | 502 S. Military Trail (Sunny Ln. Ave.) |
561-687-0161
West Palm Beach | 7101 S. Dixie Hwy. (Forest Hill Blvd.) | 561-547-8704 |
www.donramonrestaurant.com
Wellington | 11924 W. Forest Hill Blvd. (Southshore Blvd.) | 561-795-1932

They're "nothing fancy", but these "convenient" Cuban eateries
"have been around for years" dishing up "decent if unimaginative"
fare in "large portions"; service "lacks at times" and the venues
"need work" in the "atmosphere department", but there's "good
value" here; P.S. the South Dixie Highway venue is separately owned;
Clematis opened post-Survey.

Dune Deck Café ⊄ *American*
19 | 16 | 18 | $22

Lantana | 100 N. Ocean Blvd. (Ocean Ave.) | 561-582-0472 |
www.dunedeckcafe.com

Be "prepared to get sand in your shoes" at this "all-outside" oceanfront American in Lantana where you "meet the folks" for "good",
"cheap"-for-the-beach breakfasts and lunches; weekend waits can
be "long", but with that "beautiful view" to ogle, "who cares?";
P.S. cash only; no dinner.

Echo 🅼 *Asian*
23 | 22 | 22 | $59

Palm Beach | 230A Sunrise Ave. (bet. Bradley Pl. & N. County Rd.) |
561-802-4222 | www.echopalmbeach.com

"When you have The Breakers behind you, it's gotta be good", and for
the most part surveyors echo that sentiment about this resort-owned
Pan-Asian that shows Palm Beach is "not just about formal and
stodgy" (even if it is "trust-fund-baby" expensive); "excellent" fare and
"sharp" service aside, though, some pout that the "dark" dining
room can be "noisy", so opt for the "pleasant" courtyard instead.

☑ 11 Maple Street Ⓜ *American* | 28 | 23 | 26 | $60 |

Jensen Beach | 3224 NE Maple Ave. (NE Jensen Beach Blvd.) |
772-334-7714 | www.11maplestreet.net

Admittedly, you'll drive a "bit far" to get to this "fantasy house" in Jensen Beach, but it's "worth it" once chef-owner Mike Perrin's "outstanding" New American fare – and its rating as PB's No. 1 for Food – is put to the test; "farm-raised meats and veggies many can't pronounce" are "superbly" presented and paired with a "unique wine list", while "friendly yet professional" staffers and "quaint" decor seal its rep as a "charming" "gem"; P.S. also closed Tuesdays.

☑ Entre Nous Ⓢ *American* | 25 | 19 | 24 | $47 |

North Palm Beach | 123 U.S. 1 (Northlake Blvd.) | 561-863-5883 |
www.entrenousbistro.com

Supporters say "entre yes!" at "one of the real surprises in North Palm Beach", where chef-owner Jason Laudenslager "works really hard" to come up with "creative" New American fare that "borders on gourmet"; though a few say the "larger" digs (the result of a 2008 relocation) may have cost it "some charm", others find that "friendly" service and a "pleasing bar" still add up to a "relaxing atmosphere."

E.R. Bradley's Saloon ⬤ *American* | 15 | 18 | 16 | $28 |

West Palm Beach | 104 Clematis St. (Flagler Dr.) | 561-833-3520 |
www.erbradleys.com

"You never know" who'll be "dancing on the bar" late at night at this open-air West Palm Beach "party spot" with a new tiki-hut-studded garden and "amazing" Intracoastal views, perhaps the "best thing about the place"; it's definitely not the "mediocre" American chow and service, though "strong" drinks that "flow freely" and the "fun" happy hour have their fans; P.S. Sunday brunch is more family-friendly.

Figs *Italian* | 20 | 17 | 18 | $30 |

Palm Beach Gardens | Macy's at the Palm Beach Gardens Mall |
3107 PGA Blvd. (bet. Fairchild Gardens & Kew Gardens Aves.) |
561-775-2384 | www.toddenglish.com

Celeb chef Todd English offers up "creative", "contemporary" fare at this midpriced Italian in the Palm Beach Gardens Macy's that may be "as good as" the Boston original, especially the thin-crust "fig pizzas"; though some sniff it's "too cosmopolitan" and "dark", satisfied shoppers decree it's the "best place to eat in the mall."

🆕 Fiorentina *Italian* | - | - | - | M |

Lake Worth | 707 Lake Ave. (bet. J & K Sts.) | 561-588-9707

Set in the old Prime 707 space in Downtown Lake Worth (and run by one of its former managers), this small Italian turns out modern interpretations of traditional favorites, including Tuscan bread soup, rigatoni Bolognese and rosemary-rubbed steak; while the big bar and sidewalk patio bring in the younger set for late-night dining and the three-course Sunday suppers attract families, everyone's lured by the affordable prices.

	FOOD	DECOR	SERVICE	COST

☑ Five Guys *Burgers*

22 | 10 | 16 | $12

Palm Beach Gardens | Legacy Pl. | 11320 Legacy Ave.
(Fairchild Gardens Ave.) | 561-625-3888
Boca Raton | Glades Plaza | 2240 NW 19th St. (I-95)
Boynton Beach | Boynton Town Ctr. | 1000 N. Congress Ave.
(Boynton Beach Mall Access Rd.) | 561-369-4460
Wellington | The Pointe at Wellington Green | 10200 Forest Hill Blvd.
(Rte. 441) | 561-790-7500
www.fiveguys.com

These "no-frills" DC imports are the "In-N-Outs of the East", flipping "addicting" burgers with "plentiful toppings" and parceling out "large orders" of "house-cut fries" that "seal the deal"; while dissenters who "don't understand the buzz" decree it's just "greasy fast food", for many they're among the "best places" to "pig out" on a meal that's "good enough for the president"; P.S. a Stuart branch is due.

☑ Flagler Grill *Floribbean*

25 | 21 | 25 | $45

Stuart | 47 SW Flagler Ave. (bet. S. Colorado & SW St. Lucie Aves.) |
772-221-9517 | www.flaglergrill.com

"They know how to take care of a customer" at this Floribbean-American grill in "picturesque" Downtown Stuart, a "best-kept secret" whose "talented chef" creates "interesting", "regionally appropriate" fare paired with "great" vinos (its "wine dinners" also win kudos); claustrophobes fearing "tables are too close" can "eat outside", but either way, it's "very popular."

☑ Flagler Steakhouse, The *Steak*

25 | 25 | 25 | $70

Palm Beach | The Breakers | 2 S. County Rd. (bet. Royal Palm &
Royal Poinciana Ways) | 561-653-6355 | www.thebreakers.com

Exuding "class all the way", this "opulent" steakhouse run by The Breakers feels "like a private club", especially with Palm Beach's "see-and-be-seen" set sitting "on the veranda" overlooking the golf course; "impeccable service" augments an "unbelievable wine list" and fare that's "prepared, plated and presented beautifully", though you "might qualify for a government bailout" once you get the bill.

Flakowitz Bagel Inn *Deli*

- | - | - | I

Boca Raton | 1999 N. Federal Hwy. (NE 20th St.) | 561-368-0666

Flakowitz of Boynton *Deli*

Boynton Beach | Hagen Ranch Commons | 7410 W. Boynton Beach Blvd.
(Hagen Ranch Rd.) | 561-742-4144 | www.flakowitzofboynton.com

One look at the deli meats stacked a mile high at these separately owned, eat-in/take-out delis, and Manhattan transplants start pining for the mother island; prices are easy to stomach, as long as you don't bite off more than you can chew from an expansive menu encompassing everything from sable to salmon and matzo to meatloaf.

☑ Four Seasons – The Restaurant *Seafood*

26 | 27 | 26 | $76

Palm Beach | Four Seasons Resort | 2800 S. Ocean Blvd. (Lake Ave.) |
561-533-3750 | www.fourseasons.com

"Quietly elegant in every way", this "special place for a special night" offers just "what you'd expect from the Four Seasons", including "near-perfect service" (voted No. 1 in Palm Beach) that comple-ments the "spectacular setting" and "gorgeous ocean views"; chef Darryl Moiles' "flavorful" seafood is "as good as it gets", and while you may need a "second mortgage" to cover the tab, it's a "small price to pay" for an "unforgettable experience."

Gol! The Taste of Brazil Brazilian

| 20 | 18 | 21 | $52 |

Delray Beach | 411 E. Atlantic Ave. (4th Ave.) | 561-272-6565 | www.golthetasteofbrazil.com

The "mounds of food" at this Brazilian rodizio on Delray's strip are so "bountiful" you'll leave "roaring like a lion" if "you're a meat lover", though the "superb" salad bar at almost "half the price" is a draw for noncarnivores and wallet-watchers; decor is "appropriate" and the service "friendly", and while it "doesn't score a goal" for some, it's still "fun" – especially when the "drink cart lady" shows up.

Grand Lux Cafe Eclectic

| 19 | 21 | 19 | $31 |

Boca Raton | Town Center at Boca Raton | 6000 Glades Rd. (St. Andrews Blvd.) | 561-392-2141 | www.grandluxcafe.com
See review in Miami/Dade County Directory.

NEW Gratify American Gastropub American

| - | - | - | M |

West Palm Beach | 125 Datura St. (bet. Flagler Dr. & Narcissus Ave.) | 561-833-5300 | www.gratifypub.com

Downtown professionals and casual noshers alike are gratified to find this new gastropub on West Palm Beach's waterfront, where the tricked-out American eats include pulled pork sliders, flatbreads, artichoke fritters and a signature crab tower; it's set in the former Spoto's space, which has been transformed into a minimalist room (think high ceilings and brick floors) with a casual, amenable vibe and moderate prices.

Grease Burger Bar ● Burgers

| ∇ 20 | 17 | 18 | $18 |

West Palm Beach | 213 Clematis St. (Olive Ave.) | 561-651-1075 | www.greasewpb.com

The "simple hamburger" rises to a "whole new level" at this "relax-ing" patty parlor in Downtown West Palm Beach, where "organic beef" burgers (or turkey, lamb, veggie, etc.) are layered with a "va-riety of toppings"; while an "excellent" specialty-beer list keeps hopsheads happy, misers moan sandwiches "don't come with fries", making it "relatively expensive."

Grille on Congress ⊠ American

| 20 | 17 | 19 | $39 |

Boca Raton | 5101 Congress Ave. (Yamato Rd.) | 561-912-9800 | www.thegrilleoncongress.com

"Take your cuisine-challenged guests" to this "old-fashioned" Boca American for "hearty" comfort food, including "addictive biscuits"; the "owners are always there" and "treat you like royalty", and though "bad acoustics" make it "noisy", it's a "good value" nonetheless and a "favorite" for "business lunches" or an "enjoyable evening out."

	FOOD	DECOR	SERVICE	COST

Guanabanas *Floribbean*

- | - | - | M

Jupiter | 997 N. Hwy. A1A (U.S. Hwy. 1) | 561-747-8878 |
www.guanabanas.com

This waterside Jupiter alfrescan combines an island theme with
midpriced Floribbean fare to attract the Hawaiian-shirt crowd,
though the multiple bars do their part; the bamboo-and-palm–
bedecked dining areas are packed with locals who love the fish and
crustaceans, while sippers sail in for apps and drinks, and everyone
grooves to the live bands.

Hamburger Heaven 🚫 *Burgers*

20 | 12 | 18 | $19

Palm Beach | 314 S. County Rd. (bet. Brazilian Ave. & Royal Palm Way) |
561-655-5277

Both "regular guys" and islanders with "jewelry worth more than the
business" itself duck into this Palm Beach "landmark", a "retro" diner
where "perfectly done" burgers, "creamy milkshakes" and "dreamy"
"mile-high" cakes are delivered by staffers who "make you feel welcome"; alas, it's often bedeviled by "lines", so "try to go at an off time."

Harry & the Natives Ⓜ *American*

∇ 16 | 14 | 18 | $23

Hobe Sound | 11910 S. Federal Hwy. (SE Bridge Rd.) | 772-546-3061 |
www.harryandthenatives.com

"Everyone knows each other" at this Hobe Sound American, a "local
hangout" that's "Old Florida" to the core (i.e. "laid-back" with occasional "live music", "quirky decor" and outdoor seating); it may be a
"dive", but supporters shrug and dig into the "decent" eats, like modestly priced burgers and seafood, and yap with "friendly" staffers.

Havana *Cuban*

22 | 14 | 18 | $25

West Palm Beach | 6801 S. Dixie Hwy. (Forest Hill Blvd.) | 561-547-9799 |
www.havanacubanfood.com

The "outstanding" Cuban food at this "family-friendly" West Palm
Beach "staple" makes up for "what it lacks in looks", though you
never have to venture inside: there's a 24/7 "take-out window" for
"service on the run" that's "always busy" with "locals" craving
"killer" Cuban and medianoche sandwiches; wherever you order,
the staff "makes you feel at ease", as do "reasonable prices."

🅉 Henry's *American*

21 | 18 | 21 | $39

Delray Beach | Addison Pl. | 16850 Jog Rd. (bet. Clint Moore Rd. &
Linton Blvd.) | 561-638-1949 | www.henrysofbocaraton.com

Though "named for a dog", this Delray Beach American dishes up
"21st-century comfort food" that's "fit for a king", including the
"magical pea soup"; even if it's frequently "mobbed" with an "older
crowd" cashing in on "enticing" specials, most consider the "big,
noisy" place with "reliably good service" a "keeper."

Hot Pie Pizza *Pizza*

- | - | - | I

West Palm Beach | 123 S. Olive Ave. (bet. Clematis & Datura Sts.) |
561-655-2511 | www.hotpiepizza.com

West Palm Beachers hankering for John Ries' coal-fired pies turn to
this affordable pizzeria/bar Downtown; brick walls and dark woods

add to the old-time feeling, while starters like filet mignon bites, craft beers and a full bar cater to the happy-hour crowd.

☑ Houston's *American*   22 | 21 | 22 | $37

Boca Raton | 1900 NW Executive Center Circle (Glades Rd.) | 561-998-0550 | www.hillstone.com
See review in Ft. Lauderdale/Broward County Directory.

Howley's ● *Diner*   17 | 14 | 18 | $20

West Palm Beach | 4700 S. Dixie Hwy. (Russlyn Dr.) | 561-833-5691
With its "kitschy-hip" decor, "full bar" and "elevated" diner fare, it's a "real kick" to eat at this "old-fashioned" West Palm Beach American, whether you're chilling "after a hard day's night" or "sitting at the counter watching breakfast unfold"; then again, foes who cite "ok" food and service "can't figure out what all the hype is about."

Hurricane Café *American*   21 | 13 | 21 | $27

Juno Beach | 14050 U.S. 1 (Donald Ross Rd.) | 561-630-2012 | www.hurricanecafe.com
In season, "it really *is* a hurricane" at this "casual-as-hell" Juno Beach American near the surf where "locals who know" squeeze in for one of the "best breakfasts around" and other "reasonably priced" fare; if the "strip mall" site isn't all that, the "homey" atmosphere and "friendly" service win over most.

Il Bellagio *Italian*   19 | 20 | 18 | $38

West Palm Beach | CityPlace | 600 S. Rosemary Ave. (Okeechobee Blvd.) | 561-659-6160 | www.ilbellagiocityplace.com
One look at the "beautiful fountains" and you'll think you're on a "European piazza" – and not in a "lovely" trattoria at West Palm's CityPlace; while the "hearty" Italian fare and "moderate prices" are "better than you might expect in a mall", it can seem a bit "touristy", though there's no debating it's "convenient to Kravis Center" and "great for people-watching"; P.S. now serves breakfast.

Il Girasole *Italian*   22 | 18 | 23 | $54

Delray Beach | Tropics Sq. | 1911 S. Federal Hwy. (Linton Blvd.) | 561-272-3566
This "charming little" Northern Italian in a Delray Beach strip mall may be "hard to find", but groupies gush you "won't forget where it is" after sampling its "simple but high-quality" fare and "pleasant service"; the "tired" decor ("this sunflower is a little wilted") isn't as memorable, but otherwise the "old standby" "never disappoints."

Ironwood Grille *American*   ▽ – | 20 | 18 | $45

Palm Beach Gardens | PGA National Resort | 400 Ave. of the Champions (PGA Blvd.) | 561-627-2000 | www.ironwoodgrille.com
If you're puttering around the PGA National Resort, duffers and diners alike say "begin or end your night" at the "great" watering hole appended to this "lovely" (and pricey) New American grill; the word is mixed on the eatery, however: some say it's "worth a visit" for "delicious steaks and seafood", others deem it "pricey for fairly ordinary fare."

FOOD | DECOR | SERVICE | COST

Jade 🔲Ⓜ *American* ▽ 24 | 15 | 21 | $41

West Palm Beach | 422 Northwood Rd. (N. Dixie Hwy.) | 561-366-1185 | www.jadekitchen.com

The "imaginative" menu "changes often" at this West Palm Beacher whose "interesting" New American dishes – combining aspects of Indian and Italian cooking, among others – please patrons who find good value here; moreover, the small, warehouse-modern "sleeper" in the "rebounding" Northwood neighborhood offers sidewalk seating, adding to an already "enjoyable dining experience"; P.S. plans call for additional seating and a wine bar.

J. Alexander's *American* 20 | 20 | 21 | $33

Palm Beach Gardens | Midtown | 4625 PGA Blvd. (Military Trail) | 561-694-2711

Boca Raton | University Commons | 1400 Glades Rd. (Broward Ave.) | 561-347-9875

www.jalexanders.com

"Wear roomy clothing" to accommodate the "large-enough-to-share" portions of "consistently good" American fare at these "upscale" chain links whose "clubby" interiors lure everyone from "young families" to "hopping" bar-sceners; some shrug they're just "pricey" "Houston's wannabes", but with "spot-on service" and "something for everyone" (including "vegetarian selections" and a "surprisingly refined wine list"), the consensus is "they've got it down."

Jetty's *Seafood* 22 | 22 | 21 | $42

Jupiter | 1075 N. A1A (U.S. 1) | 561-743-8166

Docksiders adore the "bustling" bar scene and "spectacular view" of the Jupiter lighthouse at this "reliable" waterfront seafooder, where "always good, always fresh" fin fare is served by an "excellent" staff; natch, there's a "downside (no reservations and almost always a wait)", so "go early": the crowd of "locals and tourists" fishing for "priced-right" sunset specials "starts lining up at 4:30."

John Bull English Pub ● *American* ▽ 18 | 15 | 18 | $29

West Palm Beach | Village Commons Shopping Plaza | 801 Village Blvd. (Palm Beach Lakes Blvd.) | 561-697-2855 | www.johnbullenglishpub.com

"Fish 'n' chips and darts": that's what you'll find at this "casual" pub in central West Palm Beach, as well as other "surprisingly good" American fare; bullheaded types bark there's "nothing remarkable" here, but even they concur it's a "pleasant place for a bite"; P.S. it's a "bit noisy", so consider the "wonderful" pet-friendly patio.

🔳 John G's on the Beach ⇌ *American* 23 | 12 | 21 | $20

Lake Worth | 10 S. Ocean Blvd. (Lake Ave.) | 561-585-9860 | www.johngs.com

"Bring your sneakers" and "join the line" at this beachside Lake Worth American, a "breakfast-and-lunch" "landmark" doling out "amazing" French toast ("heaven on a plate") and perhaps the "best fish 'n' chips this side of England"; it's "hectic" , but free "chocolate-covered fruit" (Sundays) and "spectacular views" ease the pain of that "long wait"; P.S. cash only; closes at 3 PM.

	FOOD	DECOR	SERVICE	COST

Josephine's Italian Restaurant *Italian* | 20 | 21 | 20 | $45 |

Boca Raton | 5751 N. Federal Hwy. (bet. Kingsbridge & Newcastle Sts.) |
561-988-0668 | www.josephinesofboca.com

Venturing into this "romantic" Boca Italian "elegantly" adorned with
colorful murals and flowers is "like stepping back in time", with "formal" (even "aloof") service to match; however, surveyors split on the
fare: fans find it's "wonderful food at a reasonable price", while the
less-taken deem it merely "decent", and sometimes "disappointing."

Joseph's Wine Bar & Café *Mediterranean* | ▽ 24 | 24 | 25 | $37 |

Delray Beach | Pineapple Grove | 200 NE Second Ave. (NE 2nd St.) |
561-272-6100 | www.josephswinebar.com

Fans of this midpriced Delray Beach Med are "reluctant" to share
too much info for fear "it will get too busy"; but the "fresh, homemade" fare paired with "terrific" wines, owners who "make you feel
like family" and a "European ambiance" (complete with chandeliers
and floor-to-ceiling wine racks) speak for themselves.

☑ Kathy's Gazebo Restaurant ⊠ *Continental* | 25 | 21 | 24 | $63 |

Boca Raton | 4199 N. Federal Hwy. (Spanish River Blvd.) | 561-395-6033 |
www.kathysgazebo.com

"Wear a jacket" to fit in with the "older", "well-to-do" crowd that frequents this Boca Raton Continental – they're here for a "three-hour
extravaganza" of dishes like "specialty Dover sole" served by
"French waiters who know their craft"; plan to "wait" for a table
("even with a reservation") and to "leave behind part of your fortune", but for those "who enjoy elegant dining", this is the place.

☑ Kee Grill *Seafood/Steak* | 24 | 21 | 22 | $47 |

Juno Beach | 14020 US Hwy. 1 (Donald Ross Rd.) |
561-776-1167
Boca Raton | 17940 N. Military Trail (Clint Moore Rd.) |
561-995-5044

The "early bird" gets the "bargain" at these midpriced, "tropical"-
themed Boca and Juno Beach "seafood shrines" (there's also
"flavorful meat") that are "packed" with devotees digging into the
"fabulously fresh" fin fare and the "scrumptious" spinach side; while
it's "good news" they "take reservations", "unending waits" persist,
and "rushed service" in a "noisy" setting rankle some; still, for most
they're "always a treat."

Kevin's Dockside Deli ⊿ *Deli* | - | - | - | I |

Palm Beach Gardens | Harborside Plaza | 2401 PGA Blvd.
(Prosperity Farms Rd.) | 561-694-7945

Locals eagerly wait in line at this New York–style deli set in Palm
Beach Gardens' Harborside Plaza for the Dennis family's authentic
versions of such favorites as hot pastrami on rye (or corned beef,
chopped liver, etc.); it's all here by the sandwich or by the pound –
plus sides, rice pudding and specials – in a dock-themed dining
room where you order at the counter and the affordable chow is
brought to you; P.S. cash only.

	FOOD	DECOR	SERVICE	COST

Kona Grill *American/Asian* | 19 | 21 | 19 | $33 |

West Palm Beach | CityPlace | 700 S. Rosemary Ave. (Okeechobee Blvd.) | 561-253-7900 | www.konagrill.com

"Great happy hours" make West Palm Beachers positively giddy at this national chain's CityPlace outpost, especially as the "creative" Pan-Asian and American fare goes for "really low prices"; while detractors ding "inconsistent meals" and service that ranges from "friendly" to "poor", the "wonderful atmosphere" wins over many heading out for a "night at the Kravis."

NEW Kubo *Asian* | - | - | - | M |

North Palm Beach | Crystal Tree Plaza | 1201 US Hwy. 1 (PGA Blvd.) | 561-776-7248

Roy Villacrusis, Mark Militello's former sushi artist, gets his own place in North Palm Beach to spotlight his characteristically inventive raw fin fare as well as a global melange of midpriced dishes with Asian influences; diners can choose between the tile-and-dark-wood interior or large patio to enjoy the eats, accompanied by a selection of sakes, beer and wine; P.S. there's live entertainment for the late-night crowd.

La Cigale *Mediterranean* | 22 | 20 | 23 | $51 |

Delray Beach | 253 SE Fifth Ave. (bet. 2nd & 3rd Sts.) | 561-265-0600 | www.lacigaledelray.com

"From the minute you walk in", diners are enveloped in an "*American in Paris* ambiance" at this "casual" Delray Beach bistro whose "always-changing menu" of "reliably good" Med fare is served by "obliging" staffers; it's "not cheap" and a "bit noisy" (especially near the bar), but it's usually a "solid choice" for a "night out with friends"; P.S. now open for lunch on weekdays.

La Luna *Italian* | 17 | 14 | 16 | $35 |

Boca Raton | Polo Shoppes | 5030 Champion Blvd. (N. Military Trail) | 561-997-1165 | www.lalunabistro.com

"Early-birders reign supreme" at this Boca Raton "standard" churning out "large portions" of "satisfactory" if "uninventive" Italian fare (seemingly best appreciated as a 'sunset dinner'); but service that can be "snotty" and "not very good" surroundings perturb those who wonder "how it's managed to stay around as long as it has."

Z LaSpada's Original Hoagies *Deli* | 27 | 8 | 22 | $11 |

Boca Raton | Commons at Town Ctr. | 2240 NW 19th St. (bet. Butts Rd. & NW Sheraton Way) | 561-393-1434 | www.laspadashoagies.com
See review in Ft. Lauderdale/Broward County Directory.

La Tre *Vietnamese* | 21 | 10 | 19 | $35 |

Boca Raton | 249 E. Palmetto Park Rd. (Mizner Blvd.) | 561-392-4568

"Taste buds dance" at this "upscale" Vietnamese in a Boca storefront, where the "delicious, different" chow "never disappoints" and the service aims to "please"; luckily, the "food is the thing here", since an "interior decorator could really dress this place up."

FOOD | DECOR | SERVICE | COST

La Villetta *Italian*

22 | 18 | 21 | $55

Boca Raton | 4351 N. Federal Hwy. (bet. 43rd & 44th Sts.) |
561-362-8403 | www.lavillettaboca.com

"Mm-mm-good": it's a common refrain at this "long-standing" Boca Italian thanks to a "solid" menu of "fresh", "well-prepared" fare like the "whole fish baked in sea salt", its "killer" signature; expect an "upscale" scene with prices to match, but with "professional service" and a "lively" atmosphere, many vow to "go back for more."

Lazy Loggerhead Café *Seafood*

23 | 9 | 20 | $21

Jupiter | Carlin Park | 401 N. A1A (E. Indiantown Rd.) | 561-747-1134

"Don't let the yellow shack fool you" – this beachside Jupiter seafooder "packs people" in, creating "long waits" on weekends as diners queue up for "huge portions" of "reasonably priced", "creative and delicious" breakfasts and lunches; service is "helpful and quick" (so "bring your family"), making it "perfect" before a day at the shore.

Leila *Mideastern*

22 | 19 | 20 | $34

West Palm Beach | 120 S. Dixie Hwy. (Datura St.) | 561-659-7373 |
www.leilawpb.com

"If you're looking for something different", try the "standout" Mideastern fare at this Downtown West Palm Beacher that's "easy on the eye" and wallet; the chow is "just delish", with "tasty" meze and small plates that "can be a meal", plus you can "sit outside."

☑ Lemongrass Asian Bistro *Asian*

23 | 17 | 19 | $34

Boca Raton | Royal Palm Pl. | 101 Plaza Real (bet. NE 3rd & NE 5th Sts.) |
561-544-8181
Boynton Beach | 1800 N. Congress Ave. (Renaissance Dr.) | 561-733-1344
Delray Beach | 420 E. Atlantic Ave. (Federal Hwy.) | 561-278-5050
www.lemongrassasianbistro.com

"Everyone talks about the lobster monster roll – and should" gush groupies about the "otherworldly" signature sushi at this "popular" Pan-Asian chainlet featuring "lively" venues with "innovative" fare at "attractive" prices; it's "entertaining" to eat outside where it's not as "crowded or noisy", and if servers can be "overextended", they're at least "friendly"; P.S. the newer Boca branch is a bit more "upscale."

Leopard Lounge *American/Eclectic*

20 | 24 | 23 | $53

Palm Beach | Chesterfield Hotel | 363 Cocoanut Row (Australian Ave.) |
561-659-5800 | www.chesterfieldpb.com

Prepare for "botox, dyed comb-overs" and "lime-green sports coats" at this "leopard-decorated" "hoot" in Palm Beach's Chesterfield Hotel where the "people-watching" is "not to be missed"; "young and old" alike (e.g. "cougars and their male counterparts") nosh on Eclectic–New American fare that's "not bad" and enjoy "great" service, but, really, most "go for the dancing, not for the food."

☑ L'Escalier ☒Ⓜ *French*

26 | 27 | 26 | $101

Palm Beach | The Breakers | 1 S. County Rd. (Breakers Row) |
561-655-6611 | www.thebreakers.com

"Does it get much better than this?" ponder partisans of this "elegant" French in Palm Beach's "historic" Breakers resort that whispers "class all the way"; post-Survey, a new chef has instituted forays into molecular gastronomy and the "beautiful decor" has been given a softer, less-stuffy update (outdating both the Food and Decor scores), but what hasn't changed is the "world-class service" and tabs for which you should "be prepared to spend and spend."

Limoncello *Italian*
20 | 15 | 21 | $47

North Palm Beach | 11603 U.S. 1 (PGA Blvd.) | 561-622-7200 | www.limoncellorestaurant.com

Amici of this "casual" North Palm Beach Northern Italian proffering a "solid" menu of "homemade pastas", seafood and, yes, "homemade limoncello" deem it a "let's-go-back kind of place"; "tired" decor rebuffs a few, but it's a "pleasurable" "family value" nonetheless.

☑ Little Moir's Food Shack ☒ *Seafood*
26 | 14 | 21 | $34

Jupiter | Jupiter Sq. | 103 S. Hwy. 1 (E. Indiantown Rd.) | 561-741-3626

☑ Little Moir's Leftovers Café ☒ *Seafood*

Jupiter | Abacoa Bermudiana | 451 University Blvd. (Military Trail) | 561-627-6030
www.littlemoirsfoodshack.com

There's "always a line" at this "crowded" Jupiter seafooder that's so "casual" "if you're wearing something other than flip-flops you're overdressed"; sure, "it looks like a dive" (thanks to its "shopping-center" locale) and the "surf shop atmosphere isn't for everyone", but few can resist its "fabulous fresh fish" with "mix-and-match toppings, salads and sauces" – and it's "a bargain" at that; P.S. the Abacoa venture is in "nicer digs" with "less waiting" and the "same food."

Maison Carlos Ⓜ *French/Italian*
- | - | - | M

West Palm Beach | 3010 S. Dixie Hwy. (Monceaux Rd.) | 561-659-6524 | www.maisoncarlos.com

It may have moved from its Downtown West Palm perch to a quieter, smaller El Cid space in a strip mall, but this fetching French-Italian still fosters a romantic (and upscale) vibe; its popular Caprese salad, lobster crêpes, lamb chops and filet fill out a new menu, while the solid wine list and professional staff made the leap intact; P.S. thrifty sorts will find there's also less-expensive dishes to choose from.

☑ Marcello's La Sirena ☒ *Italian*
27 | 21 | 26 | $63

West Palm Beach | 6316 S. Dixie Hwy. (bet. Franklin & Nathan Hale Rds.) | 561-585-3128 | www.lasirenaonline.com

"Palm Beachers cross the bridge" for the "unbelievable" (if "expensive") Italian food at this "impress-a-date" West Palm "classic" complete with an "outstanding wine cellar", "professional service" (the "black-tie maitre d' treats each guest like royalty") and an "old-fashioned" dining room that got a boost with a remodel; no wonder regulars "go through withdrawal" when it "closes for the summer."

☑ Max's Grille *American*
22 | 20 | 21 | $42

Boca Raton | Mizner Park | 404 Plaza Real (N. Federal Hwy.) | 561-368-0080 | www.maxsgrille.com

"Still a madhouse" "after all these years", this "noisy" New American is "loaded" with "Mizner Park scenesters" downing "so delicious" grub

FOOD | DECOR | SERVICE | COST

that's "priced right" and served by "knowledgeable" staffers; a few fret the decor's "a little long in the tooth", so "sit outside" and "enjoy the parade of Boca babes and boys" – "it's about as good as the food."

MB at the Omphoy *Mediterranean*
– | – | – | VE

Palm Beach | Omphoy Resort | 2842 S. Ocean Blvd. (Lake Ave.) | 561-540-6440 | www.omphoy.com
Having conquered Miami, celeb chef Michelle Bernstein lands in Palm Beach, where her simple but flavorful Med fare incorporating Latin and Floribbean influences is in residence at the posh Omphoy Resort; a large wine and cocktail list inspires barflies to buzz in for a drink and look around the interior, which features a floor-to-ceiling Atlantic panorama that's almost as eye-popping as the prices.

McCormick & Schmick's *Seafood*
20 | 19 | 20 | $45

NEW **West Palm Beach** | CityPlace | 651 Okeechobee Blvd. (bet. S. Sapodilla & S. Quadrille Blvds.) | 561-655-6363 Ⓢ Ⓜ
Boca Raton | 1400 Glades Rd. (Airport Rd.) | 561-394-2428
www.mccormickandschmicks.com
An "endless menu" that "changes daily" reels folks into these "lively" Boca and West Palm Beach chain links, where the seafood is "fresh" ("you can almost taste the sea drip off the fish") and the atmosphere "clubby"; still, cynics sniff it's "inconsistent" and "pricey" with "waits" for plates, begging the question "why eat here in South Florida?"

Mellow Mushroom *Pizza*
23 | 18 | 20 | $22

Delray Beach | 25 SE Sixth Ave. (E. Atlantic Ave.) | 561-330-3040 | www.mellowmushroom.com
The decor's a tad "tacky" at this Delray Beach chain link, but no matter: the "groovy" pizza and "tasty toppings" trump the retro style that'll have "you thinking you're back in the '60s" (a vibe abetted by "friendly" servers who "look like R. Crumb characters"); "outstanding beers" and "reasonable prices" seal the deal.

Melting Pot *Fondue*
20 | 19 | 21 | $43

Lake Worth | Palm Coast Plaza | 3044 S. Military Trail (10th Ave. N.) | 561-967-1009
Palm Beach Gardens | 11811 US Hwy. 1 (PGA Blvd.) | 561-624-0020
Boca Raton | 5455 N. Federal Hwy. (bet. NE 51st & Newcastle Sts.) | 561-997-7472
www.meltingpot.com
"Change-of-pace" mavens and "do-it-yourself" types are fond of this "novel" fondue franchise for its "interactive" approach, i.e. the chance to "cook your own dinner"; the "long, slow meals" make it appropriate for "first dates" or "large crowds", and although the morsels are "tasty", you'll "end up spending a lot of money" for them – and you may leave "smelling like hot oil and chocolate."

Michael R. McCarty's ❶ *American*
17 | 20 | 21 | $44

Palm Beach | Royal Poinciana Plaza | 50 Cocoanut Row (Royal Poinciana Way) | 561-659-1899 | www.michaelrmccartys.com
"If you know what to order" ("try the meatloaf" for starters), this "casual" Palm Beach American with "pleasant" tropical decor can be

a "charming" "place to sit and relax"; a few pout it's all "too plain" and "inconsistent", but they're overruled by those who say it's just a "good local watering hole."

Mississippi Sweets BBQ *BBQ*

| 22 | 11 | 18 | $24 |

Lake Worth | 9859 Lake Worth Rd. (Rte. 441) | 561-642-4748
Boca Raton | 2399 N. Federal Hwy. (NE 24th St) | 561-394-6779

"Bring Handi Wipes" for the "finger-lickin' good ribs" and "out-of-this-world sweet potato fries" at these "cramped" and "casual" 'cue joints, where the service is "sweet" and prices relatively "cheap"; they're "popular", though, so "go early" or prepare for "long waits" – "your mouth will thank you."

NEW Mister Milano ⑤ *Italian*

| - | - | - | E |

Palm Beach Gardens | 6271 PGA Blvd. (Ave. of Champions) | 561-804-7747 | www.mistermilano.com

Glam decor (think mega-chandeliers and silvery footware displayed on the walls), a piano player and leather banquettes set the stage for a peerless if pricey experience at this Palm Beach Gardens Italian; what's more, there's a gregarious owner-chef who makes the rounds after dishing up Milanese dishes like osso buco pappardelle with tenderloin ragu and risotto with foie gras, washed down with a wide selection of imported vinos.

Mondo's *American/Mediterranean*

| 19 | 14 | 18 | $30 |

North Palm Beach | 713 U.S. 1 (Lighthouse Dr.) | 561-844-3396 | www.mondosnpb.com

It's "not a chain", so expect "some local neighborhood flavor" at this "casual" North Palm Beach "sports bar" that touches all the bases: "well-executed" Med–New American fare, "warm" decor (well, "too dark" for a few), a new outdoor dining space and a "friendly" staff; all that, and it "won't break the bank."

Moquila *Mexican*

| 19 | 19 | 18 | $40 |

Boca Raton | Palmetto Pl. | 88 Plaza Real S. (bet. NE 2nd & 3rd Sts.) | 561-394-9990 | www.moquila.com

This "grown-up" Mexican attracts "all ages" to its East Boca digs, a "guacamole heaven" (it's "made tableside") that quenches quaffers with *mucho* "tequila cocktails" while providing hipsters a "scene-y" ambiance; however, dissatisfied sorts who grumble about "ok" fare that leaves a big "impact on your wallet" suggest you're "better off sticking to the 'quila' part of the menu."

☑ Morton's The Steakhouse *Steak*

| 25 | 23 | 24 | $69 |

West Palm Beach | Phillips Point Office Bldg. | 777 S. Flagler Dr. (Lakeview Ave.) | 561-835-9664
Boca Raton | Boca Ctr. | 5050 Town Center Circle (Military Trail) | 561-392-7724
www.mortons.com

"Consistency abounds" at this "can't-go-wrong" steakhouse chain that pairs "well-prepared" chops that "hang off the plate" with "seriously powerful martinis"; "arm-and-a-leg" pricing comes with the territory, of course, along with a "Saran-wrapped presentation" of raw meats (accompanied by an instructional "recitation" by the waiter) – so despite "terrific" service, some "could do without the dog and pony show."

☑ New York Prime *Steak*

25 | 21 | 21 | $75

Boca Raton | 2350 Executive Center Dr. NW (Glades Rd.) | 561-998-3881 | www.newyorkprime.com

You'll need a "line of credit" to chow down at this "noisy" but "elegant" meatery where "Boca's brattiest" come for "awesome cuts" of "prime cow" that would sate "Fred Flintstone"; natterers note a "New York City edge" (read: "lots of attitude") and an "unreliable" reservations policy, but it maintains "favorite" status for many.

Nick & Johnnie's *American*

18 | 18 | 19 | $40

Palm Beach | 207 Royal Poinciana Way (N. County Rd.) | 561-655-3319 | www.nickandjohnniespb.com

"Meet and greet" and eat at this "low-key" "sidewalk cafe", a Cucina Dell' Arte sib serving "innovative", midpriced American fare amid fountains and flowers in Palm Beach; mavens mutter about "average" grub and a staff that needs a "little more training", but even some sticklers say it's "worth a try"; P.S. it's added a juice and smoothie bar into the mix.

Oakwood Grill *American*

20 | 20 | 20 | $47

Palm Beach Gardens | PGA Commons East | 4610 PGA Blvd. (Hickory Dr.) | 561-776-5778 | www.oakwoodgrill.com

Owner John Spoto "always makes you feel welcome" at his "casual" Palm Beach Gardens American, and that extends to staffers who really "try to please"; "lower prices" also please, and if some snip the "consistently good" fare is still a bit "pricey", spendthrifts can consider the "great" early-bird specials; P.S. the Food score may not reflect changes in the kitchen.

NEW Office, The *American*

- | - | - | M

Delray Beach | 201 E. Atlantic Ave. (2nd Ave.) | 561-276-3600 | www.theofficedelray.com

The team behind Vic & Angelos just across Atlantic Avenue tries its hand at upscale comfort food (e.g. fried chicken, meatloaf sandwiches, burgers) at this midpriced Delray Beach New American with a retro vibe; chic cowhide and red leather accent the inside-outside bar and dining room, while sidewalk seating provides a comfortable perch for enjoying a craft beer.

Okeechobee Steakhouse *Steak*

21 | 15 | 20 | $45

West Palm Beach | 2854 Okeechobee Blvd. (Palm Beach Lakes Blvd.) | 561-683-5151 | www.okeesteakhouse.com

"Meat eaters" get a "free steak" on their birthday at this "old-style" carnivorium that's been providing "tasty" filets, "good" early-bird deals and "fine" service to West Palm Beachers since 1947; it's "cramped, hectic" and "dark" (wags wager "there should be a discount for lack of decor"), but "regulars love the place" anyhow.

	FOOD	DECOR	SERVICE	COST

Old Calypso *American/Creole*   19 | 22 | 19 | $39

Delray Beach | 900 E. Atlantic Ave. (Venetian Dr.) | 561-279-2300 | www.oldcalypso.com

The "wonderful Intracoastal setting" is "probably the best part" of this Delray Beach American featuring a "large" (if "staid") menu of "fresh fish" prepared with a "New Orleans flair"; those who won't take the bait bemoan "food and service not up to par", though the *"Cheers"*-like bar compensates; P.S. lunch is a "better bargain."

Original Pancake House, The *American*   20 | 11 | 17 | $17

Palm Beach Gardens | 4360 Northlake Blvd. (Military Trl.) | 561-721-2213 | www.originalpancakehouse.com
Boca Raton | Del Mar Vlg. | 7146 Bera Casa Way (Palmetto Park Rd.) | 561-395-2303 | www.originalpancakehouse.com
Delray Beach | 1840 S. Federal Hwy. (Linton Blvd.) | 561-276-0769 | www.originalpancakehouseflorida.com
Royal Palm Beach | 105 S. State Rd. 7 (Southern Blvd.) | 561-296-0878 | www.originalpancakehouse.com
See review in Miami/Dade County Directory.

Outback Steakhouse *Steak*   17 | 15 | 18 | $30

Lake Worth | 6266 Lantana Rd. (Jog Rd.) | 561-963-7010
West Palm Beach | Village Commons | 871 Village Blvd. (bet. Brandywine Rd. & Community Dr.) | 561-683-1011
Stuart | 3101 SE Federal Hwy. (SE Indian St.) | 772-286-2622
Palm Beach Gardens | 10933 N. Military Trail (PGA Blvd.) | 561-625-0793
Jupiter | 103 S. U.S. 1 (Indiantown Rd.) | 561-743-6283
Boca Raton | Boca Green Shopping Ctr. | 19595 State Rd. 7 (bet. Kimberly & New England Blvds.) | 561-479-2526
Boca Raton | 6030 SW 18th St. (bet. Military Trail & Powerline Rd.) | 561-338-6283
Delray Beach | 1300 Linton Blvd. (Wallace Dr.) | 561-272-7201
Royal Palm Beach | 11101 Southern Blvd. (¼ mile west of Rte. 441) | 561-795-6663
www.outback.com
See review in Miami/Dade County Directory.

Paddy Mac's *Irish*   ∇ 22 | 17 | 23 | $29

Palm Beach Gardens | Garden Square Shoppes | 10971 N. Military Trail (PGA Blvd.) | 561-691-4366 | www.paddymacspub.com

There's a "little bit o' Dublin" in this "cheery" Palm Beach Gardens nook, courtesy of "good food at reasonable prices", "great live music" Friday–Saturday and "authentic" Emerald Isle decor; plus, the "friendly proprietor" really "knows how" to pull a Guinness – but "it's an Irish bar, so what did you expect?"

Padrino's *Cuban*   20 | 14 | 19 | $25

Boca Raton | Mission Bay Plaza | 20455 State Rd. 7 (Glades Rd.) | 561-451-1070 | www.padrinos.com

At this "reliable" South Florida chainlet, diners find "big portions" of "comforting" Cuban fare in a "plain, simple" setting; it's "pretty standard" stuff, but "prices that can't be beat" and a "family-friendly" atmosphere draw a "crowd."

	FOOD	DECOR	SERVICE	COST

◪ Palm Beach Grill *American*   25 | 22 | 23 | $48

Palm Beach | Royal Poinciana Plaza | 340 Royal Poinciana Way (Cocoanut Row) | 561-835-1077 | www.palmbeachgrill.com
Owned by the same company as the popular chain, this "Houston's in disguise" has nonetheless become a "Palm Beach must" where it's "hard to get reservations in-season" (tip: call "weeks in advance"); once in, expect "straightforward" American "comfort food" and a "young crowd" crammed into the "noisy" dining room or "chic" bar; all in all, it's a "typical highbrow scene", albeit one fueled by relatively "reasonable prices."

Palm Beach Steak House *Steak*   ▽ 23 | 19 | 21 | $53

Palm Beach | 191 Bradley Pl. (bet. Oleander & Seminole Aves.) | 561-671-4333 | www.thepalmbeachsteakhouse.com
Anxious admirers aver "more people need to discover" this Palm Beach "sleeper", if only for its "marvelous" early-bird special, which includes a "glass of wine" and wide choice of "excellent" steaks and Hellenic dishes; moreover, an "old-world courtliness" pervades the place, though that changes on "Greek night" (Thursdays), when belly dancers, a singing chef-owner and ouzo take over.

Paradiso *Italian*   21 | 18 | 21 | $61

Lake Worth | 625 Lucerne Ave. (bet. K & L Sts.) | 561-547-2500 | www.paradisolakeworth.com
Enthusiasts "enjoy the old-school formality" of this "upscale" Italian in Downtown Lake Worth, which is praised for its "talented" servers and "well-prepared" fare with a "European flavor"; but naysayers suggest it's "overpriced" and "self-impressed", with a "kitchen that doesn't quite live up to its aspirations."

Park Avenue   19 | 11 | 18 | $22
BBQ Grille *BBQ*

Lake Worth | 2401 N. Dixie Hwy. (Cornell Dr.) | 561-586-7427
West Palm Beach | 2215 Palm Beach Lakes Blvd. (Village Blvd.) | 561-689-7427
Stuart | 769 NW Federal Hwy. (Wright Rd.) | 772-692-0111
North Palm Beach | 525 U.S. 1 (Anchorage Dr.) | 561-842-7427
Tequesta | 236 U.S. 1 (bet. Glynn Mayo Hwy. & Tequesta Dr.) | 561-747-7427
NEW **Boca Raton** | 1198 N. Dixie Hwy. (Glades Rd.) | 561-416-7427
Boynton Beach | 4796 N. Congress Ave. (Hypoluxo Rd.) | 561-357-7427
Wellington | 13897 Wellington Trace (Greenview Shores Blvd.) | 561-795-7427
www.pabbqgrille.com
"Indulge your inner glutton" during "all-you-can-eat nights" at these "consistent" PB County 'cue "joints" luring everyone from families and "starving college students" to seniors "who'll knock you out of the way"; saucy sorts dis the "no-frills decor", but "surprisingly good" ribs and other BBQ staples, "fast" service and "reasonable prices" make it easy to overlook.

	FOOD	DECOR	SERVICE	COST

Z P.F. Chang's China Bistro *Chinese* | 21 | 21 | 20 | $33 |

West Palm Beach | The Gardens | 3101 PGA Blvd. (Campus Dr.) |
Palm Beach Gardens | 561-691-1610
Boca Raton | University Commons | 1400 Glades Rd. (NW 10th Ave.) |
561-393-3722
www.pfchangs.com
See review in Miami/Dade County Directory.

Pistache French Bistro *French* | 19 | 20 | 19 | $43 |

West Palm Beach | 101 N. Clematis St. (Flagler Dr.) | 561-833-5090 |
www.pistachewpb.com
"Plenty of tables, plenty of class" and plenty of "tasty", "well-priced" French fare make this "adorable", art nouveau–style bistro a "solid" addition to Downtown West Palm Beach; malcontents mumble about "spotty service" and "ok" food, but more say *non, non* – it's a "pleasure" and "we will be back."

Pizza Girls *Pizza* | 22 | 9 | 16 | $12 |

West Palm Beach | 114 S. Clematis St. (bet. Flagler Dr. & Narcissus Ave.) |
561-833-4004 | www.pizzagirls.com
"New York–style pizza" partisans profess they "gotta have" the "pretty dang good" pies proffered by this no-frills West Palm "hole-in-the-wall", as much for the "not too thick, not too thin" crusts as the "wonderful toppings"; you can "order at the counter" and take it home, but for a more "amusing" meal, "grab a slice, sit and people-watch."

Pizza Rustica ● *Pizza* | 21 | 8 | 14 | $14 |

Delray Beach | 1155 E. Atlantic Ave. (Ocean Blvd.) | 561-279-8766 |
www.pizza-rustica.com
See review in Miami/Dade County Directory.

Player's Club Restaurant *Seafood/Steak* ▽ | 19 | 19 | 18 | $49 |

Wellington | 13410 Southshore Blvd. (Greenview Shores Blvd.) |
561-795-0080 | www.playersclubrestaurant.com
Chukka fans favor this "clubby" surf 'n' turfer in Wellington, where "views of the polo fields" are unmatched and the "no-surprises" menu is "well prepared" but "expensive"; however, gourmands who grouse it's "inconsistent" suggest "going for the piano player" on weekends; P.S. a VIP cabana has been added into the mix.

Portobello *Italian* | 22 | 19 | 22 | $46 |

Jupiter | Jupiter Bay Plaza | 351 S. U.S. 1 (Indiantown Rd.) | 561-748-3224 |
www.portobellojupiter.com
"Wonderful hosts", "delicous" Italian cooking, an "attentive staff" – small wonder this "lovely" eatery in an "off-the-beaten-path" Jupiter storefront remains "popular"; it's a "little costly" compared with some of its competition, but then again, it's a "little nicer" as well.

Prime Catch *Seafood* | 21 | 20 | 19 | $41 |

Boynton Beach | 700 E. Woolbright Rd. (S. Federal Hwy.) |
561-737-8822 | www.primecatchboynton.com
Try to "sit outside" at this "lovely", oft-"busy" Boynton Beach seafooder and watch the "yachts go by" as you dig into "inven-

FOOD | DECOR | SERVICE | COST

tively prepared" "fresh fish" or the "not-to-be-missed brunch"; nevertheless, even though it's "right on the Intracoastal", a few dismiss it as purely "middle of the road", with "inconsistent" food and service.

NEW Rack's Downtown Eatery + Tavern *American*

| - | - | - | M |

Boca Raton | Mizner Park | 402 Plaza Real (Federal Hwy.) | 561-395-1662 | www.grrestaurant.com

The hip setting (e.g. chandeliers fashioned from rope) racks up points with diners digging into the old-fashioned American chow with a modern spin at this Boca newcomer from Table 42's Gary Rack; moderate prices are a further lure, hence the happy-hour denizens and late-night partyers who share plates and sample craft beers and wines by the glass.

Raindancer Steakhouse *Steak*

| 23 | 19 | 22 | $50 |

West Palm Beach | 2300 Palm Beach Lakes Blvd. (west of I-95) | 561-684-2810 | www.raindancersteakhouse.com

It's "not the fanciest place", but this longtime, dinner-only West Palm meatery is still a "winner" among beef eaters; chalk it up to "worth-the-money" steaks, a "wonderful salad bar" and "great service", all of which makes it a "classic" in its "quiet way."

RA Sushi *Japanese*

| 19 | 22 | 17 | $32 |

Palm Beach Gardens | Downtown at the Gdns. | 11701 Lake Victoria Gardens Ave. (PGA Blvd.) | 561-340-2112 | www.rasushi.com

Dining at this "cool", bamboo-imbued chain Japanese is akin to "eating in a crowded disco", but "if you can take the noise", there's a "terrific happy hour" with "half-price apps and sushi"; critics who say it just "doesn't do it" for them deem it "more of a bar than quality restaurant", and "a bit pricey" at that.

Reef Road Restaurant & Rum Bar *Seafood*

| - | - | - | M |

West Palm Beach | 223 Clematis St. (Olive Ave.) | 561-838-9099

Fresh seafood, more than 100 types of rum and nightly live entertainment are the headliners at this midpriced West Palm Beacher located on Clematis; lobster rolls and fish sandwiches swim to the top of the menu (though there's also steak, burgers and the like), while the islandlike decor adds a touch of the Caribbean.

NEW Relish *Burgers*

| - | - | - | I |

West Palm Beach | Old Northwood | 401 Northwood Rd. (Dixie Hwy.) | 561-629-5377 | www.relishburger.com

Burgeristas are relishing the plethora of patty picks (beef, lamb, turkey, vegetarian) and gourmet topping choices at this budget-friendly West Palm Beach newcomer, which also proffers quality sides, milkshakes and craft beers; order at the counter, then grab a seat on the sidewalk or stay indoors, where huge windows give the simple space an airy, sunny feel.

	FOOD	DECOR	SERVICE	COST

Renato's *Italian*

22	25	23	$62

Palm Beach | 87 Via Mizner (Worth Ave.) | 561-655-9752 |
www.renatospalmbeach.com

"Dapper, gentlemanly waiters", a "lovely courtyard", "decadent food" . . . why, it's just "like being in Europe" sigh supporters of this "romantic" Italian that's "one of the prettiest places in Palm Beach"; it's "heavy on the budget", but then again, "what isn't on Worth Avenue?"

Rhythm Café Ⓜ *American*

▽ 22	19	23	$40

West Palm Beach | 3800 S. Dixie Hwy. (Southern Blvd.) |
561-833-3406 | www.rhythmcafe.cc

"Romantic in a retro kind of way", this West Palm "bohemian" in a restored 1950s drug store is quite a pill, dishing up a "great combination" of "beautifully served" American dishes (including "outstanding Key lime chicken"); it's "quirky", for certain, but it works.

Riggin's Crabhouse *Seafood*

18	10	18	$33

Lantana | 607 Ridge Rd. (I-95, exit 61) | 561-586-3000 |
www.rigginscrabhouse.com

There's never an absence of mallets at this "real Maryland-style crab house" in Lantana, where an "attentive" staff oversees crustaceaneers "whacking" away at their meal; it's "overdue for a makeover" ("eat with your eyes closed") and the shell-shocked say they've "tasted better", but it's an "interesting place to eat in once or twice"; P.S. outdoor dining is planned.

River House, The *Seafood/Steak*

23	23	23	$50

Palm Beach Gardens | Harborside Plaza | 2373 PGA Blvd.
(Prosperity Farms Rd.) | 561-694-1188 | www.riverhouserestaurant.com

"Impress a date" at this "crowd-pleasing" Palm Beach Gardens surf 'n' turfer where "boats go by" on the Intracoastal "while you wait" for a table and nurse "great cocktails" (reservations on weekends only); happily, "solid service" and "costly but good" fare – including one of the "best salad bars in town" – leave few complaining.

Rocco's Tacos *Mexican*

22	21	20	$29

West Palm Beach | 224 Clematis St. (bet. Narcissus & Olive Aves.) |
561-650-1001 ◑
NEW Boca Raton | 5250 Town Ctr. Circle (Military Trail) |
561-416-2131
www.roccostacos.com

This "festive" Clematis Street Mexican "rocks" thanks to "terrific" owner Rocco Mangel, who occasionally "dances down the bar" and "pours free tequila" into the "young crowd"; moreover, the "creative" chow – especially the "awesome" guacamole and chips – wins over foodies, even those who call it "way too loud" and "pricey"; P.S. the Boca venue opened post-Survey; a Lauderdale branch is due.

Royal Café in Jupiter ⊅ *American/Diner*

–	–	–	I

Jupiter | Calle Vieja Shopping Ctr. | 75 E. Indiantown Rd. (Alt. A1A) |
561-747-7426

Tucked into a Jupiter shopping plaza, this family-owned diner offers Traditional American breakfast and lunch fare to locals, tourists and

VIPs alike in a down-home setting; expect generous portions at prices that won't stretch your wallet too thin and a friendly greeting from the longtime staff.

☑ Ruth's Chris Steak House *Steak*
25 | 22 | 24 | $65

West Palm Beach | CityPlace | 651 Okeechobee Blvd. (bet. S. Sapodilla & S. Quadrille Blvds.) | 561-514-3544
North Palm Beach | 661 U.S. 1 (Lighthouse Dr.) | 561-863-0660
Boca Raton | 225 NE Mizner Blvd. (NE 2nd St.) | 561-392-6746
www.ruthschris.com
See review in Miami/Dade County Directory.

Safire Ⓜ *Asian*
▽ 25 | 13 | 25 | $33

Lake Worth | 817 Lake Ave. (N. J St.) | 561-588-7768
Ok, it's "not the best looking" place, but this "under-the-radar" "gem" in Lake Worth is a "hands-down favorite" for its "unexpectedly good" Asian fusion fare; service is "highly efficient", but the venue is "teeny tiny", prompting some to suggest it's "best for takeout."

Saigon Tokyo *Japanese/Vietnamese*
▽ 22 | 13 | 16 | $22

Greenacres | 2902 Jog Rd. (10th Ave. N.) | 561-966-1288 | www.saigontokyorestaurant.com
"Huge portions" of "very good" sushi and Vietnamese dishes ("filling pho") can be found at this "always crowded" Greenacres Asian; decor and service are "nothing special", but who cares when it's "one of the best buys around."

Sailfish Marina *Seafood*
18 | 22 | 18 | $35

Palm Beach Shores | 98 Lake Dr. (¼ mi. south of Blue Heron Blvd.) | 561-842-8449 | www.sailfishmarina.com
Breakfasters, barhounds and everyone in between gather for the "beautiful water views" at this "popular" seafooder in Palm Beach Shores; the "location, location, location" ("three great reasons to visit") trumps the chow, which can be "pretty good or just fair", but the "Key West feel", "pro service" and "outstanding bar scene" make even locals who gather here feel like they're on an "island vacation."

Saito's Japanese Steakhouse *Japanese/Steak*
21 | 18 | 21 | $32

West Palm Beach | CityPlace | 700 S. Rosemary Ave. (Okeechobee Blvd.) | 561-296-8881
Palm Beach Gardens | Midtown Plaza | 4675 PGA Blvd. (Garden Square Blvd.) | 561-202-6888
Boynton Beach | 8316 Jog Rd. (bet.Gateway & Le Chalet Blvds.) | 561-369-1788
Wellington | 10240 W. Forest Hill Blvd. (Rte. 441) | 561-296-8888
www.saitosteakhouse.com
It's "dinner and a show" from the "hibachi chefs" and "fun bartenders" at these "entertaining" Japanese steakhouses, where "artfully prepared" sushi and sashimi and other "selections to please everyone" come in "large portions"; so "bring an empty stomach" and the "family", because "kids *love* this place."

	FOOD	DECOR	SERVICE	COST

Sapori *Italian*
23 | 17 | 22 | $57

Boca Raton | Royal Palm Pl. | 99 Royal Palm Pl. (Federal Hwy.) | 561-367-9779

Chef-owner Marco Pindo "comes out to greet" the regulars at his "old-fashioned" Italian in Royal Palm Place, which has "consistently put out" "wonderful" seafood and pastas that you can have "any way you want"; if there's a flaw, it's the "limited" wine list, so "bring your own."

Sara's Kitchen *American*
- | - | - | M

Palm Beach Gardens | City Ctr. | 2000 PGA Blvd. (U.S. 1) | 561-540-2822 | www.saraskitchenllc.com

Sure, it may be a bit hard to find (it's tucked inside a Palm Beach Gardens office building), but fans of this American cafe are spreading the word – and the weekend breakfast and lunch crowds attest to its burgeoning popularity; the draw: healthy omelets, big sandwiches and deep bowls of soup served by affable staffers at gentle prices.

☑ Seasons 52 *American*
23 | 24 | 23 | $41

Palm Beach Gardens | 11611 Ellison Wilson Rd. (PGA Blvd.) | 561-625-5852

Boca Raton | 2300 NW Executive Center Dr. (NW Executive Center Circle) | 561-998-9952

www.seasons52.com

See review in Ft. Lauderdale/Broward County Directory.

Sláinte Irish Pub ◐ *Irish/Pub*
14 | 18 | 15 | $26

Boynton Beach | Renaissance Commons | 1500 Gateway Blvd. (N. Congress Ave.) | 561-742-4190 | www.slaintepubs.com

"Good live music" turns this Boynton Beach Gaellic into a "Disney experience" for some, but the unenchanted contend the "loud TVs" and bar buzz just make it "incredibly noisy"; "long waits" don't help, and as for the grub, well, it's "ok Irish food in an ok Irish pub."

☑ Sloan's Ice Cream *Ice Cream*
23 | 22 | 17 | $10

West Palm Beach | 112 S. Clematis St. (S. Narcissus Ave.) | 561-833-3335

West Palm Beach | CityPlace | 700 S. Rosemary Ave. (Okeechobee Blvd.) | 561-833-4303

Palm Beach Gardens | Downtown at the Gdns. | 11701 Lake Victoria Gardens Ave. (PGA Blvd.) | 561-627-4301

Boca Raton | Mizner Park | 329 Plaza Real (N. Federal Hwy.) | 561-338-9887

www.sloansonline.com

Enveloped in an "explosion of peach colors" and home to enough "lusciously rich ice cream" to "satisfy any sweet tooth", these "cute" "soda fountains" are a "must" "with or without kids" – just beware of "long lines"; if some find the place "pricey" ("share a cone"), most feel it's "worth it", and indeed, it's PB's No. 1 Bang for the Buck.

Snappers *Seafood*
18 | 13 | 16 | $32

Boynton Beach | Oakwood Sq. | 398 N. Congress Ave. (Old Boynton Rd.) | 561-375-8600 | www.snappers.com

"There's always a line" to get into this "shopping-center" seafooder in Boynton Beach, a "hit" with "golden-agers" who come for its

	FOOD	DECOR	SERVICE	COST

"mouthwatering" cedar-planked halibut and "fair" prices; maybe so, but critics "don't get" why it's so "popular" (it's not the "mediocre" service or decor) and suggest there are "better choices available."

Solu *American*   ∇ - | 26 | 23 | M

Singer Island | Marriott Singer Island Beach Resort & Spa | 3800 N. Ocean Dr. (Bimini Ln.) | 561-340-1795 | www.solurestaurant.com
It's a "keeper in the rotation" coo converts of this "romantic" oceanfront "destination" in the Marriott on Singer Island, where a new chef is tweaking a New American menu rife in Asian, Caribbean and Latin influences – and with lower prices to boot; "gracious" service and a "gorgeous location" offer further incentive.

Sonoma Café & Bistro ☒ *American*   ∇ 20 | 17 | 20 | $44

Delray Beach | 640 E. Atlantic Ave. (Federal Hwy.) | 561-243-8581
Surveyors are of mixed mind on this "reasonably priced", Euro-inflected American in Delray Beach: supporters salute "very good" grub ("love the Wiener schnitzel") served in a "warm, inviting" atmosphere, while foes flag "average" fare in a "crowded", "noisy" space; in any case, there's "nice music on weekends" to enjoy.

Spoto's Oyster Bar *Seafood*   23 | 19 | 22 | $44

Palm Beach Gardens | 4560 PGA Blvd. (Military Trail) | 561-776-9448 | www.spotos.com
"Raw, sautéed, steamed or bouillabaissed", it's all "spot on" at John Spoto's "trendy" Palm Beach Gardens seafooder, where bivalve boosters "love watching the shuckers" work on some of the "freshest" oysters in town (though "not the cheapest"); while the "consistently delicious" fare and "knowledgeable" service "swim to the top", vets advise "sitting outside" to escape the "noise."

Station Grille, The *Seafood*   23 | 11 | 19 | $46

Lantana | 200 W. Lantana Rd. (Dixie Hwy.) | 561-547-6022

Station House *Seafood*

Lantana | 233 W. Lantana Rd. (Dixie Hwy.) | 561-547-9487
www.stationrestaurants.com
"Don't be put off" by the "weather-worn surroundings" at these Lantana twins, because claw-nivores "come here for the great lobsters" "as big as Volkswagens" and "forget everything else"; the Grille also offers steaks and the House proffers pasta, but, really, it's all about the "steamed two-pounders" here; P.S. savvy savers insist the "early-bird" prices "can't be beat."

Stir Crazy *Asian*   20 | 18 | 18 | $26

Boca Raton | Boca Raton Town Ctr. | 6000 Glades Rd. #1015
(bet. Butts Rd. & St. Andrews Blvd.) | 561-338-7500 | www.stircrazy.com
See review in Ft. Lauderdale/Broward County Directory.

Stresa *Italian*   18 | 12 | 19 | $38

West Palm Beach | 2710 Okeechobee Blvd. (bet. Congress Ave. & Palm Beach Lakes Blvd.) | 561-615-0200
The "early-bird" brigade and "pre-Kravis" diners drop into this "comfortable" Italian in West Palm Beach for "red-sauce" favorites

and "dependable service"; but "tired" trattoria-style decor and "inconsistent" fare leave many unimpressed, even if it does "try hard."

⌷ Sundy House Ⓜ *American* | 23 | 27 | 23 | $52 |

Delray Beach | Sundy House | 106 S. Swinton Ave. (Atlantic Ave.) | 561-272-5678 | www.sundyhouse.com

You're "in another world" (and PB's No. 1 for Decor) at this "gorgeous" Delray Beach estate-cum-inn, especially if seated amid the "water features" in the "exquisite" "tropical garden" for the "elaborate Sunday brunch"; service is reliably "excellent" and tabs notoriously "pricey", and if a few fret that the New American fare "doesn't match the setting", the vast majority maintains this is a "special place for a special occasion."

Sushi Jo's *Japanese* | 23 | 16 | 20 | $38 |

West Palm Beach | 319 Belvedere Rd. (Dixie Hwy.) | 561-868-7893
Palm Beach Gardens | PGA Commons | 5080 PGA Blvd. (Hickory Dr.) | 561-691-9811
Boynton Beach | Ocean Plaza | 640 E. Ocean Ave. (SE 6th Ct.) | 561-737-0606
www.sushijo.com

"Check your wallet at the door and open wide": there's "shockingly good" – and "pricey" – sushi and sakitinis to be savored at these "unique, fresh and friendly" raw-fin "treasures"; diners can "eat outdoors" at all three, a plus at the "nightclub"-y West Palm venue that features "loud music" and an interior so "dark" some advise "bringing a flashlight to read the menu."

Sushi Simon *Japanese* | - | - | - | M |

Boynton Beach | 1614 S. Federal Hwy. (off E. Woolbright Rd.) | 561-731-1819

"Sit at the bar" and "let the chef serve you" some of the "freshest" raw fish in town at this casual Boynton Beacher "near the Intracoastal"; it's a "small place", but it'll "satisfy your craving" for sushi and sashimi.

Tabica Grill *American* | 21 | 17 | 22 | $32 |

Jupiter | The Woods Shopping Plaza | 901 W. Indiantown Rd. (Pennock Ln.) | 561-747-0108 | www.tabicagrill.net

"Beef, fish, chicken or whatever", it's "always good" at this Jupiter strip-maller proffering "big portions" of "homestyle" American chow; "moderate prices", "incredible early-bird dinners" and "friendly" servers cement its status as a "locals' favorite", even if it's "loud" and "sometimes hard to get in."

NEW Table 42 *Italian* | - | - | - | M |

Boca Raton | Royal Palm Plaza | 399 SE Mizner Blvd. (Federal Hwy.) | 561-826-2625 | www.grrestaurant.com

Restaurateur Gary Rack has turned the former Coal Mine Pizza space in Boca into a chic but casual Italian where guests are encouraged to linger over dinner at booths and tables, sharing plates of pasta, coal-fired pizzas, hearty salads and bottles of wine; outdoor seating, a thumping bar scene and the budget-friendly '$5 Burger Night' draw a younger crowd that swings well after dark.

☒ Ta-boo *American/Continental*

| 21 | 22 | 22 | $54 |

Palm Beach | 221 Worth Ave. (bet. Hibiscus Ave. & S. County Rd.) | 561-835-3500 | www.tabeorestaurant.com

Put on "your Lilly or Ralph to fit in" at this Worth Avenue "experience" where "you never know who" you'll see sitting at the "premium window seat"; the "terrific" Continental–New American fare, "gorgeous" space, "attentive" staff and "semi-reasonable" prices make it a "mainstay" for "ladies who lunch", but it "gets torrid" after dark, so follow the islanders' example: "come for the food, stay for the show!"

Taso's Greek Taverna *Greek*

| 22 | 12 | 20 | $26 |

Delray Beach | 14802 S. Military Trail (Atlantic Ave.) | 561-637-7671

Sure, the "place could use some sprucing", but fans of the "great tasting", "homestyle" Greek grub at this "unpretentious" Delray Beach taverna say "you come here for the food, not the decor"; "reasonable" tabs are another reason there's usually "people waiting on line."

NEW Taste Gastropub *American*

| - | - | - | M |

Delray Beach | Pineapple Grove | 169 NE Second Ave. (NE 1st St.) | 561-274-4444 | www.tastegastropub.com

Original Mango Gangster Allen Susser ventures north to Delray's Pineapple Grove with this cheeky, thoroughly modern incarnation of a gastropub, which proffers moderately priced comfort foods like pork belly sliders and lobster mac 'n' cheese; an open-air kitchen and a charcuterie bar set the scene, while two bustling watering holes – one on the cozy patio out back – are popular gathering places during happy hour.

Taverna Kyma ◑ *Greek*

| 20 | 17 | 18 | $39 |

Boca Raton | 6298 N. Federal Hwy. (Forsyth St.) | 561-994-2828 | www.tavernakyma.com

"More locals are discovering" this "bustling" Boca taverna (a sib of Taverna Opa), where the "whole grilled fish" is a standout and "accommodating" cooks in the "open kitchen" take special orders "when they're not busy"; relatively "affordable" prices draw a "festive" crowd, though conversationalists say "sit outside" or "go midweek" to avoid the "loud music" and "tabletop belly dancers."

Taverna Opa *Greek*

| 19 | 16 | 17 | $37 |

West Palm Beach | CityPlace | 700 S. Rosemary Ave. (Okeechobee Blvd.) | 561-820-0002 | www.opapalmbeach.com

See review in Ft. Lauderdale/Broward County Directory.

Temple Orange *Italian/Mediterranean*

| - | - | - | E |

Manalapan | Ritz-Carlton Palm Beach | 100 S. Ocean Blvd. (Ocean Ave.) | 561-533-6000 | www.templeorangepalmbeach.com

The floor-to-ceiling windows of this orange-tinged Ritz-Carlton Med-Italian may offer sparkling Atlantic vistas, but it's the food that garners much of the attention – flatbreads and panini for light (and light-filled) lunches, then creamy burrata, wild mushroom risotto

FOOD | DECOR | SERVICE | COST

and the like for candlelit dinners; sip wine from a notable list and enjoy the view, but for something different, check out the monthly stargazing nights, when telescopes are set out on the terrace.

Tempura House *Asian* ∇ 20 | 16 | 15 | $36

Boca Raton | 9858 Clint Moore Rd. (Rte. 441) | 561-883-6088
With "Chinese, sushi, hibachi and some Thai" on the menu, there's "something for everyone" at this casual Boca venue (plus, of course, the "good" namesake tempura); still, it's the "tremendous portions" of raw-fin fare that win the highest praise, even if tabs can be a "bit pricey."

Thaikyo Asian Cuisine *Japanese/Thai* 22 | 18 | 21 | $34

Manalapan | Plaza Del Mar | 201 S. Ocean Blvd. (E. Ocean Ave.) | 561-588-6777 | www.thaikyo.com
This "delightful" (and "reasonable") Asian puts "all things Thai and Japanese" in the spotlight, with "satisfying" results; "fine service", "live piano music" and a "lovely" mango-hued space are other reasons Manalapan "locals seem to like it a lot."

☑ 32 East *American* 26 | 21 | 23 | $53

Delray Beach | 32 E. Atlantic Ave. (bet. 1st & Swinton Aves.) | 561-276-7868 | www.32east.com
"On the Avenue and on the ball", this "hopping" Delray Beach New American "remains a class act" thanks to "passionate chef" Nick Morfogen, who creates a "nightly changing menu" with "deliciously different twists" on "market-fresh" cuisine; expect to find a "hip crowd" alternately "people-watching", quaffing "tempting libations" and making lots of "noise" (ask the "accommodating servers" for a "quieter" table upstairs); P.S. diners deem the "half-portion" options "palatable for the pocketbook."

This Is It Café *American/Diner* - | - | - | I

West Palm Beach | Northwood Vill. | 444 24th St. (Dixie Hwy.) | 561-655-3301
This cheery, nautical-themed West Palm diner is just what you'd expect the sib of Jupiter's Royal Café to be: a friendly, casual stop for good ol' American home cooking that'll fill you up without breaking the bank; servers learn regulars' names soon, and with neighbors greeting friends and sharing local news, it all seems a bit Mayberry-esque – and that's a *good* thing.

III Forks *Seafood/Steak* 23 | 23 | 22 | $63

Palm Beach Gardens | Midtown | 4645 PGA Blvd. (Military Trail) | 561-630-3660
Boca Raton | 200 E. Palmetto Park Rd. (Mizner Blvd.) | 561-416-2185
www.iiiforks.com
"Raise your forks" at these marble-studded Texas imports in Boca, Palm Beach Gardens and Hallandale, where "y'all get a great feed" on "prime-grade beef" served with "awesome" sides; the filet-weary question "how many more steakhouses do we need?" and gripe they're too "pricey", but carnivores who like to "feel pampered" while poring over a 300-label wine list insist they'll "be back."

	FOOD	DECOR	SERVICE	COST

Tin Muffin Café, The ☒⇎ *American*

| 23 | 16 | 21 | $22 |

Boca Raton | 364 E. Palmetto Park Rd. (bet. Federal Hwy. & SE 4th Ave.) | 561-392-9446

"Ladies who lunch" – and their "husbands" too – pack this "tiny" Boca American for "wonderful" "homemade muffins, quiche, soup and desserts"; there's "sometimes a wait", but once through the door, most everyone "leaves stuffed . . . and wanting more"; P.S. cash only.

Too Bizaare *Eclectic*

| 21 | 23 | 20 | $35 |

Jupiter | 287 E. Indiantown Rd. (Intracoastal Pointe Dr.) | 561-745-6262 | www.toobizaare.com

"Everything's for sale" at this "quirky" "place to hang" in Jupiter, from the "huge variety" of "reasonably priced" wine and "creative" Eclectic fare (including "appealing" tapas and sushi) to the "couches and chairs" patrons perch on; "it works" for most, while a few find it, yep, "too bizarre."

TooJay's Original Gourmet Deli *Deli*

| 19 | 11 | 16 | $21 |

Lake Worth | 419 Lake Ave. (S. Federal Hwy.) | 561-582-8684
Palm Beach | Royal Poinciana Plaza | 313 Royal Poinciana Way (Cocoanut Row) | 561-659-7232
Palm Beach Gardens | Downtown at the Gdns. | 11701 Lake Victoria Gardens Ave. (PGA Blvd.) | 561-622-8131
Jupiter | The Bluffs | 4050 U.S. 1 (Marcinski Rd.) | 561-627-5555
Boca Raton | Glades Plaza | 2200 W. Glades Rd. (bet. Butts Rd. & Military Trail) | 561-392-4181
Boca Raton | Regency Court Plaza | 3013 Yamato Rd. (Jog Rd.) | 561-997-9911
Boca Raton | Polo Shoppes | 5030 Champion Blvd. (N. Military Trail) | 561-241-5903
Boynton Beach | Boynton Beach Mall | 801 N. Congress Ave., Ste. 602 (bet. Boynton Beach & Gateway Blvds.) | 561-740-7420
Vero Beach | Treasure Coast Plaza | 555 21st St. (6th Ave.) | 772-569-6070
Wellington | Mall at Wellington Green | 1030 W. Forest Hill Blvd. (State Rt. 441) | 561-784-9055
www.toojays.com
Additional locations throughout the Palm Beach County area

"Transplanted New Yorkers" have been spreading the news about these "solid" South Florida delis serving up "overstuffed sandwiches" – "pastrami on rye", Reubens, etc. – and "sensational" black-and-white cookies; true, guests endure "erratic service" and a "hurried" atmosphere (so consider "takeout"), but since there's "good value" here, there are also "long lines."

☑ Tramonti *Italian*

| 24 | 19 | 19 | $54 |

Delray Beach | 119 E. Atlantic Ave. (bet. SE 1st & 2nd Aves.) | 561-272-1944 | www.tramontidelray.com

"It's a zoo most nights" at this "offshoot of NY's famed Angelo's of Mulberry Street", as Delray denizens clamor for "consistently delish" Italian chow at tables "crowded so close servers can't pass by"; detractors decry "rushed meals", "excessive noise", "long waits" and "overpriced tabs", but *amici* shrug it off and dig into "satisfying portions" of "food that even New Yorkers appreciate."

	FOOD	DECOR	SERVICE	COST

☑ Trattoria Romana *Italian* 25 | 18 | 22 | $60

Boca Raton | 499 E. Palmetto Park Rd. (NE 5th Ave.) | 561-393-6715 | www.trattoriaromanaofbocaraton.com

After "taking a bite of anything", *paesani* proclaim they've "died and gone to heaven" at this "old-school Italian" featuring "fabulous, authentic" Italian fare and "unbelievable specials", plus an "outstanding antipasto bar"; there's also "attitude with a capital A", "pricey" tabs and some "noise" ("ask for a table in the back" to avoid the "hubbub"), but that's "*so* Boca."

Trevini *Italian* 22 | 20 | 21 | $61

Palm Beach | Esplanade Mall | 150 Worth Ave. (bet. Ocean Blvd. & S. County Rd.) | 561-833-3883 | www.treviniristorante.com

"Gentlemanly" service and white tablecloths add to the "old-fashioned" feel of this "classy" Palm Beach Italian offering "high-quality" cuisine; equally "high prices", however, irk practical types who say there are "better choices" for the money, while loyalists insist it's "worth it" nevertheless; P.S. design tweaks may outdate the Decor score.

Triple Eight Lounge at the Falcon House ☑ Ⓜ *American* - | - | - | M

Delray Beach | 116 NE Sixth Ave. (bet. 1st & 2nd Sts.) | 561-243-9499 | www.thefalconhouse.com

It's back to the original for this old-house-turned-lounge in Delray Beach, where restaurateur Karl Alterman (Moquila) has repainted the walls bodice-ripping crimson and brought back the affordable American small plates; add in traditional and mod drinks at the two bars – one indoors, one on the covered patio – and night owls have a good excuse to hoot it up.

☑ Truluck's *Seafood* 24 | 24 | 23 | $64

Boca Raton | Mizner Park | 351 Plaza Real (bet. E. Palmetto Park & Glades Rds.) | 561-391-0755 | www.trulucks.com

Fin-atics gush that this "upscale" Mizner Park boîte is "how Boca does seafood": with a "wide variety" of "fresh" fare that's "consistently good", especially on "all-you-can-eat crab Monday nights"; the "classy, supper-club atmosphere" with "live piano player" makes it "worth lingering" ("you won't believe it's a chain"), and the "well-trained staff" is a plus; just "bring your banker" to "cosign a loan", because this "tru winner" is truly "expensive"; P.S. the Lauderdale branch opened post-Survey; a Miami branch is due.

Two Georges Waterfront Grille *Seafood* 16 | 18 | 17 | $28

Boynton Beach | 728 Casa Loma Blvd. (SE 6th St.) | 561-736-2717 | www.twogeorgesrestaurant.com

By George, it's "all about the setting" at this "crowded", "ultra-casual" Boynton Beach seafooder that's nestled on the Intracoastal, so "bring your boat", grab a "cold beer" and "chill"; natch, the "food and service are pretty basic", but it just "doesn't get any more Florida than this."

FOOD | DECOR | SERVICE | COST

264 the Grill *American/Continental*   18 | 18 | 19 | $44

Palm Beach | 264 S. County Rd. (Royal Palm Way) | 561-833-6444 |
www.264thegrill.com

Value-seekers say the "early-bird is the way to fly" at this "casually
elegant" American, a Palm Beach "standby" that's just a "short walk
from Worth Avenue"; if "most of the pretty people have deserted it",
a "mature crowd" and "pre-theatergoers" still find the "comfort food
at comfort prices" fairly "reliable."

Uncle Julio's *Tex-Mex*   19 | 20 | 20 | $31

Boca Raton | Mizner Park | 449 Plaza Real (N. Federal Hwy.) |
561-300-3530 | www.unclejulios.com

It can be a real "madhouse" at this "upscale" Tex-Mex "favorite", a
"lively" Mizner Park outpost of the Dallas-based chain cheered by
fans for its "addictive" fare (including "fabulous guacamole" and
"fresh-made tortillas") and "yummy swirled frozen drinks"; servers
are "accommodating enough" and you get "huge portions", but critics grouch that it's all "too noisy", too "pricey" and too "average."

☒ Uncle Tai's *Chinese*   24 | 22 | 22 | $42

Boca Raton | Boca Ctr. | 5250 Town Center Circle (S. Military Trail) |
561-368-8806 | www.uncle-tais.com

"You never cry uncle" at this "grown-up Chinese", a "crown jewel"
whose "elegant service" and "beautiful" setting befit the "upscale",
"amazingly consistent" fare incorporating "quality ingredients";
portions are "smaller than expected" and "very expensive" for
some, but overall, Boca's "best Asian food" rarely "disappoints."

NEW Vagabondi Ⓜ *Italian*   – | – | – | M

West Palm Beach | 319 Belvedere Rd. (Dixie Hwy.) |
561-249-2281

Whatever you do, make reservations at this 10-table Northern
Italian hidden in a West Palm strip mall, because the word's gotten
out about its limited menu of simple standards (orecchiette with
sausage, veal saltimbocca, etc.), daily specials and global wines;
the digs are appointed with dark wood and plush banquettes, a
relatively upscale setting that belies the moderate prices;
P.S. also closed Tuesdays.

Vic & Angelos *Italian*   20 | 21 | 20 | $42

Palm Beach Gardens | PGA Commons | 4520 PGA Blvd. (Military Trail) |
561-630-9899
Delray Beach | 290 E. Atlantic Ave. (bet. 2nd & 3rd Aves.) |
561-278-9570 ●
www.vicandangelos.com

"Glimmery and bustling", the Delray outpost of the equally "lively",
"noisy" Palm Beach Gardens Italian is "fast becoming a favorite"
among townies, no surprise since it serves the same "terrific" coal-
oven–fired pizza and other "solid" fare; "spotty" service and "high
prices" perturb many, but if you enjoy "people-watching", "this is
the place for you"; P.S. both offer "outdoor tables", but take note:
"trains practically pass through" the Atlantic Avenue venue.

	FOOD	DECOR	SERVICE	COST

Village Tavern *Seafood/Steak* **20 | 20 | 20 | $32**

Boynton Beach | Renaissance Commons | 1880 N. Congress Ave. (Gateway Blvd.) | 561-853-0280 | www.villagetavern.com
See review in Ft. Lauderdale/Broward County Directory.

NEW Vivo Partenza 🖃 *Italian* **- | - | - | E**
(fka Bova)

Boca Raton | 1450 N. Federal Hwy. (15th St.) | 561-750-2120 | www.vivobocaraton.com

Restaurateur Tony Bova strikes again in his former Bova space, dishing up longtime favorites from his other eateries as well as family Italian recipes like chicken scarpiello, veal chops and penne alla vodka; white banquettes, marble tables, gauzy curtains, dramatic lighting and a dark-wood bar give the interior an upscale, oh-so-Boca vibe, while alfrescans can savor the patio out back.

Yard House ◑ *American* **19 | 19 | 19 | $28**

Palm Beach Gardens | Downtown at the Gdns. | 11701 Lake Victoria Gardens Ave. (PGA Blvd.) | 561-691-6901 | www.yardhouse.com

It takes a "huge rectangular bar" and two covered patios to handle the "noisy" Palm Beach Gardens and Coral Gables quaffers who converge on this TV-studded chain sports bar for the "amazing beer selection" ("over 100" on tap); those who froth over "overpriced" tabs for "just ok" American fare and service advise "hitting it at happy hour" for specials.

Ziree Thai & Sushi *Thai* **25 | 20 | 23 | $30**

Delray Beach | 401 W. Atlantic Ave. (bet. NW 4th & 5th Aves.) | 561-276-6549 | www.zireethai.com

"OMG, I've just died and gone to Bangkok" swoon surveyors smitten by this bright, airy Delray Beach Thai where "everything is fresh, interesting" and "reasonably" priced (including the "surprisingly good" sushi); patrons are "greeted with a smile", a harbinger of the "excellent" service to follow.

Zuccarelli's Italian Kitchen *Italian* **19 | 15 | 17 | $33**

West Palm Beach | Pine Trail Sq. | 1937 N. Military Trail (Okeechobee Blvd.) | 561-686-7739
Palm Beach Gardens | PGA Commons West | 5530 PGA Blvd. (Central Blvd.) | 561-776-9889
www.zuccarellis.com

"Mama cooks and watches the kitchen" at this West Palm "legend" that ladles out "huge portions" of "traditional Southern Italian" fare in a "comfortable, casual" setting; meanwhile, patrons of the "relatively new" Palm Beach Gardens offspring report it's "inconsistent" but "getting better"; P.S. the original is set to move across the street, while a new pizza offshoot is due in West Palm Beach.

INDEXES

All restaurants are in Miami/Dade County unless otherwise noted
(B=Broward County; K=Key West; P=Palm Beach County).

Cuisines

Includes names, locations and Food ratings.

AMERICAN

Absinthe	Boca/P	19
Ambry German	Ft. Laud/B	-
Aruba Beach	Laud-by-Sea/B	17
Atrio	Downtown	21
Bar Louie	Boynton Bch/P	17
☑ Barton G.	SoBe	23
Beach Watch	Dania Bch/B	13
Big City Tav.	Ft. Laud/B	19
Big Pink	SoBe	19
Bimini Boatyard	Ft. Laud/B	17
Bin 595	Plantation/B	22
Bistro Mezzaluna	Ft. Laud/B	25
Bistro 17	Ft. Laud/B	24
Brewzzi	multi.	18
Burger & Beer	multi.	-
By Word/Mouth	Ft. Laud/B	25
Café at Books	multi.	21
☑ Café Chardonnay	Palm Bch Gdns/P	25
☑ Cafe Marquesa	Key W./K	27
☑ Cafe Maxx	Pompano Bch/B	26
Camille's	Key W./K	22
☑ Canyon	Ft. Laud/B	26
Casablanca	Ft. Laud/B	21
Charley's Crab	Palm Bch/P	21
☑ Cheesecake	multi.	20
Copper Canyon	Boca/P	-
☑ Dada	Delray Bch/P	21
Dave's Last	Lake Worth/P	19
Dune Deck	Lantana/P	19
East City Grill	Weston/B	21
☑ 11 Maple St.	Jensen Bch/P	28
11th St. Diner	SoBe	18
☑ Entre Nous	No. Palm Bch/P	25
E.R. Bradley	W. Palm/P	15
Essensia	SoBe	-
☑ Flagler Grill	Stuart/P	25
Flanigan's	Coco Grove	20
Floridian	Ft. Laud/B	18
NEW Forge/Wine	Miami Bch	-
Front Porch	SoBe	21
Gables Diner	Coral Gables	16
Gibraltar	Coco Grove	-
Gold Coast	Coral Spgs/B	22
Gordon Biersch	Downtown	14
Grille/Congress	Boca/P	20
Grill on Alley	Aventura	22
Harry/Natives	Hobe Sound/P	16

☑ Henry's	Delray Bch/P	21
Hi-Life	Ft. Laud/B	25
Himmarshee	Ft. Laud/B	23
☑ Houston's	multi.	22
Hurricane Café	Juno Bch/P	21
Ironwood	Palm Bch Gdns/P	-
Jade	W. Palm/P	24
J. Alexander	multi.	20
Jaxson's	Dania Bch/B	22
Jimmy Buffett's	Key W./K	15
J. Mark's	multi.	21
Joe Allen	SoBe	22
John Bull	W. Palm/P	18
☑ John G's	Lake Worth/P	23
JohnMartin's	Coral Gables	17
Kaiyó	Islamorada/K	-
Kelly's Carib.	Key W./K	21
Leopard Lounge	Palm Bch/P	20
Le Tub	H'wood/B	21
Lola's	H'wood/B	24
☑ Louie's	Key W./K	25
NEW Lou's Beer	Miami Bch	-
Lucille's	Weston/B	19
Magnum	UES	21
Marker 88	Islamorada/K	22
NEW Mason Jar	Ft. Laud/B	-
☑ Max's	Boca/P	22
Meat Market	SoBe	24
Michael R.	Palm Bch/P	17
☑ Michaels	Key W./K	28
☑ Michael's	Design Dist	26
☑ Michy's	UES	27
Mondo's	No. Palm Bch/P	19
NEW Morgans	Wynwood	-
Mustard Seed	multi.	-
☑ Nemo	SoBe	24
Neomi's Grill	Sunny Is Bch	-
Nick & Johnnie's	Palm Bch/P	18
nine one five	Key W./K	25
Oakwood	Palm Bch Gdns/P	20
Oceans 234	Deerfield Bch/B	18
NEW Office	Delray Bch/P	-
Old Calypso	Delray Bch/P	19
Original Pancake	multi.	20
☑ Palm Beach Grill	Palm Bch/P	25
Pelican Café	SoBe	23
Pier Top	Ft. Laud/B	-
Pilar	Aventura	24
☑ Pisces	Key W./K	28

Prelude | **Downtown**	-|
Q American | **Design Dist**	-|
NEW Rack's Downtown | **Boca/P**	-|
ⓩ Red Light | **UES**	26|
Rhythm Café | **W. Palm/P**	22|
Rivals | **H'wood/B**	16|
Rock Fish | **Kendall**	21|
Royal Café | **Jupiter/P**	-|
ⓩ S&S | **Downtown**	21|
Sarabeth's | **Key W./K**	25|
Sara's | **Palm Bch Gdns/P**	-|
Scorch Grill | **No. Miami**	18|
Scotty's | **Coco Grove**	14|
ⓩ Seasons 52 | **multi.**	23|
Sloppy Joe's | **Key W./K**	14|
Solu | **Singer Is/P**	-|
Sonoma | **Delray Bch/P**	20|
Soyka | **UES**	20|
Square One | **Key W./K**	22|
Station Grille/Hse. | **Lantana/P**	23|
NEW STK Miami | **Miami Bch**	-|
ⓩ Sundy House | **Delray Bch/P**	23|
Sunfish | **Ft. Laud/B**	24|
Tabica Grill | **Jupiter/P**	21|
ⓩ Ta-boo | **Palm Bch/P**	21|
ⓩ 3030 Ocean | **Ft. Laud/B**	25|
ⓩ 32 East | **Delray Bch/P**	26|
This Is It Café | **W. Palm/P**	-|
Tin Muffin | **Boca/P**	23|
Titanic Brewery | **Coral Gables**	16|
Trina | **Ft. Laud/B**	-|
Triple Eight | **Delray Bch/P**	-|
Two Chefs | **So. Miami**	24|
Two Friends | **Key W./K**	19|
264 the Grill | **Palm Bch/P**	18|
Van Dyke | **SoBe**	17|
Village Grille | **Laud-by-Sea/B**	23|
Village Tav. | **multi.**	20|
NEW Water Club | **No. Miami Bch**	-|
White Lion | **Homestead**	19|
ⓩ Wish | **SoBe**	25|
Yard Hse. | **multi.**	19|
YOLO | **Ft. Laud/B**	21|

ARGENTINEAN

Argentango Grill | **H'wood/B**	21|
ⓩ Graziano's | **multi.**	26|
Las Vacas | **Miami Bch**	21|
Novecento | **multi.**	20|
Zuperpollo | **Brickell**	21|

ASIAN

Aizia | **Hallandale/B**	24|
ⓩ Asia de Cuba | **SoBe**	23|

Café Sambal | **Brickell**	23|
Café Sharaku | **Ft. Laud/B**	27|
ⓩ China Grill | **multi.**	23|
Crazy Buffet | **W. Palm/P**	15|
NEW Elle's | **Miramar/B**	-|
Indochine | **Miami Riv**	21|
Island Grill | **Islamorada/K**	22|
Kona Grill | **W. Palm/P**	19|
Lan | **So. Miami**	23|
Origin Asian | **multi.**	22|
Pei Wei | **Kendall**	19|
ⓩ Rest. at Setai | **SoBe**	22|
Stir Crazy | **multi.**	20|
Wild E. Asian | **Ft. Laud/B**	22|
Yuga | **Coral Gables**	24|

AUSTRIAN

Fin & Claw | **Lighthse Pt/B**	17|
Fritz & Franz | **Coral Gables**	16|

BAKERIES

Croissants | **Key W./K**	25|
Icebox Café | **SoBe**	23|
Paul | **multi.**	18|

BARBECUE

Bar-B-Que | **SoBe**	14|
Bulldog Barbecue | **Aventura**	20|
Mississippi | **multi.**	22|
Park Avenue BBQ Grille | **multi.**	19|
Pit Bar-B-Q | **West Dade**	20|
Shorty's | **multi.**	19|
NEW Sparky's | **Downtown**	-|
ⓩ Tom Jenkins' | **Ft. Laud/B**	25|
Turtle Kraals | **Key W./K**	19|

BRAZILIAN

ⓩ Blue Door | **SoBe**	23|
NEW Botequim Carioca | **Biscayne**	-|
Braza Lena | **multi.**	-|
Brazaviva Churrascaria | **Sunrise/B**	18|
ⓩ Chima Brazilian | **Ft. Laud/B**	24|
Fogo de Chão | **SoBe**	24|
Gol! | **Delray Bch/P**	20|
Grimpa | **Brickell**	23|
ⓩ SushiSamba | **SoBe**	23|

BRITISH

Blue Anchor | **Delray Bch/P**	19|
Kingshead Pub | **Sunrise/B**	-|

BURGERS

Brass Ring Pub | **multi.**	24|
Burger & Beer | **multi.**	-|

CUISINES

NEW CG Burgers | **Jupiter/P**	–
8 Oz. Burger | **SoBe**	20
Z Five Guys | **multi.**	22
Grease Burger | **W. Palm/P**	20
Hamburger Heaven | **Palm Bch/P**	20
Jimmy Buffett's | **Key W./K**	15
Le Tub | **H'wood/B**	21
OneBurger | **Coral Gables**	18
NEW Relish | **W. Palm/P**	–
Scotty's | **Coco Grove**	14
NEW Shake Shack | **SoBe**	–

CAJUN

Creolina's | **Davie/B**	23

CALIFORNIAN

Lime Fresh Mex. | **multi.**	21

CARIBBEAN

Aruba Beach | **Laud-by-Sea/B**	17
Bagatelle | **Key W./K**	23
Café Solé | **Key W./K**	24
Calypso | **Pompano Bch/B**	24
NEW Elle's | **Miramar/B**	–
Hot Tin Roof | **Key W./K**	23
Kelly's Carib. | **Key W./K**	21
Z Louie's | **Key W./K**	25
Martin's | **Key W./K**	24
Off the Grille | **Kendall**	–
Z Ortanique | **Coral Gables**	26
Solu | **Singer Is/P**	–
Sugar Reef | **H'wood/B**	22

CHEESE SPECIALISTS

Z Cheese Course | **Downtown**	26

CHILEAN

Viva Chile | **Davie/B**	–

CHINESE

(* dim sum specialist)

China Dumpling | **Boynton Bch/P**	22
Christina Wan's | **Ft. Laud/B**	22
Christine Lee's | **Hallandale/B**	23
Coco | **Palm Bch/P**	22
Z Hakkasan | **Miami Bch**	26
Helen Huang's | **H'wood/B**	18
NEW Indian Chillies | **Pembroke Pines/B**	–
Kon Chau* | **Westchester**	24
Mai-Kai | **Ft. Laud/B**	15
Miss Yip* | **SoBe**	19
Mr. Chow | **SoBe**	–
New Chinatown | **So. Miami**	18
Z P.F. Chang's | **multi.**	21
Philippe | **SoBe**	21

Z Rainbow Palace | **Ft. Laud/B**	26
Z Silver Pond | **Laud Lks/B**	25
Tempura Hse. | **Boca/P**	20
Toa Toa* | **Sunrise/B**	–
Tony Chan's | **Downtown**	22
Tropical Chinese* | **Westchester**	25
Z Uncle Tai's | **Boca/P**	24

COFFEE SHOPS/ DINERS

Big Pink | **SoBe**	19
Camille's | **Key W./K**	22
11th St. Diner | **SoBe**	18
Floridian | **Ft. Laud/B**	18
Gables Diner | **Coral Gables**	16
Hamburger Heaven | **Palm Bch/P**	20
Howley's | **W. Palm/P**	17
Jumbo's | **West Dade**	22
News Cafe | **SoBe**	17
Original Pancake | **multi.**	20
Royal Café | **Jupiter/P**	–
Z S&S | **Downtown**	21
This Is It Café | **W. Palm/P**	–

CONTEMPORARY LOUISIANA

Z Emeril's | **SoBe**	23

CONTINENTAL

Bistro | **Jupiter/P**	23
Bizcaya | **Coco Grove**	20
Brooks | **Deerfield Bch/B**	23
Cafe Cellini | **Palm Bch/P**	25
Z Café L'Europe | **Palm Bch/P**	25
Z Kathy's | **Boca/P**	25
Runyon's | **Coral Spgs/B**	24
Z Ta-boo | **Palm Bch/P**	21
Tatiana | **Hallandale/B**	–
264 the Grill | **Palm Bch/P**	18
Vienna Café | **Davie/B**	23
NEW Villa By Barton G. | **SoBe**	–
Wine Cellar | **Ft. Laud/B**	19

CREOLE

Creolina's | **Davie/B**	23
Old Calypso | **Delray Bch/P**	19

CUBAN

Z Asia de Cuba | **SoBe**	23
Bahamas Fish | **W. Miami**	20
Bongos Cuban | **Downtown**	17
Casa Larios | **multi.**	19
Casa Paco | **So. Miami**	20
Cuban Cafe | **multi.**	20
David's | **SoBe**	17

De Rodriguez Cuba | **SoBe** -|
Don Ramon | **multi.** 18|
El Meson | **Key W./K** 21|
El Siboney | **Key W./K** 26|
Enriqueta's | **Wynwood** 22|
Havana | **W. Palm/P** 22|
Havana Harry's | **multi.** 21|
NEW Havana's | **Cooper City/B** -|
Islas Canarias | **multi.** 20|
La Casita | **multi.** 21|
La Casona | **W. Sunset** 19|
Lario's/Beach | **SoBe** 18|
Las Culebrinas | **multi.** 22|
Las Vegas | **multi.** 21|
Little Havana | **multi.** 21|
Molina's | **Hialeah** 22|
Padrino's | **multi.** 20|
Puerto Sagua | **SoBe** 20|
Sergio's | **multi.** 20|
Uva 69 | **UES** 21|
Z Versailles | **Little Havana** 21|

DELIS

Ben's Kosher | **Boca/P** 20|
Deli Lane | **multi.** 17|
Flakowitz | **multi.** -|
Kevin's Dockside | **Palm Bch Gdns/P** -|
Z LaSpada's | **multi.** 27|
Old Heidelberg | **Ft. Laud/B** -|
TooJay's | **multi.** 19|

ECLECTIC

Acqua | **Brickell** 25|
Z Adriana | **Surfside** 26|
Aura | **SoBe** 26|
Balans | **multi.** 19|
Barracuda Grill | **Marathon/K** 23|
BED | **SoBe** 17|
Bizaare Cafe | **Lake Worth/P** 21|
Z Cafe Maxx | **Pompano Bch/B** 26|
Z Cheese Course | **multi.** 26|
Cottage | **Lake Worth/P** 16|
Z Dada | **Delray Bch/P** 21|
Dolores | **Brickell** 18|
Dynamo | **SoBe** -|
Z Eduardo/San Angel | **Ft. Laud/B** 27|
Globe Cafe | **Coral Gables** 18|
Grand Café | **Key W./K** 22|
Grand Lux | **multi.** 19|
Himmarshee | **Ft. Laud/B** 23|
Hot Tin Roof | **Key W./K** 23|
Icebox Café | **SoBe** 23|

NEW Il Mercato/Wine | **Hallandale/B** -|
Mango's Tropical | **SoBe** 15|
Mia | **Downtown** -|
Mustard Seed | **multi.** -|
Nexxt Cafe | **SoBe** 18|
Nikki | **SoBe** 17|
NEW Norman's 180 | **Coral Gables** -|
Pelican Landing | **Ft. Laud/B** 18|
Z Pierre's | **Islamorada/K** 27|
Z Santiago's | **Key W./K** 28|
NEW Sugarcane | **Downtown** -|
Sugar Reef | **H'wood/B** 22|
Sushi Blues | **H'wood/B** 23|
Tantra | **SoBe** 20|
Tasters | **Tavernier/K** -|
Too Bizaare | **Jupiter/P** 21|
Town Kit. | **So. Miami** 18|
Upper Deck | **Key W./K** 23|

EUROPEAN

NEW Angelique Euro Café | **Coral Gables** -|
Z Cheese Course | **Weston/B** 26|
Martin's | **Key W./K** 24|
Sonoma | **Delray Bch/P** 20|

FLORIBBEAN

Z Blue Heaven | **Key W./K** 24|
Z Flagler Grill | **Stuart/P** 25|
Johnny V | **Ft. Laud/B** 24|
Latitudes | **H'wood/B** 18|

FONDUE

Melting Pot | **multi.** 20|

FRENCH

Z Blue Door | **SoBe** 23|
Z Café Boulud | **Palm Bch/P** 27|
Café des Artistes | **Jupiter/P** -|
Café Pastis | **So. Miami** 24|
Café Solé | **Key W./K** 24|
Caviar Kaspia | **SoBe** -|
Chanticleer | **Islamorada/K** 24|
Charlotte Bistro | **Coral Gables** -|
Z Chez Jean-Pierre | **Palm Bch/P** 27|
DB Bistro Moderne | **Downtown** -|
Z Din. Rm./Little Palm | **Little Torch Key/K** 26|
Green/Cafe | **Coco Grove** 18|
La Sandwicherie | **SoBe** 23|
Le Bistro | **Lighthse Pt/B** 22|
Le Croisic | **Key Biscayne** 21|
Z L'Escalier | **Palm Bch/P** 26|

Maison Carlos	W. Palm/P	-
Z Michy's	UES	27
Mo's	Key W./K	21
Z Palme d'Or	Coral Gables	28
Z Pascal's	Coral Gables	27
Paul	multi.	18
Sage	multi.	22
Saint Tropez	Ft. Laud/B	-
Uva 69	UES	21

FRENCH (BISTRO)

A La Folie	SoBe	24
Banana Cafe	Key W./K	26
Bistro Bisou	So. Miami	18
Café La Bonne	Ft. Laud/B	22
Croissants	Key W./K	25
George's/Grove	Coco Grove	22
NEW George's/Sunset	So. Miami	-
Hanna's Diner	No. Miami Bch	26
La Creperie	Lauderhill/B	23
La Goulue	Bal Harbour	22
Le Bouchon du Grove	Coco Grove	23
Le Provençal	Coral Gables	22
NEW Otentic	SoBe	-
Pistache	W. Palm/P	19
Provence	Brickell	18
W Wine	Design Dist	-

GASTROPUB

NEW Gratify	American	W. Palm/P	-
NEW Lou's Beer	American	Miami Bch	-
NEW Taste	American	Delray Bch/P	-

GERMAN

Ambry German	Ft. Laud/B	-
Checkers/Munchen	Pompano Bch/B	-
Fritz & Franz	Coral Gables	16
Old Heidelberg	Ft. Laud/B	-
Royal Bavarian	UES	19

GREEK

Z Greek Islands	Ft. Laud/B	25
NEW Mandolin	Design Dist	-
Mazza	Pembroke Pines/B	23
My Big Fat Greek	Dania Bch/B	20
Mykonos	Coral Way	18
Taso's Greek	Delray Bch/P	22
Taverna Kyma	Boca/P	20
Taverna Opa	multi.	19
NEW Trata	Ft. Laud/B	-

HAITIAN

Tap Tap	SoBe	22

HEALTH FOOD

(See also Vegetarian)

Berries	Coco Grove	20
Canyon Ranch Grill	Miami Bch	23

HOT DOGS

Dogma Grill	UES	20

ICE CREAM PARLORS

Jaxson's	Dania Bch/B	22
Z Sloan's	multi.	23

INDIAN

NEW Bombay Darbar	Coco Grove	-
Guru	SoBe	24
House of India	Coral Gables	18
Imlee	Pinecrest	23
India Hse.	Plantation/B	20
NEW Indian Chillies	Pembroke Pines/B	-
Kebab Indian	No. Miami Bch	21
Madras	Pompano Bch/B	20
Mint Leaf	Coral Gables	23
Udipi	Sunrise/B	-
Woodlands	Lauderhill/B	23

INDONESIAN

Bali Café	Downtown	23

IRISH

Brogues	Lake Worth/P	16
Clarke's	SoBe	21
Finnegan's	Key W./K	18
JohnMartin's	Coral Gables	17
Paddy Mac's	Palm Bch Gdns/P	22
Sláinte Irish	Boynton Bch/P	14

ISRAELI

Pita Hut	Miami Bch	17

ITALIAN

(N=Northern; S=Southern)

Abbondanza	Key W./K	19
Acquolina	multi.	25
Ago	N	SoBe	20
Anacapri	multi.	22
Anthony's Runway	Ft. Laud/B	23
Antonia's	Key W./K	25
NEW Apicius	Lantana/P	-
Arturo's	Boca/P	23
Basilico	N	multi.	26
Bella Luna	Aventura	22
Bice	N	Palm Bch/P	21

Big Cheese | **So. Miami**	21
Bistro 555 | **Davie/B**	23
Bistro Mezzaluna | **Ft. Laud/B**	25
Blú la Pizzeria | **So. Miami**	23
Bongusto! | **Ft. Laud/B**	23
Brio Tuscan | N | **multi.**	22
Bugatti Pasta | **Coral Gables**	23
Buonasera | **Jupiter/P**	24
Cafe Avanti | **Miami Bch**	22
Café Centro | N | **W. Palm/P**	23
NEW Café Europa | **Ft. Laud/B**	-
Cafe Martorano | **multi.**	25
Café Prima | N | **Miami Bch**	23
Café Ragazzi | **Surfside**	24
Cafe Sapori | **W. Palm/P**	24
Cafe Vico | N | **Ft. Laud/B**	24
Caffe Abbracci | N | **Coral Gables**	24
Caffe Da Vinci | **Bay Harbor Is**	21
Caffé Milano | **SoBe**	19
Caffe Luna Rosa | **Delray Bch/P**	20
Caffe Vialetto | **Coral Gables**	24
Calamari | **Coco Grove**	-
Capriccio | **Pembroke Pines/B**	24
NEW Capri Rist. | **Boca/P**	-
NEW Carmine's | **Jupiter/P**	-
Carpaccio | **Bal Harbour**	22
NEW Caruso's | **Boca/P**	-
Casa Bella | **Dania Bch/B**	24
Z Casa D'Angelo | N | **multi.**	27
Z Casa Tua | N | **SoBe**	25
Cioppino | **Key Biscayne**	23
Couco Pazzo | **Lake Worth/P**	22
Cucina Dell' Arte | **Palm Bch/P**	21
Da Campo | N | **Ft. Laud/B**	24
da Leo Tratt. | **SoBe**	17
DeVito | **SoBe**	21
Dolce/Palma | **W. Palm/P**	26
Escopazzo | **SoBe**	25
Figs | **Palm Bch Gdns/P**	20
NEW Fiorentina | **Lake Worth/P**	-
Fontana | **Coral Gables**	21
Fratelli | S | **SoBe**	21
Fratelli Lyon | **Design Dist**	23
Fulvio's 1900 | **H'wood/B**	23
Gianni's | **Pompano Bch/B**	25
Gil Capa's | **Kendall**	25
NEW Giovanni's | **Pembroke Pines/B**	-
Grazie Italian | **SoBe**	24
Hosteria Romana | S | **SoBe**	20
H2O | **Ft. Laud/B**	19
Il Bellagio | **W. Palm/P**	19
Z Il Gabbiano | **Downtown**	26

Il Girasole | N | **Delray Bch/P**	22
NEW Il Grissino | **Coral Gables**	-
Il Mulino | **Ft. Laud/B**	22
Z Il Mulino NY | N | **Sunny Is Bch**	25
Il Toscano | N | **Weston/B**	22
Joey's Italian | **Wynwood**	22
Josef's | N | **Plantation/B**	25
Josephine's | N | **Boca/P**	20
kitchenetta | S | **Ft. Laud/B**	23
La Locanda | **SoBe**	23
La Loggia | N | **Downtown**	21
La Luna | **Boca/P**	17
La Palma | N | **Coral Gables**	21
La Trattoria | **Key W./K**	24
La Veranda | **Pompano Bch/B**	22
La Villetta | **Boca/P**	22
Limoncello | **No. Palm Bch/P**	20
Macaluso's | **SoBe**	23
Maison Carlos | **W. Palm/P**	-
NEW Maitardi | N | **Design Dist**	-
Mama Mia | **H'wood/B**	20
Mancini's | **Ft. Laud/B**	22
Mangia Mangia | **Key W./K**	20
Z Marcello | **W. Palm/P**	27
Mario/Baker | S | **multi.**	19
Mike's | **Kendall**	21
NEW Mr. Milano | N | **Palm Bch Gdns/P**	-
Noodles Panini | **Ft. Laud/B**	23
Oggi Caffe | **No. Bay Vill**	21
Z Osteria del Teatro | N | **SoBe**	26
Papichi | **Pinecrest**	20
Paradiso | **Lake Worth/P**	21
Peppy's | N | **Coral Gables**	20
Perricone's | **Brickell**	20
Portobello | N | **Jupiter/P**	22
Primavera | N | **Oakland Pk/B**	22
Prime Italian | **SoBe**	24
Quattro | N | **SoBe**	22
Racks Italian | **No. Miami Bch**	-
Randazzo's | **Coral Gables**	23
Renato's | **Palm Bch/P**	22
Roasted Pepper | S | **Pembroke Pines/B**	22
Z Romeo's Cafe | N | **Coral Way**	27
Rosalia's | **Aventura**	18
Rosinella | **multi.**	19
Salute! | **Key W./K**	22
Sapori | **Boca/P**	23
Sardinia | **SoBe**	23
Z Scarpetta | **Miami Bch**	25
Serafina | **Ft. Laud/B**	21
Sette Bello | **Ft. Laud/B**	27

NEW SoLita | S | Ft. Laud/B	–
Sorella | Pembroke Pines/B	–
Soya & Pomodoro | Downtown	21
Z Spiga | N | SoBe	26
Stresa | N | W. Palm/P	18
Sylvano's | SoBe	20
NEW Table 42 | Boca/P	–
Tarantella | Weston/B	24
Temple Orange | Manalapan/P	–
Timo | Sunny Is Bch	25
Timpano | Ft. Laud/B	21
Tiramesu | SoBe	21
Z Tramonti | Delray Bch/P	24
Trattoria Bella | Margate/B	–
Tratt. Luna | Pinecrest	24
Z Tratt. Romana | Boca/P	25
Tratt. Sole | So. Miami	21
Trevini | Palm Bch/P	22
Tuscan Grille | N | Ft. Laud/B	24
Tutto Pasta | Brickell	23
NEW Vagabondi | W. Palm/P	–
Z Valentino's | Ft. Laud/B	26
Z Via Luna | Ft. Laud/B	–
Vic/Angelos | multi.	20
Vigneto's | multi.	22
Villagio | multi.	20
NEW Vivo Partenza | Boca/P	–
Zuccarelli's Italian | S | multi.	19

JAPANESE

(* sushi specialist)

Abokado* | Brickell	19
Ambrosia* | Key W./K	24
Bali Café* | Downtown	23
Z Bluefin Sushi* | multi.	25
Blue Sea* | SoBe	25
Z Bond St.* | SoBe	26
Christine Lee's* | Hallandale/B	23
Doraku* | SoBe	21
Echo | Palm Bch/P	23
Eddie Hills* | Hallandale/B	22
Fuji Hana* | multi.	21
Galanga* | Wilton Manors/B	24
Hiro Japanese* | No. Miami Bch	20
Z Hiro's Yakko | No. Miami Bch	26
Ichiban* | Davie/B	20
Kaiyó | Islamorada/K	–
Kampai | multi.	21
Kiko | Plantation/B	–
NEW Kubo* | No. Palm Bch/P	–
Z Lemongrass* | Ft. Laud/B	23
Maiko* | SoBe	20
Marumi Sushi | Plantation/B	–

Z Matsuri* | So. Miami	27
Moon Thai* | Coral Gables	23
Naoe* | Sunny Is Bch	–
Z Nobu Miami Beach* | SoBe	27
Oishi Thai | No. Miami	25
Origami* | Key W./K	25
RA Sushi* | multi.	19
Saigon Tokyo* | Greenacres/P	22
Saito's | multi.	21
Sakura* | Coral Gables	22
NEW Sawa* | Coral Gables	–
Z Shibui* | Kendall	26
Shoji* | SoBe	24
Sushi Blues* | H'wood/B	23
Sushi Hse.* | No. Miami Bch	25
Sushi Jo's* | multi.	23
Sushi Maki* | multi.	20
Su Shin* | multi.	25
Su Shin Thai* | Lauderhill/B	23
Sushi Rock* | SoBe	21
Z SushiSamba* | SoBe	23
Sushi Siam* | multi.	21
Sushi Simon* | Boynton Bch/P	–
Tempura Hse. | Boca/P	20
Thai & Sushi* | W. Sunset	22
Thai Hse. II* | No. Miami Bch	24
Thaikyo Asian | Manalapan/P	22
Tokyo Sushi* | Ft. Laud/B	26
Toni's Sushi* | SoBe	25
World Resources* | SoBe	20
NEW Zuma | Downtown	–

KOREAN

(* barbecue specialist)

Myung Ga* | Weston/B	21
NEW Sakaya | Downtown	–

KOSHER/ KOSHER-STYLE

Ben's Kosher | Boca/P	20
Café Emunah | Ft. Laud/B	23
Pita Hut | Miami Bch	17

LEBANESE

Khoury's | So. Miami	22
Marhaba Med. | So. Miami	21
Mazza | Pembroke Pines/B	23

MEDITERRANEAN

Z AltaMare | SoBe	25
Z Azul | Brickell	27
Azur | Key W./K	26
Bin No. 18 | Downtown	22
Bizcaya | Coco Grove	20
Casablanca | Ft. Laud/B	21

City Cellar | **W. Palm/P**	20
Eos | **Brickell**	-
Figs | **Palm Bch Gdns/P**	20
Fontana | **Coral Gables**	21
Giorgio's Grill | **H'wood/B**	20
Green/Cafe | **Coco Grove**	18
H2O | **Ft. Laud/B**	19
Ilios | **Ft. Laud/B**	-
Joseph's Wine | **Delray Bch/P**	24
☑ La Brochette | **Cooper City/B**	27
La Cigale | **Delray Bch/P**	22
La Cofradia | **Coral Gables**	23
Lido | **SoBe**	21
Maroosh | **Coral Gables**	24
MB/Omphoy | **Palm Bch/P**	-
Mondo's | **No. Palm Bch/P**	19
nine one five | **Key W./K**	25
Oasis | **Miami Bch**	19
Pistache | **W. Palm/P**	19
Por Fin | **Coral Gables**	22
NEW Sawa | **Coral Gables**	-
Tapas & Tintos | **SoBe**	20
Taverna Yiamas | **H'wood/B**	15
Temple Orange | **Manalapan/P**	-
Timo | **Sunny Is Bch**	25

MEXICAN

Bad Boy Burrito | **Key W./K**	22
Baja Fresh | **multi.**	18
NEW Cabo Flats | **Palm Bch Gdns/P**	-
NEW Caliente Kitchen | **Delray Bch/P**	-
Cantina Laredo | **multi.**	19
Casa Maya Grill | **Deerfield Bch/B**	-
Chéen Huaye | **No. Miami**	25
Chico's Cantina | **Key W./K**	24
☑ Eduardo/San Angel | **Ft. Laud/B**	27
El Rancho | **multi.**	20
El Toro | **Homestead**	21
Lime Fresh Mex. | **multi.**	21
NEW Mercadito | **Downtown**	-
Moquila | **Boca/P**	19
Paquito's | **No. Miami Bch**	22
Rocco's Tacos | **multi.**	22
Rosa Mexicano | **Downtown**	21
NEW Talavera | **Coral Gables**	-
T-Mex Cantina | **multi.**	23

MIDDLE EASTERN

Daily Bread Pinecrest | **Pinecrest**	23
Ferdo's Grill | **Ft. Laud/B**	21
Leila | **W. Palm/P**	22

Maroosh | **Coral Gables**	24
Orig. Daily | **Coco Grove**	22
Pasha's | **multi.**	20

NEW ENGLAND

Whale Raw | **Parkland/B**	16

NEW WORLD

Morada Bay | **Islamorada/K**	23
NEW Norman's 180 | **Coral Gables**	-
☑ Ortanique | **Coral Gables**	26

NICARAGUAN

El Novillo | **multi.**	22
Guayacan | **multi.**	23
Los Ranchos | **multi.**	21

NUEVO LATINO

Cabana | **Delray Bch/P**	23
De Rodriguez Cuba | **SoBe**	-
Yuca | **SoBe**	20

PAN-LATIN

Abokado | **Brickell**	19
NEW Baru Urbano | **Brickell**	-
☑ Din. Rm./Little Palm | **Little Torch Key/K**	26
NEW Elle's | **Miramar/B**	-
Jaguar | **Coco Grove**	23
MB/Omphoy | **Palm Bch/P**	-
☑ OLA | **SoBe**	27

PERSIAN

Caspian Persian | **Plantation/B**	21
Kuluck | **Tamarac/B**	-
Rice Hse. | **multi.**	21

PERUVIAN

☑ Adriana | **Surfside**	26
El Chalán | **multi.**	22
El Gran Inka | **multi.**	21
☑ Francesco | **Coral Gables**	26
NEW Giovanni's | **Pembroke Pines/B**	-
La Cofradia | **Coral Gables**	23
Salmon | **West Dade**	23
Saxsay | **Sunrise/B**	-
☑ SushiSamba | **SoBe**	23
Tumi | **Margate/B**	-

PIZZA

☑ Andiamo! Pizza | **UES**	26
☑ Anthony's Pizza | **multi.**	23
Archie's Pizza | **multi.**	18
NEW Bellini's Pizza | **Ft. Laud/B**	-
Big Cheese | **So. Miami**	21

Blú la Pizzeria | So. Miami	23
Bugatti Pasta | Coral Gables	23
NEW Carmine's | Jupiter/P	-
Cucina Dell' Arte | Palm Bch/P	21
NEW D'Angelo | Oakland Pk/B	-
El Tamarindo | Hallandale/B	22
Fratelli | SoBe	21
Hot Pie | W. Palm/P	-
Mario/Baker | multi.	19
Mellow Mushroom | Delray Bch/P	23
Mike's | Kendall	21
Piola | multi.	22
Pizza Girls | W. Palm/P	22
Pizza Rustica | multi.	21
Pizza Volante | Design Dist	-
Rosinella | multi.	19
Spris | multi.	21
Tutto Pizza | Brickell	23
Vic/Angelos | Palm Bch Gdns/P	20

PORTUGUESE

Old Lisbon | multi.	24

PUB FOOD

Bar Louie | Boynton Bch/P	17
Blue Anchor | Delray Bch/P	19
Brass Ring Pub | multi.	24
Brogues | Lake Worth/P	16
Clarke's | SoBe	21
Dave's Last | Lake Worth/P	19
John Bull | W. Palm/P	18
JohnMartin's | Coral Gables	17
Kingshead Pub | Sunrise/B	-
Michael R. | Palm Bch/P	17
Paddy Mac's | Palm Bch Gdns/P	22
Sláinte Irish | Boynton Bch/P	14
Titanic Brewery | Coral Gables	16
NEW Waxy O'Connor's | Brickell	-

PUERTO RICAN

Old San Juan | W. Miami	19

RUSSIAN

Tatiana | Hallandale/B	-

SALVADORAN

El Atlakat | Westchester	20
El Tamarindo | multi.	22

SANDWICHES

Z Cheese Course | multi.	26
Deli Lane | multi.	17
Enriqueta's | Wynwood	22
La Sandwicherie | SoBe	23
Z LaSpada's | multi.	27

Paul | multi.	18
Perricone's | Brickell	20
Z S&S | Downtown	21
TooJay's | multi.	19

SEAFOOD

A&B Lobster | Key W./K	23
Z Adriana | Surfside	26
A Fish/Avalon | SoBe	22
Alabama Jacks | Key Largo/K	18
Z AltaMare | SoBe	25
Area 31 | Downtown	22
Aruba Beach | Laud-by-Sea/B	17
Bagatelle | Key W./K	23
Bahamas Fish | W. Miami	20
Banana Boat | Boynton Bch/P	16
Bayside Fish | Key Biscayne	13
Beach Watch | Dania Bch/B	13
Billy's Stone | H'wood/B	22
Bimini Twist | W. Palm/P	22
Z Blue Moon Fish | multi.	25
Bluepoint Grill | H'wood/B	17
Z Bonefish Grill | multi.	22
B.O.'s Fish | Key W./K	24
Bubba Gump | multi.	15
Café Emunah | Ft. Laud/B	23
Callaro's Steak | Manalapan/P	21
Calypso | Pompano Bch/B	24
Calypso's | Key Largo/K	23
Cap's | Lighthse Pt/P	19
Z Captain Charlie | Juno Bch/P	26
Captain Jim | No. Miami	25
Captain's Tav. | Pinecrest	23
Casablanca | Ft. Laud/B	21
Charley's Crab | Palm Bch/P	21
Z Chef Allen's | Aventura	26
Z Chops Lobster | Boca/P	26
City Oyster & Sushi | Delray Bch/P	21
Commodore | Key W./K	22
Conch Republic | Key W./K	19
Conchy Joe's | Jensen Bch/P	19
COOL'A | Palm Bch Gdns/P	22
Z Council Oak | H'wood/B	24
Cugini Grille | Delray Bch/P	20
Disco Fish | W. Miami	19
Dockside Sea | Lake Pk/P	19
Duffy's Steak | Key W./K	19
Z 15th St. Fish | Ft. Laud/B	19
NEW Fin | Design Dist	-
Fin & Claw | Lighthse Pt/B	17
Z Four Seasons | Palm Bch/P	26
Z Francesco | Coral Gables	26

Garcia's | **Miami Riv** — 22

Gold Coast | **Coral Spgs/B** — 22

Green Turtle Inn | **Islamorada/K** — ⎯

☑ Grille 66 | **Ft. Laud/B** — 25

Grillfish | **SoBe** — 21

Guanabanas | **Jupiter/P** — ⎯

Half Shell | **Key W./K** — 23

Ireland's | **Weston/B** — 22

Island Grill | **Islamorada/K** — 22

JB's | **Deerfield Bch/B** — 17

Jetty's | **Jupiter/P** — 22

☑ Joe's Stone | **SoBe** — 27

☑ Kee Grill | **multi.** — 24

Keys Fisheries | **Marathon/K** — 24

La Dorada | **Coral Gables** — 24

Lazy Loggerhead | **Jupiter/P** — 23

☑ Little Moir's | **Jupiter/P** — 26

Mangoes | **Key W./K** — 19

Marker 88 | **Islamorada/K** — 22

MB/Omphoy | **Palm Bch/P** — ⎯

McCormick/Schmick | **Boca/P** — 20

Monty's | **multi.** — 15

Morada Bay | **Islamorada/K** — 23

North Ocean | **Ft. Laud/B** — 18

☑ Oceanaire | **Downtown** — 24

Ocean Prime | **Aventura** — 24

Oceans 234 | **Deerfield Bch/B** — 18

Old Calypso | **Delray Bch/P** — 19

Old Florida | **Wilton Manors/B** — 21

Pelican Landing | **Ft. Laud/B** — 18

Pepe's | **Key W./K** — 24

Pilar | **Aventura** — 24

☑ Pisces | **Key W./K** — 28

Player's Club | **Wellington/P** — 19

Prime Catch | **Boynton Bch/P** — 21

☑ Prime One | **SoBe** — 26

Quinn's | **SoBe** — 25

Red Fish Grill | **Coral Gables** — 20

Reef Road | **W. Palm/P** — -

Riggin's Crab | **Lantana/P** — 18

River Hse. | **Palm Bch Gdns/P** — 23

River Oyster | **Miami Riv** — 24

Rock Fish | **Kendall** — 21

Rustic Inn | **Ft. Laud/B** — 22

Rusty Anchor | **Stock Island/K** — 21

Rusty Pelican | **Key Biscayne** — 16

Sailfish Marina | **Palm Bch Shores/P** — 18

Schooner Wharf | **Key W./K** — 15

Seafood World | **Lighthse Pt/B** — 22

Seven Fish | **Key W./K** — 26

SHOR | **Key W./K** — -

Snappers | **Boynton Bch/P** — 18

Snapper's Water. | **Key Largo/K** — 22

Southport Raw | **Ft. Laud/B** — 19

Spoto's Oyster | **Palm Bch Gdns/P** — 23

Station Grille/Hse. | **Lantana/P** — 23

Sunfish | **Ft. Laud/B** — 24

Tarpon Bend | **multi.** — 18

☑ 3030 Ocean | **Ft. Laud/B** — 25

III Forks | **Hallandale/B** — 23

Timpano | **Ft. Laud/B** — 21

Trina | **Ft. Laud/B** — -

☑ Truluck's | **multi.** — 24

Turtle Kraals | **Key W./K** — 19

Two Georges | **Boynton Bch/P** — 16

☑ Via Luna | **Ft. Laud/B** — -

Whale Raw | **Parkland/B** — 16

Whale's Rib | **Deerfield Bch/B** — 21

Ziggie/Mad Dog | **Islamorada/K** — 24

SMALL PLATES

(See also Spanish tapas specialist)

Bizaare Cafe | Eclectic | **Lake Worth/P** — 21

NEW Botequim Carioca | Brazilian | **Biscayne** — -

Cottage | Eclectic | **Lake Worth/P** — 16

NEW D'Angelo | Italian | **Oakland Pk/B** — -

NEW Elle's | Asian/Carib. | **Miramar/B** — -

☑ Hiro's Yakko | Japanese | **No. Miami Bch** — 26

Leila | Mideast. | **W. Palm/P** — 22

☑ Michy's | Med. | **UES** — 27

NEW Norman's 180 | Eclectic | **Coral Gables** — -

☑ Palme d'Or | French | **Coral Gables** — 28

River Oyster | Seafood | **Miami Riv** — 24

☑ Santiago's | Eclectic | **Key W./K** — 28

NEW Sugarcane | Eclectic | **Downtown** — -

SOUL FOOD

Mahogany | **Miami Gdns** — 23

SOUTHERN

Jumbo's | **West Dade** — 22

SOUTHWESTERN

☑ Canyon | **Ft. Laud/B** — 26

Lost & Found | **Design Dist** — 20

SPANISH

(* tapas specialist)

Cafe Seville* | **Ft. Laud/B** — 25

Casa Juancho | **Little Havana** — 25

Casa Paco* | So. Miami	20
Disco Fish | W. Miami	19
El Carajo* | Coco Grove	20
Enriqueta's | Wynwood	22
Ideas Rest. | Coco Grove	20
Ilios* | Ft. Laud/B	-
La Barraca* | H'wood/B	22
La Dorada | Coral Gables	24
Las Culebrinas | multi.	22
Por Fin | Coral Gables	22
Solea | SoBe	-
Spanish Gdns. | Islamorada/K	-
Sra. Martinez* | Design Dist	24
Tapas & Tintos* | SoBe	20
Xixón Cafe* | Coral Way	24

STEAKHOUSES

Z Abe/Louie's | Boca/P	26
BLT Steak | SoBe	24
Z Bonefish Grill | West Dade	22
Z Bourbon Steak | Aventura	25
Braza Lena | Islamorada/K	-
Callaro's Steak | Manalapan/P	21
Z Capital Grille | multi.	26
Z Chima Brazilian | Ft. Laud/B	24
Z Chops Lobster | Boca/P	26
Z Christy's | Coral Gables	25
Commodore | Key W./K	22
Z Council Oak | H'wood/B	24
Cugini Grille | Delray Bch/P	20
DeVito | SoBe	21
Duffy's Steak | Key W./K	19
El Novillo | multi.	22
5300 Chop House | Doral	-
Z Flagler Steak | Palm Bch/P	25
Fleming's Prime | Coral Gables	24
Fogo de Chão | SoBe	24
Gotham Steak | Miami Bch	22
Z Graziano's | multi.	26
Z Grille 66 | Ft. Laud/B	25
Grimpa | Brickell	23
Hollywood Prime | H'wood/B	24
Ireland's | Weston/B	22
JB's | Deerfield Bch/B	17
Z Kee Grill | multi.	24
Las Vacas | Miami Bch	21
Linda B. Steak | Key Biscayne	19
Los Ranchos | multi.	21
Meat Market | SoBe	24
Miami's Chophse. | Downtown	21
Z Morton's | multi.	25
Z NY Prime | Boca/P	25
North Ocean | Ft. Laud/B	18

Ocean Prime | Aventura	24
Okeechobee | W. Palm/P	21
Outback | multi.	17
Z Palm | Bay Harbor Is	26
Palm Beach Steak | Palm Bch/P	23
Pepe's | Key W./K	24
Player's Club | Wellington/P	19
Prime Italian | SoBe	24
Z Prime One | SoBe	26
Raindancer | W. Palm/P	23
Red Steakhouse | SoBe	25
River Hse. | Palm Bch Gdns/P	23
Z Ruth's Chris | multi.	25
Saito's | multi.	21
Scorch Grill | No. Miami	18
Shula's | multi.	21
Z Smith & Wollensky | SoBe	23
Steak 954 | Ft. Laud/B	24
NEW STK Miami | Miami Bch	-
III Forks | multi.	23
Timpano | Ft. Laud/B	21
Ziggie/Mad Dog | Islamorada/K	24

TEX-MEX

Taco Rico | Coral Gables	21
Uncle Julio's | Boca/P	19

THAI

Bangkok Bangkok | Coral Gables	20
Bangkok Bangkok | Kendall	23
Z Bluefin Sushi | multi.	25
Eddie Hills | Hallandale/B	22
Fuji Hana | multi.	21
Galanga | Wilton Manors/B	24
Jasmine Thai | Margate/B	24
Kampai | multi.	21
Kiko | Plantation/B	-
Z Lemongrass | multi.	23
Moon Thai | multi.	23
Oishi Thai | No. Miami	25
Panya Thai | No. Miami Bch	-
Safire | Lake Worth/P	25
Siam Cuisine | Wilton Manors/B	20
Siam Palace | So. Miami	25
Sukhothai | Ft. Laud/B	23
Sushi Jo's | Palm Bch Gdns/P	23
Sushi Maki | multi.	20
Su Shin Thai | Lauderhill/B	23
Sushi Siam | multi.	21
Thai & Sushi | W. Sunset	22
Thai Cuisine | Key W./K	15
Thai Hse. II | No. Miami Bch	24
Thai Hse. S. | SoBe	23

Menus, photos, voting and more – free at ZAGAT.com

Thaikyo Asian	**Manalapan/P**	22
Z Thai Spice	**Ft. Laud/B**	26
World Resources	**SoBe**	20
Ziree Thai	**Delray Bch/P**	25

TURKISH

A La Turca	**H'wood/B**	20
Hakan	**SoBe**	20
NEW Mandolin	**Design Dist**	-

URUGUAYAN

| Zuperpollo | **Brickell** | 21 |

VEGETARIAN

(* vegan)

Café	**Key W./K**	-
Helen Huang's	**H'wood/B**	18
Here/Sun	**No. Miami**	22

Julio's	**No. Miami Bch**	22
Sublime*	**Ft. Laud/B**	22
Udipi	**Sunrise/B**	-
Woodlands	**Lauderhill/B**	23

VIETNAMESE

Basilic Viet.	**Laud-by-Sea/B**	-
Cay Da	**Boca/P**	22
Z Hy-Vong	**Little Havana**	27
La Tre	**Boca/P**	21
Z Lemongrass	**multi.**	23
Little Saigon	**No. Miami Bch**	24
Miss Saigon	**multi.**	23
Pho Hoa	**Tamarac/B**	23
Pho 78	**Pembroke Pines/B**	17
Saigon Cuisine	**Margate/B**	-
Saigon Tokyo	**Greenacres/P**	22

CUISINES

Locations

Includes names, cuisines and Food ratings.

Miami/Dade County

BISCAYNE/ DOWNTOWN

(Including Brickell Area and Miami River)

Abokado	*Japanese/Pan-Latin*	19
Acqua	*Eclectic*	25
Archie's Pizza	*Pizza*	18
Area 31	*Seafood*	22
Atrio	*Amer.*	21
☑ Azul	*Med.*	27
Baja Fresh	*Mex.*	18
Balans	*Eclectic*	19
Bali Café	*Indonesian*	23
NEW Baru Urbano	*Pan-Latin*	-
Bin No. 18	*Med.*	22
Bongos Cuban	*Cuban*	17
NEW Botequim Carioca	*Brazilian*	-
Bubba Gump	*Seafood*	15
Burger & Beer	*Burgers*	-
Café Sambal	*Asian*	23
☑ Capital Grille	*Steak*	26
☑ Cheese Course	*Eclectic*	26
DB Bistro Moderne	*French*	-
Deli Lane	*Deli*	17
Dolores	*Eclectic*	18
El Gran Inka	*Peruvian*	21
Eos	*Med.*	-
Garcia's	*Seafood*	22
Gordon Biersch	*Amer.*	14
☑ Graziano's	*Argent./Steak*	26
Grimpa	*Brazilian/Steak*	23
☑ Il Gabbiano	*Italian*	26
Indochine	*Asian*	21
La Loggia	*Italian*	21
Las Culebrinas	*Cuban/Spanish*	22
Lime Fresh Mex.	*Cal./Mex.*	21
Los Ranchos	*S Amer./Steak*	21
Mario/Baker	*Italian/Pizza*	19
NEW Mercadito	*Mex.*	-
Mia	*Eclectic*	-
Miami's Chophse.	*Steak*	21
☑ Morton's	*Steak*	25
Novecento	*Argent.*	20
☑ Oceanaire	*Seafood*	24
Pasha's	*Med.*	20
Perricone's	*Italian*	20
☑ P.F. Chang's	*Chinese*	21

Piola	*Pizza*	22
Prelude	*Amer.*	-
Provence	*French*	18
River Oyster	*Seafood*	24
Rosa Mexicano	*Mex.*	21
Rosinella	*Italian*	19
NEW Sakaya	*Korean*	-
☑ S&S	*Diner*	21
Soya & Pomodoro	*Italian*	21
NEW Sparky's	*BBQ*	-
NEW Sugarcane	*Eclectic*	-
Sushi Maki	*Japanese/Thai*	20
Tony Chan's	*Chinese*	22
Tutto Pasta	*Italian*	23
Tutto Pizza	*Pizza*	23
NEW Waxy O'Connor's	*Pub*	-
NEW Zuma	*Japanese*	-
Zuperpollo	*S Amer.*	21

CORAL GABLES

Anacapri	*Italian*	22
NEW Angelique Euro Café	*Euro.*	-
Archie's Pizza	*Pizza*	18
Baja Fresh	*Mex.*	18
Bangkok Bangkok	*Thai*	20
Bugatti Pasta	*Italian*	23
Café at Books	*Amer.*	21
Caffe Abbracci	*Italian*	24
Caffe Vialetto	*Italian*	24
Charlotte Bistro	*French*	-
☑ Christy's	*Steak*	25
Fleming's Prime	*Steak*	24
Fontana	*Italian*	21
☑ Francesco	*Peruvian*	26
Fritz & Franz	*German*	16
Gables Diner	*Diner*	16
Globe Cafe	*Eclectic*	18
☑ Graziano's	*Argent./Steak*	26
Havana Harry's	*Cuban*	21
House of India	*Indian*	18
☑ Houston's	*Amer.*	22
NEW Il Grissino	*Italian*	-
JohnMartin's	*Amer./Irish*	17
La Casita	*Cuban*	21
La Cofradia	*Peruvian*	23
La Dorada	*Seafood/Spanish*	24
La Palma	*Italian*	21
Le Provençal	*French*	22
Mario/Baker	*Italian/Pizza*	19

Maroosh	*Med./Mideast.*	24
Mint Leaf	*Indian*	23
Miss Saigon	*Viet.*	23
Moon Thai	*Japanese/Thai*	23
☑ Morton's	*Steak*	25
NEW Norman's 180	*Eclectic*	-
OneBurger	*Burgers*	18
☑ Ortanique	*Carib./New World*	26
☑ Palme d'Or	*French*	28
☑ Pascal's	*French*	27
Pasha's	*Med.*	20
Peppy's	*Italian*	20
Por Fin	*Med./Spanish*	22
Randazzo's	*Italian*	23
Red Fish Grill	*Seafood*	20
☑ Ruth's Chris	*Steak*	25
Sakura	*Japanese*	22
NEW Sawa	*Japanese/Med.*	-
Spris	*Pizza*	21
Sushi Maki	*Japanese/Thai*	20
Su Shin	*Japanese*	25
Taco Rico	*Tex-Mex*	21
NEW Talavera	*Mex.*	-
Tarpon Bend	*Seafood*	18
Titanic Brewery	*Amer.*	16
Villagio	*Italian*	20
Yard Hse.	*Amer.*	19
Yuga	*Asian*	24

CORAL WAY/ LITTLE HAVANA

Casa Juancho	*Spanish*	25
Guayacan	*Nicaraguan*	23
☑ Hy-Vong	*Viet.*	27
Islas Canarias	*Cuban*	20
Las Vegas	*Cuban*	21
Mykonos	*Greek*	18
Old Lisbon	*Portug.*	24
Outback	*Steak*	17
☑ Romeo's Cafe	*Italian*	27
Sergio's	*Cuban*	20
☑ Versailles	*Cuban*	21
Xixón Cafe	*Spanish*	24

DESIGN DISTRICT/ UPPER EAST SIDE

☑ Andiamo! Pizza	*Pizza*	26
Balans	*Eclectic*	19
Dogma Grill	*Hot Dogs*	20
NEW Fin	*Seafood*	-
Fratelli Lyon	*Italian*	23
Lost & Found	*SW*	20
Magnum	*Amer./Eclectic*	21
NEW Maitardi	*Italian*	-

NEW Mandolin	*Greek*	-
Mario/Baker	*Italian/Pizza*	19
☑ Michael's	*Amer.*	26
☑ Michy's	*Amer./French*	27
Pasha's	*Med.*	20
Pizza Volante	*Pizza*	-
Q American	*Amer.*	-
☑ Red Light	*Amer.*	26
Royal Bavarian	*German*	19
Soyka	*Amer.*	20
Sra. Martinez	*Spanish*	24
Uva 69	*Cuban/French*	21
W Wine	*French*	-

KEY BISCAYNE

Archie's Pizza	*Pizza*	18
Bayside Fish	*Seafood*	13
Cioppino	*Italian*	23
El Gran Inka	*Peruvian*	21
Le Croisic	*French*	21
Linda B. Steak	*Steak*	19
Novecento	*Argent.*	20
Origin Asian	*Asian*	22
Rusty Pelican	*Seafood*	16
Sushi Siam	*Japanese/Thai*	21

MIAMI BEACH

(Including Bal Harbour, Bay Harbor Island, Little Haiti, Sunny Isles Beach, Surfside, Wynwood; see also South Beach)

☑ Adriana	*Eclectic/Seafood*	26
Cafe Avanti	*Italian*	22
Café Prima	*Italian*	23
Café Ragazzi	*Italian*	24
Caffe Da Vinci	*Italian*	21
Canyon Ranch Grill	*Health*	23
Carpaccio	*Italian*	22
El Rancho	*Mex.*	20
Enriqueta's	*Sandwiches*	22
NEW Forge/Wine	*Amer.*	-
Gotham Steak	*Steak*	22
☑ Hakkasan	*Chinese*	26
☑ Il Mulino NY	*Italian*	25
Joey's Italian	*Italian*	22
La Goulue	*French*	22
Las Vacas	*Argent./Steak*	21
NEW Lou's Beer	*Amer.*	-
NEW Morgans	*Amer.*	-
☑ Morton's	*Steak*	25
Naoe	*Japanese*	-
Neomi's Grill	*Amer.*	-
Oasis	*Med.*	19
Oggi Caffe	*Italian*	21
☑ Palm	*Steak*	26

LOCATIONS

Paul	*Bakery/Sandwiches*	18
Pita Hut	*Israeli*	17
Z Scarpetta	*Italian*	25
Shula's	*Steak*	21
NEW STK Miami	*Amer./Steak*	-
Timo	*Italian/Med.*	25

NORTH DADE

(Including Aventura, Miami Gardens, North Miami and North Miami Beach)

Z Anthony's Pizza	*Pizza*	23
Bella Luna	*Italian*	22
Z Bourbon Steak	*Steak*	25
Bulldog Barbecue	*BBQ*	20
Captain Jim	*Seafood*	25
Chéen Huaye	*Mex.*	25
Z Cheesecake	*Amer.*	20
Z Chef Allen's	*Seafood*	26
El Gran Inka	*Peruvian*	21
Fuji Hana	*Japanese/Thai*	21
Grand Lux	*Eclectic*	19
Grill on Alley	*Amer.*	22
Hanna's Diner	*French*	26
Here/Sun	*Veg.*	22
Hiro Japanese	*Japanese*	20
Z Hiro's Yakko	*Japanese*	26
Z Houston's	*Amer.*	22
Julio's	*Veg.*	22
Kampai	*Japanese/Thai*	21
Kebab Indian	*Indian*	21
Lime Fresh Mex.	*Cal./Mex.*	21
Little Havana	*Cuban*	21
Little Saigon	*Viet.*	24
Mahogany	*Soul Food*	23
Mario/Baker	*Italian/Pizza*	19
Melting Pot	*Fondue*	20
Z Morton's	*Steak*	25
Ocean Prime	*Seafood/Steak*	24
Oishi Thai	*Japanese/Thai*	25
Original Pancake	*Amer.*	20
Outback	*Steak*	17
Panya Thai	*Thai*	-
Paquito's	*Mex.*	22
Pasha's	*Med.*	20
Paul	*Bakery/Sandwiches*	18
Z P.F. Chang's	*Chinese*	21
Pilar	*Amer./Seafood*	24
Racks Italian	*Italian*	-
Rosalia's	*Italian*	18
Scorch Grill	*Steak*	18
Sushi Hse.	*Asian/Japanese*	25
Thai Hse. II	*Thai*	24
NEW Water Club	*Amer.*	-

SOUTH BEACH

A Fish/Avalon	*Seafood*	22
Ago	*Italian*	20
A La Folie	*French*	24
Z AltaMare	*Seafood*	25
Z Asia de Cuba	*Asian/Cuban*	23
Aura	*Eclectic*	26
Balans	*Eclectic*	19
Bar-B-Que	*BBQ*	14
Z Barton G.	*Amer.*	23
BED	*Eclectic*	17
Big Pink	*Diner*	19
BLT Steak	*Steak*	24
Z Blue Door	*Brazilian/French*	23
Blue Sea	*Japanese*	25
Z Bond St.	*Japanese*	26
Burger & Beer	*Burgers*	-
Café at Books	*Amer.*	21
Caffé Milano	*Italian*	19
Z Casa Tua	*Italian*	25
Caviar Kaspia	*French*	-
Z China Grill	*Asian*	23
Clarke's	*Irish*	21
da Leo Tratt.	*Italian*	17
David's	*Cuban*	17
De Rodriguez Cuba	*Cuban*	-
DeVito	*Italian/Steak*	21
Doraku	*Japanese*	21
Dynamo	*Eclectic*	-
8 Oz. Burger	*Amer.*	20
El Chalán	*Peruvian*	22
11th St. Diner	*Diner*	18
El Rancho	*Mex.*	20
Z Emeril's	*Contemp. LA*	23
Escopazzo	*Italian*	25
Essensia	*Amer.*	-
Fogo de Chão	*Brazilian/Steak*	24
Fratelli	*Italian*	21
Front Porch	*Amer.*	21
Grazie Italian	*Italian*	24
Grillfish	*Seafood*	21
Guru	*Indian*	24
Hakan	*Turkish*	20
Hosteria Romana	*Italian*	20
Icebox Café	*Bakery/Eclectic*	23
Joe Allen	*Amer.*	22
Z Joe's Stone	*Seafood*	27
La Locanda	*Italian*	23
Lario's/Beach	*Cuban*	18
La Sandwicherie	*French/Sandwiches*	23
Lido	*Med.*	21
Lime Fresh Mex.	*Cal./Mex.*	21

Macaluso's	*Italian*	23
Maiko	*Japanese*	20
Mango's Tropical	*Eclectic*	15
Meat Market	*Steak*	24
Miss Saigon	*Viet.*	23
Miss Yip	*Chinese*	19
Monty's	*Seafood*	15
Mr. Chow	*Chinese*	-
☑ Nemo	*Amer.*	24
News Cafe	*Diner*	17
Nexxt Cafe	*Eclectic*	18
Nikki	*Eclectic*	17
☑ Nobu Miami Beach	*Japanese*	27
☑ OLA	*Pan-Latin*	27
☑ Osteria del Teatro	*Italian*	26
NEW Otentic	*French*	-
Pasha's	*Med.*	20
Pelican Café	*Amer.*	23
Philippe	*Chinese*	21
Piola	*Pizza*	22
Pizza Rustica	*Pizza*	21
Prime Italian	*Italian/Steak*	24
☑ Prime One	*Seafood/Steak*	26
Puerto Sagua	*Cuban*	20
Quattro	*Italian*	22
Quinn's	*Seafood*	25
Red Steakhouse	*Steak*	25
☑ Rest. at Setai	*Asian*	22
Rice Hse.	*Persian*	21
Rosinella	*Italian*	19
Sardinia	*Italian*	23
NEW Shake Shack	*Burgers*	-
Shoji	*Japanese*	24
☑ Smith & Wollensky	*Steak*	23
Solea	*Spanish*	-
☑ Spiga	*Italian*	26
Spris	*Pizza*	21
Sushi Rock	*Japanese*	21
☑ SushiSamba	*Japanese/S Amer.*	23
Sushi Siam	*Japanese/Thai*	21
Sylvano's	*Italian*	20
Tantra	*Eclectic*	20
Tapas & Tintos	*Med./Spanish*	20
Tap Tap	*Haitian*	22
Taverna Opa	*Greek*	19
Thai Hse. S.	*Thai*	23
Tiramesu	*Italian*	21
T-Mex Cantina	*Mex.*	23
Toni's Sushi	*Japanese*	25
Van Dyke	*Amer.*	17
NEW Villa By Barton G.	*Continental*	-
☑ Wish	*Amer.*	25

World Resources	*Japanese/Thai*	20
Yuca	*Nuevo Latino*	20

SOUTH DADE

(Including Coconut Grove, Cutler Ridge, Dadeland, Homestead, Kendall, Palmetto Bay, Pinecrest, South Miami and West Sunset)

Anacapri	*Italian*	22
☑ Anthony's Pizza	*Pizza*	23
Bangkok Bangkok	*Thai*	23
Berries	*Health*	20
Big Cheese	*Pizza*	21
Bistro Bisou	*French*	18
Bizcaya	*Continental/Med.*	20
Blú la Pizzeria	*Pizza*	23
NEW Bombay Darbar	*Indian*	-
☑ Bonefish Grill	*Seafood*	22
Café Pastis	*French*	24
Calamari	*Italian*	-
Captain's Tav.	*Seafood*	23
Casa Larios	*Cuban*	19
Casa Paco	*Cuban/Spanish*	20
☑ Cheesecake	*Amer.*	20
Daily Bread Pinecrest	*Mideast.*	23
Deli Lane	*Deli*	17
El Carajo	*Spanish*	20
El Rancho Grande	*Mex.*	20
El Toro	*Mex.*	21
Flanigan's	*Amer.*	20
Fuji Hana	*Japanese/Thai*	21
George's/Grove	*French*	22
NEW George's/Sunset	*French/Med.*	-
Gibraltar	*Amer.*	-
Gil Capa's	*Italian*	25
Green/Cafe	*French/Med.*	18
Havana Harry's	*Cuban*	21
Ideas Rest.	*Spanish*	20
Imlee	*Indian*	23
Jaguar	*Pan-Latin*	23
Kampai	*Japanese/Thai*	21
Khoury's	*Lebanese*	22
La Casona	*Cuban*	19
Lan	*Asian*	23
Las Culebrinas	*Cuban/Spanish*	22
Le Bouchon du Grove	*French*	23
Lime Fresh Mex.	*Cal./Mex.*	21
Los Ranchos	*S Amer./Steak*	21
Marhaba Med.	*Lebanese*	21
☑ Matsuri	*Japanese*	27
Melting Pot	*Fondue*	20
Mike's	*Pizza*	21
Miss Saigon	*Viet.*	23

LOCATIONS

Monty's | *Seafood*	15
Moon Thai | *Japanese/Thai*	23
New Chinatown | *Chinese*	18
Novecento | *Argent.*	20
Off the Grille | *Carib.*	-
Old Lisbon | *Portug.*	24
Orig. Daily | *Mideast.*	22
Original Pancake | *Amer.*	20
Origin Asian | *Asian*	22
Outback | *Steak*	17
Papichi | *Italian*	20
Pei Wei | *Asian*	19
☑ P.F. Chang's | *Chinese*	21
Pizza Rustica | *Pizza*	21
RA Sushi | *Japanese*	19
Rice Hse. | *Persian*	21
Rock Fish | *Amer.*	21
Scotty's | *Amer.*	14
Sergio's | *Cuban*	20
☑ Shibui | *Japanese*	26
Shorty's | *BBQ*	19
Siam Palace | *Thai*	25
Sushi Maki | *Japanese/Thai*	20
Su Shin | *Japanese*	25
Sushi Siam | *Japanese/Thai*	21
Thai & Sushi | *Thai*	22
Town Kit. | *Eclectic*	18
Tratt. Luna | *Italian*	24
Tratt. Sole | *Italian*	21
Two Chefs | *Amer.*	24
White Lion | *Amer.*	19

WEST DADE

(Including the Airport, Doral, Hialeah, Miami Lakes, Westchester and West Miami)

Anacapri | *Italian*	22
☑ Anthony's Pizza | *Pizza*	23
Archie's Pizza | *Pizza*	18
Bahamas Fish | *Seafood*	20
Basilico | *Italian*	26
☑ Bonefish Grill | *Seafood*	22
Casa Larios | *Cuban*	19
Disco Fish | *Seafood/Spanish*	19
El Atlakat | *Salvadoran*	20
El Chalán | *Peruvian*	22
El Novillo | *Nicaraguan/Steak*	22
5300 Chop House | *Steak*	-
☑ Graziano's | *Argent./Steak*	26
Guayacan | *Nicaraguan*	23
Islas Canarias | *Cuban*	20
Jumbo's | *Diner*	22
Kon Chau | *Chinese*	24
La Casita | *Cuban*	21

Las Culebrinas | *Cuban/Spanish*	22
Los Ranchos | *S Amer./Steak*	21
Molina's | *Cuban*	22
Old San Juan | *Puerto Rican*	19
Original Pancake | *Amer.*	20
Outback | *Steak*	17
Pit Bar-B-Q | *BBQ*	20
Rice Hse. | *Persian*	21
Salmon | *Peruvian*	23
Sergio's | *Cuban*	20
Shorty's | *BBQ*	19
Shula's | *Steak*	21
Tropical Chinese | *Chinese*	25

Keys

KEY WEST

A&B Lobster | *Seafood*	23
Abbondanza | *Italian*	19
Ambrosia | *Japanese*	24
Antonia's | *Italian*	25
Azur | *Med.*	26
Bad Boy Burrito | *Mexican*	22
Bagatelle | *Carib./Seafood*	23
Banana Cafe | *French*	26
☑ Blue Heaven | *Floribbean*	24
B.O.'s Fish | *Seafood*	24
Braza Lena | *Brazilian*	-
Café | *Veg.*	-
☑ Cafe Marquesa | *Amer.*	27
Café Solé | *Carib./French*	24
Camille's | *Amer.*	22
Chico's Cantina | *Mex.*	24
Commodore | *Seafood/Steak*	22
Conch Republic | *Seafood*	19
Croissants | *Bakery/French*	25
Duffy's Steak | *Seafood/Steak*	19
El Meson | *Cuban*	21
El Siboney | *Cuban*	26
Finnegan's | *Irish*	18
Grand Café | *Eclectic*	22
Half Shell | *Seafood*	23
Hot Tin Roof | *Carib./Eclectic*	23
Jimmy Buffett's | *Amer.*	15
Kelly's Carib. | *Amer./Carib.*	21
La Trattoria | *Italian*	24
☑ Louie's | *Amer./Carib.*	25
Mangia Mangia | *Italian*	20
Mangoes | *Seafood*	19
Martin's | *Carib./Euro.*	24
☑ Michaels | *Amer.*	28
Mo's | *French*	21
nine one five | *Amer./Med.*	25

Origami | *Japanese*	25
Outback | *Steak*	17
Pepe's | *Seafood/Steak*	24
☑ Pisces | *Amer./Seafood*	28
Salute! | *Italian/Seafood*	22
☑ Santiago's | *Eclectic*	28
Sarabeth's | *Amer.*	25
Schooner Wharf | *Seafood*	15
Seven Fish | *Seafood*	26
SHOR | *Seafood*	-
Sloppy Joe's | *Amer.*	14
Square One | *Amer.*	22
Thai Cuisine | *Thai*	15
Turtle Kraals | *BBQ/Seafood*	19
Two Friends | *Amer.*	19
Upper Deck | *Eclectic*	23

OTHER KEYS

(Including Islamorada, Key Largo, Little Torch Key and Marathon)

Alabama Jacks | *Seafood*	18
Barracuda Grill | *Eclectic*	23
Braza Lena | *Brazilian*	-
Calypso's | *Seafood*	23
Chanticleer | *French*	24
☑ Din. Rm./Little Palm | *French/Pan-Latin*	26
Green Turtle Inn | *Seafood*	-
Island Grill | *Asian/Seafood*	22
Kaiyó | *Amer./Asian*	-
Keys Fisheries | *Seafood*	24
Marker 88 | *Amer.*	22
Morada Bay | *New World*	23
☑ Pierre's | *Eclectic*	27
Rusty Anchor | *Seafood*	21
Snapper's Water. | *Seafood*	22
Spanish Gdns. | *Spanish*	-
Tasters | *Eclectic*	-
Ziggie/Mad Dog | *Seafood/Steak*	24

Ft. Lauderdale/ Broward County

FT. LAUDERDALE

Ambry German | *Amer./German*	-
☑ Anthony's Pizza | *Pizza*	23
Anthony's Runway | *Italian*	23
NEW Bellini's Pizza | *Pizza*	-
Big City Tav. | *Amer.*	19
Bimini Boatyard | *Amer.*	17
Bistro Mezzaluna | *Amer./Italian*	25
Bistro 17 | *Amer.*	24
☑ Bonefish Grill | *Seafood*	22
Bongusto! | *Italian*	23

Bubba Gump | *Seafood*	15
By Word/Mouth | *Amer.*	25
Café Emunah | *Seafood*	23
NEW Café Europa | *Italian*	-
Café La Bonne | *French*	22
Cafe Martorano | *Italian*	25
Cafe Seville | *Spanish*	25
Café Sharaku | *Asian*	27
Cafe Vico | *Italian*	24
☑ Canyon | *SW*	26
☑ Capital Grille | *Steak*	26
Casablanca | *Amer./Med.*	21
☑ Casa D'Angelo | *Italian*	27
☑ Cheesecake | *Amer.*	20
☑ Chima Brazilian | *Brazilian/Steak*	24
☑ China Grill | *Asian*	23
Christina Wan's | *Chinese*	22
Da Campo | *Italian*	24
☑ Eduardo/San Angel | *Eclectic/Mex.*	27
El Tamarindo | *Salvadoran*	22
Ferdo's Grill | *Mideast.*	21
☑ 15th St. Fish | *Seafood*	19
Floridian | *Diner*	18
☑ Greek Islands | *Greek*	25
☑ Grille 66 | *Seafood/Steak*	25
Hi-Life | *Amer.*	25
Himmarshee | *Amer./Eclectic*	23
H2O | *Italian/Med.*	19
Ilios | *Med./Spanish*	-
Il Mulino | *Italian*	22
J. Alexander | *Amer.*	20
J. Mark's | *Amer.*	21
Johnny V | *Floribbean*	24
kitchenetta | *Italian*	23
Las Vegas | *Cuban*	21
☑ Lemongrass | *Asian*	23
Mai-Kai | *Chinese*	15
Mancini's | *Italian*	22
NEW Mason Jar | *Amer.*	-
Melting Pot | *Fondue*	20
☑ Morton's | *Steak*	25
Noodles Panini | *Italian*	23
North Ocean | *Seafood/Steak*	18
Old Heidelberg | *German*	-
Original Pancake | *Amer.*	20
Outback | *Steak*	17
Pelican Landing | *Eclectic*	18
☑ P.F. Chang's | *Chinese*	21
Pier Top | *Amer.*	-
Pizza Rustica | *Pizza*	21
☑ Rainbow Palace | *Chinese*	26

LOCATIONS

Rustic Inn	*Seafood*	22
❷ Ruth's Chris	*Steak*	25
Sage	*French*	22
Saint Tropez	*French*	-
❷ Seasons 52	*Amer.*	23
Serafina	*Italian*	21
Sette Bello	*Italian*	27
Shula's	*Steak*	21
NEW SoLita	*Italian*	-
Southport Raw	*Seafood*	19
Steak 954	*Steak*	24
Sublime	*Vegan*	22
Sukhothai	*Thai*	23
Sunfish	*Amer./Seafood*	24
Tarpon Bend	*Seafood*	18
❷ Thai Spice	*Thai*	26
❷ 3030 Ocean	*Amer./Seafood*	25
Timpano	*Italian/Steak*	21
T-Mex Cantina	*Mex.*	23
Tokyo Sushi	*Japanese*	26
❷ Tom Jenkins'	*BBQ*	25
NEW Trata	*Greek*	-
Trina	*Amer.*	-
❷ Truluck's	*Seafood*	24
Tuscan Grille	*Italian*	24
❷ Valentino's	*Italian*	26
❷ Via Luna	*Italian*	-
Wild E. Asian	*Asian*	22
Wine Cellar	*Continental*	19
YOLO	*Amer.*	21

GREATER FT. LAUDERDALE

(Including Lauderdale-by-the-Sea, Oakland Park and Wilton Manors)

Aruba Beach	*Amer./Carib.*	17
Basilic Viet.	*Viet.*	-
❷ Blue Moon Fish	*Seafood*	25
NEW D'Angelo	*Pizza*	-
Galanga	*Japanese/Thai*	24
❷ LaSpada's	*Deli*	27
Old Florida	*Seafood*	21
Primavera	*Italian*	22
Siam Cuisine	*Thai*	20
Village Grille	*Amer.*	23

NORTHEAST BROWARD COUNTY

(Including Deerfield Beach, Lighthouse Point and Pompano Beach)

❷ Anthony's Pizza	*Pizza*	23
Brooks	*Continental*	23
❷ Cafe Maxx	*Amer./Eclectic*	26
Calypso	*Carib./Seafood*	24
Cap's	*Seafood*	19
Casa Maya Grill	*Mex.*	-
Checkers/Munchen	*German*	-
Fin & Claw	*Austrian/Seafood*	17
Gianni's	*Italian*	25
❷ Houston's	*Amer.*	22
JB's	*Seafood/Steak*	17
J. Mark's	*Amer.*	21
La Veranda	*Italian*	22
Le Bistro	*French*	22
Little Havana	*Cuban*	21
Madras	*Indian*	20
Oceans 234	*Seafood*	18
Seafood World	*Seafood*	22
Shorty's	*BBQ*	19
Whale's Rib	*Seafood*	21

NORTHWEST BROWARD COUNTY

(Including Coconut Creek, Coral Springs, Margate, Parkland and Tamarac)

❷ Anthony's Pizza	*Pizza*	23
❷ Bluefin Sushi	*Japanese/Thai*	25
❷ Blue Moon Fish	*Seafood*	25
❷ Bonefish Grill	*Seafood*	22
Gold Coast	*Seafood*	22
Jasmine Thai	*Thai*	24
Kuluck	*Persian*	-
❷ LaSpada's	*Deli*	27
Lime Fresh Mex.	*Cal./Mex.*	21
Melting Pot	*Fondue*	20
Moon Thai	*Japanese/Thai*	23
Original Pancake	*Amer.*	20
Outback	*Steak*	17
Pho Hoa	*Viet.*	23
Runyon's	*Continental*	24
Saigon Cuisine	*Viet.*	-
Saito's	*Japanese/Steak*	21
TooJay's	*Deli*	19
Trattoria Bella	*Italian*	-
Tumi	*Peruvian*	-
Whale Raw	*New Eng.*	16

SOUTHEAST BROWARD COUNTY

(Including Dania Beach, Hallandale and Hollywood)

Acqualina	*Italian*	25
Aizia	*Asian*	24
A La Turca	*Turkish*	20
Argentango Grill	*Argent.*	21
Beach Watch	*Amer./Seafood*	13
Billy's Stone	*Seafood*	22
Bluepoint Grill	*Seafood*	17

Brio Tuscan | *Italian* 22
Cafe Martorano | *Italian* 25
Cantina Laredo | *Mex.* 19
Casa Bella | *Italian* 24
Ω Cheese Course | *Eclectic* 26
Christine Lee's | *Chinese* 23
Ω Council Oak | *Steak* 24
Eddie Hills | *Japanese/Thai* 22
El Tamarindo | *Salvadoran/Pizza* 22
Fulvio's 1900 | *Italian* 23
Giorgio's Grill | *Med.* 20
Helen Huang's | *Chinese* 18
Hollywood Prime | *Steak* 24
NEW Il Mercato/Wine | *Eclectic* -
Jaxson's | *Ice Cream* 22
La Barraca | *Spanish* 22
Las Vegas | *Cuban* 21
Latitudes | *Floribbean* 18
Le Tub | *Burgers* 21
Lola's | *Amer.* 24
Mama Mia | *Italian* 20
Mario/Baker | *Italian/Pizza* 19
My Big Fat Greek | *Greek* 20
Padrino's | *Cuban* 20
Pizza Rustica | *Pizza* 21
Rivals | *Amer.* 16
Sage | *French* 22
Sugar Reef | *Carib.* 22
Sushi Blues | *Eclectic* 23
Tatiana | *Continental/Russian* -
Taverna Opa | *Greek* 19
Taverna Yiamas | *Med.* 15
III Forks | *Seafood/Steak* 23

SOUTHWEST BROWARD COUNTY

(Including Cooper City, Miramar and Pembroke Pines)
Ω Anthony's Pizza | *Pizza* 23
Brio Tuscan | *Italian* 22
Capriccio | *Italian* 24
NEW Elle's | *Asian/Caib.* -
NEW Giovanni's | *Italian/Peruvian* -
NEW Havana's | *Cuban* -
NEW Indian Chillies | *Chinese/Indian* -
Ω La Brochette | *Med.* 27
Las Vegas | *Cuban* 21
Lime Fresh Mex. | *Cal./Mex.* 21
Mazza | *Greek/Lebanese* 23
Melting Pot | *Fondue* 20
Mustard Seed | *Amer./Eclectic* -
Outback | *Steak* 17
Pho 78 | *Viet.* 17

RA Sushi | *Japanese* 19
Roasted Pepper | *Italian* 22
Sorella | *Italian* -
Stir Crazy | *Asian* 20
Village Tav. | *Amer.* 20

WEST BROWARD COUNTY

(Including Davie and Weston)
Acquolina | *Italian* 25
Ω Anthony's Pizza | *Pizza* 23
Bistro 555 | *Italian* 23
Ω Bonefish Grill | *Seafood* 22
Ω Cheese Course | *Eclectic* 26
Creolina's | *Cajun/Creole* 23
East City Grill | *Amer.* 21
Ichiban | *Japanese* 20
Il Toscano | *Italian* 22
Ireland's | *Seafood/Steak* 22
Ω LaSpada's | *Deli* 27
Lucille's | *Amer.* 19
Moon Thai | *Japanese/Thai* 23
Myung Ga | *Korean* 21
Original Pancake | *Amer.* 20
Shorty's | *BBQ* 19
Tarantella | *Italian* 24
Vienna Café | *Continental* 23
Vigneto's | *Italian* 22
Viva Chile | *Chilean* -

WEST CENTRAL BROWARD COUNTY

(Including Lauderdale Lakes, Lauderhill, Plantation and Sunrise)
Ω Anthony's Pizza | *Pizza* 23
Bin 595 | *Amer.* 22
Ω Bonefish Grill | *Seafood* 22
Brazaviva Churrascaria | *Brazilian* 18
Caspian Persian | *Persian* 21
Ω Cheesecake | *Amer.* 20
Grand Lux | *Eclectic* 19
India Hse. | *Indian* 20
J. Alexander | *Amer.* 20
Josef's | *Italian* 25
Kiko | *Japanese/Thai* -
Kingshead Pub | *British* -
La Creperie | *French* 23
Las Vegas | *Cuban* 21
Mario/Baker | *Italian/Pizza* 19
Marumi Sushi | *Japanese* -
Mustard Seed | *Amer./Eclectic* -
Original Pancake | *Amer.* 20
Outback | *Steak* 17
Padrino's | *Cuban* 20

Paul | *Bakery/Sandwiches* 18
🛂 P.F. Chang's | *Chinese* 21
Saxsay | *Peruvian* -
🛂 Silver Pond | *Chinese* 25
Su Shin Thai | *Japanese/Thai* 23
Toa Toa | *Chinese* -
TooJay's | *Deli* 19
Udipi | *Indian/Veg.* -
Vigneto's | *Italian* 22
Villagio | *Italian* 20
Woodlands | *Indian* 23

Palm Beach/Palm Beach County & Environs

CENTRAL PALM BEACH COUNTY

(Including Greenacres, Lake Worth, Lantana and Palm Beach)

🆕 Apicius | *Italian* -
Bice | *Italian* 21
Bimini Twist | *Seafood* 22
Bizaare Cafe | *Eclectic* 21
Brewzzi | *Amer./Italian* 18
Brogues | *Pub* 16
Cabana | *Nuevo Latino* 23
🛂 Café Boulud | *French* 27
Cafe Cellini | *Continental* 25
Café Centro | *Italian* 23
🛂 Café L'Europe | *Continental* 25
Cafe Sapori | *Italian* 24
Callaro's Steak | *Steak* 21
Charley's Crab | *Seafood* 21
🛂 Cheesecake | *Amer.* 20
🛂 Chez Jean-Pierre | *French* 27
City Cellar | *Med.* 20
Coco | *Asian* 22
Cottage | *Eclectic* 16
Couco Pazzo | *Italian* 22
Crazy Buffet | *Asian* 15
Cucina Dell' Arte | *Italian* 21
Dave's Last | *Amer* 19
Dolce/Palma | *Italian* 26
Don Ramon | *Cuban* 18
Dune Deck | *Amer.* 19
Echo | *Asian* 23
E.R. Bradley | *Amer.* 15
🆕 Fiorentina | *Italian* -
🛂 Flagler Steak | *Steak* 25
🛂 Four Seasons | *Seafood* 26
🆕 Gratify | *Amer.* -
Grease Burger | *Burgers* 20
Hamburger Heaven | *Burgers* 20

Havana | *Cuban* 22
Hot Pie | *Pizza* -
Howley's | *Diner* 17
Il Bellagio | *Italian* 19
Jade | *Amer.* 24
John Bull | *Amer.* 18
🛂 John G's | *Amer.* 23
Kona Grill | *Amer./Asian* 19
Leila | *Mideast.* 22
Leopard Lounge | *Amer./Eclectic* 20
🛂 L'Escalier | *French* 26
Maison Carlos | *French/Italian* -
🛂 Marcello | *Italian* 27
MB/Omphoy | *Med.* -
McCormick/Schmick | *Seafood* 20
Melting Pot | *Fondue* 20
Michael R. | *Amer.* 17
Mississippi | *BBQ* 22
🛂 Morton's | *Steak* 25
Nick & Johnnie's | *Amer.* 18
Okeechobee | *Steak* 21
Outback | *Steak* 17
🛂 Palm Beach Grill | *Amer.* 25
Palm Beach Steak | *Steak* 23
Paradiso | *Italian* 21
Park Avenue BBQ Grille | *BBQ* 19
🛂 P.F. Chang's | *Chinese* 21
Pistache | *French* 19
Pizza Girls | *Pizza* 22
Raindancer | *Steak* 23
Reef Road | *Seafood* -
🆕 Relish | *Burgers* -
Renato's | *Italian* 22
Rhythm Café | *Amer.* 22
Riggin's Crab | *Seafood* 18
Rocco's Tacos | *Mex.* 22
🛂 Ruth's Chris | *Steak* 25
Safire | *Asian* 25
Saigon Tokyo | *Japanese/Viet.* 22
Saito's | *Japanese/Steak* 21
🛂 Sloan's | *Ice Cream* 23
Station Grille/Hse. | *Seafood* 23
Stresa | *Italian* 18
Sushi Jo's | *Japanese* 23
🛂 Ta-boo | *Amer./Continental* 21
Taverna Opa | *Greek* 19
Temple Orange | *Italian/Med.* -
Thaikyo Asian | *Japanese/Thai* 22
This Is It Café | *Amer./Diner* -
TooJay's | *Deli* 19
Trevini | *Italian* 22
264 the Grill | *Amer./Continental* 18

NEW Vagabondi	*Italian*	⌐
Zuccarelli's Italian	*Italian*	19

MARTIN COUNTY

(Including Jensen Beach and Stuart)

Z Anthony's Pizza	*Pizza*	23
Z Bonefish Grill	*Seafood*	22
Conchy Joe's	*Seafood*	19
Z 11 Maple St.	*Amer.*	28
Z Flagler Grill	*Floribbean*	25
Outback	*Steak*	17
Park Avenue BBQ Grille	*BBQ*	19

NORTH CENTRAL PALM BEACH COUNTY

(Including Lake Park, N. Palm Beach, Palm Beach Gardens, Palm Beach Shores and Riviera Beach)

Z Anthony's Pizza	*Pizza*	23
Z Bonefish Grill	*Seafood*	22
Brass Ring Pub	*Pub*	24
NEW Cabo Flats	*Mex.*	⌐
Z Café Chardonnay	*Amer.*	25
Cantina Laredo	*Mex.*	19
Z Capital Grille	*Steak*	26
Z Cheesecake	*Amer.*	20
COOL'A	*Seafood*	22
Dockside Sea	*Seafood*	19
Z Entre Nous	*Amer.*	25
Figs	*Italian*	20
Z Five Guys	*Burgers*	22
Ironwood	*Amer.*	⌐
J. Alexander	*Amer.*	20
Kevin's Dockside	*Deli*	⌐
NEW Kubo	*Asian*	⌐
Limoncello	*Italian*	20
Melting Pot	*Fondue*	20
NEW Mr. Milano	*Italian*	⌐
Mondo's	*Amer./Med.*	19
Oakwood	*Amer.*	20
Original Pancake	*Amer.*	20
Outback	*Steak*	17
Paddy Mac's	*Irish*	22
Park Avenue BBQ Grille	*BBQ*	19
RA Sushi	*Japanese*	19
River Hse.	*Seafood/Steak*	23
Z Ruth's Chris	*Steak*	25
Sailfish Marina	*Seafood*	18
Saito's	*Japanese/Steak*	21
Sara's	*Amer.*	⌐
Z Seasons 52	*Amer.*	23
Z Sloan's	*Ice Cream*	23
Solu	*Amer.*	⌐

Spoto's Oyster	*Seafood*	23
Sushi Jo's	*Japanese*	23
III Forks	*Seafood/Steak*	23
TooJay's	*Deli*	19
Vic/Angelos	*Italian*	20
Yard Hse.	*Amer.*	19
Zuccarelli's Italian	*Italian*	19

NORTH PALM BEACH COUNTY

(Including Hobe Sound, Juno Beach, Jupiter and Tequesta)

Bistro	*Continental*	23
Buonasera	*Italian*	24
Café des Artistes	*French*	⌐
Z Captain Charlie	*Seafood*	26
NEW Carmine's	*Italian/Pizza*	⌐
NEW CG Burgers	*Burgers*	⌐
Guanabanas	*Floribbean*	⌐
Harry/Natives	*Amer.*	16
Hurricane Café	*Amer.*	21
Jetty's	*Seafood*	22
Z Kee Grill	*Seafood/Steak*	24
Lazy Loggerhead	*Seafood*	23
Z Little Moir's	*Seafood*	26
Outback	*Steak*	17
Park Avenue BBQ Grille	*BBQ*	19
Portobello	*Italian*	22
Royal Café	*Amer./Diner*	⌐
Tabica Grill	*Amer.*	21
Too Bizaare	*Eclectic*	21
TooJay's	*Deli*	19

SOUTH PALM BEACH COUNTY

(Including Boca Raton, Boynton Beach and Delray Beach)

Z Abe/Louie's	*Steak*	26
Absinthe	*Amer.*	19
Z Anthony's Pizza	*Pizza*	23
Arturo's	*Italian*	23
Banana Boat	*Seafood*	16
Bar Louie	*Amer.*	17
Ben's Kosher	*Deli/Jewish*	20
Blue Anchor	*Pub*	19
Z Bluefin Sushi	*Japanese/Thai*	25
Z Bonefish Grill	*Seafood*	22
Brewzzi	*Amer./Italian*	18
Cabana	*Nuevo Latino*	23
Caffe Luna Rosa	*Italian*	20
NEW Caliente Kitchen	*Mex.*	⌐
Z Capital Grille	*Steak*	26
NEW Capri Rist.	*Italian*	⌐
NEW Caruso's	*Italian*	⌐

LOCATIONS

🔼 Casa D'Angelo	Italian	27
Cay Da	Viet.	22
🔼 Cheesecake	Amer.	20
🔼 Cheese Course	Eclectic	26
China Dumpling	Chinese	22
🔼 Chops Lobster	Seafood/Steak	26
City Oyster & Sushi	Seafood	21
Copper Canyon	Amer.	-
Cuban Cafe	Cuban	20
Cugini Grille	Seafood/Steak	20
🔼 Dada	Amer./Eclectic	21
🔼 Five Guys	Burgers	22
Flakowitz	Deli	-
Gol!	Brazilian	20
Grand Lux	Eclectic	19
Grille/Congress	Amer.	20
🔼 Henry's	Amer.	21
🔼 Houston's	Amer.	22
Il Girasole	Italian	22
J. Alexander	Amer.	20
Josephine's	Italian	20
Joseph's Wine	Med.	24
🔼 Kathy's	Continental	25
🔼 Kee Grill	Seafood/Steak	24
La Cigale	Med.	22
La Luna	Italian	17
🔼 LaSpada's	Deli	27
La Tre	Viet.	21
La Villetta	Italian	22
🔼 Lemongrass	Asian	23
🔼 Max's	Amer.	22
McCormick/Schmick	Seafood	20
Mellow Mushroom	Pizza	23
Melting Pot	Fondue	20
Mississippi	BBQ	22
Moquila	Mex.	19
🔼 Morton's	Steak	25
🔼 NY Prime	Steak	25
NEW Office	Amer.	-
Old Calypso	Amer./Creole	19
Original Pancake	Amer.	20
Outback	Steak	17
Padrino's	Cuban	20
Park Avenue BBQ Grille	BBQ	19
🔼 P.F. Chang's	Chinese	21
Pizza Rustica	Pizza	21
Prime Catch	Seafood	21
NEW Rack's Downtown	Amer.	-
Rocco's Tacos	Mex.	22

🔼 Ruth's Chris	Steak	25
Saito's	Japanese/Steak	21
Sapori	Italian	23
🔼 Seasons 52	Amer.	23
Sláinte Irish	Irish/Pub	14
🔼 Sloan's	Ice Cream	23
Snappers	Seafood	18
Sonoma	Amer.	20
Stir Crazy	Asian	20
🔼 Sundy House	Amer.	23
Sushi Jo's	Japanese	23
Sushi Simon	Japanese	-
NEW Table 42	Italian	-
Taso's Greek	Greek	22
NEW Taste	Amer.	-
Taverna Kyma	Greek	20
Tempura Hse.	Asian	20
🔼 32 East	Amer.	26
III Forks	Seafood/Steak	23
Tin Muffin	Amer.	23
TooJay's	Deli	19
🔼 Tramonti	Italian	24
🔼 Tratt. Romana	Italian	25
Triple Eight	Amer.	-
🔼 Truluck's	Seafood	24
Two Georges	Seafood	16
Uncle Julio's	Tex-Mex	19
🔼 Uncle Tai's	Chinese	24
Vic/Angelos	Italian	20
Village Tav.	Seafood/Steak	20
NEW Vivo Partenza	Italian	-
Ziree Thai	Thai	25

ST. LUCIE COUNTY

TooJay's	Deli	19

WESTERN PALM BEACH COUNTY

(Including Royal Palm Beach and Wellington)

🔼 Anthony's Pizza	Pizza	23
Brass Ring Pub	Pub	24
Don Ramon	Cuban	18
🔼 Five Guys	Burgers	22
Original Pancake	Amer.	20
Outback	Steak	17
Park Avenue BBQ Grille	BBQ	19
Player's Club	Seafood/Steak	19
Saito's	Japanese/Steak	21
TooJay's	Deli	19

Special Features

Listings cover the best in each category and include names, locations and Food ratings. Multi-location restaurants' features may vary by branch.

ADDITIONS

(Properties added since the last edition of the book)

Ambry German | **Ft. Laud/B**
Angelique Euro Café | **Coral Gables**
Apicius | **Lantana/P**
Baru Urbano | **Brickell**
Bellini's Pizza | **Ft. Laud/B**
Bombay Darbar | **Coco Grove**
Botequim Carioca | **Biscayne**
Cabo Flats | **Palm Bch Gdns/P**
Café des Artistes | **Jupiter/P**
Café Europa | **Ft. Laud/B**
Caliente Kitchen | **Delray Bch/P**
Capri Rist. | **Boca/P**
Carmine's | **Jupiter/P**
Caruso's | **Boca/P**
Casa Maya Grill | **Deerfield Bch/B**
CG Burgers | **Jupiter/P**
Checkers/Munchen | **Pompano Bch/B**
D'Angelo | **Oakland Pk/B**
De Rodriguez Cuba | **SoBe**
Elle's | **Miramar/B**
Fin | **Design Dist**
Fiorentina | **Lake Worth/P**
Forge/Wine | **Miami Bch**
George's/Sunset | **So. Miami**
Gibraltar | **Coco Grove**
Giovanni's | **Pembroke Pines/B**
Gratify | **W. Palm/P**
Havana's | **Cooper City/B**
Il Grissino | **Coral Gables**
Il Mercato/Wine | **Hallandale/B**
Indian Chillies | **Pembroke Pines/B**
Kevin's Dockside | **Palm Bch Gdns/P**
Kiko | **Plantation/B**
Kingshead Pub | **Sunrise/B**
Kubo | **No. Palm Bch/P**
Lou's Beer | **Miami Bch**
Maison Carlos | **W. Palm/P**
Maitardi | **Design Dist**
Mandolin | **Design Dist**
Mason Jar | **Ft. Laud/B**
Mercadito | **Downtown**
Mr. Milano | **Palm Bch Gdns/P**
Morgans | **Wynwood**

Norman's 180 | **Coral Gables**
Office | **Delray Bch/P**
Old Heidelberg | **Ft. Laud/B**
Otentic | **SoBe**
Rack's Downtown | **Boca/P**
Relish | **W. Palm/P**
Royal Café | **Jupiter/P**
Sakaya | **Downtown**
Sara's | **Palm Bch Gdns/P**
Sawa | **Coral Gables**
Saxsay | **Sunrise/B**
Shake Shack | **SoBe**
SoLita | **Ft. Laud/B**
Sparky's | **Downtown**
STK Miami | **Miami Bch**
Sugarcane | **Downtown**
Table 42 | **Boca/P**
Talavera | **Coral Gables**
Taste | **Delray Bch/P**
Temple Orange | **Manalapan/P**
This Is It Café | **W. Palm/P**
Trata | **Ft. Laud/B**
Vagabondi | **W. Palm/P**
Villa By Barton G. | **SoBe**
Vivo Partenza | **Boca/P**
Water Club | **No. Miami Bch**
Waxy O'Connor's | **Brickell**
Zuma | **Downtown**

BOAT DOCKING FACILITIES

Alabama Jacks	**Key Largo/K**	18
Banana Boat	**Boynton Bch/P**	16
Bayside Fish	**Key Biscayne**	13
Beach Watch	**Dania Bch/B**	13
☑ Blue Moon Fish	**Laud-by-Sea/B**	25
Calypso's	**Key Largo/K**	23
Commodore	**Key W./K**	22
Conchy Joe's	**Jensen Bch/P**	19
Da Campo	**Ft. Laud/B**	24
☑ Din. Rm./Little Palm	**Little Torch Key/K**	26
☑ 15th St. Fish	**Ft. Laud/B**	19
Garcia's	**Miami Riv**	22
Giorgio's Grill	**H'wood/B**	20
☑ Grille 66	**Ft. Laud/B**	25
Half Shell	**Key W./K**	23

SPECIAL FEATURES

Houston's	**Pompano Bch/B**	22	John G's	**Lake Worth/P**	23
Island Grill	**Islamorada/K**	22	La Casita	**Sweetwater**	21
Jetty's	**Jupiter/P**	22	La Casona	**W. Sunset**	19
Keys Fisheries	**Marathon/K**	24	Lazy Loggerhead	**Jupiter/P**	23
Lido	**SoBe**	21	Mustard Seed	**Cooper City/B**	–
Marker 88	**Islamorada/K**	22	News Cafe	**SoBe**	17
Monty's	**multi.**	15	Nexxt Cafe	**SoBe**	18
Morada Bay	**Islamorada/K**	23	Original Pancake	**multi.**	20
Old Calypso	**Delray Bch/P**	19	Pepe's	**Key W./K**	24
Pelican Landing	**Ft. Laud/B**	18	Puerto Sagua	**SoBe**	20
Pierre's	**Islamorada/K**	27	Sailfish Marina	**Palm Bch Shores/P**	18
Prime Catch	**Boynton Bch/P**	21	S&S	**Downtown**	21
Red Fish Grill	**Coral Gables**	20	Sarabeth's	**Key W./K**	25
River Hse.	**Palm Bch Gdns/P**	23	Sergio's	**multi.**	20
Rustic Inn	**Ft. Laud/B**	22	Square One	**Key W./K**	22
Sailfish Marina	**Palm Bch Shores/P**	18	Sugar Reef	**H'wood/B**	22
Schooner Wharf	**Key W./K**	15	TooJay's	**multi.**	19
Seasons 52	**Palm Bch Gdns/P**	23	Van Dyke	**SoBe**	17
Snapper's Water.	**Key Largo/K**	22	Versailles	**Little Havana**	21
Southport Raw	**Ft. Laud/B**	19			
Tony Chan's	**Downtown**	22			
Turtle Kraals	**Key W./K**	19			
Two Georges	**Boynton Bch/P**	16			

BREAKFAST

(See also Hotel Dining)

A La Folie	**SoBe**	24
Bagatelle	**Key W./K**	23
Balans	**SoBe**	19
Banana Cafe	**Key W./K**	26
Berries	**Coco Grove**	20
Big Pink	**SoBe**	19
Blue Heaven	**Key W./K**	24
Café at Books	**multi.**	21
Café La Bonne	**Ft. Laud/B**	22
Caffe Luna Rosa	**Delray Bch/P**	20
Camille's	**Key W./K**	22
Croissants	**Key W./K**	25
David's	**SoBe**	17
Deli Lane	**multi.**	17
Dune Deck	**Lantana/P**	19
11th St. Diner	**SoBe**	18
Floridian	**Ft. Laud/B**	18
Green/Cafe	**Coco Grove**	18
Hamburger Heaven	**Palm Bch/P**	20
Howley's	**W. Palm/P**	17
Hurricane Café	**Juno Bch/P**	21
Islas Canarias	**Little Havana**	20

New listings from first column:

NEW Water Club	**No. Miami Bch**	–
NEW Waxy O'Connor's	**Brickell**	
Wild E. Asian	**Ft. Laud/B**	22
NEW Zuma	**Downtown**	–

BRUNCH

Abe's/Louie's	**Boca/P**	26
Aruba Beach	**Laud-by-Sea/B**	17
Balans	**SoBe**	19
Bizcaya	**Coco Grove**	20
Blue Heaven	**Key W./K**	24
Blue Moon Fish	**multi.**	25
Café Boulud	**Palm Bch/P**	27
Café Solé	**Key W./K**	24
Caffe Luna Rosa	**Delray Bch/P**	20
Camille's	**Key W./K**	22
Charley's Crab	**Palm Bch/P**	21
Deli Lane	**multi.**	17
11th St. Diner	**SoBe**	18
E.R. Bradley	**W. Palm/P**	15
Giorgio's Grill	**H'wood/B**	20
Icebox Café	**SoBe**	23
Joe Allen	**SoBe**	22
La Palma	**Coral Gables**	21
Louie's	**Key W./K**	25
Martin's	**Key W./K**	24
Nemo	**SoBe**	24
Nexxt Cafe	**SoBe**	18
Nikki	**SoBe**	17
Perricone's	**Brickell**	20
Rusty Pelican	**Key Biscayne**	16
Sage	**Ft. Laud/B**	22
Sailfish Marina	**Palm Bch Shores/P**	18
Sarabeth's	**Key W./K**	25
Sergio's	**multi.**	20
Soyka	**UES**	20

Sugar Reef | H'wood/B	22
☑ Sundy House | Delray Bch/P	23
☑ SushiSamba | SoBe	23
☑ Ta-boo | Palm Bch/P	21

BUFFET

(Check availability)

Acqua | Brickell	25
Aruba Beach | Laud-by-Sea/B	17
Bin 595 | Plantation/B	22
Bizcaya | Coco Grove	20
☑ Blue Moon Fish | Laud-by-Sea/B	25
Braza Lena | multi.	-
Brazaviva Churrascaria | Sunrise/B	18
Caspian Persian | Plantation/B	21
Cioppino | Key Biscayne	23
☑ Council Oak | H'wood/B	24
Crazy Buffet | W. Palm/P	15
☑ Din. Rm./Little Palm | Little Torch Key/K	26
E.R. Bradley | W. Palm/P	15
Essensia | SoBe	-
Giorgio's Grill | H'wood/B	20
Gol! | Delray Bch/P	20
House of India | Coral Gables	18
Imlee | Pinecrest	23
India Hse. | Plantation/B	20
Kaiyó | Islamorada/K	-
Kebab Indian | No. Miami Bch	21
Kuluck | Tamarac/B	-
La Palma | Coral Gables	21
Madras | Pompano Bch/B	20
☑ Nemo | SoBe	24
Nikki | SoBe	17
North Ocean | Ft. Laud/B	18
Old San Juan | W. Miami	19
Padrino's | multi.	20
Perricone's | Brickell	20
Rusty Pelican | Key Biscayne	16
Sailfish Marina | Palm Bch Shores/P	18
☑ Sundy House | Delray Bch/P	23
Udipi | Sunrise/B	-
Woodlands | Lauderhill/B	23

BUSINESS DINING

☑ Abe/Louie's | Boca/P	26
Aizia | Hallandale/B	24
Ambry German | Ft. Laud/B	-
Arturo's | Boca/P	23
Bice | Palm Bch/P	21
Bizcaya | Coco Grove	20

☑ Blue Door | SoBe	23
Bluepoint Grill | H'wood/B	17
☑ Bonefish Grill | Plantation/B	22
☑ Bourbon Steak | Aventura	25
Brio Tuscan | multi.	22
☑ Café Boulud | Palm Bch/P	27
☑ Café Chardonnay | Palm Bch Gdns/P	25
☑ Café L'Europe | Palm Bch/P	25
Cafe Martorano | H'wood/B	25
☑ Cafe Maxx | Pompano Bch/B	26
Café Sambal | Brickell	23
Cafe Sapori | W. Palm/P	24
Cafe Seville | Ft. Laud/B	25
Caffe Abbracci | Coral Gables	24
Caffé Milano | SoBe	19
Callaro's Steak | Manalapan/P	21
☑ Capital Grille | multi.	26
NEW Caruso's | Boca/P	-
☑ Casa D'Angelo | Ft. Laud/B	27
☑ Chima Brazilian | Ft. Laud/B	24
☑ Chops Lobster | Boca/P	26
☑ Christy's | Coral Gables	25
Cioppino | Key Biscayne	23
Coco | Palm Bch/P	22
Copper Canyon | Boca/P	-
☑ Council Oak | H'wood/B	24
Da Campo | Ft. Laud/B	24
Dolores | Brickell	18
Don Ramon | W. Palm/P	18
East City Grill | Weston/B	21
Echo | Palm Bch/P	23
☑ Eduardo/San Angel | Ft. Laud/B	27
NEW Elle's | Miramar/B	-
El Novillo | Miami Lks	22
☑ Emeril's | SoBe	23
☑ 15th St. Fish | Ft. Laud/B	19
☑ Flagler Steak | Palm Bch/P	25
Fontana | Coral Gables	21
Gibraltar | Coco Grove	-
Gold Coast | Coral Spgs/B	22
☑ Graziano's | Westchester	26
☑ Grille 66 | Ft. Laud/B	25
Grill on Alley | Aventura	22
Havana Harry's | Coral Gables	21
Himmarshee | Ft. Laud/B	23
☑ Il Gabbiano | Downtown	26
Ireland's | Weston/B	22
Ironwood | Palm Bch Gdns/P	-
Jaguar | Coco Grove	23
J. Alexander | Palm Bch Gdns/P	20
☑ Joe's Stone | SoBe	27

Johnny V	**Ft. Laud/B**	24
🅩 Kathy's	**Boca/P**	25
🆕 Kubo	**No. Palm Bch/P**	-
La Cigale	**Delray Bch/P**	22
La Dorada	**Coral Gables**	24
Leila	**W. Palm/P**	22
🅩 L'Escalier	**Palm Bch/P**	26
Linda B. Steak	**Key Biscayne**	19
Little Havana	**No. Miami**	21
🅩 Louie's	**Key W./K**	25
Mai-Kai	**Ft. Laud/B**	15
Maison Carlos	**W. Palm/P**	-
MB/Omphoy	**Palm Bch/P**	-
McCormick/Schmick	**Boca/P**	20
Monty's	**multi.**	15
Moquila	**Boca/P**	19
🅩 Morton's	**multi.**	25
🅩 NY Prime	**Boca/P**	25
Oakwood	**Palm Bch Gdns/P**	20
🅩 Oceanaire	**Downtown**	24
🆕 Office	**Delray Bch/P**	-
Oishi Thai	**No. Miami**	25
Okeechobee	**W. Palm/P**	21
🅩 Ortanique	**Coral Gables**	26
🅩 Osteria del Teatro	**SoBe**	26
🅩 Palm	**Bay Harbor Is**	26
🅩 Palm Beach Grill	**Palm Bch/P**	25
🅩 Palme d'Or	**Coral Gables**	28
Paradiso	**Lake Worth/P**	21
🅩 Pascal's	**Coral Gables**	27
Perricone's	**Brickell**	20
🅩 P.F. Chang's	**No. Miami Bch**	21
🅩 Pierre's	**Islamorada/K**	27
Pistache	**W. Palm/P**	19
Prime Catch	**Boynton Bch/P**	21
🅩 Prime One	**SoBe**	26
Provence	**Brickell**	18
🅩 Rainbow Palace	**Ft. Laud/B**	26
Rosinella	**Brickell**	19
🅩 Ruth's Chris	**multi.**	25
Sakura	**Coral Gables**	22
🅩 Scarpetta	**Miami Bch**	25
🅩 Seasons 52	**Boca/P**	23
🅩 Shibui	**Kendall**	26
Shula's	**multi.**	21
🅩 Smith & Wollensky	**SoBe**	23
Solu	**Singer Is/P**	-
Spoto's Oyster	**Palm Bch Gdns/P**	23
🆕 STK Miami	**Miami Bch**	-
Sunfish	**Ft. Laud/B**	24
🆕 Table 42	**Boca/P**	-
🅩 Ta-boo	**Palm Bch/P**	21

🆕 Taste	**Delray Bch/P**	-
Temple Orange	**Manalapan/P**	-
🅩 3030 Ocean	**Ft. Laud/B**	25
🅩 32 East	**Delray Bch/P**	26
III Forks	**multi.**	23
Timpano	**Ft. Laud/B**	21
Tony Chan's	**Downtown**	22
Tratt. Sole	**So. Miami**	21
🅩 Truluck's	**Ft. Laud/B**	24
🅩 Via Luna	**Ft. Laud/B**	-
Villagio	**multi.**	20
Wild E. Asian	**Ft. Laud/B**	22
Yuca	**SoBe**	20

CELEBRITY CHEFS

Tim Andriola	
Timo	**Sunny Is Bch**	25
Zach Bell	
🅩 Café Boulud	**Palm Bch/P**	27
Michelle Bernstein	
MB/Omphoy	**Palm Bch/P**	-
🅩 Michy's	**UES**	27
Sra. Martinez	**Design Dist**	24
Daniel Boulud	
🅩 Café Boulud	**Palm Bch/P**	27
DB Bistro Moderne	**Downtown**	-
Darrel Broek	
🅩 Cafe Maxx	**Pompano Bch/B**	26
Philippe Chow	
Philippe	**SoBe**	21
Scott Conant	
🅩 Scarpetta	**Miami Bch**	25
Andrea Curto-Randazzo	
🆕 Water Club	**No. Miami Bch**	-
Jonathan Eismann	
🆕 Fin	**Design Dist**	-
Angelo Elia	
🅩 Casa D'Angelo	**multi.**	27
🆕 D'Angelo	**Oakland Pk/B**	-
Todd English	
Da Campo	**Ft. Laud/B**	24
Figs	**Palm Bch Gdns/P**	20
Marcello Fiorentino	
🅩 Marcello	**W. Palm/P**	27
Cindy Hutson	
🅩 Ortanique	**Coral Gables**	26
Emeril Lagasse	
🅩 Emeril's	**SoBe**	23
Dewey LoSasso	
🆕 Forge/Wine	**Miami Bch**	-

Todd Mark Miller
NEW STK Miami | **Miami Bch** – |

Steve Martorano
Cafe Martorano | **H'wood/B** 25 |

Nobu Matsuhisa
Z Nobu Miami Beach | **SoBe** 27 |

Dean James Max
Z 3030 Ocean | **Ft. Laud/B** 25 |

Nick Morfogen
Z 32 East | **Delray Bch/P** 26 |

Pascal Oudin
Z Pascal's | **Coral Gables** 27 |

Mike Perrin
Z 11 Maple St. | **Jensen Bch/P** 28 |

Alfred Portale
Gotham Steak | **Miami Bch** 22 |

Eduardo Pria
Z Eduardo/San Angel | **Ft. Laud/B** 27 |

Michael Psilakis
Eos | **Brickell** – |

Douglas Rodriguez
De Rodriguez Cuba | **SoBe** – |
Z OLA | **SoBe** 27 |

Philippe Ruiz
Z Palme d'Or | **Coral Gables** 28 |

Oliver Saucy
Z Cafe Maxx | **Pompano Bch/B** 26 |

Michael Schwartz
Z Michael's | **Design Dist** 26 |

Allen Susser
Z Chef Allen's | **Aventura** 26 |
NEW Taste | **Delray Bch/P** – |

Claude Troisgros
Z Blue Door | **SoBe** 23 |

Norman Van Aken
NEW Norman's 180 | **Coral Gables** – |

Johnny Vinczencz
Johnny V | **Ft. Laud/B** 24 |

CHILD-FRIENDLY

(Alternatives to the usual fast-food places; * children's menu available)

Abbondanza | **Key W./K** 19 |
Z Andiamo! Pizza | **UES** 26 |
Z Anthony's Pizza | **multi.** 23 |
Antonia's | **Key W./K** 25 |
Archie's Pizza* | **multi.** 18 |
Aura | **SoBe** 26 |
Bagatelle* | **Key W./K** 23 |
Bahamas Fish* | **W. Miami** 20 |
Baja Fresh* | **multi.** 18 |
Balans | **SoBe** 19 |

Banana Boat* | **Boynton Bch/P** 16 |
Banana Cafe | **Key W./K** 26 |
Bangkok Bangkok | **Coral Gables** 20 |
Bangkok Bangkok | **Kendall** 23 |
Barracuda Grill* | **Marathon/K** 23 |
Bayside Fish* | **Key Biscayne** 13 |
Bella Luna | **Aventura** 22 |
Berries | **Coco Grove** 20 |
Big Cheese* | **So. Miami** 21 |
Big Pink* | **SoBe** 19 |
Bizcaya* | **Coco Grove** 20 |
Z Blue Heaven* | **Key W./K** 24 |
Z Bonefish Grill* | **Kendall** 22 |
Bongos Cuban* | **Downtown** 17 |
Bongusto! | **Ft. Laud/B** 23 |
B.O.'s Fish | **Key W./K** 24 |
Brogues* | **Lake Worth/P** 16 |
Café at Books | **SoBe** 21 |
Café Ragazzi | **Surfside** 24 |
Café Sambal* | **Brickell** 23 |
Café Solé* | **Key W./K** 24 |
Caffe Abbracci | **Coral Gables** 24 |
Callaro's Steak* | **Manalapan/P** 21 |
Calypso's* | **Key Largo/K** 23 |
Camille's* | **Key W./K** 22 |
Capriccio | **Pembroke Pines/B** 24 |
Captain's Tav.* | **Pinecrest** 23 |
NEW Carmine's | **Jupiter/P** – |
Carpaccio | **Bal Harbour** 22 |
Casa Paco* | **So. Miami** 20 |
Caspian Persian | **Plantation/B** 21 |
Cay Da | **Boca/P** 22 |
NEW CG Burgers | **Jupiter/P** – |
Charley's Crab* | **Palm Bch/P** 21 |
Z Cheesecake | **multi.** 20 |
Chico's Cantina* | **Key W./K** 24 |
Christina Wan's | **Ft. Laud/B** 22 |
Cioppino* | **Key Biscayne** 23 |
Conch Republic* | **Key W./K** 19 |
Conchy Joe's* | **Jensen Bch/P** 19 |
Crazy Buffet | **W. Palm/P** 15 |
Croissants | **Key W./K** 25 |
Daily Bread Pinecrest | **Pinecrest** 23 |
da Leo Tratt. | **SoBe** 17 |
David's* | **SoBe** 17 |
Deli Lane* | **multi.** 17 |
Dogma Grill | **UES** 20 |
Don Ramon* | **multi.** 18 |
Doraku | **SoBe** 21 |
Duffy's Steak* | **Key W./K** 19 |
Dune Deck* | **Lantana/P** 19 |
East City Grill* | **Weston/B** 21 |

El Chalán* | multi.	22
11th St. Diner | SoBe	18
El Meson* | Key W./K	21
El Novillo* | multi.	22
El Rancho* | SoBe	20
Ferdo's Grill* | Ft. Laud/B	21
Finnegan's* | Key W./K	18
🅩 Five Guys | Palm Bch Gdns/P	22
Fleming's Prime | Coral Gables	24
Floridian | Ft. Laud/B	18
Front Porch | SoBe	21
Fuji Hana | Aventura	21
Gables Diner* | Coral Gables	16
Garcia's | Miami Riv	22
Gil Capa's | Kendall	25
Gordon Biersch* | Downtown	14
Grand Café* | Key W./K	22
Grazie Italian | SoBe	24
🅩 Greek Islands | Ft. Laud/B	25
Green/Cafe* | Coco Grove	18
Guayacan* | multi.	23
Half Shell* | Key W./K	23
Hamburger Heaven | Palm Bch/P	20
Hanna's Diner* | No. Miami Bch	26
Harry/Natives* | Hobe Sound/P	16
Havana* | W. Palm/P	22
Havana Harry's* | Coral Gables	21
Helen Huang's | H'wood/B	18
🅩 Henry's* | Delray Bch/P	21
Here/Sun* | No. Miami	22
Hiro Japanese | No. Miami Bch	20
🅩 Hiro's Yakko | No. Miami Bch	26
Hosteria Romana | SoBe	20
House of India | Coral Gables	18
🅩 Houston's* | multi.	22
Howley's* | W. Palm/P	17
Hurricane Café* | Juno Bch/P	21
Icebox Café | SoBe	23
Ichiban* | Davie/B	20
Il Mulino* | Ft. Laud/B	22
Il Toscano | Weston/B	22
Islas Canarias* | multi.	20
Jaguar | Coco Grove	23
Jasmine Thai | Margate/B	24
Jaxson's* | Dania Bch/B	22
JB's* | Deerfield Bch/B	17
Jetty's* | Jupiter/P	22
🅩 Joe's Stone | SoBe	27
🅩 John G's | Lake Worth/P	23
Kaiyó* | Islamorada/K	-
Kampai* | multi.	21
Kelly's Carib.* | Key W./K	21

Kevin's Dockside | Palm Bch Gdns/P	-
Khoury's | So. Miami	22
La Casita* | multi.	21
La Casona* | W. Sunset	19
La Dorada* | Coral Gables	24
La Loggia | Downtown	21
Lan | So. Miami	23
La Palma | Coral Gables	21
La Sandwicherie | SoBe	23
Las Culebrinas* | multi.	22
🅩 LaSpada's | multi.	27
Las Vegas* | multi.	21
La Trattoria | Key W./K	24
Lazy Loggerhead | Jupiter/P	23
Le Bistro | Lighthse Pt/B	22
Le Bouchon du Grove | Coco Grove	23
🅩 Lemongrass | Delray Bch/P	23
Le Provençal | Coral Gables	22
Linda B. Steak* | Key Biscayne	19
Little Havana* | multi.	21
🅩 Little Moir's* | Jupiter/P	26
Los Ranchos* | multi.	21
Madras* | Pompano Bch/B	20
Mai-Kai* | Ft. Laud/B	15
Mangoes* | Key W./K	19
Marhaba Med. | So. Miami	21
Mario/Baker* | multi.	19
Maroosh | Coral Gables	24
Martin's | Key W./K	24
Mellow Mushroom | Delray Bch/P	23
Melting Pot | multi.	20
🅩 Michaels* | Key W./K	28
Miss Saigon | multi.	23
Miss Yip | SoBe	19
Morada Bay* | Islamorada/K	23
Mo's | Key W./K	21
Mykonos | Coral Way	18
🅩 Nemo* | SoBe	24
New Chinatown | So. Miami	18
News Cafe | SoBe	17
Oceans 234* | Deerfield Bch/B	18
Oggi Caffe* | No. Bay Vill	21
Old Florida* | Wilton Manors/B	21
Outback* | multi.	17
Paddy Mac's* | Palm Bch Gdns/P	22
Padriño's* | multi.	20
Papichi | Pinecrest	20
Park Avenue BBQ Grille* | multi.	19
Pasha's | multi.	20
Pelican Café | SoBe	23
Pepe's* | Key W./K	24

Menus, photos, voting and more – free at ZAGAT.com

Peppy's | **Coral Gables**	20
Piola | **SoBe**	22
Pit Bar-B-Q* | **West Dade**	20
Pizza Girls | **W. Palm/P**	22
Pizza Rustica | **multi.**	21
Puerto Sagua | **SoBe**	20
Randazzo's | **Coral Gables**	23
Riggin's Crab* | **Lantana/P**	18
River Oyster | **Miami Riv**	24
Roasted Pepper* | **Pembroke Pines/B**	22
Rosalia's | **Aventura**	18
Rosinella | **multi.**	19
Royal Café | **Jupiter/P**	-
Rustic Inn* | **Ft. Laud/B**	22
Rusty Anchor | **Stock Island/K**	21
Rusty Pelican* | **Key Biscayne**	16
Sailfish Marina* | **Palm Bch Shores/P**	18
Salute! | **Key W./K**	22
Scorch Grill* | **No. Miami**	18
Seafood World* | **Lighthse Pt/B**	22
Sergio's* | **multi.**	20
☑ Shibui* | **Kendall**	26
SHOR* | **Key W./K**	-
Shorty's* | **multi.**	19
Shula's* | **multi.**	21
Siam Cuisine | **Wilton Manors/B**	20
Siam Palace | **So. Miami**	25
☑ Silver Pond | **Laud Lks/B**	25
☑ Sloan's | **multi.**	23
Snappers* | **Boynton Bch/P**	18
Soyka* | **UES**	20
☑ Spiga | **SoBe**	26
Spris* | **multi.**	21
Sukhothai | **Ft. Laud/B**	23
Su Shin* | **multi.**	25
Su Shin Thai | **Lauderhill/B**	23
Sushi Rock | **SoBe**	21
Sushi Siam | **multi.**	21
Taco Rico* | **Coral Gables**	21
Tap Tap | **SoBe**	22
Tarantella* | **Weston/B**	24
Taverna Opa | **SoBe**	19
Thai & Sushi | **W. Sunset**	22
Thai Cuisine* | **Key W./K**	15
Thai Hse. S. | **SoBe**	23
☑ Thai Spice | **Ft. Laud/B**	26
This Is It Café | **W. Palm/P**	-
Timpano* | **Ft. Laud/B**	21
Tiramesu | **SoBe**	21
Titanic Brewery* | **Coral Gables**	16
T-Mex Cantina | **SoBe**	23

Tokyo Sushi | **Ft. Laud/B**	26
☑ Tom Jenkins' | **Ft. Laud/B**	25
Toni's Sushi | **SoBe**	25
Tony Chan's | **Downtown**	22
Too Bizaare | **Jupiter/P**	21
TooJay's* | **multi.**	19
Tratt. Luna | **Pinecrest**	24
Tratt. Sole | **So. Miami**	21
Tropical Chinese | **Westchester**	25
Tumi | **Margate/B**	-
Turtle Kraals* | **Key W./K**	19
Tutto Pasta | **Brickell**	23
Tutto Pizza | **Brickell**	23
Two Chefs | **So. Miami**	24
Two Friends* | **Key W./K**	19
Uva 69 | **UES**	21
Van Dyke | **SoBe**	17
☑ Versailles* | **Little Havana**	21
Whale's Rib* | **Deerfield Bch/B**	21
White Lion* | **Homestead**	19
Wine Cellar* | **Ft. Laud/B**	19

DANCING

Banana Boat | **Boynton Bch/P**	16
Bayside Fish | **Key Biscayne**	13
BED | **SoBe**	17
Bongos Cuban | **Downtown**	17
Cucina Dell' Arte | **Palm Bch/P**	21
Cugini Grille | **Delray Bch/P**	20
Dolores | **Brickell**	18
El Meson | **Key W./K**	21
E.R. Bradley | **W. Palm/P**	15
Giorgio's Grill | **H'wood/B**	20
JB's | **Deerfield Bch/B**	17
Jimmy Buffett's | **Key W./K**	15
Kuluck | **Tamarac/B**	-
Leopard Lounge | **Palm Bch/P**	20
Mango's Tropical | **SoBe**	15
Mia | **Downtown**	-
Monty's | **multi.**	15
My Big Fat Greek | **Dania Bch/B**	20
Nikki | **SoBe**	17
Pelican Landing | **Ft. Laud/B**	18
Sloppy Joe's | **Key W./K**	14
NEW SoLita | **Ft. Laud/B**	-
Tantra | **SoBe**	20
Tapas & Tintos | **SoBe**	20
Tarpon Bend | **Ft. Laud/B**	18
Taverna Opa | **multi.**	19
Timpano | **Ft. Laud/B**	21
NEW Water Club | **No. Miami Bch**	-
Yuca | **SoBe**	20

SPECIAL FEATURES

DESSERT SPECIALISTS

A La Folie | SoBe	24
🅩 Azul | Brickell	27
🅩 Barton G. | SoBe	23
Big Pink | SoBe	19
Billy's Stone | H'wood/B	22
🅩 Blue Heaven | Key W./K	24
By Word/Mouth | Ft. Laud/B	25
🅩 Café Boulud | Palm Bch/P	27
🅩 Café L'Europe | Palm Bch/P	25
🅩 Cafe Maxx | Pompano Bch/B	26
Café Ragazzi | Surfside	24
Captain's Tav. | Pinecrest	23
🅩 Cheesecake | multi.	20
🅩 Chef Allen's | Aventura	26
Cioppino | Key Biscayne	23
Conch Republic | Key W./K	19
Croissants | Key W./K	25
Daily Bread Pinecrest | Pinecrest	23
🅩 Emeril's | SoBe	23
Escopazzo | SoBe	25
Fin & Claw | Lighthse Pt/B	17
Fontana | Coral Gables	21
🅩 Four Seasons | Palm Bch/P	26
🅩 Graziano's | Westchester	26
Hanna's Diner | No. Miami Bch	26
Hi-Life | Ft. Laud/B	25
Hot Tin Roof | Key W./K	23
🅩 Houston's | multi.	22
Icebox Café | SoBe	23
Jaguar | Coco Grove	23
Jaxson's | Dania Bch/B	22
Joe Allen | SoBe	22
Josef's | Plantation/B	25
Lan | So. Miami	23
🅩 L'Escalier | Palm Bch/P	26
🅩 Michaels | Key W./K	28
🅩 Morton's | multi.	25
🅩 Nemo | SoBe	24
Old Calypso | Delray Bch/P	19
🅩 Ortanique | Coral Gables	26
🅩 Palme d'Or | Coral Gables	28
Paul | multi.	18
Pepe's | Key W./K	24
Portobello | Jupiter/P	22
🅩 Prime One | SoBe	26
Royal Bavarian | UES	19
🅩 Ruth's Chris | Coral Gables	25
Seven Fish | Key W./K	26
🅩 Sloan's | multi.	23
🅩 Smith & Wollensky | SoBe	23

Soyka | UES	20
🅩 SushiSamba | SoBe	23
Temple Orange | Manalapan/P	-
🅩 32 East | Delray Bch/P	26
Timo | Sunny Is Bch	25
TooJay's | multi.	19
🅩 Wish | SoBe	25
🆕 Zuma | Downtown	-

DINING ALONE

(Other than hotels and places with counter service)

A La Folie | SoBe	24
🆕 Angelique Euro Café | Coral Gables	-
🅩 Anthony's Pizza | Plantation/B	23
Baja Fresh | Coral Gables	18
Balans | SoBe	19
Beach Watch | Dania Bch/B	13
Bella Luna | Aventura	22
Big Pink | SoBe	19
Bizaare Cafe | Lake Worth/P	21
Brass Ring Pub | multi.	24
Cabana | W. Palm/P	23
🆕 Cabo Flats | Palm Bch Gdns/P	-
Café at Books | multi.	21
Cafe Cellini | Palm Bch/P	25
🅩 Café Chardonnay | Palm Bch Gdns/P	25
Café des Artistes | Jupiter/P	-
Café Emunah | Ft. Laud/B	23
🆕 Caliente Kitchen | Delray Bch/P	-
🆕 Carmine's | Jupiter/P	-
🆕 CG Burgers | Jupiter/P	-
🅩 Cheese Course | Weston/B	26
COOL'A | Palm Bch Gdns/P	22
Creolina's | Davie/B	23
Croissants | Key W./K	25
Cuban Cafe | Boca/P	20
🅩 Dada | Delray Bch/P	21
Dockside Sea | Lake Pk/P	19
Dogma Grill | UES	20
Don Ramon | W. Palm/P	18
Dune Deck | Lantana/P	19
Echo | Palm Bch/P	23
11th St. Diner | SoBe	18
El Tamarindo | Ft. Laud/B	22
🅩 15th St. Fish | Ft. Laud/B	19
Fin & Claw | Lighthse Pt/B	17
🅩 Five Guys | Palm Bch Gdns/P	22
Garcia's | Miami Riv	22
🆕 Gratify | W. Palm/P	-

Menus, photos, voting and more - free at ZAGAT.com

Green/Cafe	**Coco Grove**	18
Grillfish	**SoBe**	21
Hanna's Diner	**No. Miami Bch**	26
Here/Sun	**No. Miami**	22
☑ Hiro's Yakko	**No. Miami Bch**	26
☑ Houston's	**multi.**	22
Howley's	**W. Palm/P**	17
Icebox Café	**SoBe**	23
Jaguar	**Coco Grove**	23
Jaxson's	**Dania Bch/B**	22
Joe Allen	**SoBe**	22
☑ Joe's Stone	**SoBe**	27
John Bull	**W. Palm/P**	18
☑ Kathy's	**Boca/P**	25
Kelly's Carib.	**Key W./K**	21
Kevin's Dockside	**Palm Bch Gdns/P**	-
NEW Kubo	**No. Palm Bch/P**	-
Lan	**So. Miami**	23
☑ LaSpada's	**multi.**	27
Las Vegas	**Little Havana**	21
Le Croisic	**Key Biscayne**	21
Le Tub	**H'wood/B**	21
Lime Fresh Mex.	**SoBe**	21
Little Havana	**No. Miami**	21
Maiko	**SoBe**	20
Mangoes	**Key W./K**	19
Marker 88	**Islamorada/K**	22
☑ Michy's	**UES**	27
Monty's	**multi.**	15
☑ Morton's	**Brickell**	25
Mykonos	**Coral Way**	18
News Cafe	**SoBe**	17
NEW Office	**Delray Bch/P**	-
Off the Grille	**Kendall**	-
Okeechobee	**W. Palm/P**	21
OneBurger	**Coral Gables**	18
Origami	**Key W./K**	25
NEW Otentic	**SoBe**	-
Outback	**Delray Bch/P**	17
Paddy Mac's	**Palm Bch Gdns/P**	22
☑ Palm Beach Grill	**Palm Bch/P**	25
Paquito's	**No. Miami Bch**	22
Park Avenue BBQ Grille	**Boca/P**	19
Paul	**multi.**	18
Pei Wei	**Kendall**	19
☑ P.F. Chang's	**multi.**	21
Pizza Rustica	**multi.**	21
☑ Rainbow Palace	**Ft. Laud/B**	26
NEW Relish	**W. Palm/P**	-
Rhythm Café	**W. Palm/P**	22
Riggin's Crab	**Lantana/P**	18
Royal Café	**Jupiter/P**	-

Sailfish Marina	**Palm Bch Shores/P**	18
Sakura	**Coral Gables**	22
☑ S&S	**Downtown**	21
Sara's	**Palm Bch Gdns/P**	-
☑ Seasons 52	**Ft. Laud/B**	23
Shoji	**SoBe**	24
Shula's	**Miami Lks**	21
☑ Smith & Wollensky	**SoBe**	23
Southport Raw	**Ft. Laud/B**	19
Station Grille/Hse.	**Lantana/P**	23
Sunfish	**Ft. Laud/B**	24
NEW Taste	**Delray Bch/P**	-
Taverna Kyma	**Boca/P**	20
Tempura Hse.	**Boca/P**	20
Thai & Sushi	**W. Sunset**	22
This Is It Café	**W. Palm/P**	-
Titanic Brewery	**Coral Gables**	16
Toni's Sushi	**SoBe**	25
Too Bizaare	**Jupiter/P**	21
TooJay's	**multi.**	19
Two Georges	**Boynton Bch/P**	16
Uva 69	**UES**	21
Villagio	**Coral Gables**	20
Zuccarelli's Italian	**W. Palm/P**	19

EARLY-BIRD MENUS

A Fish/Avalon	**SoBe**	22
Bimini Twist	**W. Palm/P**	22
Bistro	**Jupiter/P**	23
Cafe Avanti	**Miami Bch**	22
Café Emunah	**Ft. Laud/B**	23
Café Prima	**Miami Bch**	23
Callaro's Steak	**Manalapan/P**	21
NEW Capri Rist.	**Boca/P**	-
☑ Captain Charlie	**Juno Bch/P**	26
Charley's Crab	**Palm Bch/P**	21
Christina Wan's	**Ft. Laud/B**	22
Cugini Grille	**Delray Bch/P**	20
Dockside Sea	**Lake Pk/P**	19
Don Ramon	**W. Palm/P**	18
☑ Entre Nous	**No. Palm Bch/P**	25
☑ 15th St. Fish	**Ft. Laud/B**	19
Fontana	**Coral Gables**	21
Helen Huang's	**H'wood/B**	18
☑ Henry's	**Delray Bch/P**	21
Here/Sun	**No. Miami**	22
Hurricane Café	**Juno Bch/P**	21
Jetty's	**Jupiter/P**	22
☑ Kee Grill	**Boca/P**	24
La Luna	**Boca/P**	17
Mai-Kai	**Ft. Laud/B**	15

Z Max's | **Boca/P**	22
Z Michaels | **Key W./K**	28
Mondo's | **No. Palm Bch/P**	19
NEW Morgans | **Wynwood**	-
Nick & Johnnie's | **Palm Bch/P**	18
Okeechobee | **W. Palm/P**	21
Old Florida | **Wilton Manors/B**	21
Z Osteria del Teatro | **SoBe**	26
Palm Beach Steak | **Palm Bch/P**	23
Peppy's | **Coral Gables**	20
Primavera | **Oakland Pk/B**	22
Riggin's Crab | **Lantana/P**	18
Spoto's Oyster | **Palm Bch Gdns/P**	23
Sunfish | **Ft. Laud/B**	24
Tabica Grill | **Jupiter/P**	21
Taverna Kyma | **Boca/P**	20
Taverna Opa | **W. Palm/P**	19
Tiramesu | **SoBe**	21
Trattoria Bella | **Margate/B**	-
Tumi | **Margate/B**	-
Two Friends | **Key W./K**	19
Two Georges | **Boynton Bch/P**	16
264 the Grill | **Palm Bch/P**	18
Z Uncle Tai's | **Boca/P**	24
Vic/Angelos | **multi.**	20

ENTERTAINMENT

(Call for days and times
of performances)

A Fish/Avalon | varies | **SoBe**	22
Aruba Beach | live music | **Laud-by-Sea/B**	17
Bayside Fish | varies | **Key Biscayne**	13
Blue Anchor | live music | **Delray Bch/P**	19
Z Blue Heaven | solo guitarist | **Key W./K**	24
Bongos Cuban | DJ/salsa | **Downtown**	17
Brogues | Irish folk | **Lake Worth/P**	16
Cafe Avanti | pianist | **Miami Bch**	22
Casa Juancho | Spanish | **Little Havana**	25
El Meson | salsa | **Key W./K**	21
Finnegan's | Irish/local bands | **Key W./K**	18
Fritz & Franz | bands | **Coral Gables**	16
Gordon Biersch | live music | **Downtown**	14
JB's | live music | **Deerfield Bch/B**	17
Jimmy Buffett's | bands | **Key W./K**	15

JohnMartin's | karaoke/live music | **Coral Gables**	17
La Barraca | flamenco | **H'wood/B**	22
La Dorada | live music | **Coral Gables**	24
Lario's/Beach | Latin music | **SoBe**	18
Leila | belly dancing | **W. Palm/P**	22
Magnum | piano bar | **UES**	21
Mai-Kai | Polynesian | **Ft. Laud/B**	15
Mango's Tropical | live music | **SoBe**	15
Marhaba Med. | belly dancing | **So. Miami**	21
Monty's | varies | **multi.**	15
Nikki | DJ | **SoBe**	17
Paddy Mac's | folk | **Palm Bch Gdns/P**	22
Perricone's | varies | **Brickell**	20
Rusty Pelican | piano | **Key Biscayne**	16
Sloppy Joe's | rock | **Key W./K**	14
Spoto's Oyster | jazz | **Palm Bch Gdns/P**	23
Square One | piano | **Key W./K**	22
Sushi Blues | blues | **H'wood/B**	23
Z SushiSamba | DJ | **SoBe**	23
Tantra | DJ/drummer | **SoBe**	20
Tap Tap | Haitian folk jazz | **SoBe**	22
Tatiana | cabaret | **Hallandale/B**	-
Taverna Opa | varies | **multi.**	19
Titanic Brewery | live music | **Coral Gables**	16
Van Dyke | live music | **SoBe**	17
Village Grille | live music | **Laud-by-Sea/B**	23
Yuca | varies | **SoBe**	20
Zuperpollo | International music | **Brickell**	21

GREEN/LOCAL/ORGANIC

Berries | **Coco Grove**	20
Z Bourbon Steak | **Aventura**	25
Café | **Key W./K**	-
Café Emunah | **Ft. Laud/B**	23
Z Cafe Maxx | **Pompano Bch/B**	26
Calypso's | **Key Largo/K**	23
Canyon Ranch Grill | **Miami Bch**	23
Z 11 Maple St. | **Jensen Bch/P**	28
Escopazzo | **SoBe**	25
Fontana | **Coral Gables**	21
Z Four Seasons | **Palm Bch/P**	26
Fratelli Lyon | **Design Dist**	23

Z Graziano's | **Westchester** 26
Here/Sun | **No. Miami** 22
Julio's | **No. Miami Bch** 22
MB/Omphoy | **Palm Bch/P** –
Meat Market | **SoBe** 24
Z Nobu Miami Beach | **SoBe** 27
Z Oceanaire | **Downtown** 24
Palm Beach Steak | **Palm Bch/P** 23
Z Palme d'Or | **Coral Gables** 28
Paradiso | **Lake Worth/P** 21
Sublime | **Ft. Laud/B** 22
Z 32 East | **Delray Bch/P** 26

HISTORIC PLACES
(Year opened; * building)

1877 | El Meson* | **Key W./K** 21
1884 | Bagatelle* | **Key W./K** 23
1890 | Turtle Kraals* | **Key W./K** 19
1902 | Sundy House* | 23
  Delray Bch/P
1903 | nine one five* | **Key W./K** 25
1905 | 11 Maple St.* | 28
  Jensen Bch/P
1909 | Pepe's | **Key W./K** 24
1910 | Louie's* | **Key W./K** 25
1912 | Casa Bella* | **Dania Bch/B** 24
1913 | Joe's Stone | **SoBe** 27
1917 | Sloppy Joe's* | **Key W./K** 14
1920 | Café* | **Key W./K** –
1920 | Café Solé* | **Key W./K** 24
1920 | Michaels* | **Key W./K** 28
1920 | Uva 69* | **UES** 21
1922 | Soya & Pomodoro* | 21
  Downtown
1924 | Dada* | **Delray Bch/P** 21
1924 | La Palma* | **Coral Gables** 21
1925 | Triple Eight* | –
  Delray Bch/P
1926 | L'Escalier* | **Palm Bch/P** 26
1926 | Palme d'Or* | 28
  Coral Gables
1927 | Casablanca* | **Ft. Laud/B** 21
1928 | Cap's* | **Lighthse Pt/B** 19
1930 | Mandolin* | **Design Dist** –
1930 | Morgans* | **Wynwood** –
1933 | Gol!* | **Delray Bch/P** 20
1937 | Floridian* | **Ft. Laud/B** 18
1938 | S&S | **Downtown** 21
1940 | Cafe Avanti* | **Miami Bch** 22
1941 | Ta-boo | **Palm Bch/P** 21
1945 | Hamburger Heaven | 20
  Palm Bch/P
1947 | Alabama Jacks | 18
  Key Largo/K

1947 | Blue Door* | **SoBe** 23
1947 | Green Turtle Inn | –
  Islamorada/K
1947 | Okeechobee | **W. Palm/P** 21
1948 | 11th St. Diner* | **SoBe** 18
1950 | Blú la Pizzeria* | **So. Miami** –
1950 | Howley's | **W. Palm/P** 17
1951 | Shorty's | **multi.** 19
1952 | Harry/Natives | 16
  Hobe Sound/P
1952 | Sailfish Marina | 18
  Palm Bch Shores/P
1955 | Jumbo's | **West Dade** 22
1955 | Rustic Inn | **Ft. Laud/B** 22
1955 | Two Georges | 16
  Boynton Bch/P
1956 | Jaxson's | **Dania Bch/B** 22
1956 | Mai-Kai | **Ft. Laud/B** 15
1957 | Pelican Landing* | 18
  Ft. Laud/B
1960 | Ambry German | –
  Ft. Laud/B

HOLIDAY MEALS
(Special prix fixe meals offered at
major holidays)

Z Adriana | **Surfside** 26
A La Folie | **SoBe** 24
Antonia's | **Key W./K** 25
Z Azul | **Brickell** 27
Brooks | **Deerfield Bch/B** 23
Bugatti Pasta | **Coral Gables** 23
Capriccio | **Pembroke Pines/B** 24
Casa Bella | **Dania Bch/B** 24
Casa Juancho | **Little Havana** 25
Z Chef Allen's | **Aventura** 26
Cioppino | **Key Biscayne** 23
Escopazzo | **SoBe** 25
Fontana | **Coral Gables** 21
Gables Diner | **Coral Gables** 16
La Dorada | **Coral Gables** 24
La Palma | **Coral Gables** 21
Lario's/Beach | **SoBe** 18
Las Vacas | **Miami Bch** 21
Z L'Escalier | **Palm Bch/P** 26
Z Michael's | **Design Dist** 26
Z Michy's | **UES** 27
Mr. Chow | **SoBe** –
Z Nemo | **SoBe** 24
Neomi's Grill | **Sunny Is Bch** –
Z Ortanique | **Coral Gables** 26
Z Palme d'Or | **Coral Gables** 28
Z Pascal's | **Coral Gables** 27
Z Rest. at Setai | **SoBe** 22

Z Ruth's Chris | **Coral Gables**	25
Sardinia | **SoBe**	23
Z Scarpetta | **Miami Bch**	25
Z SushiSamba | **SoBe**	23
Tap Tap | **SoBe**	22
Timo | **Sunny Is Bch**	25
TooJay's | **multi.**	19
Z Wish | **SoBe**	25

HOTEL DINING

Acqualina Hotel
Z Il Mulino NY \| **Sunny Is Bch** — 25

Alexander Hotel
Shula's \| **Miami Bch** — 21

Astor Hotel
De Rodriguez Cuba \| **SoBe** — ▔

Atlantic, The
Trina \| **Ft. Laud/B** — ▔

Avalon
A Fish/Avalon \| **SoBe** — 22

Betsy Hotel, The
BLT Steak \| **SoBe** — 24

Biltmore Hotel
Fontana \| **Coral Gables** — 21
Z Palme d'Or \| **Coral Gables** — 28

Blu, Motel
Z Red Light \| **UES** — 26

Boca Raton Marriott
Absinthe \| **Boca/P** — 19

Bradley Park Hotel
Coco \| **Palm Bch/P** — 22

Brazilian Court Hotel
Z Café Boulud \| **Palm Bch/P** — 27

Breakers, The
Z Flagler Steak \| **Palm Bch/P** — 25
Z L'Escalier \| **Palm Bch/P** — 26

Canyon Ranch Living
Canyon Ranch Grill \| **Miami Bch** — 23

Casa Tua
Z Casa Tua \| **SoBe** — 25

Chesterfield Hotel
Leopard Lounge \| **Palm Bch/P** — 20

Conrad Miami Hotel
Atrio \| **Downtown** — 21

Crown at Miami Beach, The
Z Morton's \| **Miami Bch** — 25

Delano Hotel
Z Blue Door \| **SoBe** — 23
Blue Sea \| **SoBe** — 25

Epic Hotel
Area 31 \| **Downtown** — 22
NEW Zuma \| **Downtown** — ▔

Fairmont Turnberry Isle Resort & Club
Z Bourbon Steak \| **Aventura** — 25

Fontainebleau Miami Beach
Gotham Steak \| **Miami Bch** — 22
Z Hakkasan \| **Miami Bch** — 26
Z Scarpetta \| **Miami Bch** — 25

Four Seasons
Acqua \| **Brickell** — 25
Pasha's \| **Brickell** — 20

Four Seasons Resort
Z Four Seasons \| **Palm Bch/P** — 26

Gansevoort South Beach Hotel
Philippe \| **SoBe** — 21
NEW STK Miami \| **Miami Bch** — ▔

Grand Doubletree Hotel
Tony Chan's \| **Downtown** — 22

Grove Isle Hotel & Spa
Gibraltar \| **Coco Grove** — ▔

Harbor Beach Marriott Resort & Spa
Z 3030 Ocean \| **Ft. Laud/B** — 25

Hilton Bentley Miami/South Beach
Prime Italian \| **SoBe** — 24

Hilton Ft. Lauderdale Beach Resort
Ilios \| **Ft. Laud/B** — ▔

Hilton Ft. Lauderdale Marina
Z China Grill \| **Ft. Laud/B** — 23

Hollywood Beach Marriott
Latitudes \| **H'wood/B** — 18

Hotel, The
Z Wish \| **SoBe** — 25

Hyatt Key West Resort
SHOR \| **Key W./K** — ▔

Hyatt Regency Bonaventure Conference Center & Spa
Ireland's \| **Weston/B** — 22

Hyatt Regency Pier 66
Z Grille 66 \| **Ft. Laud/B** — 25
Pelican Landing \| **Ft. Laud/B** — 18
Pier Top \| **Ft. Laud/B** — ▔

Il Lugano Hotel
Da Campo \| **Ft. Laud/B** — 24

JW Marriott Marquis Miami
DB Bistro Moderne \| **Downtown** — ▔

Little Palm Island Resort
Z Din. Rm./Little Palm \| **Little Torch Key/K** — 26

Loews Miami Beach Hotel
Z Emeril's \| **SoBe** — 23

Mandarin Oriental Hotel
Z Azul \| **Brickell** — 27
Café Sambal \| **Brickell** — 23

Marquesa Hotel
 🔀 Cafe Marquesa | Key W./K   27

Marriott Singer Island Beach Resort & Spa
 Solu | Singer Is/P   -

Mondrian South Beach
 🔀 Asia de Cuba | SoBe   23

New Hotel
 NEW Lou's Beer | Miami Bch   -

Ocean Key Resort
 Hot Tin Roof | Key W./K   23

Omphoy Resort
 MB/Omphoy | Palm Bch/P   -

Palms Hotel & Spa, The
 Essensia | SoBe   -

Park Central Hotel
 Quinn's | SoBe   25

Pelican Beach Resort
 North Ocean | Ft. Laud/B   18

Pelican Hotel
 Pelican Café | SoBe   23

Penguin Hotel
 Front Porch | SoBe   21

PGA National Resort
 Ironwood | Palm Bch Gdns/P   -

Quality Inn
 India Hse. | Plantation/B   20

Renaissance Hotel
 Bin 595 | Plantation/B   22
 Bistro 17 | Ft. Laud/B   24

Ritz-Carlton Coconut Grove
 Bizcaya | Coco Grove   20

Ritz-Carlton Ft. Lauderdale
 🔀 Via Luna | Ft. Laud/B   -

Ritz-Carlton Key Biscayne
 Cioppino | Key Biscayne   23

Ritz-Carlton Palm Beach
 Temple Orange | Manalapan/P   -

Sanctuary Hotel
 🔀 OLA | SoBe   27

Santa Maria Suites Resort
 Ambrosia | Key W./K   24

Seminole Paradise at Hard Rock Hotel & Casino
 Bluepoint Grill | H'wood/B   17
 Cafe Martorano | H'wood/B   25
 🔀 Council Oak | H'wood/B   24

Setai, The
 🔀 Rest. at Setai | SoBe   22

Shore Club
 Ago | SoBe   20
 🔀 Nobu Miami Beach | SoBe   27

Standard, The
 Lido | SoBe   21

Sundy House
 🔀 Sundy House | Delray Bch/P   23

Townhouse Hotel
 🔀 Bond St. | SoBe   26

Trump Int'l Sonesta Beach
 Neomi's Grill | Sunny Is Bch   -

Viceroy Hotel, The
 Eos | Brickell   -

Westin Beach Resort
 Shula's | Ft. Laud/B   21

Westin Colonnade
 NEW Norman's 180 | Coral Gables   -

Westin Diplomat Resort
 Hollywood Prime | H'wood/B   24
 Rivals | H'wood/B   16

W Ft. Lauderdale
 Steak 954 | Ft. Laud/B   24

W South Beach
 Mr. Chow | SoBe   -
 Solea | SoBe   -

LATE DINING

(Weekday closing hour)

Ago | 12 AM | SoBe   20

A La Folie | 12 AM | SoBe   24

Argentango Grill | 12 AM | H'wood/B   21

Aura | 12 AM | SoBe   26

Balans | 12 AM | SoBe   19

Banana Boat | 12 AM | Boynton Bch/P   16

Bar-B-Que | 2 AM | SoBe   14

Bar Louie | varies | Boynton Bch/P   17

NEW Baru Urbano | varies | Brickell   -

BED | 12:30 AM | SoBe   17

Big Pink | 12 AM | SoBe   19

🔀 Blue Door | 1 AM | SoBe   23

Blue Sea | 12 AM | SoBe   25

Brass Ring Pub | 1 AM | multi.   24

Burger & Beer | 1 AM | multi.   -

NEW Cabo Flats | varies | Palm Bch Gdns/P   -

Cafe Martorano | varies | H'wood/B   25

Café Prima | 12 AM | Miami Bch   23

Café Ragazzi | 12 AM | Surfside   24

Caffe Abbracci | varies | Coral Gables   24

Caffè Milano | 12 AM | SoBe   19

Restaurant	Details	Rating
☑ Cheesecake | varies | **Coco Grove**		20
☑ China Grill | 12 AM | **SoBe**		23
Christine Lee's | 12 AM | **Hallandale/B**		23
Clarke's | 12 AM | **SoBe**		21
Cottage | 1:30 AM | **Lake Worth/P**		16
Cucina Dell' Arte | 3 AM | **Palm Bch/P**		21
☑ Dada | 1:30 AM | **Delray Bch/P**		21
Dave's Last | 1 AM | **Lake Worth/P**		19
David's | 24 hrs. | **SoBe**		17
DeVito | varies | **SoBe**		21
Dolores | 12 AM | **Brickell**		18
8 Oz. Burger | 12 AM | **SoBe**		20
El Atlakat | 12 AM | **Westchester**		20
11th St. Diner | 12 AM | **SoBe**		18
E.R. Bradley | 3 AM | **W. Palm/P**		15
Escopazzo | 12 AM | **SoBe**		25
Finnegan's | 2 AM | **Key W./K**		18
Flanigan's | 4 AM | **Coco Grove**		20
Floridian | 24 hrs. | **Ft. Laud/B**		18
Fratelli | 12 AM | **SoBe**		21
Gordon Biersch | 12 AM | **Downtown**		14
Grease Burger | 12 AM | **W. Palm/P**		20
Hakan | 12 AM | **SoBe**		20
Hiro Japanese | 3:30 AM | **No. Miami Bch**		20
☑ Hiro's Yakko | 3:30 AM | **No. Miami Bch**		26
Hosteria Romana | 12 AM | **SoBe**		20
Howley's | 2 AM | **W. Palm/P**		17
Jimmy Buffett's | varies | **Key W./K**		15
John Bull | 12 AM | **W. Palm/P**		18
Jumbo's | 24 hrs. | **West Dade**		22
Kingshead Pub | varies | **Sunrise/B**		-
La Casona | 12 AM | **W. Sunset**		19
La Locanda | 12 AM | **SoBe**		23
La Palma | 12 AM | **Coral Gables**		21
La Sandwicherie | 6 AM | **SoBe**		23
Las Vacas | 12 AM | **Miami Bch**		21
Latitudes | 12AM | **H'wood/B**		18
Le Tub | 3:30 AM | **H'wood/B**		21
Lido | 12 AM | **SoBe**		21
Little Saigon | 1 AM | **No. Miami Bch**		24
NEW Lou's Beer | 2 AM | **Miami Bch**		-
Macaluso's | 12 AM | **SoBe**		23
Mama Mia | 12 AM | **H'wood/B**		20
Mango's Tropical | 4 AM | **SoBe**		15
Marumi Sushi | 1:30 AM | **Plantation/B**		-
Meat Market | 12 AM | **SoBe**		24
NEW Mercadito | 12 AM | **Downtown**		-
Mia | 2 AM | **Downtown**		-
Mr. Chow | 11:30 PM | **SoBe**		-
☑ Nemo | 12 AM | **SoBe**		24
News Cafe | 24 hrs. | **SoBe**		17
☑ Nobu Miami Beach | 12 AM | **SoBe**		27
Novecento | 12 AM | **multi.**		20
NEW Otentic | 12 AM | **SoBe**		-
Pasha's | varies | **SoBe**		20
Paul | 12 AM | **Miami Bch**		18
Pelican Café | 1 AM | **SoBe**		23
Philippe | 12 AM | **SoBe**		21
Piola | varies | **multi.**		22
Pizza Rustica | varies | **multi.**		21
Prelude | 12 AM | **Downtown**		-
Prime Italian | 12 AM | **SoBe**		24
☑ Prime One | 12 AM | **SoBe**		26
Puerto Sagua | 2 AM | **SoBe**		20
Quattro | 12 AM | **SoBe**		22
Racks Italian | 12 AM | **No. Miami Bch**		-
☑ Red Light | 2 AM | **UES**		26
Rosinella | 12 AM | **SoBe**		19
Sardinia | 12 AM | **SoBe**		23
Sergio's | 12 AM | **multi.**		20
NEW Shake Shack | 1 AM | **SoBe**		-
Shoji | 12 AM | **SoBe**		24
Shula's | 12 AM | **Miami Lks**		21
Sláinte Irish | 1 AM | **Boynton Bch/P**		14
☑ Smith & Wollensky | 2 AM | **SoBe**		23
Southport Raw | varies | **Ft. Laud/B**		19
Spris | 1 AM | **SoBe**		21
NEW Sugarcane | varies | **Downtown**		-
Sushi Hse. | 3 AM | **No. Miami Bch**		25
Sushi Rock | 12 AM | **SoBe**		21
☑ SushiSamba | 12 AM | **SoBe**		23
Sylvano's | 12 AM | **SoBe**		20
Tantra | 12 AM | **SoBe**		20
Tapas & Tintos | 3:30 AM | **SoBe**		20
Tatiana | 2 AM | **Hallandale/B**		-
Taverna Kyma | 12 AM | **Boca/P**		20
Taverna Opa | varies | **multi.**		19
Thai Hse. S. | 12 AM | **SoBe**		23
Tiramesu | 12 AM | **SoBe**		21

Restaurant	Score
Titanic Brewery | 1 AM | **Coral Gables**	16
T-Mex Cantina | varies | **multi.**	23
Toni's Sushi | 12 AM | **SoBe**	25
Two Friends | 1 AM | **Key W./K**	19
Van Dyke | 2 AM | **SoBe**	17
Z Versailles | 1 AM | **Little Havana**	21
Vic/Angelos | 12 AM | **Delray Bch/P**	20
NEW Water Club | varies | **No. Miami Bch**	-
NEW Waxy O'Connor's | 1 AM | **Brickell**	-
Yard Hse. | varies | **Coral Gables**	19
NEW Zuma | 12 AM | **Downtown**	-
Zuperpollo | 12 AM | **Brickell**	21

MICROBREWERIES

Restaurant	Score
Brewzzi | **multi.**	18
Gordon Biersch | **Downtown**	14
Kelly's Carib. | **Key W./K**	21
Titanic Brewery | **Coral Gables**	16

OFFBEAT

Restaurant	Score
Abbondanza | **Key W./K**	19
Ambrosia | **Key W./K**	24
Z Andiamo! Pizza | **UES**	26
Bahamas Fish | **W. Miami**	20
Bali Café | **Downtown**	23
Banana Cafe | **Key W./K**	26
NEW Baru Urbano | **Brickell**	-
Bayside Fish | **Key Biscayne**	13
Beach Watch | **Dania Bch/B**	13
BED | **SoBe**	17
Berries | **Coco Grove**	20
Bizaare Cafe | **Lake Worth/P**	21
Z Blue Door | **SoBe**	23
Z Blue Heaven | **Key W./K**	24
B.O.'s Fish | **Key W./K**	24
By Word/Mouth | **Ft. Laud/B**	25
Café Emunah | **Ft. Laud/B**	23
Cafe Martorano | **multi.**	25
Café Pastis | **So. Miami**	24
NEW Caliente Kitchen | **Delray Bch/P**	-
Calypso | **Pompano Bch/B**	24
Calypso's | **Key Largo/K**	23
Cap's | **Lighthse Pt/B**	19
Z Cheese Course | **Weston/B**	26
COOL'A | **Palm Bch Gdns/P**	22
Z Dada | **Delray Bch/P**	21
David's | **SoBe**	17
11th St. Diner | **SoBe**	18
Ferdo's Grill | **Ft. Laud/B**	21
Gables Diner | **Coral Gables**	16
Garcia's | **Miami Riv**	22
NEW George's/Sunset | **So. Miami**	-
Gil Capa's | **Kendall**	25
Gol! | **Delray Bch/P**	20
Half Shell | **Key W./K**	23
Hanna's Diner | **No. Miami Bch**	26
Howley's | **W. Palm/P**	17
Z Hy-Vong | **Little Havana**	27
Jaxson's | **Dania Bch/B**	22
Jumbo's | **West Dade**	22
Z La Brochette | **Cooper City/B**	27
Lario's/Beach | **SoBe**	18
Le Tub | **H'wood/B**	21
Little Saigon | **No. Miami Bch**	24
NEW Lou's Beer | **Miami Bch**	-
Mai-Kai | **Ft. Laud/B**	15
NEW Maitardi | **Design Dist**	-
Mango's Tropical | **SoBe**	15
Melting Pot | **multi.**	20
Miss Saigon | **Coral Gables**	23
Monty's | **Coco Grove**	15
Mo's | **Key W./K**	21
Mustard Seed | **Plantation/B**	-
Nikki | **SoBe**	17
Pepe's | **Key W./K**	24
Puerto Sagua | **SoBe**	20
Rhythm Café | **W. Palm/P**	22
Z Romeo's Cafe | **Coral Way**	27
Rusty Anchor | **Stock Island/K**	21
Salute! | **Key W./K**	22
Z S&S | **Downtown**	21
NEW Sawa | **Coral Gables**	-
Scotty's | **Coco Grove**	14
Seven Fish | **Key W./K**	26
Shorty's | **multi.**	19
Sloppy Joe's | **Key W./K**	14
NEW Sparky's | **Downtown**	-
Sushi Blues | **H'wood/B**	23
Tantra | **SoBe**	20
Tap Tap | **SoBe**	22
Taverna Opa | **multi.**	19
Titanic Brewery | **Coral Gables**	16
T-Mex Cantina | **SoBe**	23
Triple Eight | **Delray Bch/P**	-
Turtle Kraals | **Key W./K**	19
Tuscan Grille | **Ft. Laud/B**	24
Two Friends | **Key W./K**	19
Z Versailles | **Little Havana**	21
Villagio | **Coral Gables**	20
White Lion | **Homestead**	19
Zuperpollo | **Brickell**	21

OUTDOOR DINING

(G=garden; P=patio; S=sidewalk; T=terrace)

A&B Lobster | P, T | Key W./K — 23
Acqua | T | Brickell — 25
Acquolina | P | Weston/B — 25
A Fish/Avalon | S, T | SoBe — 22
Ago | T | SoBe — 20
A La Folie | G, T | SoBe — 24
🔟 AltaMare | S | SoBe — 25
🔟 Andiamo! Pizza | P | UES — 26
Aruba Beach | P | Laud-by-Sea/B — 17
Bagatelle | G, T | Key W./K — 23
Balans | S, T | SoBe — 19
Banana Boat | P | Boynton Bch/P — 16
Banana Cafe | P | Key W./K — 26
Barracuda Grill | P | Marathon/K — 23
🔟 Barton G. | G | SoBe — 23
Bayside Fish | P | Key Biscayne — 13
Berries | G | Coco Grove — 20
Bice | P | Palm Bch/P — 21
Bimini Boatyard | P | Ft. Laud/B — 17
Bizaare Cafe | T | Lake Worth/P — 21
Bizcaya | T | Coco Grove — 20
🔟 Blue Door | T | SoBe — 23
🔟 Blue Heaven | G, P | Key W./K — 24
🔟 Blue Moon Fish | T | Laud-by-Sea/B — 25
Bongos Cuban | T | Downtown — 17
Brewzzi | P | multi. — 18
Brogues | P | Lake Worth/P — 16
Buonasera | P | Jupiter/P — 24
Cabana | S | Delray Bch/P — 23
Café at Books | G, S | multi. — 21
🔟 Café Boulud | G, T | Palm Bch/P — 27
🔟 Café Chardonnay | S | Palm Bch Gdns/P — 25
Café Pastis | S | So. Miami — 24
Café Prima | P | Miami Bch — 23
Café Sambal | P | Brickell — 23
Cafe Sapori | P | W. Palm/P — 24
Café Solé | G, T | Key W./K — 24
Caffe Da Vinci | S | Bay Harbor Is — 21
Caffé Milano | P, S | SoBe — 19
Caffe Luna Rosa | P | Delray Bch/P — 20
Callaro's Steak | P | Manalapan/P — 21
Carpaccio | P | Bal Harbour — 22
Casablanca | P | Ft. Laud/B — 21
🔟 Casa Tua | T | SoBe — 25
🔟 Cheesecake | P | multi. — 20
Chico's Cantina | P | Key W./K — 24
Cioppino | T | Key Biscayne — 23

City Cellar | P | W. Palm/P — 20
City Oyster & Sushi | S | Delray Bch/P — 21
Coco | P | Palm Bch/P — 22
Cottage | P | Lake Worth/P — 16
Couco Pazzo | S | Lake Worth/P — 22
Croissants | P | Key W./K — 25
Cucina Dell' Arte | P | Palm Bch/P — 21
🔟 Dada | G, P | Delray Bch/P — 21
Deli Lane | P, S | multi. — 17
De Rodriguez Cuba | P | SoBe — -
Dogma Grill | P | UES — 20
Dolores | T | Brickell — 18
Dune Deck | T | Lantana/P — 19
Echo | G, T | Palm Bch/P — 23
🔟 11 Maple St. | P | Jensen Bch/P — 28
11th St. Diner | P | SoBe — 18
El Meson | G, P | Key W./K — 21
El Toro | P | Homestead — 21
🔟 Emeril's | T | SoBe — 23
E.R. Bradley | T | W. Palm/P — 15
🔟 Flagler Steak | T | Palm Bch/P — 25
Fontana | G | Coral Gables — 21
Front Porch | T | SoBe — 21
Garcia's | P | Miami Riv — 22
Giorgio's Grill | P | H'wood/B — 20
Globe Cafe | S | Coral Gables — 18
Gordon Biersch | P | Downtown — 14
Grand Café | G | Key W./K — 22
Green/Cafe | S | Coco Grove — 18
🔟 Grille 66 | P | Ft. Laud/B — 25
Half Shell | P, T | Key W./K — 23
Harry/Natives | P | Hobe Sound/P — 16
🔟 Henry's | P | Delray Bch/P — 21
Hollywood Prime | P | H'wood/B — 24
Hosteria Romana | S | SoBe — 20
🔟 Houston's | P | multi. — 22
Howley's | P | W. Palm/P — 17
Hurricane Café | P | Juno Bch/P — 21
Il Bellagio | P | W. Palm/P — 19
JB's | P | Deerfield Bch/B — 17
Jetty's | P | Jupiter/P — 22
🔟 John G's | P | Lake Worth/P — 23
Johnny V | P | Ft. Laud/B — 24
Kelly's Carib. | G, P | Key W./K — 21
Khoury's | P | So. Miami — 22
Lario's/Beach | P | SoBe — 18
Las Vacas | S | Miami Bch — 21
Latitudes | T | H'wood/B — 18
Lazy Loggerhead | P | Jupiter/P — 23
Leila | P | W. Palm/P — 22
🔟 Lemongrass | P | Delray Bch/P — 23

Le Tub | P | H'wood/B — 21
Lime Fresh Mex. | P | SoBe — 21
Limoncello | P | No. Palm Bch/P — 20
Z Louie's | T | Key W./K — 25
NEW Maitardi | P | Design Dist — _
Mangia Mangia | G | Key W./K — 20
Mangoes | G, P | Key W./K — 19
Mango's Tropical | P | SoBe — 15
Maroosh | T | Coral Gables — 24
Martin's | G | Key W./K — 24
Z Max's | P | Boca/P — 22
Z Michaels | G | Key W./K — 28
Monty's | P | multi. — 15
Moquila | P | Boca/P — 19
Morada Bay | P | Islamorada/K — 23
Z Nemo | P | SoBe — 24
News Cafe | G, S | SoBe — 17
Nexxt Cafe | P, S | SoBe — 18
Nikki | G | SoBe — 17
nine one five | P | Key W./K — 25
Oakwood | P | Palm Bch Gdns/P — 20
Oceans 234 | P | Deerfield Bch/B — 18
Origami | P | Key W./K — 25
Paddy Mac's | P | Palm Bch Gdns/P — 22
Paradiso | S | Lake Worth/P — 21
Pasha's | P | multi. — 20
Pelican Landing | P | Ft. Laud/B — 18
Pepe's | P | Key W./K — 24
Perricone's | G, T | Brickell — 20
Z P.F. Chang's | P | multi. — 21
Z Pisces | P | Key W./K — 28
Pizza Girls | S | W. Palm/P — 22
Player's Club | P | Wellington/P — 19
Portobello | P | Jupiter/P — 22
Prime Catch | P | Boynton Bch/P — 21
Red Fish Grill | P | Coral Gables — 20
Renato's | T | Palm Bch/P — 22
Z Rest. at Setai | P | SoBe — 22
Rivals | P | H'wood/B — 16
River Oyster | S | Miami Riv — 24
Rustic Inn | P | Ft. Laud/B — 22
Rusty Pelican | T | Key Biscayne — 16
Safire | S | Lake Worth/P — 25
Sailfish Marina | P | Palm Bch Shores/P — 18
Salute! | P | Key W./K — 22
Sapori | P, T | Boca/P — 23
Scorch Grill | P | No. Miami — 18
Scotty's | P | Coco Grove — 14
Serafina | P | Ft. Laud/B — 21
Shula's | P | Ft. Laud/B — 21
Z Smith & Wollensky | P | SoBe — 23

Spoto's Oyster | P | Palm Bch Gdns/P — 23
Spris | S | multi. — 21
Square One | T | Key W./K — 22
Steak 954 | T | Ft. Laud/B — 24
Sugar Reef | S | H'wood/B — 22
Z Sundy House | G | Delray Bch/P — 23
Sushi Jo's | S | W. Palm/P — 23
Sushi Rock | P | SoBe — 21
Z SushiSamba | S | SoBe — 23
Sushi Siam | P, S | multi. — 21
Tabica Grill | S | Jupiter/P — 21
Tap Tap | P | SoBe — 22
Thaikyo Asian | P, T | Manalapan/P — 22
Z Thai Spice | G, P | Ft. Laud/B — 26
Z 32 East | P, S | Delray Bch/P — 26
Tin Muffin | S | Boca/P — 23
Tiramesu | G, P, S | SoBe — 21
Z Tramonti | P, S | Delray Bch/P — 24
Tratt. Sole | S | So. Miami — 21
Trevini | S | Palm Bch/P — 22
Trina | T | Ft. Laud/B — _
Triple Eight | P | Delray Bch/P — _
Turtle Kraals | G, P, T | Key W./K — 19
Two Friends | P | Key W./K — 19
Z Uncle Tai's | P | Boca/P — 24
Uva 69 | T | UES — 21
Van Dyke | G, P, S | SoBe — 17
Z Via Luna | T | Ft. Laud/B — _
NEW Water Club | P | No. Miami Bch — _
White Lion | G, P | Homestead — 19
Wild E. Asian | T | Ft. Laud/B — 22
Z Wish | G, T | SoBe — 25
World Resources | P, S | SoBe — 20
YOLO | P, S | Ft. Laud/B — 21
Yuca | S | SoBe — 20

PEOPLE-WATCHING

A&B Lobster | Key W./K — 23
Absinthe | Boca/P — 19
A Fish/Avalon | SoBe — 22
Ago | SoBe — 20
NEW Angelique Euro Café | Coral Gables — _
Anthony's Runway | Ft. Laud/B — 23
NEW Apicius | Lantana/P — _
Aruba Beach | Laud-by-Sea/B — 17
Z Asia de Cuba | SoBe — 23
Aura | SoBe — 26
Bahamas Fish | W. Miami — 20

Restaurant	Location	Rating
Balans	SoBe	19
☑ Barton G.	SoBe	23
Beach Watch	Dania Bch/B	13
Bice	Palm Bch/P	21
Big City Tav.	Ft. Laud/B	19
Bimini Boatyard	Ft. Laud/B	17
Bistro Mezzaluna	Ft. Laud/B	25
☑ Blue Door	SoBe	23
☑ Blue Heaven	Key W./K	24
Blue Sea	SoBe	25
Brio Tuscan	Hallandale/B	22
NEW Cabo Flats	Palm Bch Gdns/P	-
Café at Books	multi.	21
Café Centro	W. Palm/P	23
NEW Café Europa	Ft. Laud/B	-
☑ Café L'Europe	Palm Bch/P	25
Cafe Martorano	multi.	25
Caffé Milano	SoBe	19
NEW Caliente Kitchen	Delray Bch/P	-
Cantina Laredo	Hallandale/B	19
Carpaccio	Bal Harbour	22
☑ Casa Tua	SoBe	25
☑ Cheese Course	Weston/B	26
☑ China Grill	multi.	23
☑ Chops Lobster	Boca/P	26
Christine Lee's	Hallandale/B	23
City Cellar	W. Palm/P	20
Commodore	Key W./K	22
☑ Council Oak	H'wood/B	24
Cucina Dell' Arte	Palm Bch/P	21
Da Campo	Ft. Laud/B	24
da Leo Tratt.	SoBe	17
NEW D'Angelo	Oakland Pk/B	-
Dave's Last	Lake Worth/P	19
Doraku	SoBe	21
Echo	Palm Bch/P	23
☑ Emeril's	SoBe	23
E.R. Bradley	W. Palm/P	15
Floridian	Ft. Laud/B	18
NEW Forge/Wine	Miami Bch	-
Fratelli Lyon	Design Dist	23
Front Porch	SoBe	21
Garcia's	Miami Riv	22
Globe Cafe	Coral Gables	18
Gotham Steak	Miami Bch	22
NEW Gratify	W. Palm/P	-
Green/Cafe	Coco Grove	18
Guanabanas	Jupiter/P	-
Half Shell	Key W./K	23
Havana Harry's	Coral Gables	21
Himmarshee	Ft. Laud/B	23
Hosteria Romana	SoBe	20
H2O	Ft. Laud/B	19
Ilios	Ft. Laud/B	-
JB's	Deerfield Bch/B	17
Joe Allen	SoBe	22
☑ Joe's Stone	SoBe	27
Johnny V	Ft. Laud/B	24
Joseph's Wine	Delray Bch/P	24
☑ Kathy's	Boca/P	25
Lario's/Beach	SoBe	18
Las Vacas	Miami Bch	21
Latitudes	H'wood/B	18
La Trattoria	Key W./K	24
Le Bouchon du Grove	Coco Grove	23
Le Croisic	Key Biscayne	21
Leopard Lounge	Palm Bch/P	20
Le Tub	H'wood/B	21
Mancini's	Ft. Laud/B	22
Mangoes	Key W./K	19
Mango's Tropical	SoBe	15
☑ Max's	Boca/P	22
MB/Omphoy	Palm Bch/P	-
Miss Yip	SoBe	19
Monty's	Coco Grove	15
Moquila	Boca/P	19
☑ Morton's	multi.	25
☑ Nemo	SoBe	24
News Cafe	SoBe	17
☑ NY Prime	Boca/P	25
Nexxt Cafe	SoBe	18
Nikki	SoBe	17
☑ Nobu Miami Beach	SoBe	27
NEW Office	Delray Bch/P	-
☑ Palm	Bay Harbor Is	26
☑ Palm Beach Grill	Palm Bch/P	25
Palm Beach Steak	Palm Bch/P	23
☑ Palme d'Or	Coral Gables	28
Perricone's	Brickell	20
Pistache	W. Palm/P	19
Player's Club	Wellington/P	19
☑ Prime One	SoBe	26
NEW Rack's Downtown	Boca/P	-
NEW Relish	W. Palm/P	-
Rivals	H'wood/B	16
Rosinella	SoBe	19
☑ S&S	Downtown	21
Sardinia	SoBe	23
☑ Scarpetta	Miami Bch	25
Shoji	SoBe	24
Shula's	Miami Lks	21
Sloppy Joe's	Key W./K	14
NEW SoLita	Ft. Laud/B	-

Soyka	**UES**	20
Spris	**SoBe**	21
Sra. Martinez	**Design Dist**	24
Sushi Rock	**SoBe**	21
Z SushiSamba	**SoBe**	23
Sushi Siam	**SoBe**	21
NEW Table 42	**Boca/P**	–
Z Ta-boo	**Palm Bch/P**	21
Tantra	**SoBe**	20
NEW Taste	**Delray Bch/P**	–
Tatiana	**Hallandale/B**	–
Taverna Opa	**multi.**	19
Z 32 East	**Delray Bch/P**	26
III Forks	**multi.**	23
Tiramesu	**SoBe**	21
Toni's Sushi	**SoBe**	25
Z Tramonti	**Delray Bch/P**	24
Triple Eight	**Delray Bch/P**	–
Two Georges	**Boynton Bch/P**	16
264 the Grill	**Palm Bch/P**	18
Van Dyke	**SoBe**	17
Z Versailles	**Little Havana**	21
Z Via Luna	**Ft. Laud/B**	–
Vic/Angelos	**Palm Bch Gdns/P**	20
Village Grille	**Laud-by-Sea/B**	23
Villagio	**multi.**	20
NEW Vivo Partenza	**Boca/P**	–
Z Wish	**SoBe**	25
World Resources	**SoBe**	20
Yuca	**SoBe**	20

POWER SCENES

Acqua	**Brickell**	25
Ago	**SoBe**	20
Antonia's	**Key W./K**	25
Z Asia de Cuba	**SoBe**	23
Z Azul	**Brickell**	27
Big City Tav.	**Ft. Laud/B**	19
Bistro Mezzaluna	**Ft. Laud/B**	25
Z Blue Door	**SoBe**	23
Cafe Martorano	**H'wood/B**	25
Caffe Abbracci	**Coral Gables**	24
Caffe Da Vinci	**Bay Harbor Is**	21
Z Capital Grille	**multi.**	26
Carpaccio	**Bal Harbour**	22
Z Casa D'Angelo	**Ft. Laud/B**	27
Casa Juancho	**Little Havana**	25
Z Casa Tua	**SoBe**	25
Z Chef Allen's	**Aventura**	26
Z Chima Brazilian	**Ft. Laud/B**	24
Z China Grill	**Ft. Laud/B**	23
Z Chops Lobster	**Boca/P**	26
Christine Lee's	**Hallandale/B**	23

Cioppino	**Key Biscayne**	23
Da Campo	**Ft. Laud/B**	24
NEW D'Angelo	**Oakland Pk/B**	–
Echo	**Palm Bch/P**	23
Z Emeril's	**SoBe**	23
Z Flagler Steak	**Palm Bch/P**	25
NEW Forge/Wine	**Miami Bch**	–
Z Four Seasons	**Palm Bch/P**	26
Fratelli Lyon	**Design Dist**	23
Gibraltar	**Coco Grove**	–
Gordon Biersch	**Downtown**	14
Z Graziano's	**Westchester**	26
Havana Harry's	**Coral Gables**	21
Himmarshee	**Ft. Laud/B**	23
Ireland's	**Weston/B**	22
Joe Allen	**SoBe**	22
Z Joe's Stone	**SoBe**	27
Johnny V	**Ft. Laud/B**	24
La Palma	**Coral Gables**	21
Le Croisic	**Key Biscayne**	21
Le Provençal	**Coral Gables**	22
Z Morton's	**multi.**	25
Z NY Prime	**Boca/P**	25
Z Nobu Miami Beach	**SoBe**	27
NEW Norman's 180	**Coral Gables**	–
Oakwood	**Palm Bch Gdns/P**	20
Z Oceanaire	**Downtown**	24
NEW Office	**Delray Bch/P**	–
Oggi Caffe	**No. Bay Vill**	21
Z Ortanique	**Coral Gables**	26
Z Palm	**Bay Harbor Is**	26
Z Palme d'Or	**Coral Gables**	28
Z Pascal's	**Coral Gables**	27
Perricone's	**Brickell**	20
Player's Club	**Wellington/P**	19
Z Prime One	**SoBe**	26
Quattro	**SoBe**	22
NEW Rack's Downtown	**Boca/P**	–
Rivals	**H'wood/B**	16
Z Ruth's Chris	**Coral Gables**	25
Sardinia	**SoBe**	23
Z Scarpetta	**Miami Bch**	25
Seven Fish	**Key W./K**	26
Z Shibui	**Kendall**	26
Shula's	**multi.**	21
Z Smith & Wollensky	**SoBe**	23
Sra. Martinez	**Design Dist**	24
NEW STK Miami	**Miami Bch**	–
Z Ta-boo	**Palm Bch/P**	21
Tantra	**SoBe**	20
Z 32 East	**Delray Bch/P**	26
Toni's Sushi	**SoBe**	25

Z Truluck's | **Ft. Laud/B** — 24

Z Versailles | **Little Havana** — 21

Z Via Luna | **Ft. Laud/B** — –

NEW Vivo Partenza | **Boca/P** — –

PRIVATE ROOMS

(Restaurants charge less at off times; call for capacity)

Absinthe | **Boca/P** — 19

Antonia's | **Key W./K** — 25

Bice | **Palm Bch/P** — 21

Bimini Boatyard | **Ft. Laud/B** — 17

Bin 595 | **Plantation/B** — 22

Bizcaya | **Coco Grove** — 20

Z Blue Door | **SoBe** — 23

Z Blue Moon Fish | **Coral Spgs/B** — 25

Z Bourbon Steak | **Aventura** — 25

Brogues | **Lake Worth/P** — 16

Brooks | **Deerfield Bch/B** — 23

Cabana | **Delray Bch/P** — 23

Z Café Boulud | **Palm Bch/P** — 27

Z Café L'Europe | **Palm Bch/P** — 25

Z Cafe Maxx | **Pompano Bch/B** — 26

Z Capital Grille | **Brickell** — 26

Charley's Crab | **Palm Bch/P** — 21

Z Chef Allen's | **Aventura** — 26

Z Chez Jean-Pierre | **Palm Bch/P** — 27

Coco | **Palm Bch/P** — 22

Z Dada | **Delray Bch/P** — 21

DeVito | **SoBe** — 21

East City Grill | **Weston/B** — 21

Echo | **Palm Bch/P** — 23

El Novillo | **Miami Lks** — 22

Escopazzo | **SoBe** — 25

Z Four Seasons | **Palm Bch/P** — 26

Giorgio's Grill | **H'wood/B** — 20

Globe Cafe | **Coral Gables** — 18

Gold Coast | **Coral Spgs/B** — 22

Z Graziano's | **multi.** — 26

Z Grille 66 | **Ft. Laud/B** — 25

Hollywood Prime | **H'wood/B** — 24

Il Bellagio | **W. Palm/P** — 19

Z Kathy's | **Boca/P** — 25

Kelly's Carib. | **Key W./K** — 21

La Casona | **W. Sunset** — 19

La Creperie | **Lauderhill/B** — 23

La Dorada | **Coral Gables** — 24

La Palma | **Coral Gables** — 21

Leopard Lounge | **Palm Bch/P** — 20

Z L'Escalier | **Palm Bch/P** — 26

Little Havana | **No. Miami** — 21

Z Louie's | **Key W./K** — 25

Mai-Kai | **Ft. Laud/B** — 15

Mangoes | **Key W./K** — 19

Martin's | **Key W./K** — 24

Melting Pot | **multi.** — 20

Z Michaels | **Key W./K** — 28

Z Morton's | **multi.** — 25

Z Nemo | **SoBe** — 24

nine one five | **Key W./K** — 25

Oakwood | **Palm Bch Gdns/P** — 20

Z Oceanaire | **Downtown** — 24

Old Lisbon | **Coral Way** — 24

Z Ortanique | **Coral Gables** — 26

Paddy Mac's | **Palm Bch Gdns/P** — 22

Z Palme d'Or | **Coral Gables** — 28

Paradiso | **Lake Worth/P** — 21

Pier Top | **Ft. Laud/B** — –

Z Pisces | **Key W./K** — 28

Z Prime One | **SoBe** — 26

Z Rainbow Palace | **Ft. Laud/B** — 26

Raindancer | **W. Palm/P** — 23

Renato's | **Palm Bch/P** — 22

River Hse. | **Palm Bch Gdns/P** — 23

Rustic Inn | **Ft. Laud/B** — 22

Z Ruth's Chris | **Ft. Laud/B** — 25

Sage | **H'wood/B** — 22

Z Smith & Wollensky | **SoBe** — 23

Stresa | **W. Palm/P** — 18

Sublime | **Ft. Laud/B** — 22

Tap Tap | **SoBe** — 22

Z 3030 Ocean | **Ft. Laud/B** — 25

Z 32 East | **Delray Bch/P** — 26

Timpano | **Ft. Laud/B** — 21

Trevini | **Palm Bch/P** — 22

Trina | **Ft. Laud/B** — –

Z Truluck's | **multi.** — 24

Two Chefs | **So. Miami** — 24

Z Uncle Tai's | **Boca/P** — 24

Yuca | **SoBe** — 20

PRIX FIXE MENUS

(Call for prices and times)

Anacapri | **Coral Gables** — 22

Brooks | **Deerfield Bch/B** — 23

Z Café Boulud | **Palm Bch/P** — 27

Z Chef Allen's | **Aventura** — 26

Z Din. Rm./Little Palm | **Little Torch Key/K** — 26

Z Emeril's | **SoBe** — 23

Le Bistro | **Lighthse Pt/B** — 22

Z L'Escalier | **Palm Bch/P** — 26

Maroosh | **Coral Gables** — 24

Melting Pot | **multi.** — 20

Z Nobu Miami Beach | **SoBe** — 27

Origami | **Key W./K** — 25

Renato's | **Palm Bch/P**	22
🅉 Romeo's Cafe | **Coral Way**	27
Sushi Blues | **H'wood/B**	23
🅉 SushiSamba | **SoBe**	23

QUICK BITES

🆕 Angelique Euro Café | **Coral Gables**	-
🅉 Anthony's Pizza | **multi.**	23
Baja Fresh | **Coral Gables**	18
Basilic Viet. | **Laud-by-Sea/B**	-
🆕 Bellini's Pizza | **Ft. Laud/B**	-
Berries | **Coco Grove**	20
Big Cheese | **So. Miami**	21
🆕 Botequim Carioca | **Biscayne**	-
Brass Ring Pub | **Royal Palm Bch/P**	24
Brewzzi | **multi.**	18
Bugatti Pasta | **Coral Gables**	23
🆕 Cabo Flats | **Palm Bch Gdns/P**	-
Café Centro | **W. Palm/P**	23
Café des Artistes | **Jupiter/P**	-
Café Emunah | **Ft. Laud/B**	23
🆕 Café Europa | **Ft. Laud/B**	-
🆕 Caliente Kitchen | **Delray Bch/P**	-
Camille's | **Key W./K**	22
🆕 Carmine's | **Jupiter/P**	-
🆕 CG Burgers | **Jupiter/P**	-
🅉 Cheese Course | **multi.**	26
Copper Canyon | **Boca/P**	-
Cottage | **Lake Worth/P**	16
Creolina's | **Davie/B**	23
Cuban Cafe | **Boca/P**	20
Daily Bread Pinecrest | **Pinecrest**	23
David's | **SoBe**	17
Deli Lane | **multi.**	17
Dockside Sea | **Lake Pk/P**	19
Dogma Grill | **UES**	20
11th St. Diner | **SoBe**	18
El Siboney | **Key W./K**	26
El Toro | **Homestead**	21
Eos | **Brickell**	-
E.R. Bradley | **W. Palm/P**	15
Finnegan's | **Key W./K**	18
🅉 Five Guys | **Palm Bch Gdns/P**	22
Floridian | **Ft. Laud/B**	18
Front Porch | **SoBe**	21
Gordon Biersch | **Downtown**	14
🆕 Gratify | **W. Palm/P**	-
Green/Cafe | **Coco Grove**	18
Guanabanas | **Jupiter/P**	-

Hamburger Heaven | **Palm Bch/P**	20
Havana | **W. Palm/P**	22
Havana Harry's | **Coral Gables**	21
Hot Pie | **W. Palm/P**	-
Icebox Café | **SoBe**	23
🆕 Il Grissino | **Coral Gables**	-
Joey's Italian | **Wynwood**	22
🅉 John G's | **Lake Worth/P**	23
Kebab Indian | **No. Miami Bch**	21
Kevin's Dockside | **Palm Bch Gdns/P**	-
La Casita | **multi.**	21
La Casona | **W. Sunset**	19
Lan | **So. Miami**	23
La Sandwicherie | **SoBe**	23
🅉 LaSpada's | **multi.**	27
Las Vegas | **Little Havana**	21
Latitudes | **H'wood/B**	18
Le Tub | **H'wood/B**	21
Lime Fresh Mex. | **SoBe**	21
Maiko | **SoBe**	20
Marumi Sushi | **Plantation/B**	-
🆕 Mason Jar | **Ft. Laud/B**	-
🅉 Michael's | **Design Dist**	26
Miss Saigon | **SoBe**	23
Molina's | **Hialeah**	22
Mykonos | **Coral Way**	18
Myung Ga | **Weston/B**	21
News Cafe | **SoBe**	17
North Ocean | **Ft. Laud/B**	18
🆕 Office | **Delray Bch/P**	-
OneBurger | **Coral Gables**	18
Orig. Daily | **Coco Grove**	22
🆕 Otentic | **SoBe**	-
Paquito's | **No. Miami Bch**	22
Park Avenue BBQ Grille | **multi.**	19
Pasha's | **multi.**	20
Paul | **multi.**	18
Pelican Landing | **Ft. Laud/B**	18
🅉 P.F. Chang's | **multi.**	21
Pho 78 | **Pembroke Pines/B**	17
Piola | **SoBe**	22
Pistache | **W. Palm/P**	19
Pit Bar-B-Q | **West Dade**	20
Pizza Girls | **W. Palm/P**	22
Pizza Rustica | **multi.**	21
Puerto Sagua | **SoBe**	20
🆕 Rack's Downtown | **Boca/P**	-
RA Sushi | **Palm Bch Gdns/P**	19
🆕 Relish | **W. Palm/P**	-
Rice Hse. | **SoBe**	21
Royal Café | **Jupiter/P**	-
Saigon Cuisine | **Margate/B**	-

NEW Sakaya | Downtown	-
Sara's | Palm Bch Gdns/P	-
Saxsay | Sunrise/B	-
Sergio's | multi.	20
NEW Shake Shack | SoBe	-
Shorty's | multi.	19
Southport Raw | Ft. Laud/B	19
Spris | multi.	21
Sushi Jo's | W. Palm/P	23
Sushi Siam | SoBe	21
NEW Table 42 | Boca/P	-
Taco Rico | Coral Gables	21
NEW Taste | Delray Bch/P	-
Taverna Kyma | Boca/P	20
Taverna Opa | W. Palm/P	19
Tempura Hse. | Boca/P	20
This Is It Café | W. Palm/P	-
T-Mex Cantina | SoBe	23
Tokyo Sushi | Ft. Laud/B	26
Z Tom Jenkins' | Ft. Laud/B	25
TooJay's | multi.	19
Tutto Pasta | Brickell	23
Tutto Pizza | Brickell	23
Z Versailles | Little Havana	21
Village Grille | Laud-by-Sea/B	23
Wild E. Asian | Ft. Laud/B	22
Zuccarelli's Italian | Palm Bch Gdns/P	19
Zuperpollo | Brickell	21

QUIET CONVERSATION

Acqua | Brickell	25
Z AltaMare | SoBe	25
Ambry German | Ft. Laud/B	-
Antonia's | Key W./K	25
Arturo's | Boca/P	23
Bagatelle | Key W./K	23
Balans | SoBe	19
Bali Café | Downtown	23
Bangkok Bangkok | Coral Gables	20
Bangkok Bangkok | Kendall	23
Barracuda Grill | Marathon/K	23
Bistro 555 | Davie/B	23
Bizaare Cafe | Lake Worth/P	21
BLT Steak | SoBe	24
Z Bonefish Grill | Plantation/B	22
Brazaviva Churrascaria | Sunrise/B	18
Cafe Avanti | Miami Bch	22
Cafe Cellini | Palm Bch/P	25
Z Café Chardonnay | Palm Bch Gdns/P	25
Café Emunah | Ft. Laud/B	23

Z Cafe Marquesa | Key W./K	27
Café Sambal | Brickell	23
Cafe Sapori | W. Palm/P	24
Cafe Seville | Ft. Laud/B	25
Café Sharaku | Ft. Laud/B	27
Caffe Da Vinci | Bay Harbor Is	21
Caffe Vialetto | Coral Gables	24
Canyon Ranch Grill | Miami Bch	23
Z Capital Grille | Palm Bch Gdns/P	26
NEW Capri Rist. | Boca/P	-
NEW Caruso's | Boca/P	-
Casa Maya Grill | Deerfield Bch/B	-
Z Chef Allen's | Aventura	26
Z Chez Jean-Pierre | Palm Bch/P	27
Da Campo | Ft. Laud/B	24
Z Eduardo/San Angel | Ft. Laud/B	27
NEW Elle's | Miramar/B	-
El Tamarindo | Ft. Laud/B	22
Z Entre Nous | No. Palm Bch/P	25
Escopazzo | SoBe	25
Z 15th St. Fish | Ft. Laud/B	19
Fin & Claw | Lighthse Pt/B	17
Z Francesco | Coral Gables	26
NEW Giovanni's | Pembroke Pines/B	-
Gold Coast | Coral Spgs/B	22
Green/Cafe | Coco Grove	18
Grillfish | SoBe	21
Grill on Alley | Aventura	22
Guru | SoBe	24
Hi-Life | Ft. Laud/B	25
Z Hy-Vong | Little Havana	27
Icebox Café | SoBe	23
Ichiban | Davie/B	20
Ilios | Ft. Laud/B	-
NEW Il Mercato/Wine | Hallandale/B	-
Il Toscano | Weston/B	22
India Hse. | Plantation/B	20
NEW Indian Chillies | Pembroke Pines/B	-
Joey's Italian | Wynwood	22
Josef's | Plantation/B	25
Kelly's Carib. | Key W./K	21
La Cigale | Delray Bch/P	22
La Dorada | Coral Gables	24
Las Vegas | multi.	21
Latitudes | H'wood/B	18
La Tre | Boca/P	21
Le Bistro | Lighthse Pt/B	22
Z Lemongrass | Ft. Laud/B	23

Leopard Lounge | **Palm Bch/P**	20
Z L'Escalier | **Palm Bch/P**	26
Lola's | **H'wood/B**	24
Maiko | **SoBe**	20
Maison Carlos | **W. Palm/P**	-
Mancini's | **Ft. Laud/B**	22
Martin's | **Key W./K**	24
Marumi Sushi | **Plantation/B**	-
NEW Mason Jar | **Ft. Laud/B**	-
MB/Omphoy | **Palm Bch/P**	-
NEW Mr. Milano | **Palm Bch Gdns/P**	-
Mustard Seed | **multi.**	-
Z Nemo | **SoBe**	24
North Ocean | **Ft. Laud/B**	18
Oceans 234 | **Deerfield Bch/B**	18
Oishi Thai | **No. Miami**	25
Z Palm Beach Grill | **Palm Bch/P**	25
Palm Beach Steak | **Palm Bch/P**	23
Z Palme d'Or | **Coral Gables**	28
Z Pascal's | **Coral Gables**	27
Peppy's | **Coral Gables**	20
Pho Hoa | **Tamarac/B**	23
Pier Top | **Ft. Laud/B**	-
Portobello | **Jupiter/P**	22
Provence | **Brickell**	18
Z Rainbow Palace | **Ft. Laud/B**	26
Renato's | **Palm Bch/P**	22
Z Romeo's Cafe | **Coral Way**	27
Z Ruth's Chris | **Coral Gables**	25
Safire | **Lake Worth/P**	25
Sage | **Ft. Laud/B**	22
Saigon Cuisine | **Margate/B**	-
Saxsay | **Sunrise/B**	-
Z Seasons 52 | **Ft. Laud/B**	23
Serafina | **Ft. Laud/B**	21
Seven Fish | **Key W./K**	26
Shoji | **SoBe**	24
Solu | **Singer Is/P**	-
Stresa | **W. Palm/P**	18
Sukhothai | **Ft. Laud/B**	23
Z Sundy House | **Delray Bch/P**	23
Sunfish | **Ft. Laud/B**	24
Tarpon Bend | **Coral Gables**	18
Temple Orange | **Manalapan/P**	-
Thai Hse. S. | **SoBe**	23
III Forks | **Hallandale/B**	23
Toa Toa | **Sunrise/B**	-
Toni's Sushi | **SoBe**	25
NEW Trata | **Ft. Laud/B**	-
Tratt. Luna | **Pinecrest**	24
Z Truluck's | **Ft. Laud/B**	24
Two Chefs | **So. Miami**	24

264 the Grill | **Palm Bch/P**	18
Udipi | **Sunrise/B**	-
NEW Vagabondi | **W. Palm/P**	-
Z Valentino's | **Ft. Laud/B**	26
Z Via Luna | **Ft. Laud/B**	-
NEW Villa By Barton G. | **SoBe**	-
Village Grille | **Laud-by-Sea/B**	23
Villagio | **Sunrise/B**	20
Viva Chile | **Davie/B**	-
Wild E. Asian | **Ft. Laud/B**	22

RAW BARS

Z Azul | **Brickell**	27
Z Blue Moon Fish | **multi.**	25
Charley's Crab | **Palm Bch/P**	21
City Oyster & Sushi | **Delray Bch/P**	21
Conch Republic | **Key W./K**	19
Conchy Joe's | **Jensen Bch/P**	19
Crazy Buffet | **W. Palm/P**	15
Dave's Last | **Lake Worth/P**	19
Gotham Steak | **Miami Bch**	22
Half Shell | **Key W./K**	23
Harry/Natives | **Hobe Sound/P**	16
Meat Market | **SoBe**	24
Z Michy's | **UES**	27
Monty's | **multi.**	15
Z Nemo | **SoBe**	24
Z Oceanaire | **Downtown**	24
Old Florida | **Wilton Manors/B**	21
Pepe's | **Key W./K**	24
Prime Catch | **Boynton Bch/P**	21
Prime Italian | **SoBe**	24
Quinn's | **SoBe**	25
NEW Rack's Downtown | **Boca/P**	-
River Oyster | **Miami Riv**	24
Sage | **multi.**	22
Sailfish Marina | **Palm Bch Shores/P**	18
Schooner Wharf | **Key W./K**	15
Southport Raw | **Ft. Laud/B**	19
Spoto's Oyster | **Palm Bch Gdns/P**	23
Steak 954 | **Ft. Laud/B**	24
NEW Sugarcane | **Downtown**	-
Tarpon Bend | **Coral Gables**	18
Z 3030 Ocean | **Ft. Laud/B**	25
Z Truluck's | **Boca/P**	24
Whale Raw | **Parkland/B**	16
Whale's Rib | **Deerfield Bch/B**	21

ROMANTIC PLACES

Acqua | **Brickell**	25
Ago | **SoBe**	20

Restaurant	Rating
A La Folie | **SoBe**	24
Z AltaMare | **SoBe**	25
NEW Angelique Euro Café | **Coral Gables**	-
Antonia's | **Key W./K**	25
Arturo's | **Boca/P**	23
Z Asia de Cuba | **SoBe**	23
Atrio | **Downtown**	21
Z Azul | **Brickell**	27
Bagatelle | **Key W./K**	23
Beach Watch | **Dania Bch/B**	13
BED | **SoBe**	17
BLT Steak | **SoBe**	24
Z Blue Moon Fish | **Laud-by-Sea/B**	25
Z Bourbon Steak | **Aventura**	25
Brooks | **Deerfield Bch/B**	23
Buonasera | **Jupiter/P**	24
Z Café Boulud | **Palm Bch/P**	27
Z Café Chardonnay | **Palm Bch Gdns/P**	25
Café des Artistes | **Jupiter/P**	-
NEW Café Europa | **Ft. Laud/B**	-
Z Café L'Europe | **Palm Bch/P**	25
Z Cafe Marquesa | **Key W./K**	27
Cafe Sapori | **W. Palm/P**	24
Cafe Seville | **Ft. Laud/B**	25
Café Sharaku | **Ft. Laud/B**	27
Caffe Vialetto | **Coral Gables**	24
Canyon Ranch Grill | **Miami Bch**	23
NEW Capri Rist. | **Boca/P**	-
NEW Caruso's | **Boca/P**	-
Casa Bella | **Dania Bch/B**	24
Casablanca | **Ft. Laud/B**	21
Z Casa D'Angelo | **multi.**	27
Z Casa Tua | **SoBe**	25
Z Chez Jean-Pierre | **Palm Bch/P**	27
Cioppino | **Key Biscayne**	23
Creolina's | **Davie/B**	23
Da Campo | **Ft. Laud/B**	24
De Rodriguez Cuba | **SoBe**	-
Z Din. Rm./Little Palm | **Little Torch Key/K**	26
Dolores | **Brickell**	18
Z Eduardo/San Angel | **Ft. Laud/B**	27
NEW Elle's | **Miramar/B**	-
Z Entre Nous | **No. Palm Bch/P**	25
Escopazzo | **SoBe**	25
Z 15th St. Fish | **Ft. Laud/B**	19
Z Flagler Steak | **Palm Bch/P**	25
Fontana | **Coral Gables**	21
Z Four Seasons | **Palm Bch/P**	26
Z Francesco | **Coral Gables**	26
Gibraltar | **Coco Grove**	-
Z Grille 66 | **Ft. Laud/B**	25
Hi-Life | **Ft. Laud/B**	25
Hot Tin Roof | **Key W./K**	23
Z Houston's | **multi.**	22
Z Il Gabbiano | **Downtown**	26
Johnny V | **Ft. Laud/B**	24
Josef's | **Plantation/B**	25
Z Kathy's | **Boca/P**	25
Kelly's Carib. | **Key W./K**	21
Z La Brochette | **Cooper City/B**	27
La Cigale | **Delray Bch/P**	22
La Palma | **Coral Gables**	21
Latitudes | **H'wood/B**	18
La Veranda | **Pompano Bch/B**	22
Leopard Lounge | **Palm Bch/P**	20
Le Provençal | **Coral Gables**	22
Z L'Escalier | **Palm Bch/P**	26
Z Louie's | **Key W./K**	25
Maison Carlos | **W. Palm/P**	-
NEW Maitardi | **Design Dist**	-
Mancini's | **Ft. Laud/B**	22
NEW Mandolin | **Design Dist**	-
Marker 88 | **Islamorada/K**	22
Martin's | **Key W./K**	24
Melting Pot | **multi.**	20
Z Michaels | **Key W./K**	28
NEW Mr. Milano | **Palm Bch Gdns/P**	-
Morada Bay | **Islamorada/K**	23
NEW Morgans | **Wynwood**	-
Z Morton's | **Brickell**	25
Mustard Seed | **Cooper City/B**	-
Naoe | **Sunny Is Bch**	-
nine one five | **Key W./K**	25
North Ocean | **Ft. Laud/B**	18
Oceans 234 | **Deerfield Bch/B**	18
Z OLA | **SoBe**	27
Old Lisbon | **Coral Way**	24
Z Palme d'Or | **Coral Gables**	28
Peppy's | **Coral Gables**	20
Perricone's | **Brickell**	20
Z Pierre's | **Islamorada/K**	27
Portobello | **Jupiter/P**	22
Primavera | **Oakland Pk/B**	22
Z Rainbow Palace | **Ft. Laud/B**	26
Red Fish Grill | **Coral Gables**	20
Renato's | **Palm Bch/P**	22
Z Rest. at Setai | **SoBe**	22
Z Romeo's Cafe | **Coral Way**	27
Sage | **Ft. Laud/B**	22
Saint Tropez | **Ft. Laud/B**	-

Serafina | **Ft. Laud/B** — 21

Seven Fish | **Key W./K** — 26

☑ Smith & Wollensky | **SoBe** — 23

Solu | **Singer Is/P** — -

☑ Spiga | **SoBe** — 26

Sra. Martinez | **Design Dist** — 24

Sugar Reef | **H'wood/B** — 22

☑ Sundy House | **Delray Bch/P** — 23

☑ Ta-boo | **Palm Bch/P** — 21

Tantra | **SoBe** — 20

Temple Orange | **Manalapan/P** — -

☑ 3030 Ocean | **Ft. Laud/B** — 25

III Forks | **Hallandale/B** — 23

Toni's Sushi | **SoBe** — 25

NEW Trata | **Ft. Laud/B** — -

Tratt. Luna | **Pinecrest** — 24

☑ Tratt. Romana | **Boca/P** — 25

Tratt. Sole | **So. Miami** — 21

Trevini | **Palm Bch/P** — 22

Trina | **Ft. Laud/B** — -

☑ Truluck's | **Ft. Laud/B** — 24

Tuscan Grille | **Ft. Laud/B** — 24

☑ Valentino's | **Ft. Laud/B** — 26

☑ Via Luna | **Ft. Laud/B** — -

NEW Villa By Barton G. | **SoBe** — -

Villagio | **Sunrise/B** — 20

Wild E. Asian | **Ft. Laud/B** — 22

☑ Wish | **SoBe** — 25

SINGLES SCENES

Absinthe | **Boca/P** — 19

Ago | **SoBe** — 20

Aruba Beach | **Laud-by-Sea/B** — 17

☑ Asia de Cuba | **SoBe** — 23

Banana Boat | **Boynton Bch/P** — 16

Beach Watch | **Dania Bch/B** — 13

Big City Tav. | **Ft. Laud/B** — 19

Bimini Boatyard | **Ft. Laud/B** — 17

☑ Blue Door | **SoBe** — 23

☑ Blue Heaven | **Key W./K** — 24

NEW Botequim Carioca | **Biscayne** — -

Brio Tuscan | **multi.** — 22

Cabana | **Delray Bch/P** — 23

NEW Cabo Flats | **Palm Bch Gdns/P** — -

Cafe Martorano | **multi.** — 25

Caffé Milano | **SoBe** — 19

NEW Caliente Kitchen | **Delray Bch/P** — -

Cantina Laredo | **multi.** — 19

☑ China Grill | **multi.** — 23

Cottage | **Lake Worth/P** — 16

☑ Dada | **Delray Bch/P** — 21

Dave's Last | **Lake Worth/P** — 19

East City Grill | **Weston/B** — 21

11th St. Diner | **SoBe** — 18

E.R. Bradley | **W. Palm/P** — 15

Fleming's Prime | **Coral Gables** — 24

NEW Forge/Wine | **Miami Bch** — -

Fratelli Lyon | **Design Dist** — 23

Front Porch | **SoBe** — 21

Giorgio's Grill | **H'wood/B** — 20

Globe Cafe | **Coral Gables** — 18

NEW Gratify | **W. Palm/P** — -

Guanabanas | **Jupiter/P** — -

Half Shell | **Key W./K** — 23

Himmarshee | **Ft. Laud/B** — 23

☑ Houston's | **multi.** — 22

H2O | **Ft. Laud/B** — 19

Ilios | **Ft. Laud/B** — -

JB's | **Deerfield Bch/B** — 17

Jimmy Buffett's | **Key W./K** — 15

JohnMartin's | **Coral Gables** — 17

Johnny V | **Ft. Laud/B** — 24

Kelly's Carib. | **Key W./K** — 21

NEW Kubo | **No. Palm Bch/P** — -

Lario's/Beach | **SoBe** — 18

Latitudes | **H'wood/B** — 18

Le Tub | **H'wood/B** — 21

Mango's Tropical | **SoBe** — 15

Mellow Mushroom | **Delray Bch/P** — 23

Monty's | **Coco Grove** — 15

Moquila | **Boca/P** — 19

☑ Nemo | **SoBe** — 24

Nikki | **SoBe** — 17

Novecento | **Key Biscayne** — 20

Oceans 234 | **Deerfield Bch/B** — 18

NEW Office | **Delray Bch/P** — -

Pistache | **W. Palm/P** — 19

☑ Prime One | **SoBe** — 26

NEW Rack's Downtown | **Boca/P** — -

RA Sushi | **Palm Bch Gdns/P** — 19

Rhythm Café | **W. Palm/P** — 22

Rivals | **H'wood/B** — 16

Royal Bavarian | **UES** — 19

NEW Sawa | **Coral Gables** — -

☑ Smith & Wollensky | **SoBe** — 23

NEW SoLita | **Ft. Laud/B** — -

Soyka | **UES** — 20

NEW Sugarcane | **Downtown** — -

Sushi Blues | **H'wood/B** — 23

Sushi Rock | **SoBe** — 21

NEW Table 42 | **Boca/P** — -

☑ Ta-boo | **Palm Bch/P** — 21

NEW Talavera | Coral Gables	–
Tantra | SoBe	20
Tarpon Bend | Ft. Laud/B	18
NEW Taste | Delray Bch/P	–
Taverna Opa | multi.	19
Thai Hse. S. | SoBe	23
☑ 32 East | Delray Bch/P	26
Titanic Brewery | Coral Gables	16
Triple Eight | Delray Bch/P	–
☑ Truluck's | Ft. Laud/B	24
Turtle Kraals | Key W./K	19
Two Georges | Boynton Bch/P	16
Van Dyke | SoBe	17
NEW Waxy O'Connor's | Brickell	–
Wild E. Asian | Ft. Laud/B	22

SLEEPERS

(Good food, but little known)

Aizia | Hallandale/B	24
Ambrosia | Key W./K	24
Azur | Key W./K	26
Bali Café | Downtown	23
Basilico | multi.	26
Bistro | Jupiter/P	23
Bistro 555 | Davie/B	23
Bistro 17 | Ft. Laud/B	24
Buonasera | Jupiter/P	24
Café Emunah | Ft. Laud/B	23
Calypso's | Key Largo/K	23
Cay Da | Boca/P	22
Chanticleer | Islamorada/K	24
Chéen Huaye | No. Miami	25
Chico's Cantina | Key W./K	24
Coco | Palm Bch/P	22
Commodore | Key W./K	22
Creolina's | Davie/B	23
Croissants | Key W./K	25
El Chalán | multi.	22
El Tamarindo | multi.	22
Enriqueta's | Wynwood	22
Grazie Italian | SoBe	24
Guayacan | multi.	23
Guru | SoBe	24
Hot Tin Roof | Key W./K	23
Il Girasole | Delray Bch/P	22
Ireland's | Weston/B	22
Jade | W. Palm/P	24
Josef's | Plantation/B	25
Joseph's Wine | Delray Bch/P	24
Julio's | No. Miami Bch	22
Kon Chau | Westchester	24
La Barraca | H'wood/B	22
La Locanda | SoBe	23

Lan | So. Miami	23
Le Bistro | Lighthse Pt/B	22
Leila | W. Palm/P	22
Little Saigon | No. Miami Bch	24
Mahogany | Miami Gdns	23
Mancini's | Ft. Laud/B	22
Martin's | Key W./K	24
Mazza | Pembroke Pines/B	23
Molina's | Hialeah	22
Origami | Key W./K	25
Orig. Daily | Coco Grove	22
Palm Beach Steak | Palm Bch/P	23
Pho Hoa | Tamarac/B	23
Pilar | Aventura	24
Rhythm Café | W. Palm/P	22
Safire | Lake Worth/P	25
Saigon Tokyo | Greenacres/P	22
Sakura | Coral Gables	22
Salmon | West Dade	23
Salute! | Key W./K	22
Seafood World | Lighthse Pt/B	22
Siam Palace | So. Miami	25
Sukhothai | Ft. Laud/B	23
Sushi Hse. | No. Miami Bch	25
Su Shin | multi.	25
Su Shin Thai | Lauderhill/B	23
Taso's Greek | Delray Bch/P	22
Thai & Sushi | W. Sunset	22
Thai Hse. S. | SoBe	23
Thaikyo Asian | Manalapan/P	22
T-Mex Cantina | multi.	23
Tokyo Sushi | Ft. Laud/B	26
Trevini | Palm Bch/P	22
Wild E. Asian | Ft. Laud/B	22
Woodlands | Lauderhill/B	23
Yuga | Coral Gables	24
Ziggie/Mad Dog | Islamorada/K	24
Ziree Thai | Delray Bch/P	25

SPECIAL OCCASIONS

A&B Lobster | Key W./K	23
Absinthe | Boca/P	19
Ago | SoBe	20
Arturo's | Boca/P	23
☑ Asia de Cuba | SoBe	23
☑ Blue Moon Fish | Laud-by-Sea/B	25
Brooks | Deerfield Bch/B	23
☑ Café Boulud | Palm Bch/P	27
☑ Café L'Europe | Palm Bch/P	25
☑ Cafe Marquesa | Key W./K	27
Cafe Martorano | multi.	25
Café Sharaku | Ft. Laud/B	27

🔲 Casa D'Angelo	Ft. Laud/B	27
🔲 Casa Tua	SoBe	25
🔲 Chef Allen's	Aventura	26
🔲 Chima Brazilian	Ft. Laud/B	24
🔲 China Grill	Ft. Laud/B	23
Cioppino	Key Biscayne	23
Commodore	Key W./K	22
Da Campo	Ft. Laud/B	24
🔲 Din. Rm./Little Palm	Little Torch Key/K	26
🔲 Eduardo/San Angel	Ft. Laud/B	27
NEW Elle's	Miramar/B	-
Escopazzo	SoBe	25
🔲 15th St. Fish	Ft. Laud/B	19
Fontana	Coral Gables	21
Fratelli Lyon	Design Dist	23
NEW George's/Sunset	So. Miami	-
Gibraltar	Coco Grove	-
🔲 Grille 66	Ft. Laud/B	25
Himmarshee	Ft. Laud/B	23
Hot Tin Roof	Key W./K	23
Ireland's	Weston/B	22
Ironwood	Palm Bch Gdns/P	-
Johnny V	Ft. Laud/B	24
Josef's	Plantation/B	25
🔲 La Brochette	Cooper City/B	27
La Cigale	Delray Bch/P	22
🔲 L'Escalier	Palm Bch/P	26
🔲 Louie's	Key W./K	25
Marker 88	Islamorada/K	22
Martin's	Key W./K	24
Melting Pot	Palm Bch Gdns/P	20
🔲 Nobu Miami Beach	SoBe	27
🔲 Oceanaire	Downtown	24
🔲 Pierre's	Islamorada/K	27
Pier Top	Ft. Laud/B	-
Renato's	Palm Bch/P	22
🔲 Rest. at Setai	SoBe	22
🔲 Ruth's Chris	Ft. Laud/B	25
🔲 Scarpetta	Miami Bch	25
Serafina	Ft. Laud/B	21
Sra. Martinez	Design Dist	24
NEW STK Miami	Miami Bch	-
Tatiana	Hallandale/B	-
🔲 3030 Ocean	Ft. Laud/B	25
III Forks	multi.	23
🔲 Truluck's	Ft. Laud/B	24
🔲 Via Luna	Ft. Laud/B	-
NEW Villa By Barton G.	SoBe	-
NEW Vivo Partenza	Boca/P	-
Wild E. Asian	Ft. Laud/B	22

TEEN APPEAL

Abbondanza	Key W./K	19
🔲 Anthony's Pizza	multi.	23
Archie's Pizza	multi.	18
Aruba Beach	Laud-by-Sea/B	17
Baja Fresh	Coral Gables	18
Berries	Coco Grove	20
Big Pink	SoBe	19
🔲 Blue Heaven	Key W./K	24
🔲 Cheesecake	multi.	20
Dave's Last	Lake Worth/P	19
11th St. Diner	SoBe	18
El Rancho Grande	Kendall	20
Floridian	Ft. Laud/B	18
Front Porch	SoBe	21
Hamburger Heaven	Palm Bch/P	20
🔲 Hiro's Yakko	No. Miami Bch	26
Hot Pie	W. Palm/P	-
Il Mulino	Ft. Laud/B	22
Jaxson's	Dania Bch/B	22
Kelly's Carib.	Key W./K	21
La Casona	W. Sunset	19
La Sandwicherie	SoBe	23
🔲 LaSpada's	multi.	27
Mangoes	Key W./K	19
Mario/Baker	multi.	19
Mellow Mushroom	Delray Bch/P	23
Melting Pot	multi.	20
News Cafe	SoBe	17
OneBurger	Coral Gables	18
Outback	multi.	17
Paquito's	No. Miami Bch	22
🔲 P.F. Chang's	multi.	21
Piola	SoBe	22
Pit Bar-B-Q	West Dade	20
Pizza Girls	W. Palm/P	22
Pizza Rustica	multi.	21
Randazzo's	Coral Gables	23
Salmon	West Dade	23
NEW Shake Shack	SoBe	-
🔲 Sloan's	multi.	23
Spris	multi.	21
Stir Crazy	multi.	20
Sushi Maki	multi.	20
Taco Rico	Coral Gables	21
Vic/Angelos	Palm Bch Gdns/P	20
Zuccarelli's Italian	W. Palm/P	19

THEME RESTAURANTS

Ambry German	Ft. Laud/B	-
Brogues	Lake Worth/P	16
Bubba Gump	Ft. Laud/B	15

NEW Cabo Flats | **Palm Bch Gdns/P**	_-_
Café Emunah | **Ft. Laud/B**	23
Cafe Martorano | **H'wood/B**	25
NEW Caliente Kitchen | **Delray Bch/P**	_-_
Cantina Laredo | **multi.**	19
Cap's | **Lighthse Pt/B**	19
Casa Maya Grill | **Deerfield Bch/B**	_-_
Checkers/Munchen | **Pompano Bch/B**	_-_
Z Chima Brazilian | **Ft. Laud/B**	24
Z China Grill | **Ft. Laud/B**	23
Copper Canyon | **Boca/P**	_-_
El Meson | **Key W./K**	21
Fogo de Chão | **SoBe**	24
Guanabanas | **Jupiter/P**	_-_
NEW Havana's | **Cooper City/B**	_-_
NEW Indian Chillies | **Pembroke Pines/B**	_-_
Jaxson's | **Dania Bch/B**	22
Jimmy Buffett's | **Key W./K**	15
Kiko | **Plantation/B**	_-_
Kingshead Pub | **Sunrise/B**	_-_
Kuluck | **Tamarac/B**	_-_
La Tre | **Boca/P**	21
Mai-Kai | **Ft. Laud/B**	15
Melting Pot | **multi.**	20
Moquila | **Boca/P**	19
My Big Fat Greek | **Dania Bch/B**	20
Naoe | **Sunny Is Bch**	_-_
Z Oceanaire | **Downtown**	24
Old Heidelberg | **Ft. Laud/B**	_-_
Outback | **multi.**	17
Paddy Mac's | **Palm Bch Gdns/P**	22
Z P.F. Chang's | **multi.**	21
RA Sushi | **Palm Bch Gdns/P**	19
Saxsay | **Sunrise/B**	_-_
Shula's | **Ft. Laud/B**	21
Sloppy Joe's | **Key W./K**	14
Sublime | **Ft. Laud/B**	22
Tatiana | **Hallandale/B**	_-_
Taverna Opa | **multi.**	19
Villagio | **Coral Gables**	20

TRANSPORTING EXPERIENCES

A La Folie | **SoBe**	24
Z Azul | **Brickell**	27
Z Café Boulud | **Palm Bch/P**	27
Café Emunah | **Ft. Laud/B**	23
Cafe Martorano | **Ft. Laud/B**	25

Camille's | **Key W./K**	22
Cap's | **Lighthse Pt/B**	19
Z Casa D'Angelo | **Ft. Laud/B**	27
Casa Larios | **multi.**	19
Caspian Persian | **Plantation/B**	21
Creolina's | **Davie/B**	23
Z Din. Rm./Little Palm | **Little Torch Key/K**	26
Echo | **Palm Bch/P**	23
Z Eduardo/San Angel | **Ft. Laud/B**	27
El Chalán | **SoBe**	22
El Tamarindo | **Ft. Laud/B**	22
Escopazzo | **SoBe**	25
Ferdo's Grill | **Ft. Laud/B**	21
Fontana | **Coral Gables**	21
Galanga | **Wilton Manors/B**	24
Z Graziano's | **Westchester**	26
Hosteria Romana | **SoBe**	20
Z Hy-Vong | **Little Havana**	27
Imlee | **Pinecrest**	23
India Hse. | **Plantation/B**	20
Jaxson's | **Dania Bch/B**	22
Kingshead Pub | **Sunrise/B**	_-_
Kuluck | **Tamarac/B**	_-_
La Barraca | **H'wood/B**	22
La Dorada | **Coral Gables**	24
La Palma | **Coral Gables**	21
Las Culebrinas | **multi.**	22
Las Vacas | **Miami Bch**	21
Las Vegas | **Little Havana**	21
La Tre | **Boca/P**	21
Le Bouchon du Grove | **Coco Grove**	23
Z L'Escalier | **Palm Bch/P**	26
Madras | **Pompano Bch/B**	20
Mai-Kai | **Ft. Laud/B**	15
Mango's Tropical | **SoBe**	15
Miss Saigon | **Coral Gables**	23
Morada Bay | **Islamorada/K**	23
Old Heidelberg | **Ft. Laud/B**	_-_
Z Palme d'Or | **Coral Gables**	28
Z Pascal's | **Coral Gables**	27
Z Pierre's | **Islamorada/K**	27
Z Rest. at Setai | **SoBe**	22
Z Romeo's Cafe | **Coral Way**	27
Saxsay | **Sunrise/B**	_-_
Z SushiSamba | **SoBe**	23
Tantra | **SoBe**	20
Tap Tap | **SoBe**	22
Thai & Sushi | **W. Sunset**	22
Z 32 East | **Delray Bch/P**	26
Tropical Chinese | **Westchester**	25

Wine Cellar	**Ft. Laud/B**	19
Zuperpollo	**Brickell**	21

TRENDY

Absinthe	**Boca/P**	19
Ago	**SoBe**	20
NEW Apicius	**Lantana/P**	-
Z Asia de Cuba	**SoBe**	23
Z Azul	**Brickell**	27
Balans	**SoBe**	19
Z Barton G.	**SoBe**	23
NEW Bellini's Pizza	**Ft. Laud/B**	-
Big City Tav.	**Ft. Laud/B**	19
Big Pink	**SoBe**	19
Bistro Mezzaluna	**Ft. Laud/B**	25
Z Blue Door	**SoBe**	23
Z Blue Heaven	**Key W./K**	24
Blue Sea	**SoBe**	25
Z Bond St.	**SoBe**	26
NEW Botequim Carioca	**Biscayne**	-
Brio Tuscan	**multi.**	22
Cabana	**Delray Bch/P**	23
Cafe Martorano	**multi.**	25
Café Prima	**Miami Bch**	23
Caffe Abbracci	**Coral Gables**	24
NEW Caliente Kitchen	**Delray Bch/P**	-
Cantina Laredo	**Hallandale/P**	19
Z Canyon	**Ft. Laud/B**	26
Z Capital Grille	**Ft. Laud/B**	26
Carpaccio	**Bal Harbour**	22
Z Casa Tua	**SoBe**	25
Z Chima Brazilian	**Ft. Laud/B**	24
Z China Grill	**multi.**	23
Z Chops Lobster	**Boca/P**	26
Coco	**Palm Bch/P**	22
Cottage	**Lake Worth/P**	16
Da Campo	**Ft. Laud/B**	24
Z Dada	**Delray Bch/P**	21
NEW D'Angelo	**Oakland Pk/B**	-
DeVito	**SoBe**	21
Dolce/Palma	**W. Palm/P**	26
Echo	**Palm Bch/P**	23
E.R. Bradley	**W. Palm/P**	15
Floridian	**Ft. Laud/B**	18
NEW Forge/Wine	**Miami Bch**	-
Fratelli Lyon	**Design Dist**	23
Globe Cafe	**Coral Gables**	18
Grand Lux	**multi.**	19
NEW Gratify	**W. Palm/P**	-
Hi-Life	**Ft. Laud/B**	25
Himmarshee	**Ft. Laud/B**	23

Z Houston's	**multi.**	22
Ilios	**Ft. Laud/B**	-
Jade	**W. Palm/P**	24
JB's	**Deerfield Bch/B**	17
Joe Allen	**SoBe**	22
Joey's Italian	**Wynwood**	22
Johnny V	**Ft. Laud/B**	24
Joseph's Wine	**Delray Bch/P**	24
Kaiyó	**Islamorada/K**	-
Kiko	**Plantation/B**	-
NEW Kubo	**No. Palm Bch/P**	-
Lario's/Beach	**SoBe**	18
Latitudes	**H'wood/B**	18
Leila	**W. Palm/P**	22
Leopard Lounge	**Palm Bch/P**	20
Lime Fresh Mex.	**SoBe**	21
Z Little Moir's	**Jupiter/P**	26
Lola's	**H'wood/B**	24
Mangoes	**Key W./K**	19
Mango's Tropical	**SoBe**	15
MB/Omphoy	**Palm Bch/P**	-
NEW Mercadito	**Downtown**	-
Moquila	**Boca/P**	19
Z Nemo	**SoBe**	24
Nikki	**SoBe**	17
NEW Norman's 180	**Coral Gables**	-
Oakwood	**Palm Bch Gdns/P**	20
NEW Office	**Delray Bch/P**	-
Oggi Caffe	**No. Bay Vill**	21
Z Ortanique	**Coral Gables**	26
NEW Rack's Downtown	**Boca/P**	-
RA Sushi	**Palm Bch Gdns/P**	19
NEW Relish	**W. Palm/P**	-
Z Rest. at Setai	**SoBe**	22
Safire	**Lake Worth/P**	25
Sardinia	**SoBe**	23
NEW Sawa	**Coral Gables**	-
Z Scarpetta	**Miami Bch**	25
Z Seasons 52	**Ft. Laud/B**	23
Seven Fish	**Key W./K**	26
NEW Shake Shack	**SoBe**	-
NEW SoLita	**Ft. Laud/B**	-
Soyka	**UES**	20
Spoto's Oyster	**Palm Bch Gdns/P**	23
Sra. Martinez	**Design Dist**	24
Sublime	**Ft. Laud/B**	22
NEW Sugarcane	**Downtown**	-
Sushi Blues	**H'wood/B**	23
Sushi Jo's	**W. Palm/P**	23
Sushi Rock	**SoBe**	21
NEW Table 42	**Boca/P**	-
Z Ta-boo	**Palm Bch/P**	21

SPECIAL FEATURES

Tantra	SoBe	20
NEW Taste	Delray Bch/P	-
Taverna Opa	multi.	19
☑ 32 East	Delray Bch/P	26
Toni's Sushi	SoBe	25
☑ Tratt. Romana	Boca/P	25
Triple Eight	Delray Bch/P	-
☑ Truluck's	Ft. Laud/B	24
Turtle Kraals	Key W./K	19
Van Dyke	SoBe	17
☑ Via Luna	Ft. Laud/B	-
Villagio	multi.	20
Wild E. Asian	Ft. Laud/B	22

VIEWS

A&B Lobster	Key W./K	23
Abokado	Brickell	19
Acqua	Brickell	25
Acquolina	Weston/B	25
Ago	SoBe	20
Aruba Beach	Laud-by-Sea/B	17
Atrio	Downtown	21
☑ Azul	Brickell	27
Bagatelle	Key W./K	23
Balans	Brickell	19
Banana Boat	Boynton Bch/P	16
Bayside Fish	Key Biscayne	13
Beach Watch	Dania Bch/B	13
Billy's Stone	H'wood/B	22
Bimini Boatyard	Ft. Laud/B	17
☑ Blue Moon Fish	Laud-by-Sea/B	25
☑ Café Boulud	Palm Bch/P	27
Café Sambal	Brickell	23
Caffe Luna Rosa	Delray Bch/P	20
Calypso's	Key Largo/K	23
Cap's	Lighthse Pt/B	19
Charley's Crab	Palm Bch/P	21
☑ China Grill	Ft. Laud/B	23
Christine Lee's	Hallandale/B	23
Cioppino	Key Biscayne	23
Commodore	Key W./K	22
Conch Republic	Key W./K	19
Conchy Joe's	Jensen Bch/P	19
☑ Din. Rm./Little Palm	Little Torch Key/K	26
Dockside Sea	Lake Pk/P	19
Dune Deck	Lantana/P	19
☑ Emeril's	SoBe	23
Eos	Brickell	-
E.R. Bradley	W. Palm/P	15
☑ 15th St. Fish	Ft. Laud/B	19
☑ Flagler Steak	Palm Bch/P	25

☑ Four Seasons	Palm Bch/P	26
Front Porch	SoBe	21
Garcia's	Miami Riv	22
Gibraltar	Coco Grove	-
Giorgio's Grill	H'wood/B	20
☑ Grille 66	Ft. Laud/B	25
Half Shell	Key W./K	23
Hot Tin Roof	Key W./K	23
☑ Houston's	No. Miami Bch	22
H2O	Ft. Laud/B	19
Il Bellagio	W. Palm/P	19
☑ Il Gabbiano	Downtown	26
Ilios	Ft. Laud/B	-
☑ Il Mulino NY	Sunny Is Bch	25
Island Grill	Islamorada/K	22
JB's	Deerfield Bch/B	17
Jetty's	Jupiter/P	22
☑ John G's	Lake Worth/P	23
Kevin's Dockside	Palm Bch Gdns/P	-
Keys Fisheries	Marathon/K	24
Lario's/Beach	SoBe	18
Latitudes	H'wood/B	18
Lazy Loggerhead	Jupiter/P	23
Le Tub	H'wood/B	21
Lido	SoBe	21
Los Ranchos	Biscayne	21
☑ Louie's	Key W./K	25
Marker 88	Islamorada/K	22
☑ Max's	Boca/P	22
MB/Omphoy	Palm Bch/P	-
Meat Market	SoBe	24
Monty's	multi.	15
Morada Bay	Islamorada/K	23
☑ Morton's	Miami Bch	25
My Big Fat Greek	Dania Bch/B	20
Neomi's Grill	Sunny Is Bch	-
Nikki	SoBe	17
Oceans 234	Deerfield Bch/B	18
Old Calypso	Delray Bch/P	19
Pelican Landing	Ft. Laud/B	18
☑ Pierre's	Islamorada/K	27
Pier Top	Ft. Laud/B	-
Prime Catch	Boynton Bch/P	21
Quinn's	SoBe	25
Red Fish Grill	Coral Gables	20
☑ Red Light	UES	26
Rivals	H'wood/B	16
River Hse.	Palm Bch Gdns/P	23
Rusty Pelican	Key Biscayne	16
Sailfish Marina	Palm Bch Shores/P	18
Schooner Wharf	Key W./K	15

Scotty's | **Coco Grove**	14
ⓩ Seasons 52 | **Palm Bch Gdns/P**	23
Serafina | **Ft. Laud/B**	21
SHOR | **Key W./K**	-
Shula's | **multi.**	21
ⓩ Smith & Wollensky | **SoBe**	23
Snapper's Water. | **Key Largo/K**	22
Solu | **Singer Is/P**	-
Steak 954 | **Ft. Laud/B**	24
Sugar Reef | **H'wood/B**	22
ⓩ Sundy House | **Delray Bch/P**	23
Temple Orange | **Manalapan/P**	-
ⓩ 3030 Ocean | **Ft. Laud/B**	25
Tony Chan's | **Downtown**	22
Trina | **Ft. Laud/B**	-
Turtle Kraals | **Key W./K**	19
Two Georges | **Boynton Bch/P**	16
ⓩ Via Luna | **Ft. Laud/B**	-
NEW Waxy O'Connor's | **Brickell**	-
Whale Raw | **Parkland/B**	16
Wild E. Asian | **Ft. Laud/B**	22
NEW Zuma | **Downtown**	-

VISITORS ON EXPENSE ACCOUNT

ⓩ Abe/Louie's | **Boca/P**	26
Absinthe | **Boca/P**	19
NEW Apicius | **Lantana/P**	-
Arturo's | **Boca/P**	23
ⓩ Asia de Cuba | **SoBe**	23
ⓩ Azul | **Brickell**	27
BED | **SoBe**	17
Bice | **Palm Bch/P**	21
Bistro 17 | **Ft. Laud/B**	24
ⓩ Bourbon Steak | **Aventura**	25
Brazaviva Churrascaria | **Sunrise/B**	18
ⓩ Café Boulud | **Palm Bch/P**	27
ⓩ Café Chardonnay | **Palm Bch Gdns/P**	25
ⓩ Café L'Europe | **Palm Bch/P**	25
ⓩ Cafe Marquesa | **Key W./K**	27
Cafe Martorano | **multi.**	25
ⓩ Cafe Maxx | **Pompano Bch/B**	26
Cafe Sapori | **W. Palm/P**	24
Caffe Abbracci | **Coral Gables**	24
Caffé Milano | **SoBe**	19
ⓩ Capital Grille | **multi.**	26
Carpaccio | **Bal Harbour**	22
ⓩ Casa D'Angelo | **Ft. Laud/B**	27
ⓩ Casa Tua | **SoBe**	25
ⓩ Chef Allen's | **Aventura**	26

ⓩ Chez Jean-Pierre | **Palm Bch/P**	27
ⓩ Chima Brazilian | **Ft. Laud/B**	24
ⓩ China Grill | **multi.**	23
ⓩ Chops Lobster | **Boca/P**	26
Christine Lee's | **Hallandale/B**	23
ⓩ Christy's | **Coral Gables**	25
Cioppino | **Key Biscayne**	23
Coco | **Palm Bch/P**	22
ⓩ Council Oak | **H'wood/B**	24
Da Campo | **Ft. Laud/B**	24
Echo | **Palm Bch/P**	23
ⓩ Eduardo/San Angel | **Ft. Laud/B**	27
Escopazzo | **SoBe**	25
ⓩ Flagler Grill | **Stuart/P**	25
Fontana | **Coral Gables**	21
ⓩ Four Seasons | **Palm Bch/P**	26
Gibraltar | **Coco Grove**	-
Gotham Steak | **Miami Bch**	22
ⓩ Grille 66 | **Ft. Laud/B**	25
Himmarshee | **Ft. Laud/B**	23
Hollywood Prime | **H'wood/B**	24
ⓩ Il Gabbiano | **Downtown**	26
Ireland's | **Weston/B**	22
Ironwood | **Palm Bch Gdns/P**	-
ⓩ Joe's Stone | **SoBe**	27
Joey's Italian | **Wynwood**	22
Johnny V | **Ft. Laud/B**	24
ⓩ Kathy's | **Boca/P**	25
La Cigale | **Delray Bch/P**	22
Leopard Lounge | **Palm Bch/P**	20
Le Provençal | **Coral Gables**	22
ⓩ L'Escalier | **Palm Bch/P**	26
ⓩ Louie's | **Key W./K**	25
Mai-Kai | **Ft. Laud/B**	15
NEW Mr. Milano | **Palm Bch Gdns/P**	-
Monty's | **Coco Grove**	15
Moquila | **Boca/P**	19
ⓩ Morton's | **multi.**	25
ⓩ NY Prime | **Boca/P**	25
ⓩ Nobu Miami Beach | **SoBe**	27
Oakwood | **Palm Bch Gdns/P**	20
ⓩ Oceanaire | **Downtown**	24
ⓩ Ortanique | **Coral Gables**	26
ⓩ Osteria del Teatro | **SoBe**	26
ⓩ Palm | **Bay Harbor Is**	26
ⓩ Palme d'Or | **Coral Gables**	28
ⓩ Pascal's | **Coral Gables**	27
ⓩ Pierre's | **Islamorada/K**	27
Pier Top | **Ft. Laud/B**	-
ⓩ Prime One | **SoBe**	26

☑ Rest. at Setai | SoBe	22
☑ Ruth's Chris | multi.	25
☑ Scarpetta | Miami Bch	25
Shula's | multi.	21
☑ Smith & Wollensky | SoBe	23
NEW SoLita | Ft. Laud/B	-
Solu | Singer Is/P	-
Square One | Key W./K	22
NEW STK Miami | Miami Bch	-
☑ SushiSamba | SoBe	23
☑ Ta-boo | Palm Bch/P	21
☑ 3030 Ocean | Ft. Laud/B	25
☑ 32 East | Delray Bch/P	26
III Forks | multi.	23
Timpano | Ft. Laud/B	21
Tony Chan's | Downtown	22
Trina | Ft. Laud/B	-
☑ Truluck's | Ft. Laud/B	24
☑ Via Luna | Ft. Laud/B	-
NEW Villa By Barton G. | SoBe	-
NEW Zuma | Downtown	-

WATERSIDE

Acquolina | Weston/B	25
Alabama Jacks | Key Largo/K	18
Area 31 | Downtown	22
Aruba Beach | Laud-by-Sea/B	17
☑ Azul | Brickell	27
Banana Boat | Boynton Bch/P	16
Bayside Fish | Key Biscayne	13
Beach Watch | Dania Bch/B	13
Billy's Stone | H'wood/B	22
Bimini Boatyard | Ft. Laud/B	17
☑ Blue Moon Fish | Laud-by-Sea/B	25
Bluepoint Grill | H'wood/B	17
Café Sambal | Brickell	23
Caffe Luna Rosa | Delray Bch/P	20
Calypso's | Key Largo/K	23
Cap's | Lighthse Pt/B	19
Charley's Crab | Palm Bch/P	21
☑ China Grill | Ft. Laud/B	23
Commodore | Key W./K	22
Conch Republic | Key W./K	19
Conchy Joe's | Jensen Bch/P	19
☑ Din. Rm./Little Palm | Little Torch Key/K	26
Dockside Sea | Lake Pk/P	19
Dune Deck | Lantana/P	19
East City Grill | Weston/B	21
☑ Emeril's | SoBe	23
E.R. Bradley | W. Palm/P	15

☑ 15th St. Fish | Ft. Laud/B	19
Garcia's | Miami Riv	22
Gibraltar | Coco Grove	-
Giorgio's Grill | H'wood/B	20
☑ Grille 66 | Ft. Laud/B	25
Half Shell | Key W./K	23
Hollywood Prime | H'wood/B	24
Hot Tin Roof | Key W./K	23
☑ Houston's | Pompano Bch/B	22
H2O | Ft. Laud/B	19
Ilios | Ft. Laud/B	-
☑ Il Mulino NY | Sunny Is Bch	25
Il Toscano | Weston/B	22
Island Grill | Islamorada/K	22
JB's | Deerfield Bch/B	17
Jetty's | Jupiter/P	22
☑ John G's | Lake Worth/P	23
Kevin's Dockside | Palm Bch Gdns/P	-
Keys Fisheries | Marathon/K	24
Latitudes | H'wood/B	18
Lazy Loggerhead | Jupiter/P	23
Le Tub | H'wood/B	21
Lido | SoBe	21
Los Ranchos | Biscayne	21
☑ Louie's | Key W./K	25
NEW Lou's Beer | Miami Bch	-
Marker 88 | Islamorada/K	22
Monty's | multi.	15
Morada Bay | Islamorada/K	23
☑ Morton's | Miami Bch	25
Mr. Chow | SoBe	-
My Big Fat Greek | Dania Bch/B	20
Neomi's Grill | Sunny Is Bch	-
Nikki | SoBe	17
North Ocean | Ft. Laud/B	18
Oceans 234 | Deerfield Bch/B	18
Pelican Landing | Ft. Laud/B	18
Philippe | SoBe	21
☑ Pierre's | Islamorada/K	27
Prime Catch | Boynton Bch/P	21
Racks Italian | No. Miami Bch	-
Red Fish Grill | Coral Gables	20
☑ Red Light | UES	26
River Hse. | Palm Bch Gdns/P	23
Rustic Inn | Ft. Laud/B	22
Sailfish Marina | Palm Bch Shores/P	18
Salute! | Key W./K	22
Schooner Wharf | Key W./K	15
Scotty's | Coco Grove	14
☑ Seasons 52 | Palm Bch Gdns/P	23
Serafina | Ft. Laud/B	21

SHOR | **Key W./K**	-‌
Shula's | **multi.**	21
☑ Smith & Wollensky | **SoBe**	23
Snapper's Water. | **Key Largo/K**	22
Solu | **Singer Is/P**	-‌
Southport Raw | **Ft. Laud/B**	19
Steak 954 | **Ft. Laud/B**	24
Sublime | **Ft. Laud/B**	22
Sugar Reef | **H'wood/B**	22
☑ 3030 Ocean | **Ft. Laud/B**	25
Tony Chan's | **Downtown**	22
Trina | **Ft. Laud/B**	-‌
Turtle Kraals | **Key W./K**	19
Two Georges | **Boynton Bch/P**	16
Upper Deck | **Key W./K**	23
☑ Via Luna | **Ft. Laud/B**	-‌
Village Grille | **Laud-by-Sea/B**	23
NEW Water Club | **No. Miami Bch**	-‌
Whale Raw | **Parkland/B**	16
Wild E. Asian | **Ft. Laud/B**	22
NEW Zuma | **Downtown**	-‌

WINNING WINE LISTS

Absinthe | **Boca/P**	19
Acqua | **Brickell**	25
☑ AltaMare | **SoBe**	25
Anacapri | **Pinecrest**	22
NEW Angelique Euro Café | **Coral Gables**	-‌
☑ Azul | **Brickell**	27
☑ Blue Heaven | **Key W./K**	24
Blú la Pizzeria | **So. Miami**	23
Brio Tuscan | **Pembroke Pines/B**	22
Bugatti Pasta | **Coral Gables**	23
☑ Café Boulud | **Palm Bch/P**	27
☑ Café Chardonnay | **Palm Bch Gdns/P**	25
☑ Café L'Europe | **Palm Bch/P**	25
☑ Cafe Marquesa | **Key W./K**	27
☑ Cafe Maxx | **Pompano Bch/B**	26
Café Sambal | **Brickell**	23
Cafe Sapori | **W. Palm/P**	24
Cafe Seville | **Ft. Laud/B**	25
Caffe Abbracci | **Coral Gables**	24
Caffe Da Vinci | **Bay Harbor Is**	21
Caffé Milano | **SoBe**	19
Canyon Ranch Grill | **Miami Bch**	23
☑ Captain Charlie | **Juno Bch/P**	26
Captain's Tav. | **Pinecrest**	23
Carpaccio | **Bal Harbour**	22
☑ Casa D'Angelo | **Boca/P**	27
Casa Juancho | **Little Havana**	25

☑ Chef Allen's | **Aventura**	26
Cioppino | **Key Biscayne**	23
City Cellar | **W. Palm/P**	20
Da Campo | **Ft. Laud/B**	24
NEW D'Angelo | **Oakland Pk/B**	-‌
☑ Din. Rm./Little Palm | **Little Torch Key/K**	26
Doraku | **SoBe**	21
East City Grill | **Weston/B**	21
☑ 11 Maple St. | **Jensen Bch/P**	28
NEW Elle's | **Miramar/B**	-‌
Escopazzo | **SoBe**	25
☑ Flagler Grill | **Stuart/P**	25
Fontana | **Coral Gables**	21
☑ Four Seasons | **Palm Bch/P**	26
Fratelli Lyon | **Design Dist**	23
Globe Cafe | **Coral Gables**	18
Gold Coast | **Coral Spgs/B**	22
☑ Graziano's | **Westchester**	26
Grazie Italian | **SoBe**	24
☑ Grille 66 | **Ft. Laud/B**	25
Hanna's Diner | **No. Miami Bch**	26
☑ Henry's | **Delray Bch/P**	21
Himmarshee | **Ft. Laud/B**	23
Hot Tin Roof | **Key W./K**	23
Ideas Rest. | **Coco Grove**	20
NEW Il Mercato/Wine | **Hallandale/B**	-‌
Ireland's | **Weston/B**	22
☑ Joe's Stone | **SoBe**	27
Joey's Italian | **Wynwood**	22
Johnny V | **Ft. Laud/B**	24
Kelly's Carib. | **Key W./K**	21
kitchenetta | **Ft. Laud/B**	23
La Trattoria | **Key W./K**	24
Le Bistro | **Lighthse Pt/B**	22
☑ L'Escalier | **Palm Bch/P**	26
Lola's | **H'wood/B**	24
☑ Louie's | **Key W./K**	25
Mangia Mangia | **Key W./K**	20
☑ Marcello | **W. Palm/P**	27
Marker 88 | **Islamorada/K**	22
Melting Pot | **Boca/P**	20
☑ Michaels | **Key W./K**	28
☑ Michael's | **Design Dist**	26
☑ Michy's | **UES**	27
Morada Bay | **Islamorada/K**	23
☑ Morton's | **multi.**	25
☑ Nemo | **SoBe**	24
☑ NY Prime | **Boca/P**	25
nine one five | **Key W./K**	25
Oakwood | **Palm Bch Gdns/P**	20
☑ Oceanaire | **Downtown**	24

SPECIAL FEATURES

Z Ortanique | **Coral Gables** 26
Z Palm | **Bay Harbor Is** 26
Z Palme d'Or | **Coral Gables** 28
Z Pascal's | **Coral Gables** 27
Z Pierre's | **Islamorada/K** 27
Z Prime One | **SoBe** 26
Quattro | **SoBe** 22
Z Rest. at Setai | **SoBe** 22
Salute! | **Key W./K** 22
Sardinia | **SoBe** 23
Z Scarpetta | **Miami Bch** 25
Shula's | **multi.** 21
Z Smith & Wollensky | **SoBe** 23

Snappers | **Boynton Bch/P** 18
Square One | **Key W./K** 22
NEW STK Miami | **Miami Bch** -
Z 3030 Ocean | **Ft. Laud/B** 25
Z 32 East | **Delray Bch/P** 26
III Forks | **Hallandale/B** 23
Timo | **Sunny Is Bch** 25
Trina | **Ft. Laud/B** -
Z Truluck's | **Ft. Laud/B** 24
Z Via Luna | **Ft. Laud/B** -
Vienna Café | **Davie/B** 23
NEW Villa By Barton G. | **SoBe** -
W Wine | **Design Dist** -

ALPHABETICAL
PAGE INDEX

ALPHA INDEX

ALPHA INDEX

Wine Vintage Chart

This chart is based on our 0 to 30 scale. The ratings (by U. of South Carolina law professor **Howard Stravitz**) reflect vintage quality and the wine's readiness to drink. A dash means the wine is past its peak or too young to rate. Loire ratings are for dry whites.

Whites	95	96	97	98	99	00	01	02	03	04	05	06	07	08	09
France:															
Alsace	24	23	23	25	23	25	26	23	21	24	25	24	26	25	25
Burgundy	27	26	22	21	24	24	24	27	23	26	27	25	26	25	25
Loire Valley	-	-	-	-	-	-	-	26	21	23	27	23	24	24	26
Champagne	26	27	24	23	25	24	21	26	21	-	-	-	-	-	-
Sauternes	21	23	25	23	24	24	29	24	26	21	26	24	27	25	27
California:															
Chardonnay	-	-	-	-	22	21	25	26	22	26	29	24	27	25	-
Sauvignon Blanc	-	-	-	-	-	-	-	-	-	26	25	27	25	24	25
Austria:															
Grüner V./Riesl.	22	-	25	22	25	21	22	25	26	25	24	26	25	23	27
Germany:	21	26	21	22	24	20	29	25	26	27	28	25	27	25	25

Reds	95	96	97	98	99	00	01	02	03	04	05	06	07	08	09
France:															
Bordeaux	26	25	23	25	24	29	26	24	26	25	28	24	23	25	27
Burgundy	26	27	25	24	27	22	24	27	25	23	28	25	25	24	26
Rhône	26	22	23	27	26	27	26	-	26	25	27	25	26	23	26
Beaujolais	-	-	-	-	-	-	-	-	-	-	27	24	25	23	27
California:															
Cab./Merlot	27	25	28	23	25	-	27	26	25	24	26	23	26	23	25
Pinot Noir	-	-	-	-	-	-	25	26	25	26	24	23	27	25	24
Zinfandel	-	-	-	-	-	-	25	23	27	22	24	21	21	25	23
Oregon:															
Pinot Noir	-	-	-	-	-	-	-	26	24	26	25	24	23	27	25
Italy:															
Tuscany	25	24	29	24	27	24	27	-	25	27	26	26	25	24	-
Piedmont	21	27	26	25	26	28	27	-	24	27	26	25	26	26	-
Spain:															
Rioja	26	24	25	-	25	24	28	-	23	27	26	24	24	-	26
Ribera del Duero/Priorat	26	27	25	24	25	24	27	-	24	27	26	24	26	-	-
Australia:															
Shiraz/Cab.	24	26	25	28	24	24	27	27	25	26	27	25	23	-	-
Chile:	-	-	-	-	25	23	26	24	25	24	27	25	24	26	-
Argentina:															
Malbec	-	-	-	-	-	-	-	-	-	25	26	27	25	24	-